# DEMON

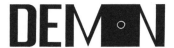

# DEM○N

VOLUME 2

JASON SHIGA

First Second

New York

First Second

Copyright © 2017 by Jason Shiga

Penciled with a Bic ballpoint on letter-size copy paper. Inked with a size 2 Windsor & Newton brush and black India ink on more copy paper. Colored digitally with Photoshop. Production help from Jackie Lo.

Published by First Second
First Second is an imprint of Roaring Brook Press,
a division of Holtzbrinck Publishing Holdings Limited Partnership
175 Fifth Avenue, New York, New York 10010

Library of Congress Control Number: 2016938724

ISBN 978-1-62672-453-2

Our books may be purchased in bulk for promotional, educational, or business use. Please contact your local bookseller or the Macmillan Corporate and Premium Sales Department at (800) 221-7945 ext. 5442 or by e-mail at MacmillanSpecialMarkets@macmillan.com.

First edition 2017
Book design by John Green

Printed in China
10 9 8 7 6 5 4 3 2 1

To my wife, Alina, who's still mad at me
for dedicating the first volume to her

# THE STORY SO FAR

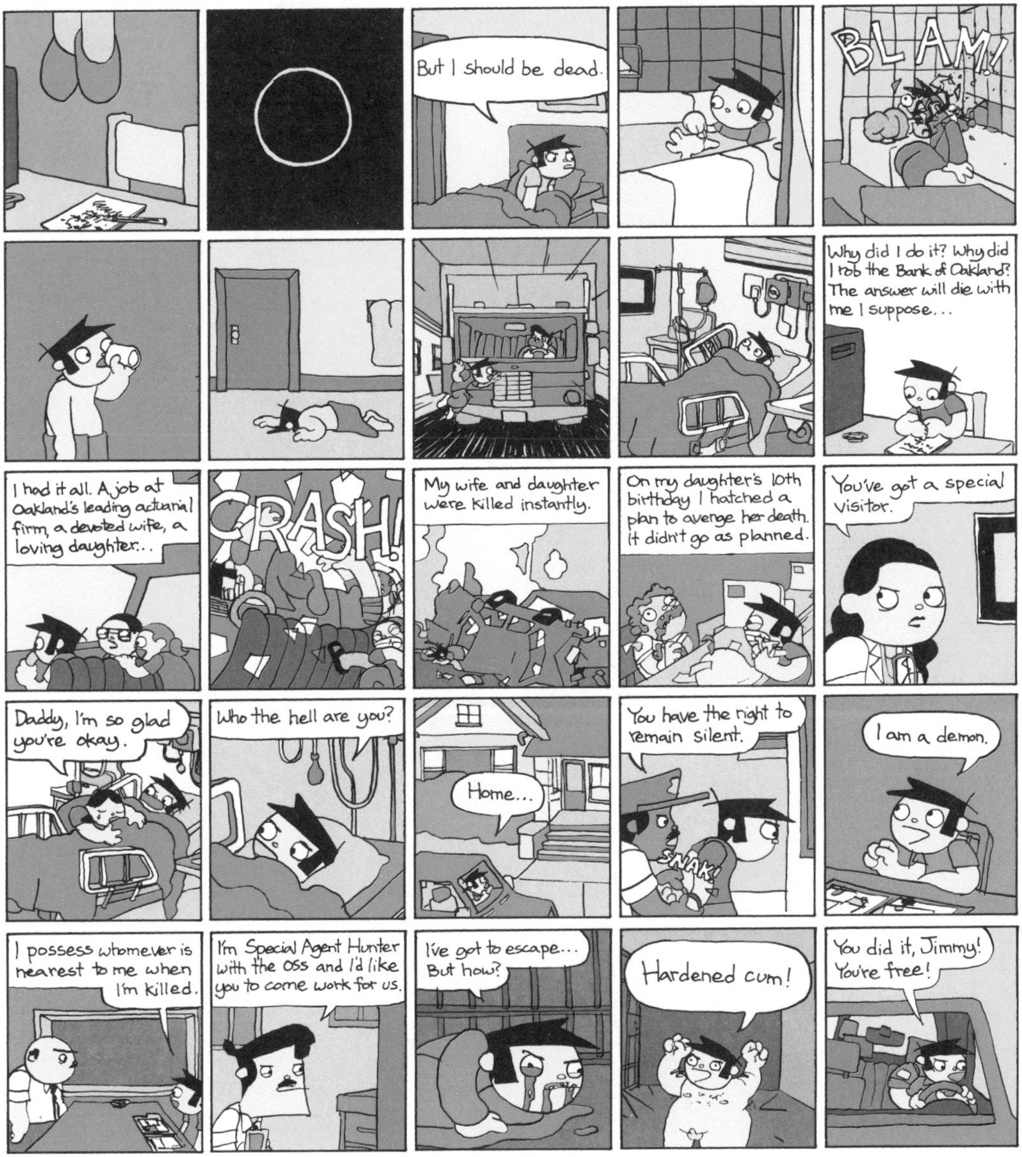
But I should be dead.
BLAM!
Why did I do it? Why did I rob the Bank of Oakland? The answer will die with me I suppose...
I had it all. A job at Oakland's leading actuarial firm, a devoted wife, a loving daughter...
CRASH!
My wife and daughter were killed instantly.
On my daughter's 10th birthday I hatched a plan to avenge her death. It didn't go as planned.
You've got a special visitor.
Daddy, I'm so glad you're okay.
Who the hell are you?
Home...
You have the right to remain silent.
SNAK!
I am a demon.
I possess whomever is nearest to me when I'm killed.
I'm Special Agent Hunter with the OSS and I'd like you to come work for us.
I've got to escape... But how?
Hardened cum!
You did it, Jimmy! You're free!

# CHAPTER 6

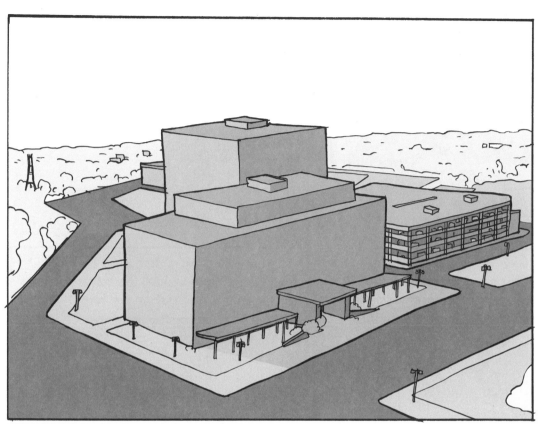

What do we know?

His original identity was Jimmy Yee, 44 years of age, born and raised in Oakland, California.

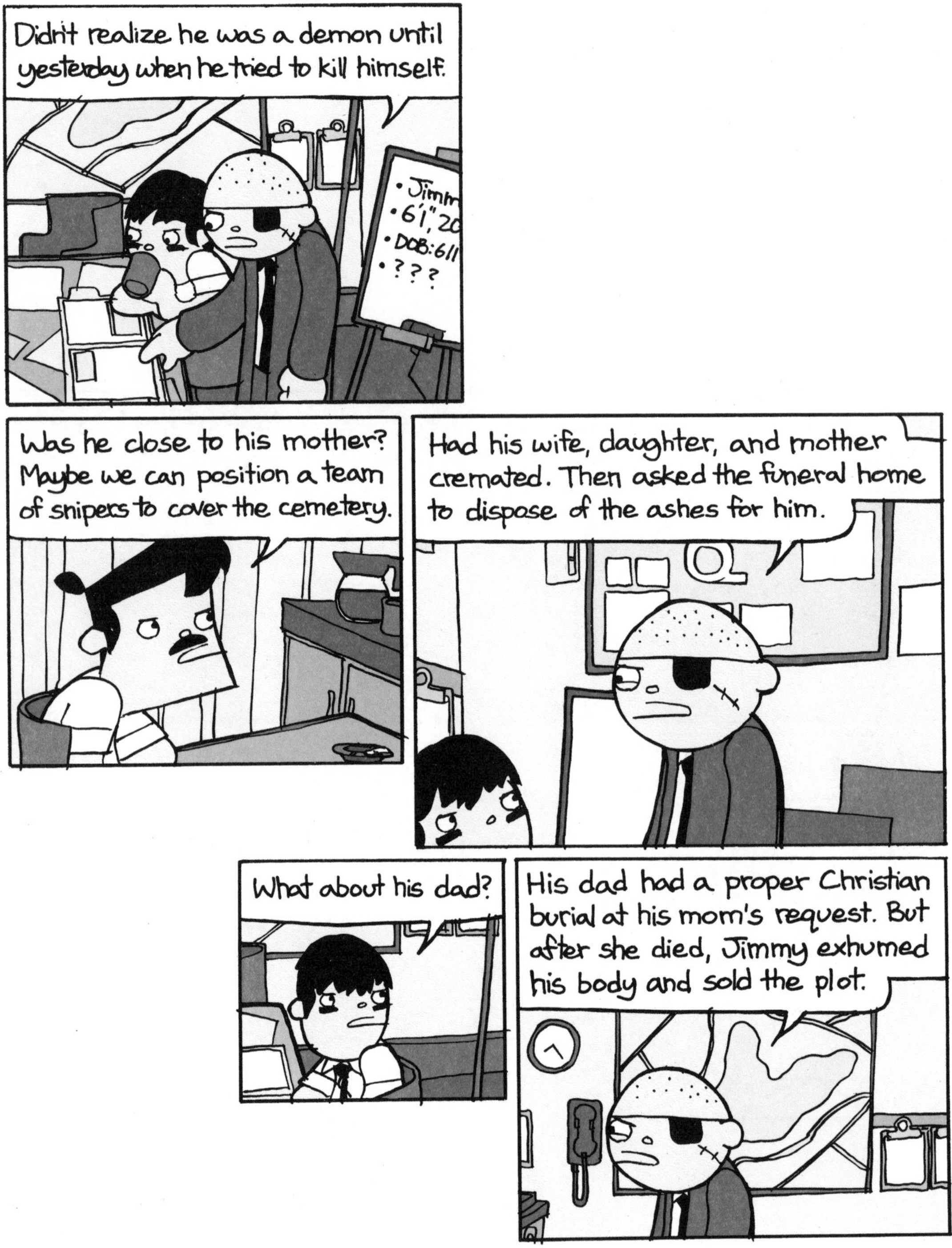
Didn't realize he was a demon until yesterday when he tried to kill himself.
Was he close to his mother? Maybe we can position a team of snipers to cover the cemetery.
Had his wife, daughter, and mother cremated. Then asked the funeral home to dispose of the ashes for him.
What about his dad?
His dad had a proper Christian burial at his mom's request. But after she died, Jimmy exhumed his body and sold the plot.

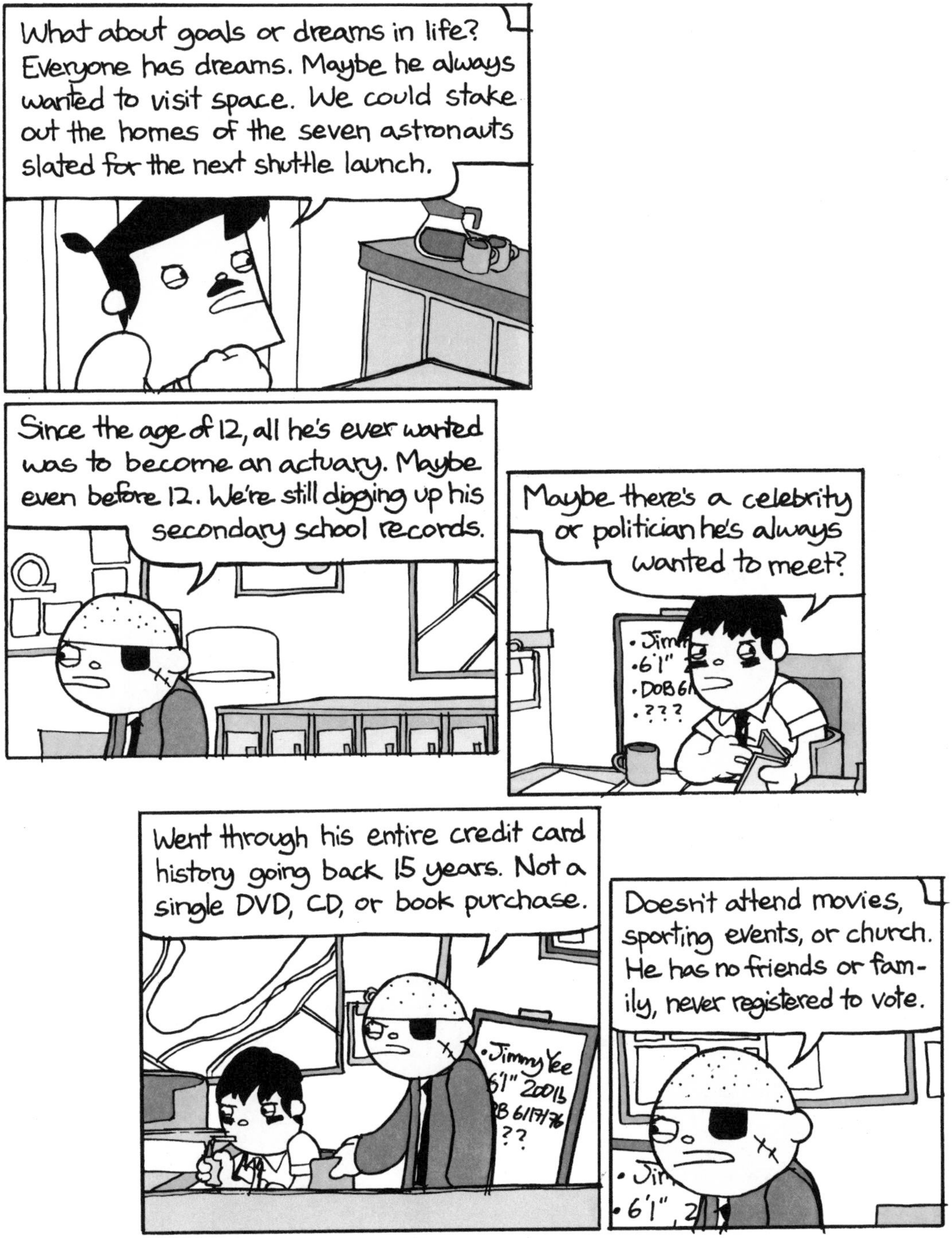
What about goals or dreams in life? Everyone has dreams. Maybe he always wanted to visit space. We could stake out the homes of the seven astronauts slated for the next shuttle launch.
Since the age of 12, all he's ever wanted was to become an actuary. Maybe even before 12. We're still digging up his secondary school records.
Maybe there's a celebrity or politician he's always wanted to meet?
Went through his entire credit card history going back 15 years. Not a single DVD, CD, or book purchase.
• Jimmy Yee
6'1" 200lb
Doesn't attend movies, sporting events, or church. He has no friends or family, never registered to vote.

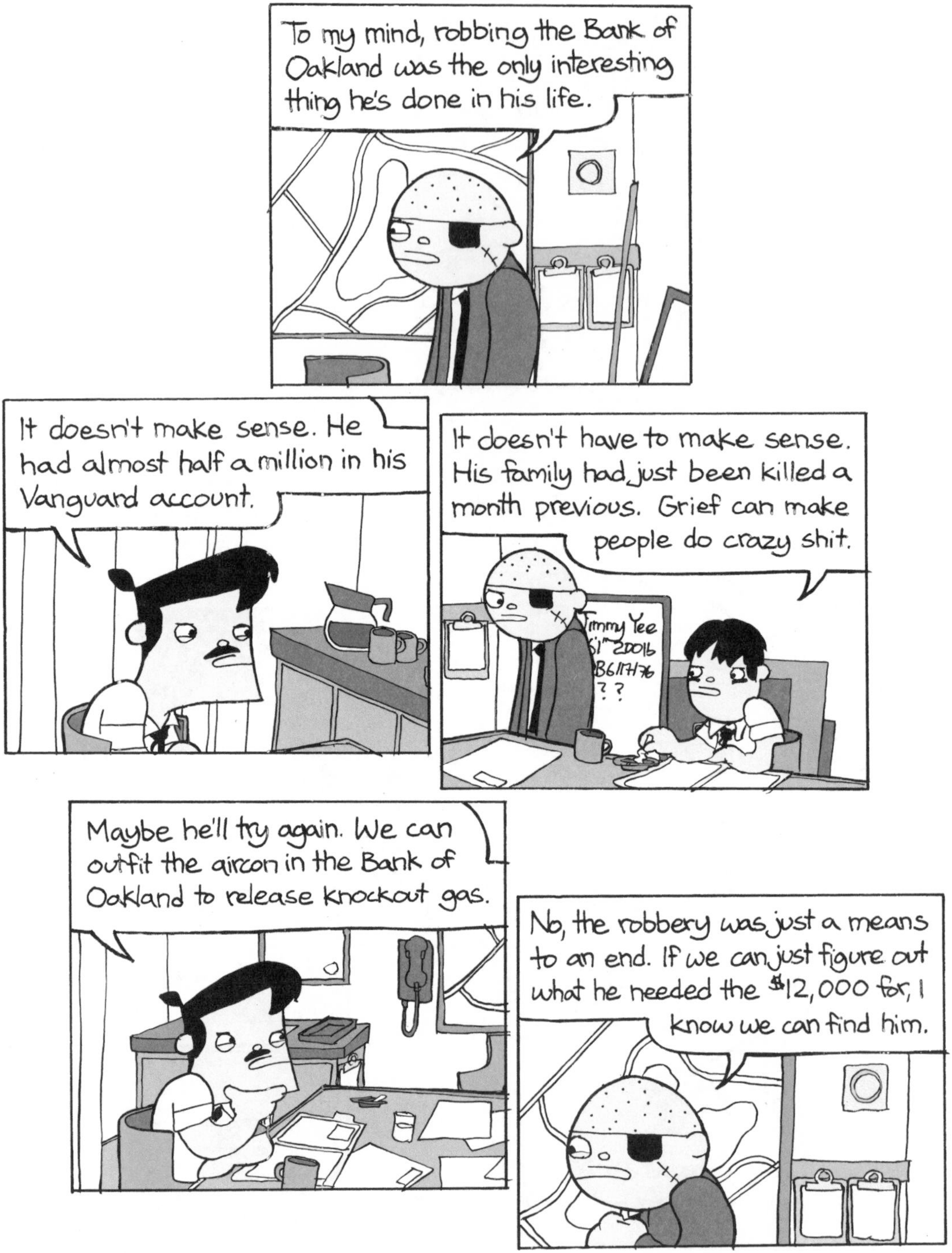
To my mind, robbing the Bank of Oakland was the only interesting thing he's done in his life.
It doesn't make sense. He had almost half a million in his Vanguard account.
It doesn't have to make sense. His family had just been killed a month previous. Grief can make people do crazy shit.
Timmy Yee
5'1" 200lb
B6/17/76
? ?
Maybe he'll try again. We can outfit the aircon in the Bank of Oakland to release knockout gas.
No, the robbery was just a means to an end. If we can just figure out what he needed the $12,000 for, I know we can find him.

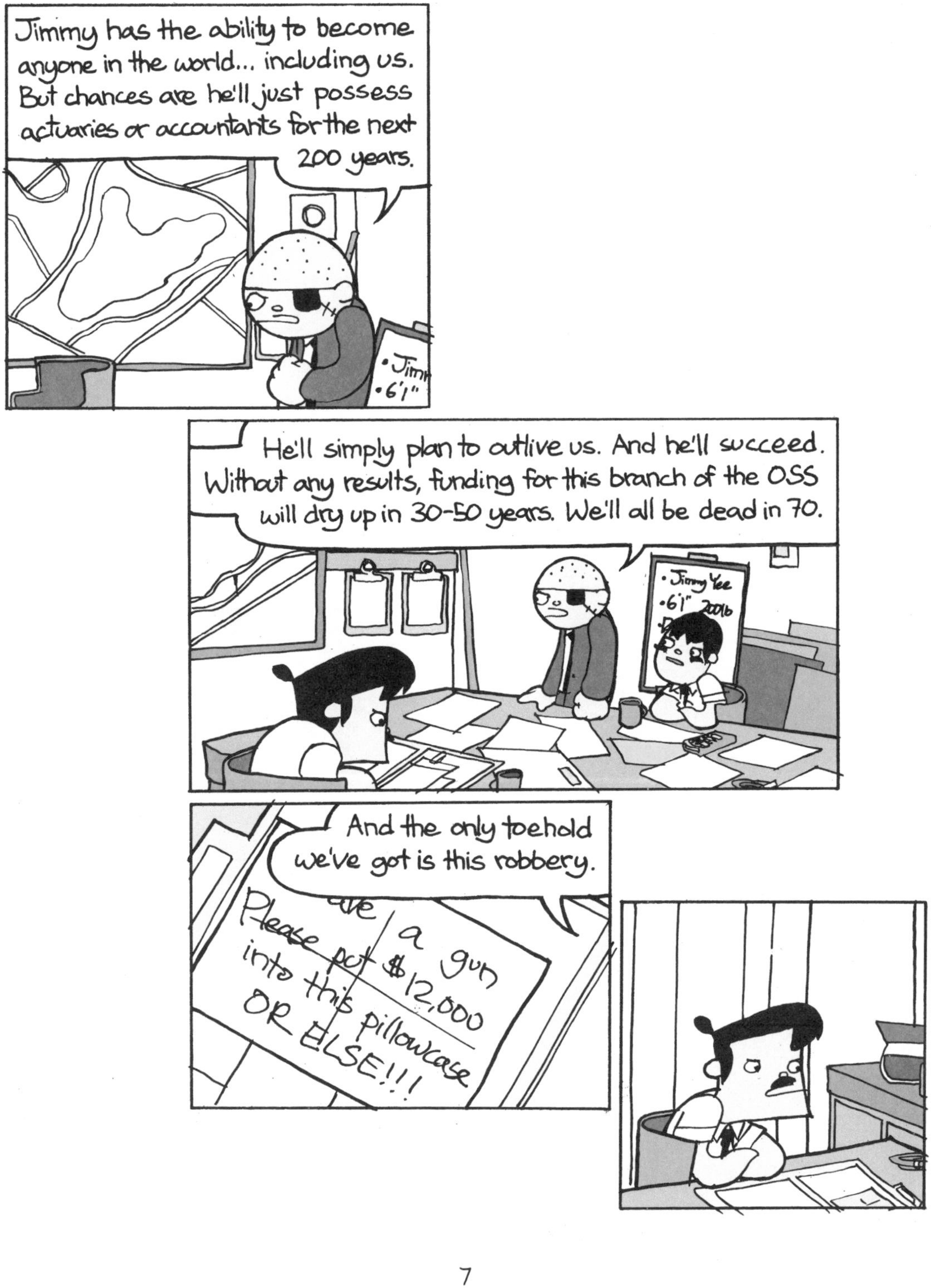

Jimmy has the ability to become anyone in the world... including us. But chances are he'll just possess actuaries or accountants for the next 200 years.
He'll simply plan to outlive us. And he'll succeed. Without any results, funding for this branch of the OSS will dry up in 30-50 years. We'll all be dead in 70.
• Jimmy Yee
• 6'1" 2016
And the only toehold we've got is this robbery.
Please put
a gun
$12,000
into this pillowcase
OR ELSE!!!

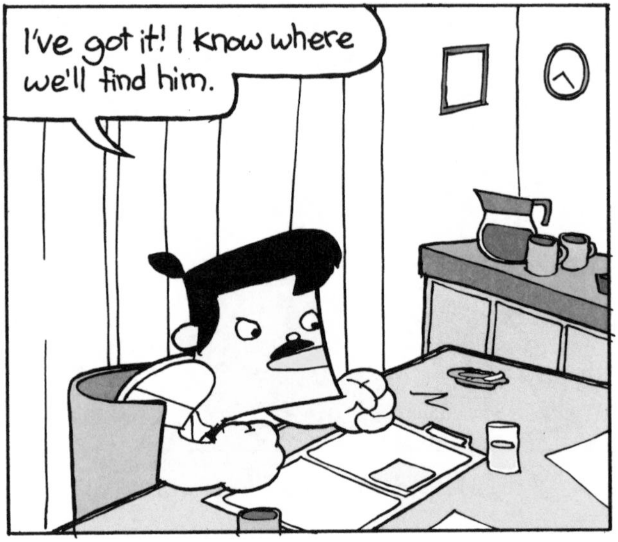
I've got it! I know where we'll find him.

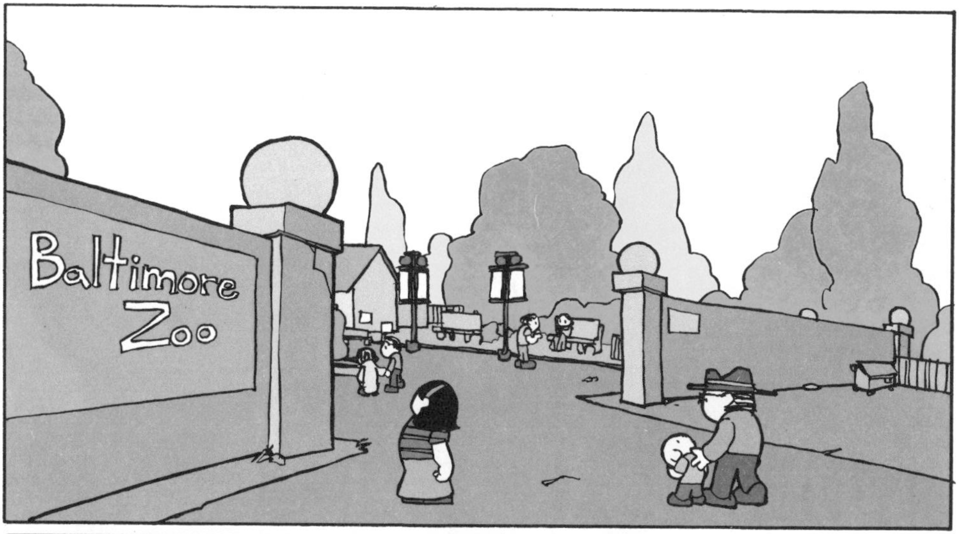
Baltimore Zoo

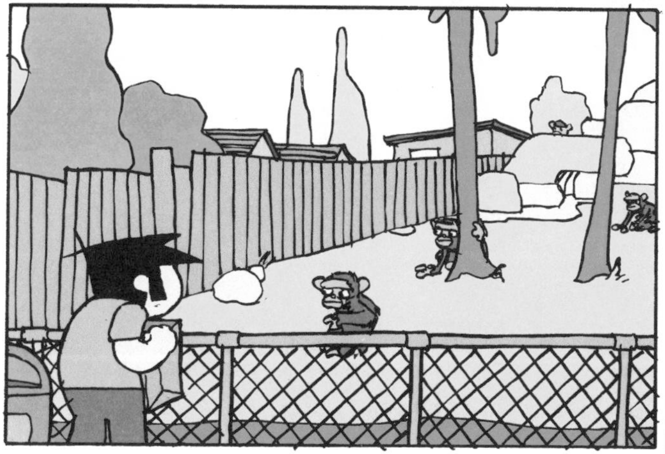

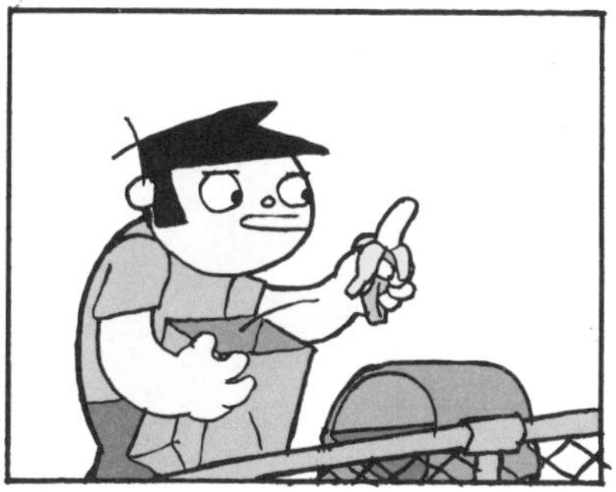

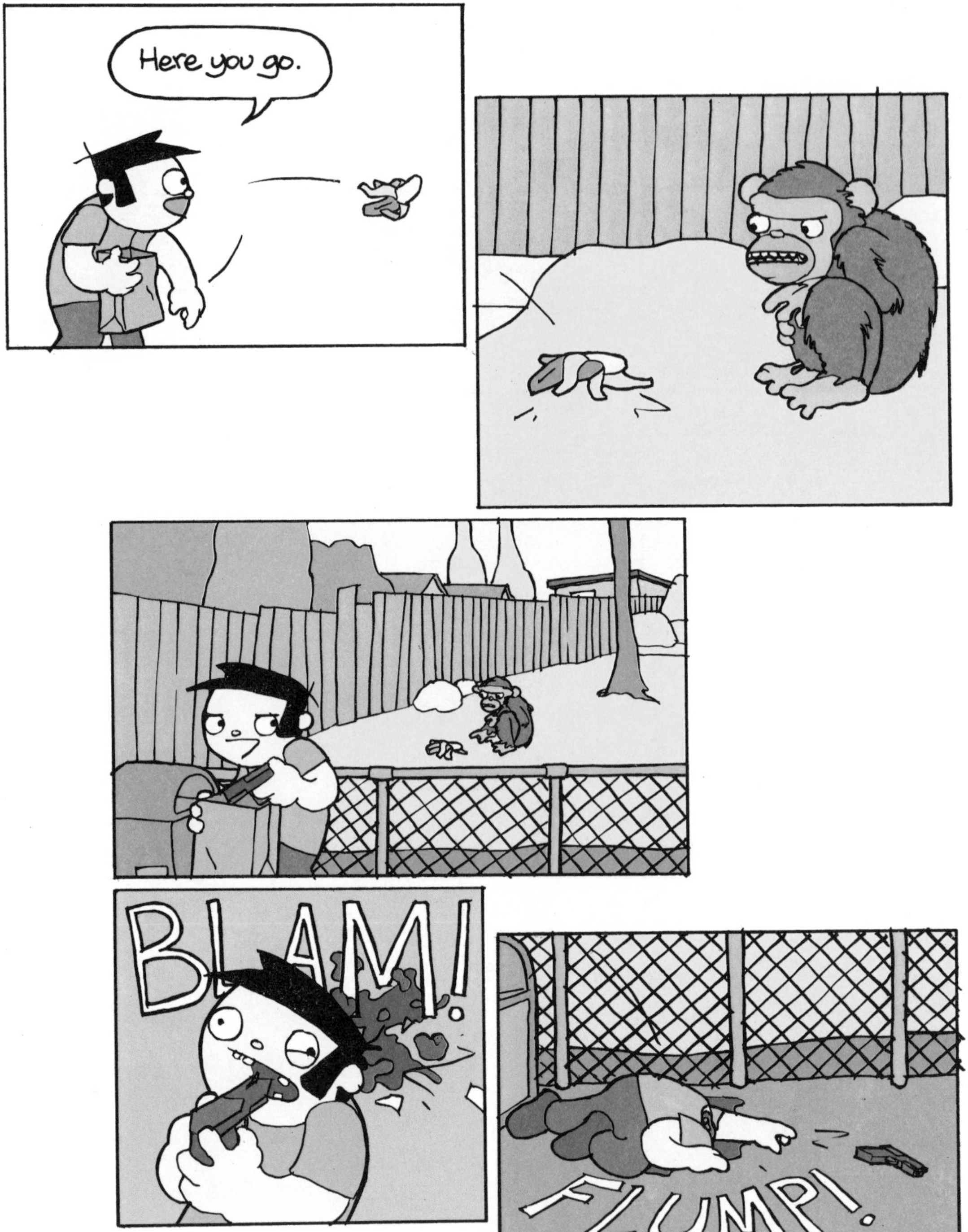
Here you go.
BLAM!
FLUMP!

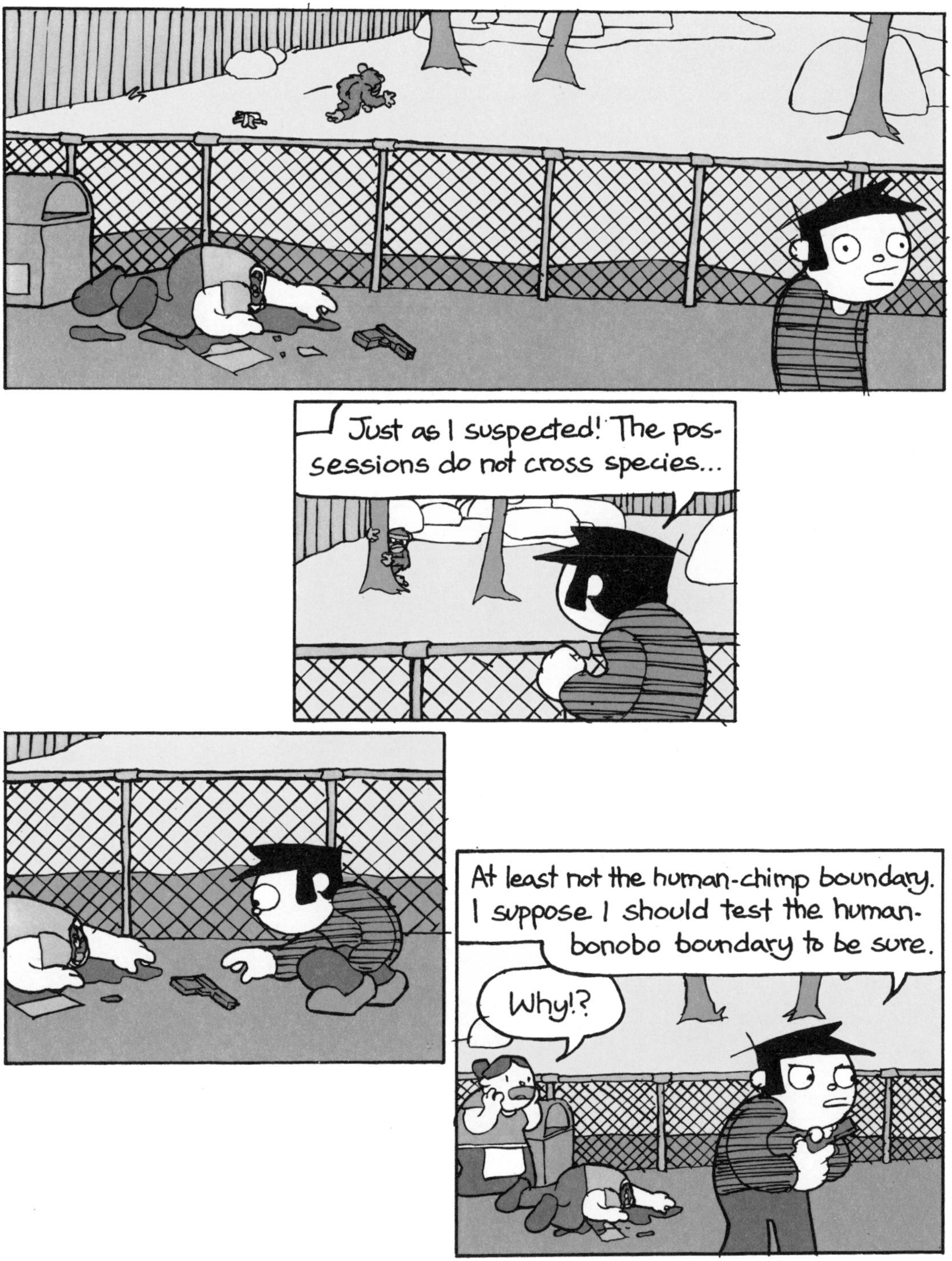

Just as I suspected! The possessions do not cross species...
At least not the human-chimp boundary. I suppose I should test the human-bonobo boundary to be sure.
Why!?

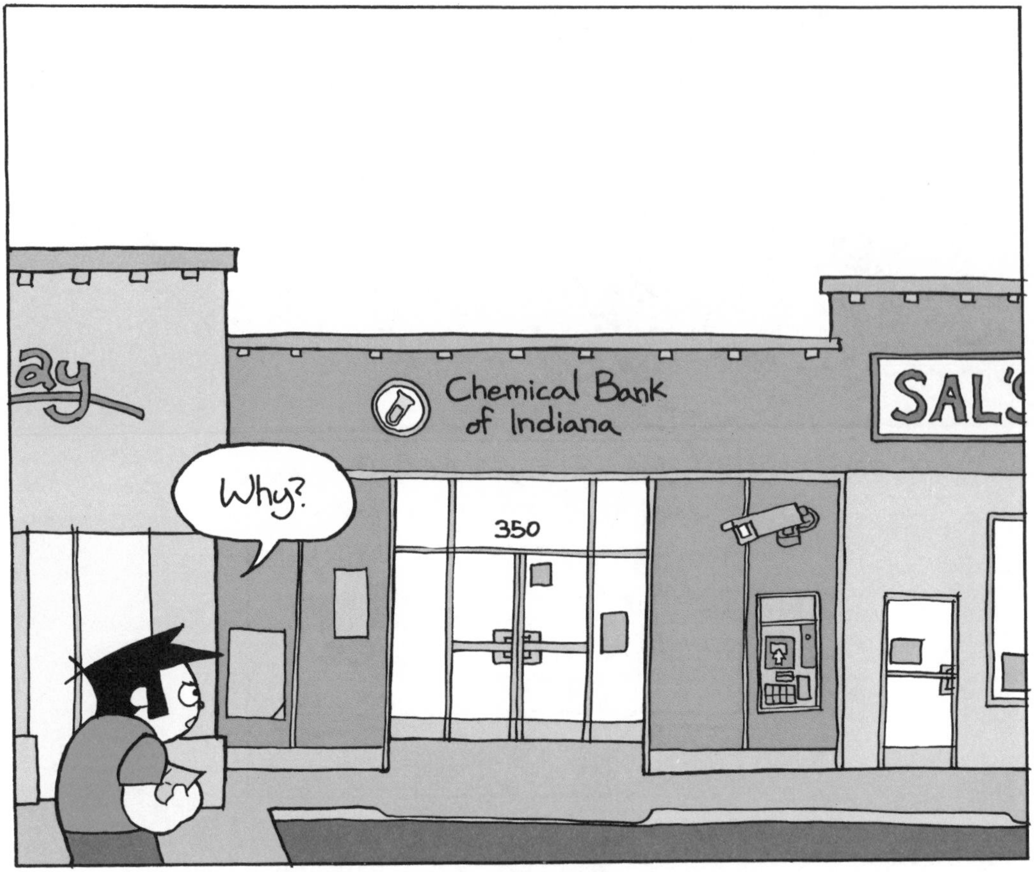
ay
Chemical Bank of Indiana
SAL'S
Why?
350

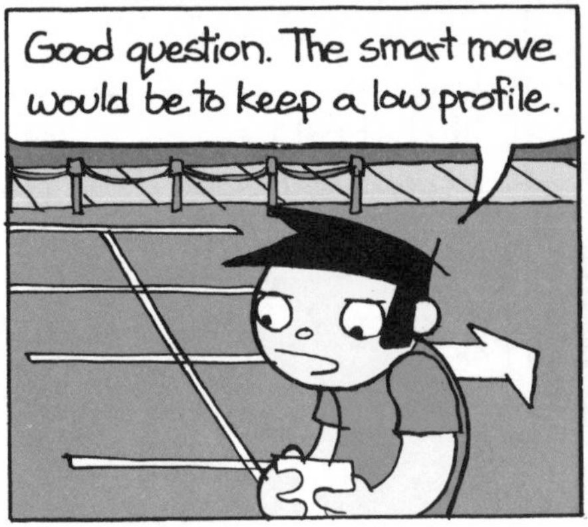
Good question. The smart move would be to keep a low profile.

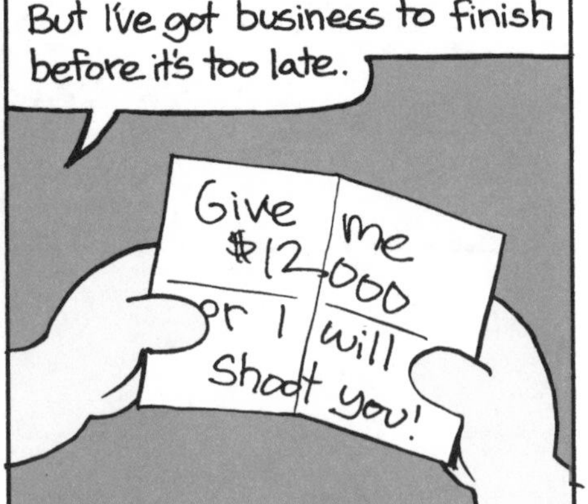
But I've got business to finish before it's too late.
Give me $12,000 or I will shoot you!

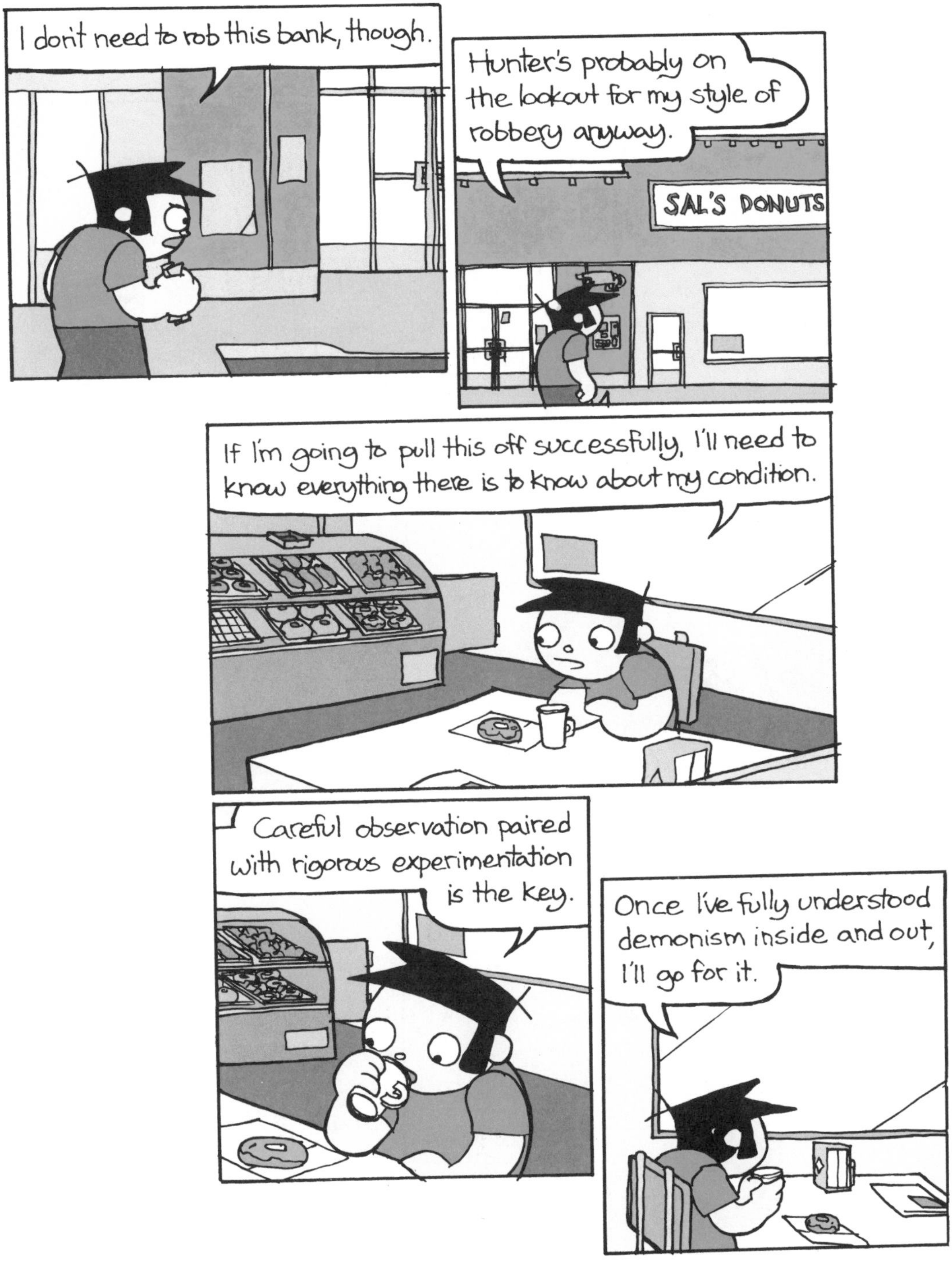
I don't need to rob this bank, though.
Hunter's probably on the lookout for my style of robbery anyway.
SAL'S DONUTS
If I'm going to pull this off successfully, I'll need to know everything there is to know about my condition.
Careful observation paired with rigorous experimentation is the key.
Once I've fully understood demonism inside and out, I'll go for it.

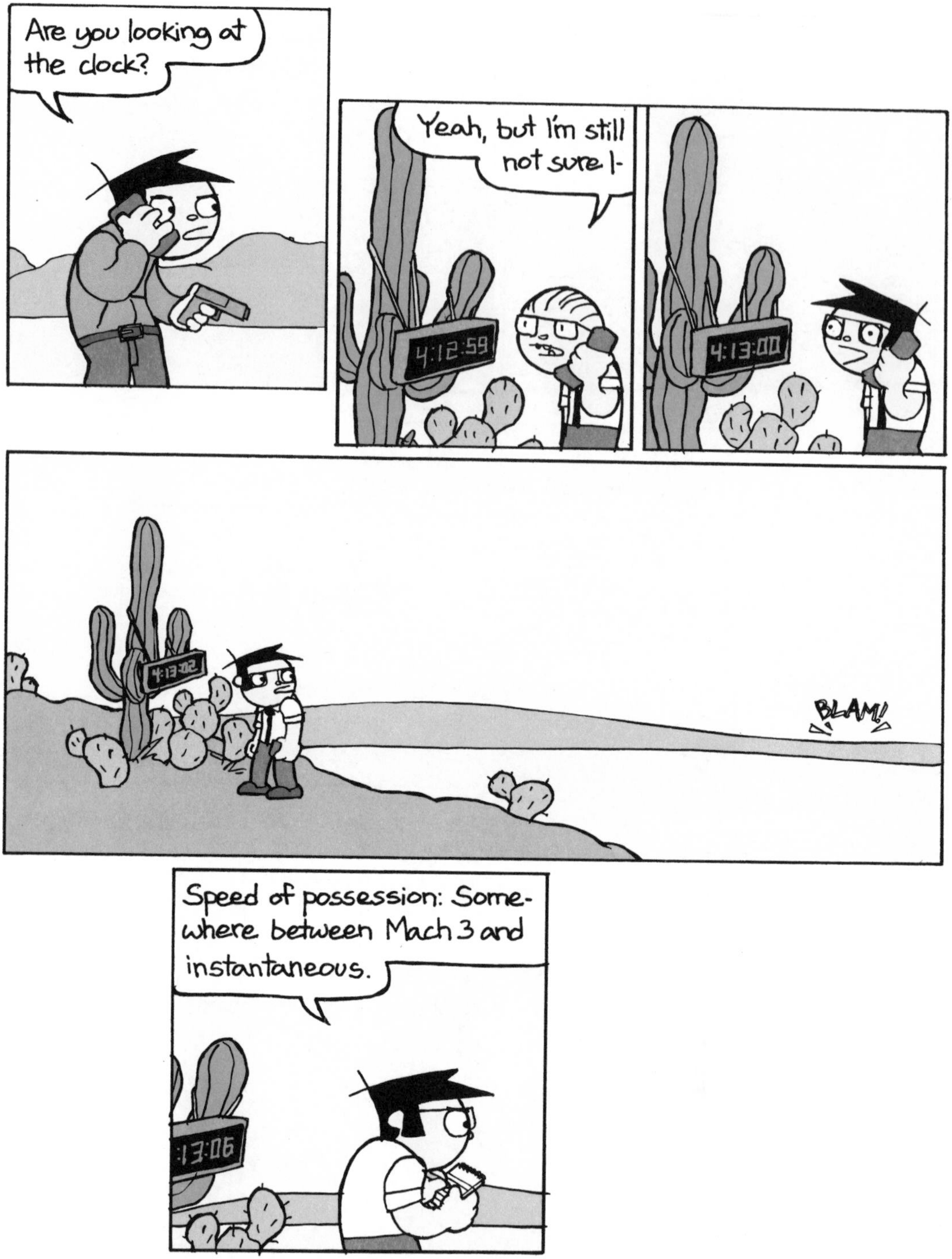
Are you looking at the clock?
Yeah, but I'm still not sure I-
4:12:59
4:13:00
4:13:02
BLAM!
Speed of possession: Somewhere between Mach 3 and instantaneous.
:13:06

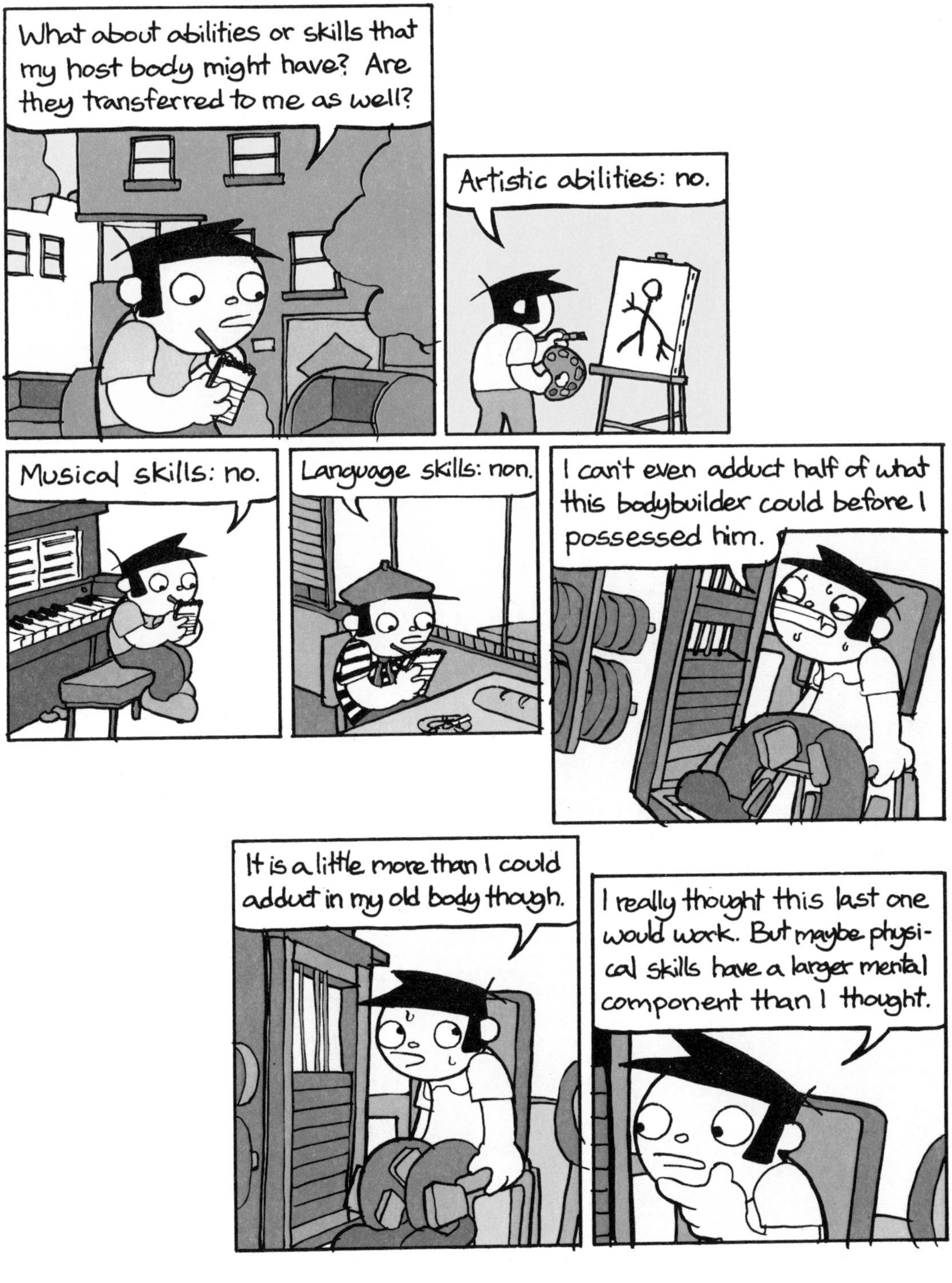
What about abilities or skills that my host body might have? Are they transferred to me as well?
Artistic abilities: no.
Musical skills: no.
Language skills: non.
I can't even adduct half of what this bodybuilder could before I possessed him.
It is a little more than I could adduct in my old body though.
I really thought this last one would work. But maybe physical skills have a larger mental component than I thought.

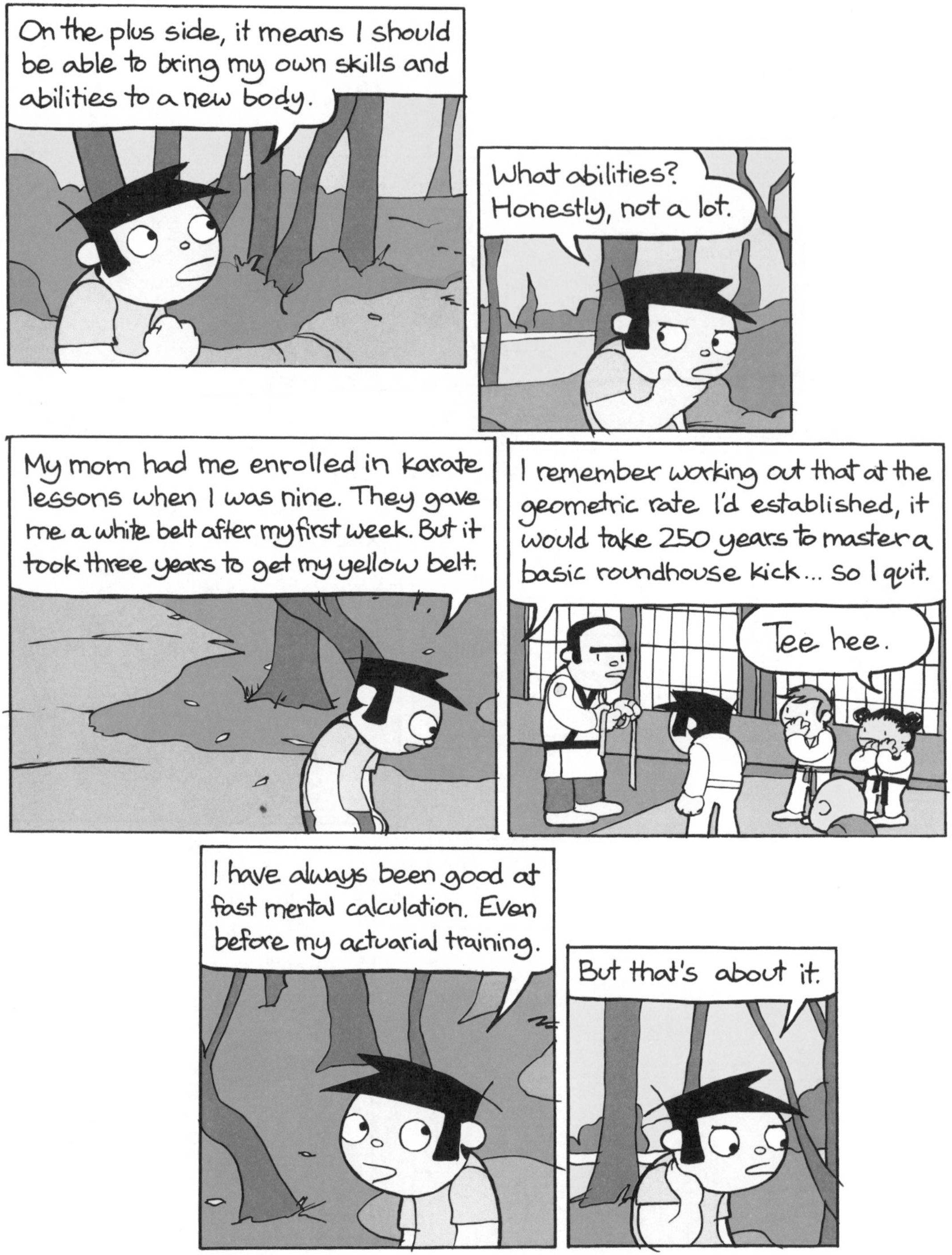
On the plus side, it means I should be able to bring my own skills and abilities to a new body.
What abilities? Honestly, not a lot.
My mom had me enrolled in karate lessons when I was nine. They gave me a white belt after my first week. But it took three years to get my yellow belt.
I remember working out that at the geometric rate I'd established, it would take 250 years to master a basic roundhouse kick... so I quit.
Tee hee.
I have always been good at fast mental calculation. Even before my actuarial training.
But that's about it.

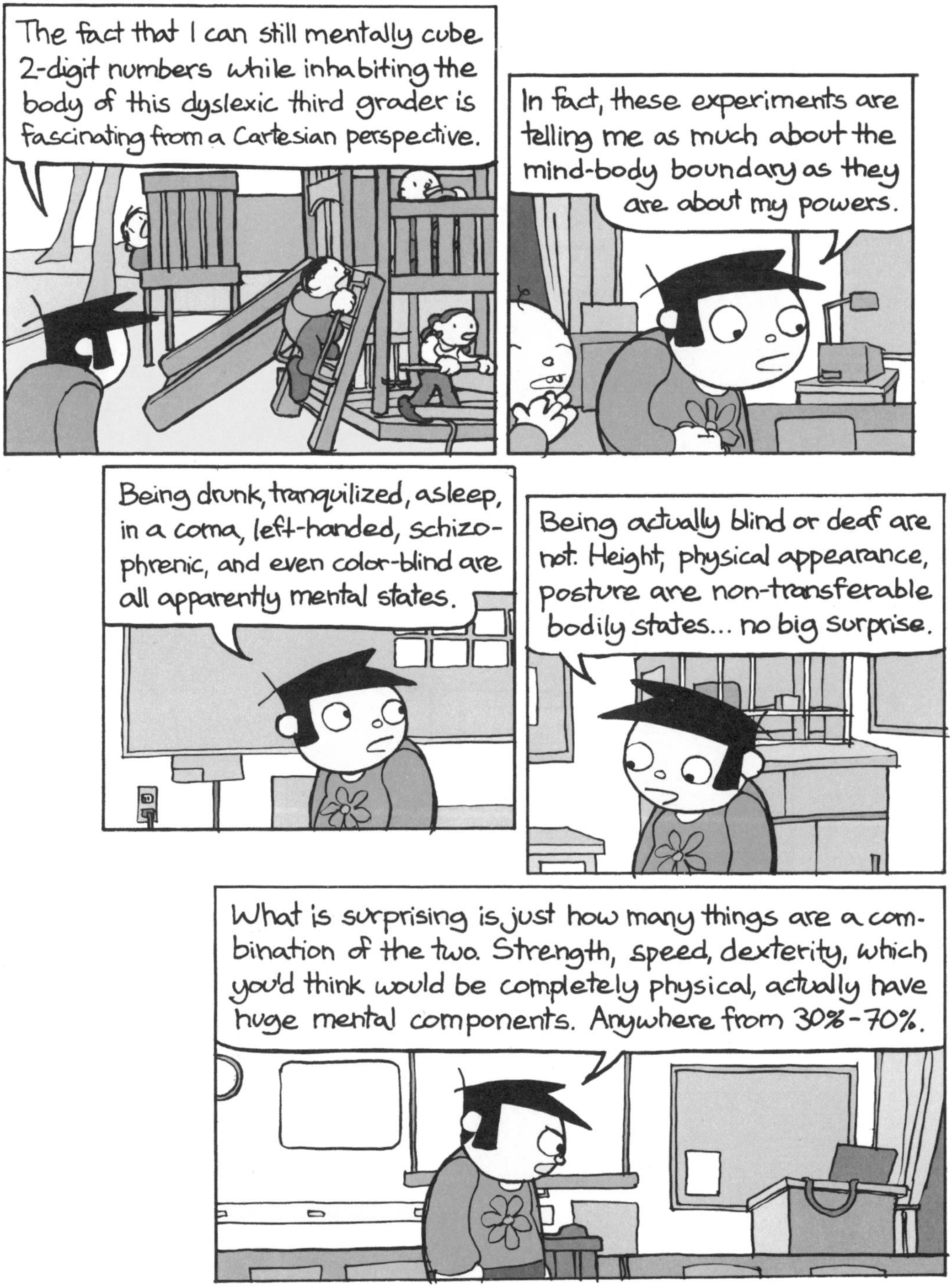
The fact that I can still mentally cube 2-digit numbers while inhabiting the body of this dyslexic third grader is fascinating from a Cartesian perspective.
In fact, these experiments are telling me as much about the mind-body boundary as they are about my powers.
Being drunk, tranquilized, asleep, in a coma, left-handed, schizophrenic, and even color-blind are all apparently mental states.
Being actually blind or deaf are not. Height, physical appearance, posture are non-transferable bodily states... no big surprise.
What is surprising is just how many things are a combination of the two. Strength, speed, dexterity, which you'd think would be completely physical, actually have huge mental components. Anywhere from 30%-70%.

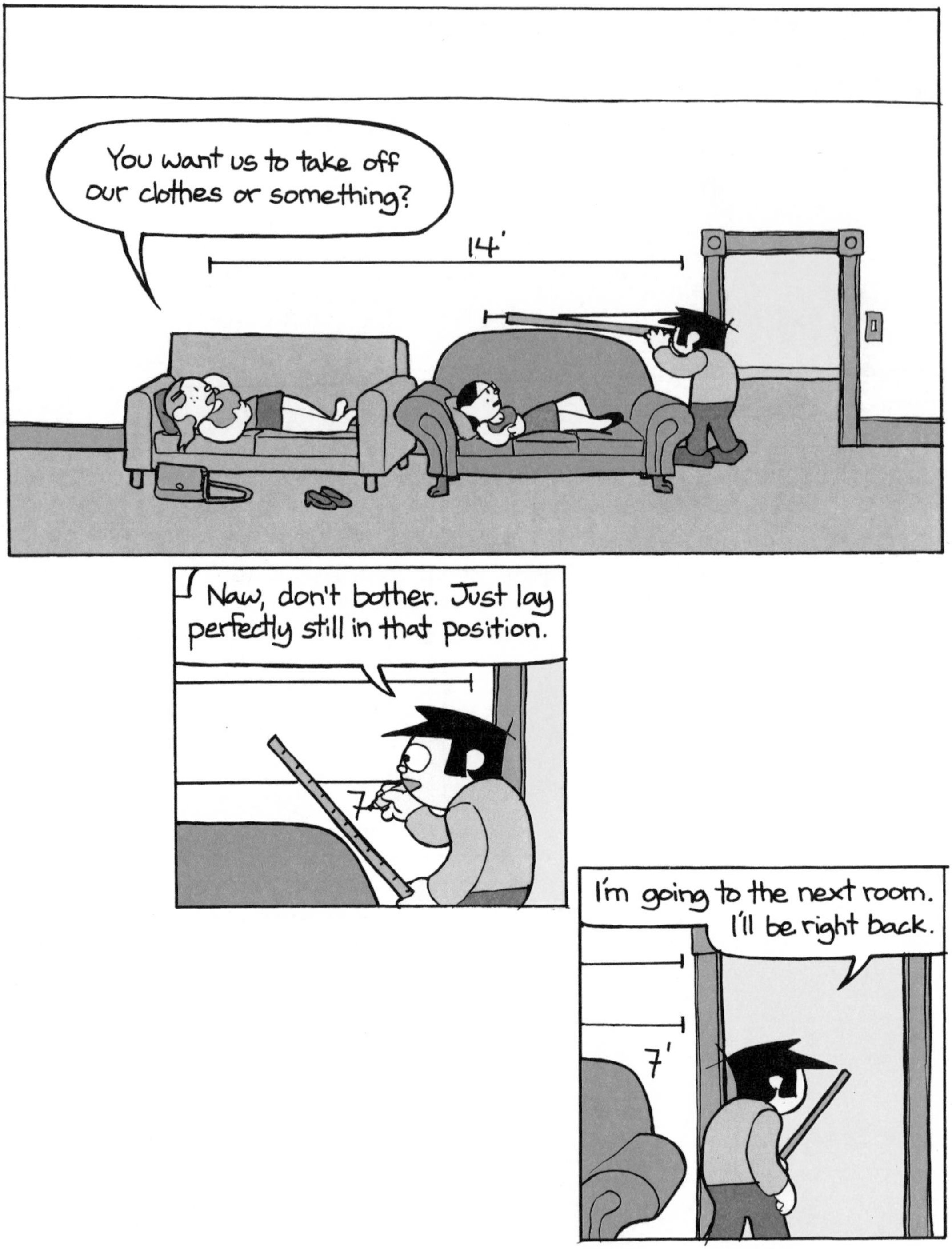
You want us to take off our clothes or something?
14'
Naw, don't bother. Just lay perfectly still in that position.
7
I'm going to the next room. I'll be right back.
7'

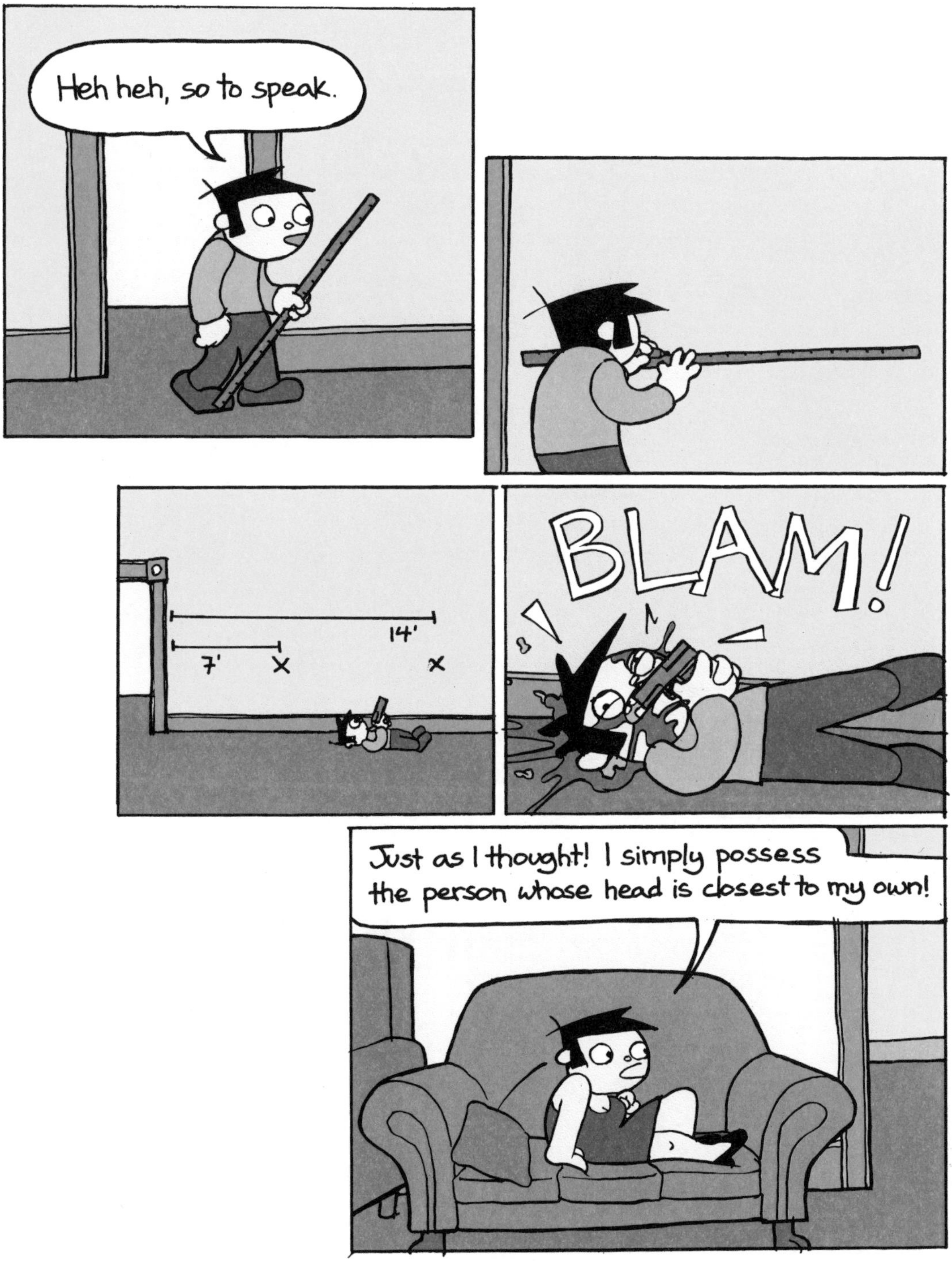

Heh heh, so to speak.
14'
7'
BLAM!
Just as I thought! I simply possess the person whose head is closest to my own!

It all has a certain logic to it, I suppose.

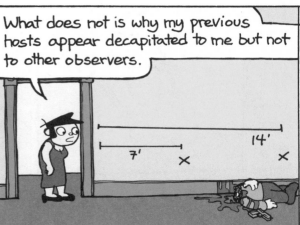

What does not is why my previous hosts appear decapitated to me but not to other observers.

7' ✕ 14' ✕

I can even feel their head as if it were still there, just invisible.

✕ 14' ✕

I'm sure it's related to the fact that when I look in the mirror, I still see my own head on my host's body.

Quick! Where's the bathroom?

Down the hall.

7' 14'

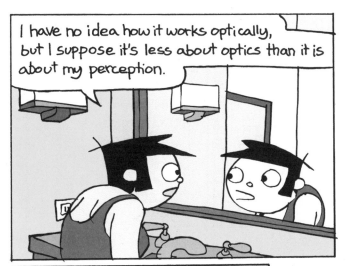

I have no idea how it works optically, but I suppose it's less about optics than it is about my perception.

It's weird. I can't see it in the mirror but I can feel this prostitute's face on my own. Her nose, her mole, even her long hair.

There's gotta be some explanation that ties it all together.

I know I'll get it eventually. For now, I suppose the theory is less important than the application.

For example, other than killing myself, is there any way to control when I leave my body?

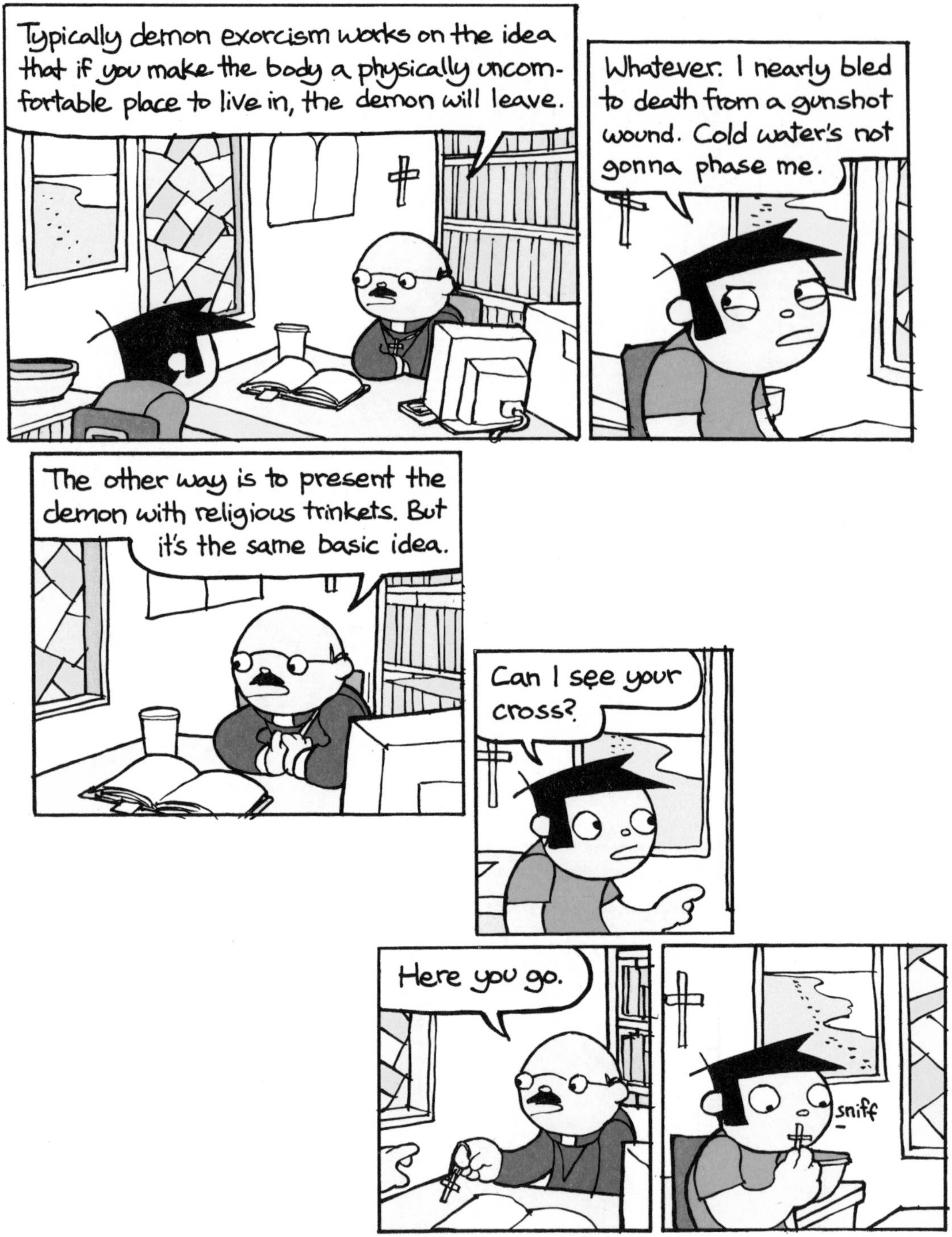
Typically demon exorcism works on the idea that if you make the body a physically uncomfortable place to live in, the demon will leave.
Whatever. I nearly bled to death from a gunshot wound. Cold water's not gonna phase me.
The other way is to present the demon with religious trinkets. But it's the same basic idea.
Can I see your cross?
Here you go.
sniff

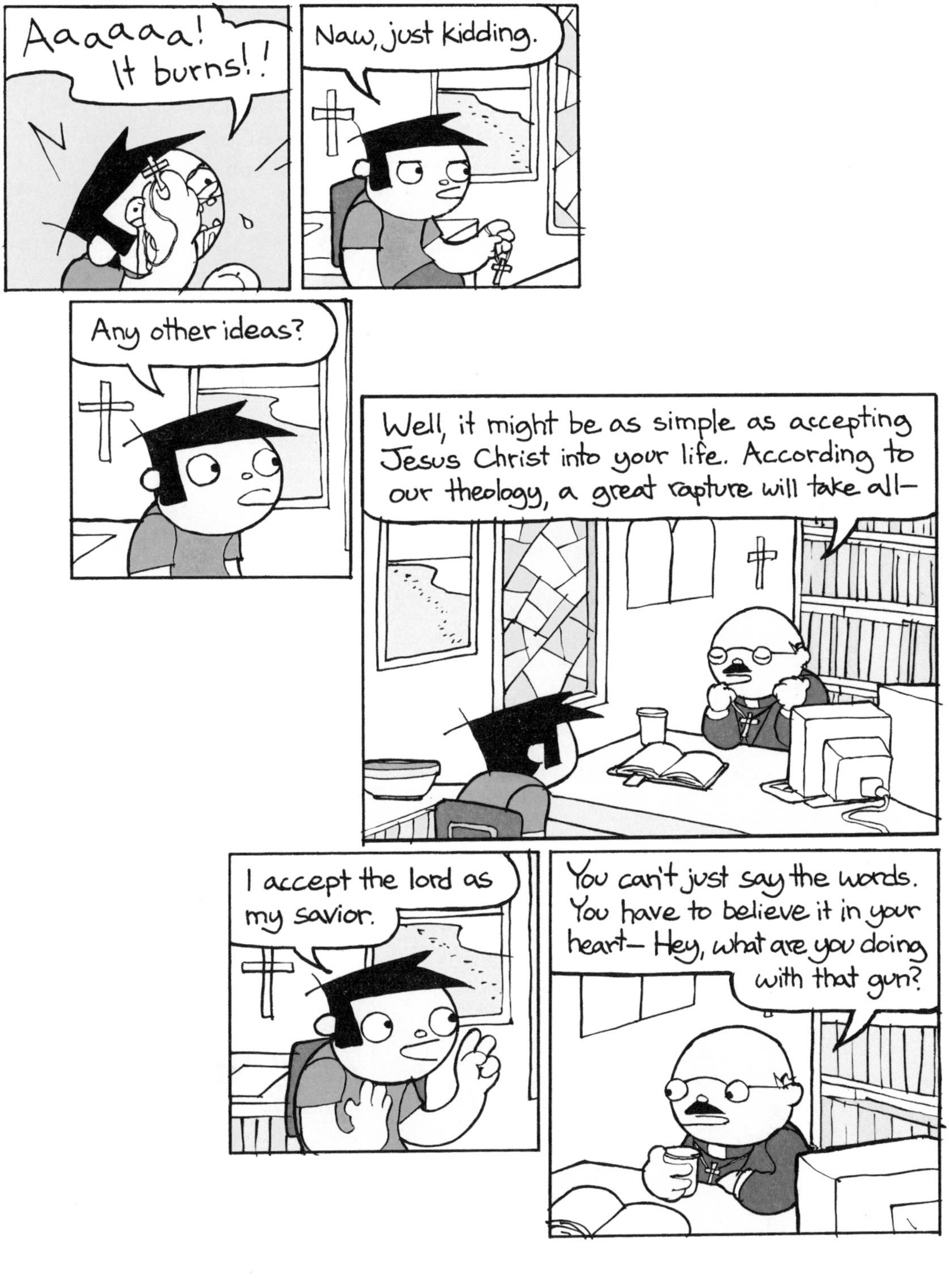

Aaaaaa! It burns!!
Naw, just kidding.
Any other ideas?
Well, it might be as simple as accepting Jesus Christ into your life. According to our theology, a great rapture will take all—
I accept the lord as my savior.
You can't just say the words. You have to believe it in your heart— Hey, what are you doing with that gun?

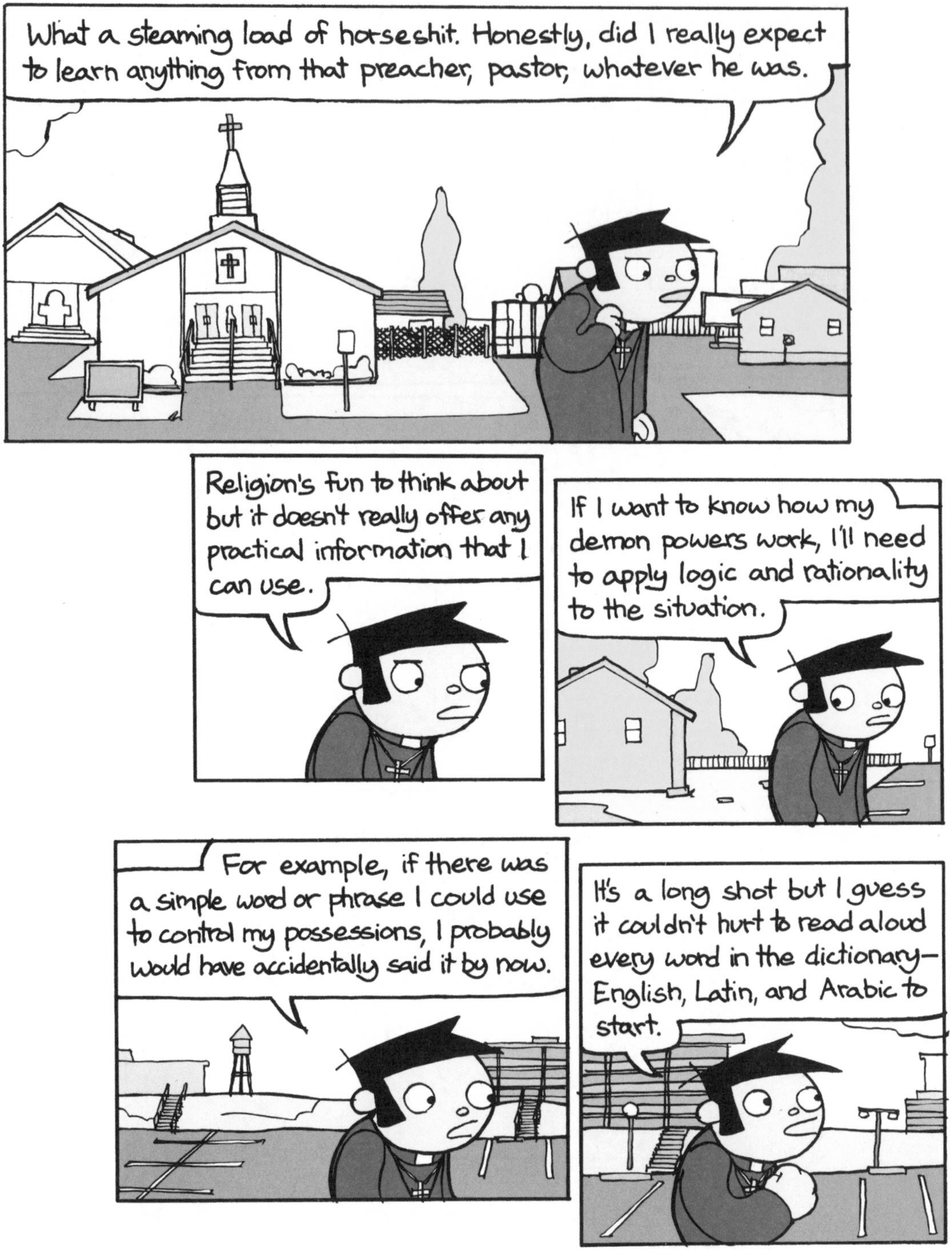

What a steaming load of horseshit. Honestly, did I really expect to learn anything from that preacher, pastor, whatever he was.
Religion's fun to think about but it doesn't really offer any practical information that I can use.
If I want to know how my demon powers work, I'll need to apply logic and rationality to the situation.
For example, if there was a simple word or phrase I could use to control my possessions, I probably would have accidentally said it by now.
It's a long shot but I guess it couldn't hurt to read aloud every word in the dictionary— English, Latin, and Arabic to start.

I suppose there's also the question of how I became a demon to begin with.

I had a pretty uneventful childhood. Boring, really.

I've started a list of every weird or unusual thing that's ever happened to me in my life. But even this list is kinda boring.

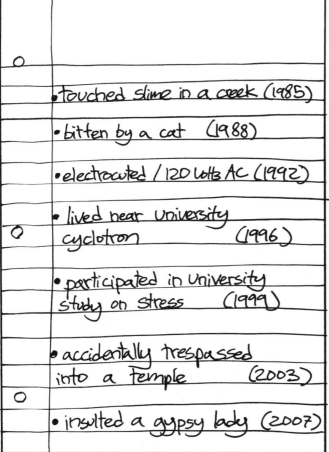

- touched slime in a creek (1985)
- bitten by a cat (1988)
- electrocuted / 120 volts AC (1992)
- lived near university cyclotron (1996)
- participated in university study on stress (1999)
- accidentally trespassed into a temple (2003)
- insulted a gypsy lady (2007)

Could my powers be hereditary?

No. My mom or dad would still be around. My daughter...

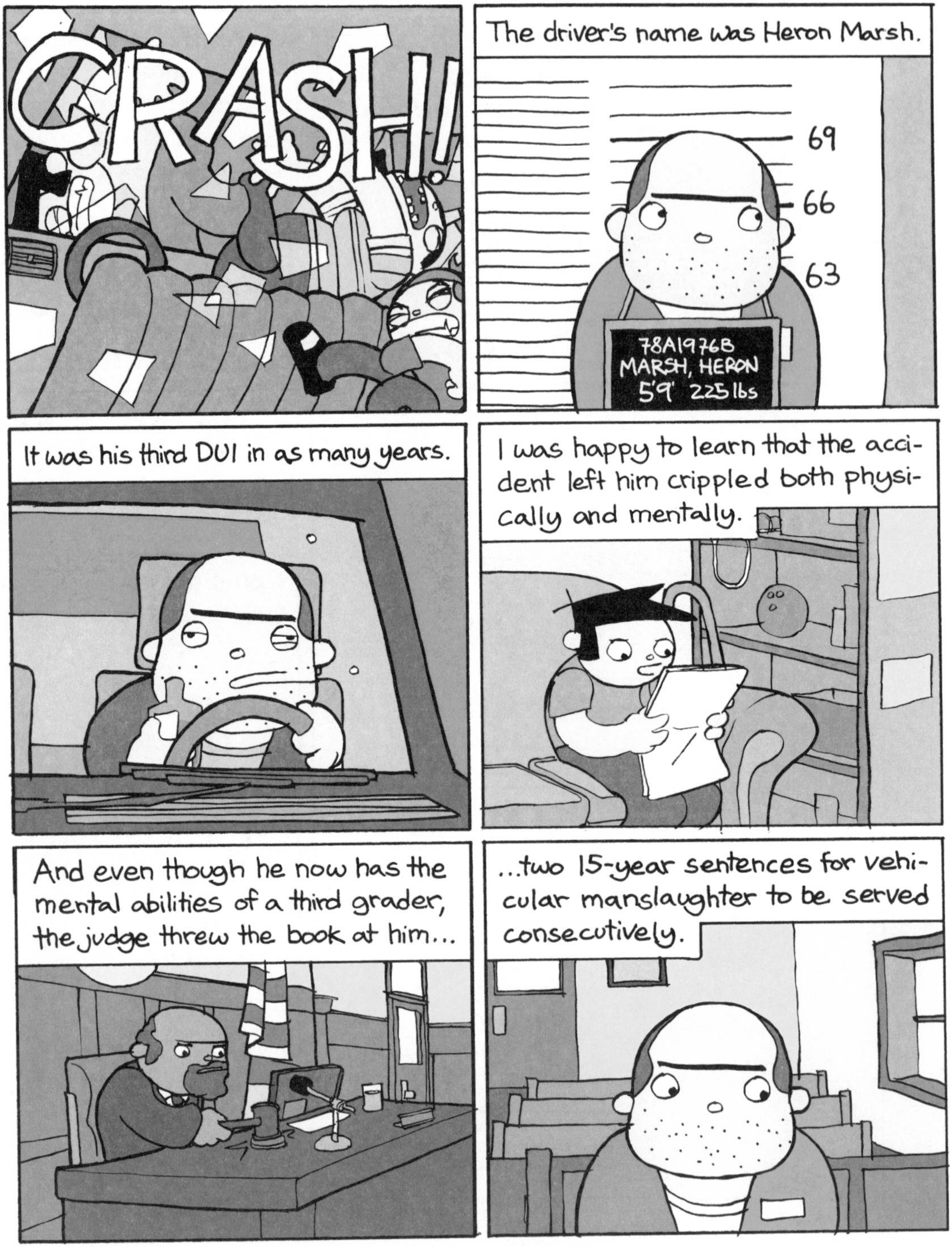
CRASH!!
The driver's name was Heron Marsh.
69
66
63
78A1976B
MARSH, HERON
5'9' 225 lbs
It was his third DUI in as many years.
I was happy to learn that the accident left him crippled both physically and mentally.
And even though he now has the mental abilities of a third grader, the judge threw the book at him...
...two 15-year sentences for vehicular manslaughter to be served consecutively.

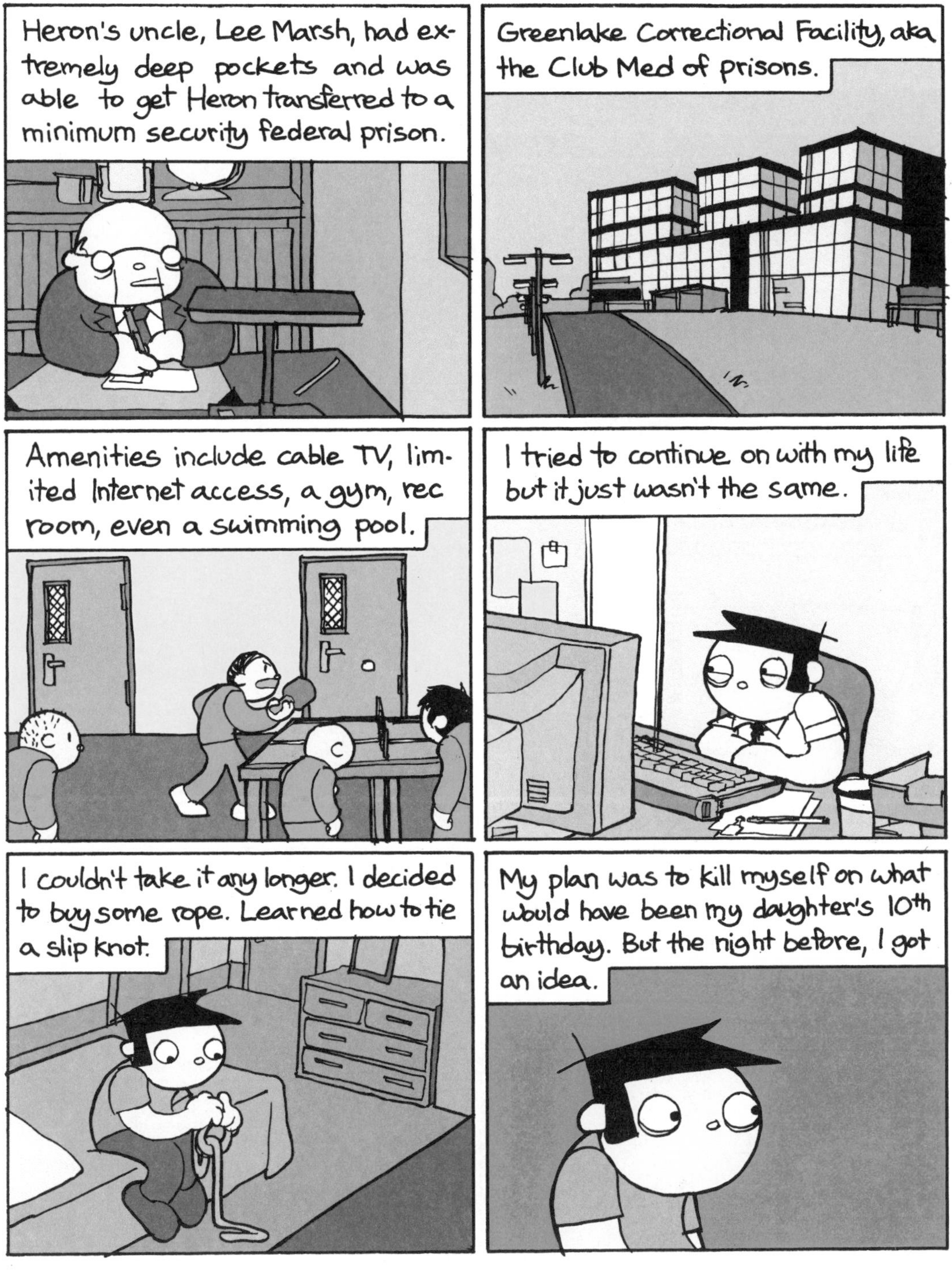
Heron's uncle, Lee Marsh, had extremely deep pockets and was able to get Heron transferred to a minimum security federal prison.
Greenlake Correctional Facility, aka the Club Med of prisons.
Amenities include cable TV, limited Internet access, a gym, rec room, even a swimming pool.
I tried to continue on with my life but it just wasn't the same.
I couldn't take it any longer. I decided to buy some rope. Learned how to tie a slip knot.
My plan was to kill myself on what would have been my daughter's 10th birthday. But the night before, I got an idea.

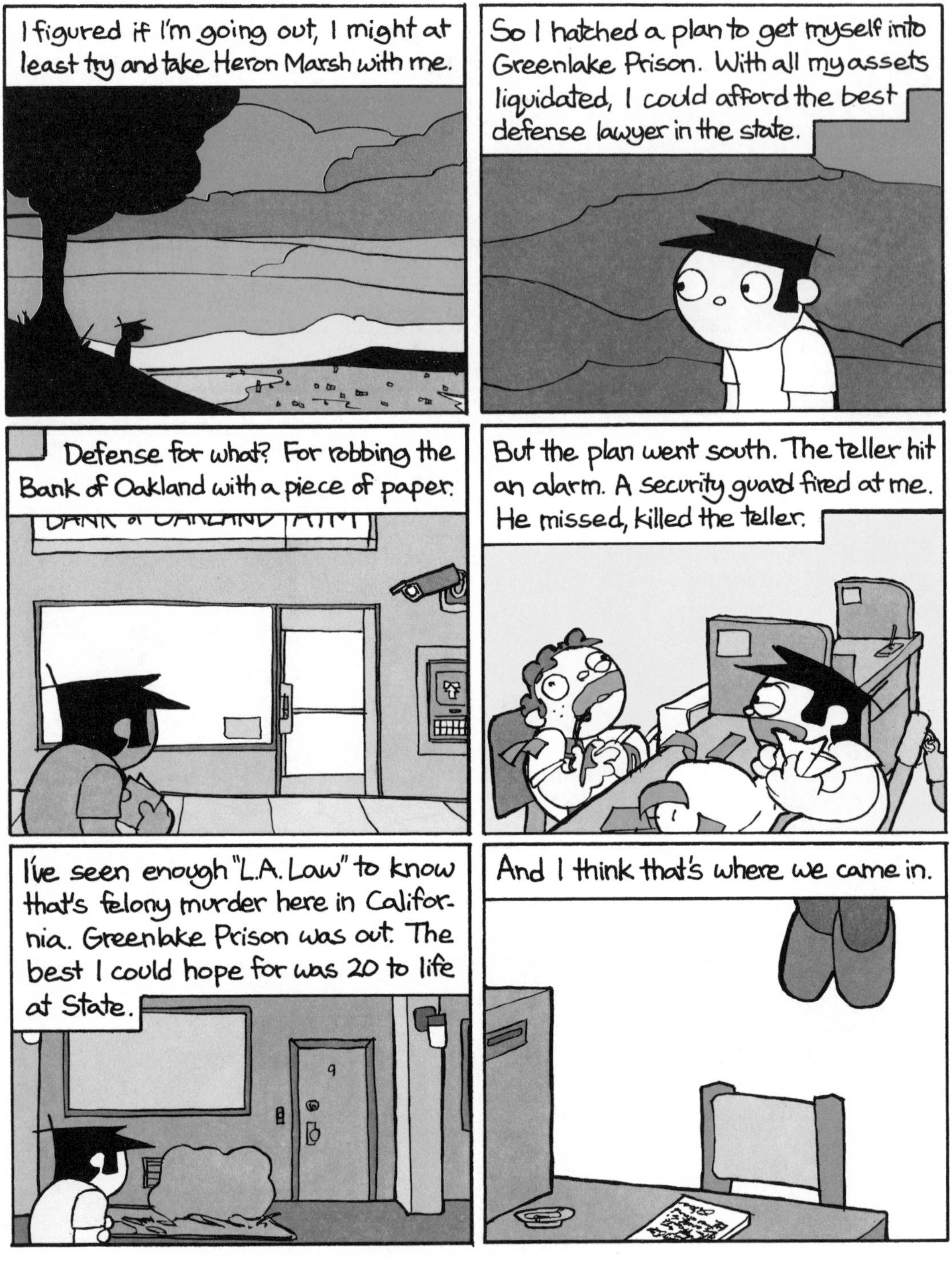
I figured if I'm going out, I might at least try and take Heron Marsh with me.
So I hatched a plan to get myself into Greenlake Prison. With all my assets liquidated, I could afford the best defense lawyer in the state.
Defense for what? For robbing the Bank of Oakland with a piece of paper.
But the plan went south. The teller hit an alarm. A security guard fired at me. He missed, killed the teller.
I've seen enough "L.A. Law" to know that's felony murder here in California. Greenlake Prison was out. The best I could hope for was 20 to life at State.
And I think that's where we came in.

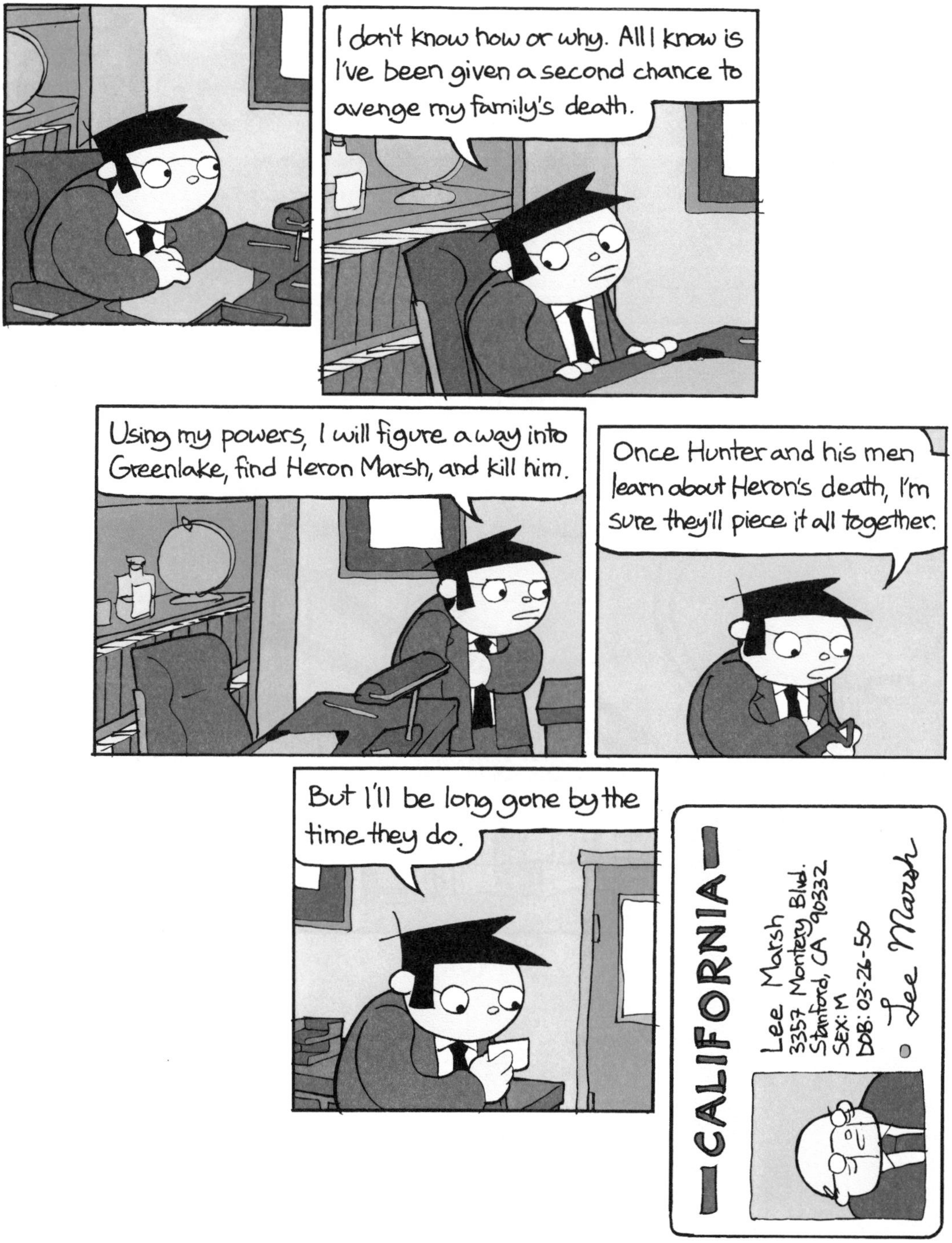
I don't know how or why. All I know is I've been given a second chance to avenge my family's death.
Using my powers, I will figure a way into Greenlake, find Heron Marsh, and kill him.
Once Hunter and his men learn about Heron's death, I'm sure they'll piece it all together.
But I'll be long gone by the time they do.
CALIFORNIA
Lee Marsh
3357 Montery Blvd.
Stanford, CA 90332
SEX: M
DOB: 03-26-50
Lee Marsh

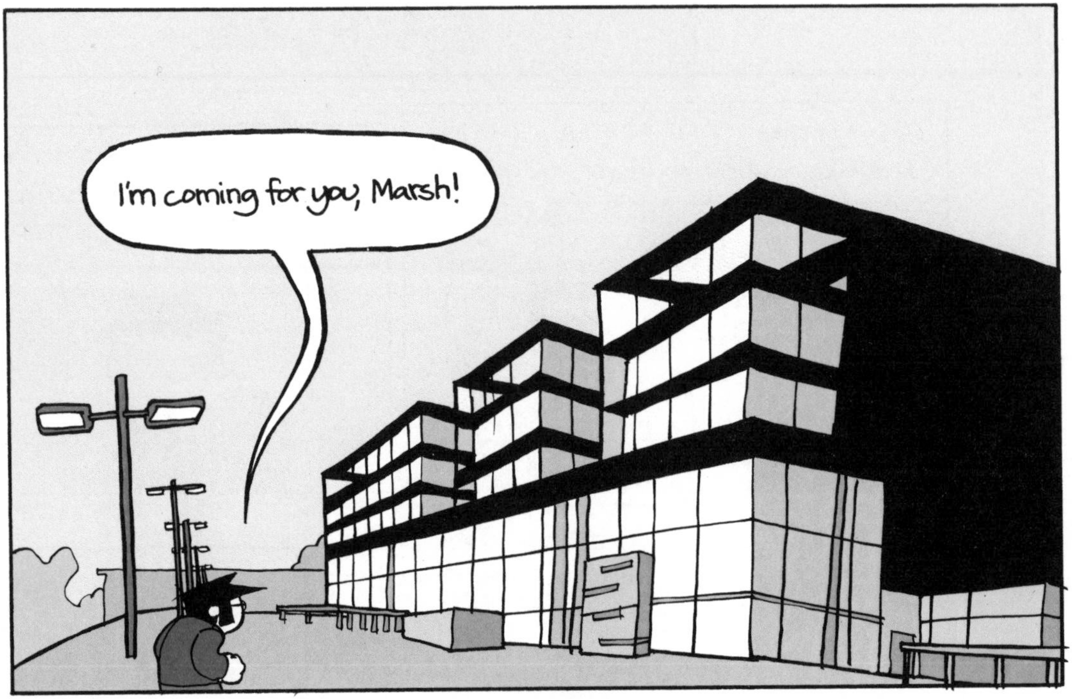
I'm coming for you, Marsh!

# CHAPTER 7

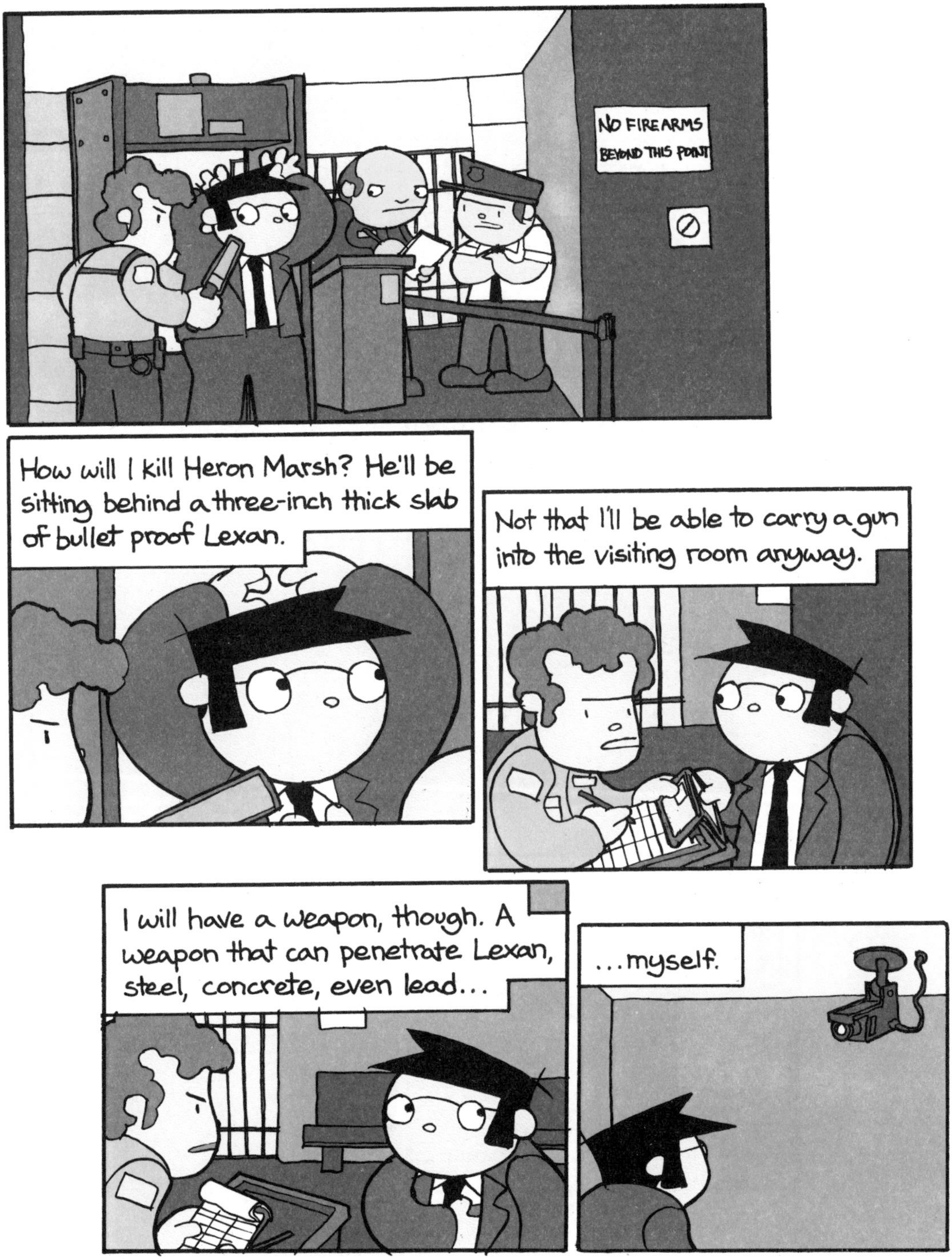
NO FIREARMS
BEYOND THIS POINT
How will I kill Heron Marsh? He'll be sitting behind a three-inch thick slab of bullet proof Lexan.
Not that I'll be able to carry a gun into the visiting room anyway.
I will have a weapon, though. A weapon that can penetrate Lexan, steel, concrete, even lead...
...myself.

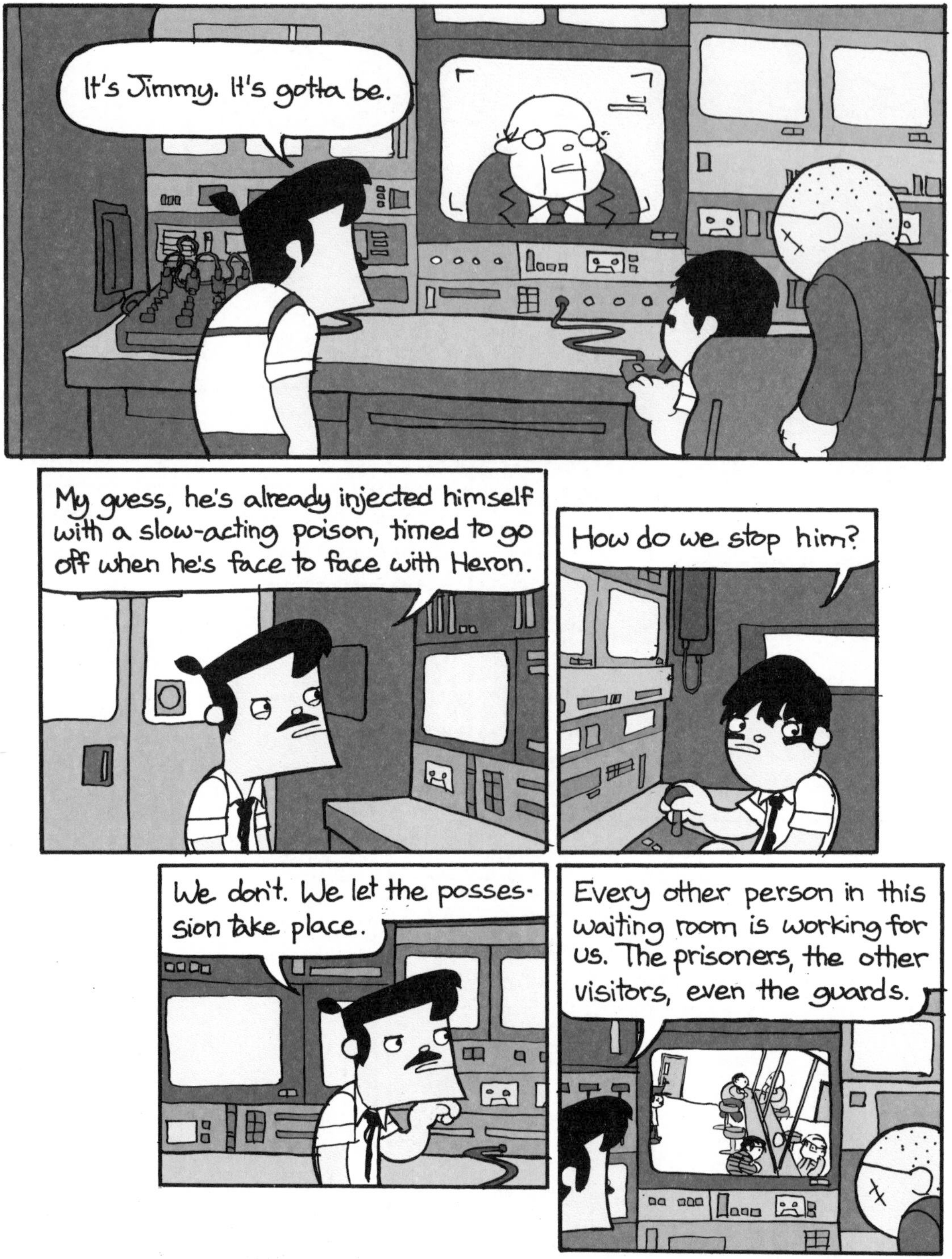
It's Jimmy. It's gotta be.
My guess, he's already injected himself with a slow-acting poison, timed to go off when he's face to face with Heron.
How do we stop him?
We don't. We let the posses-sion take place.
Every other person in this waiting room is working for us. The prisoners, the other visitors, even the guards.

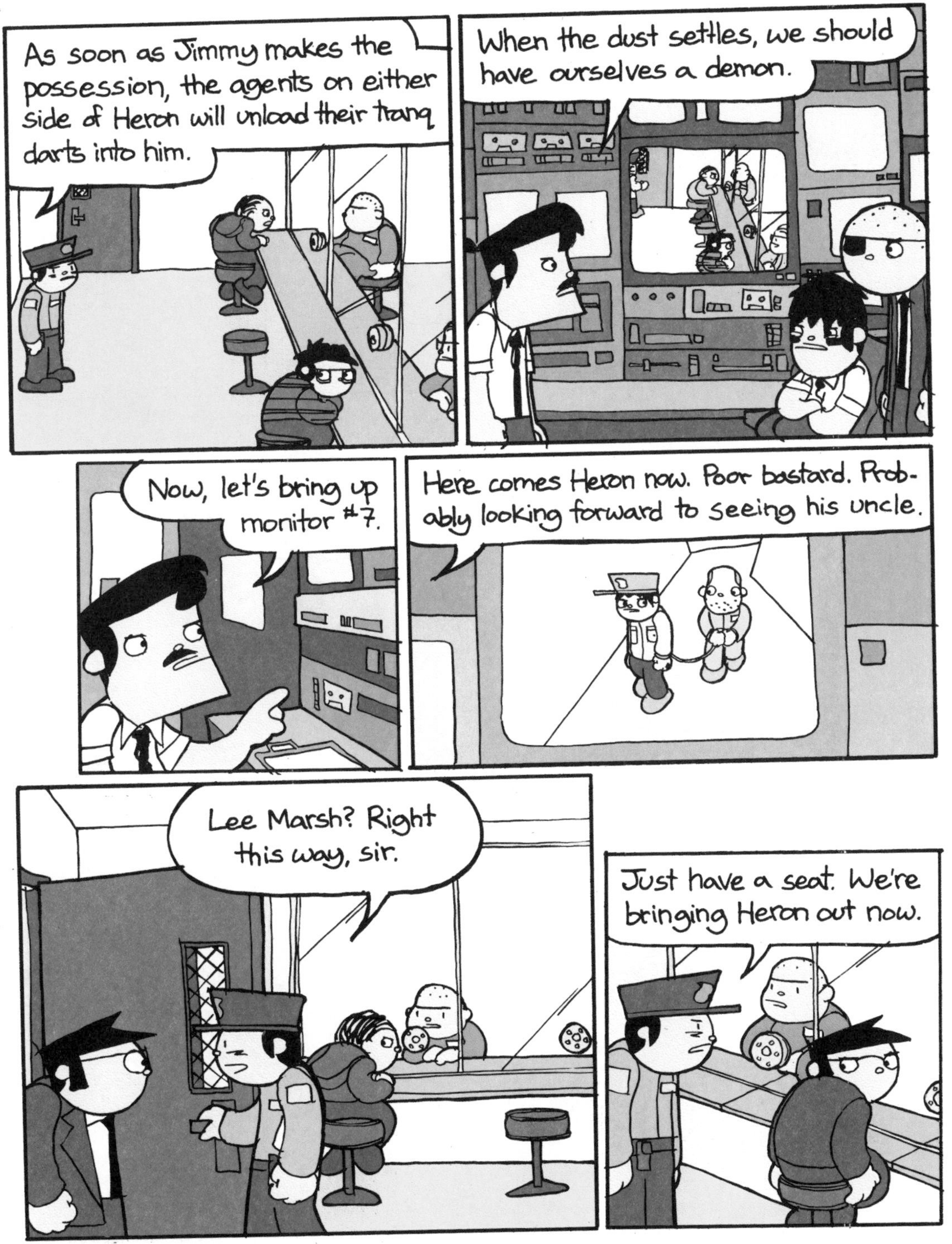
As soon as Jimmy makes the possession, the agents on either side of Heron will unload their tranq darts into him.
When the dust settles, we should have ourselves a demon.
Now, let's bring up monitor #7.
Here comes Heron now. Poor bastard. Probably looking forward to seeing his uncle.
Lee Marsh? Right this way, sir.
Just have a seat. We're bringing Heron out now.

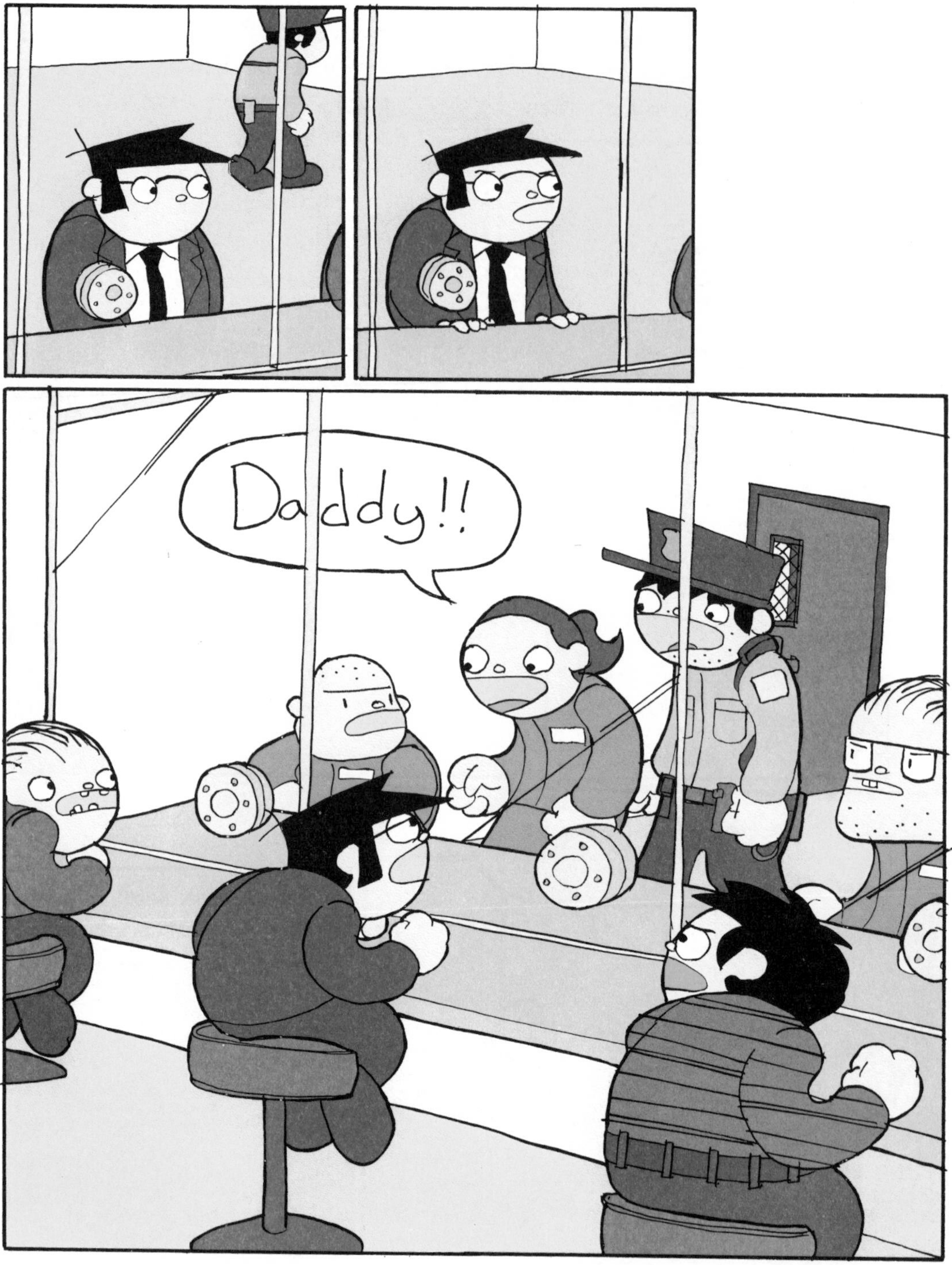
Daddy!!

# CHAPTER 8

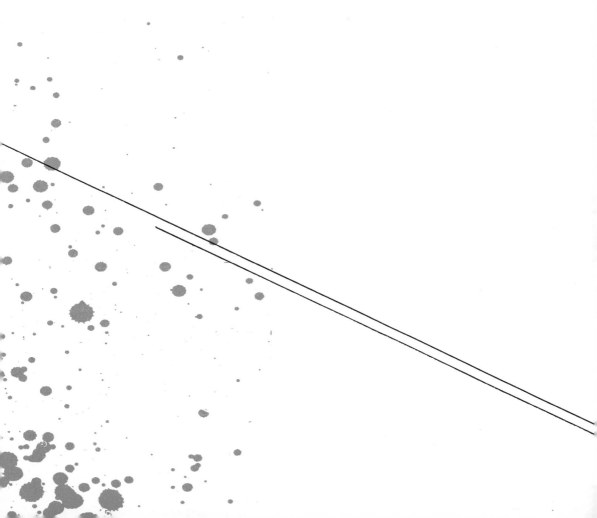

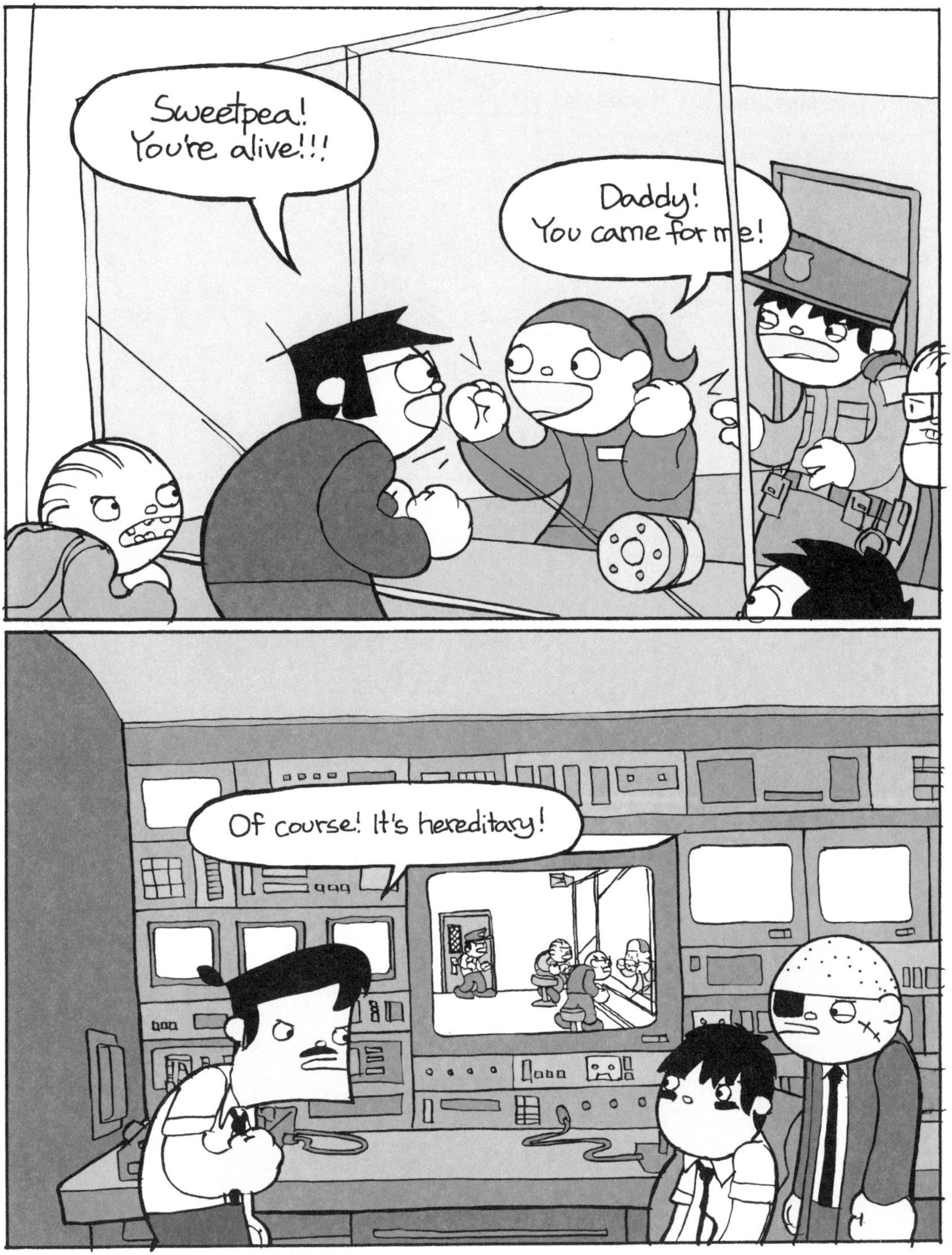
Sweetpea! You're alive!!!
Daddy! You came for me!
Of course! It's hereditary!

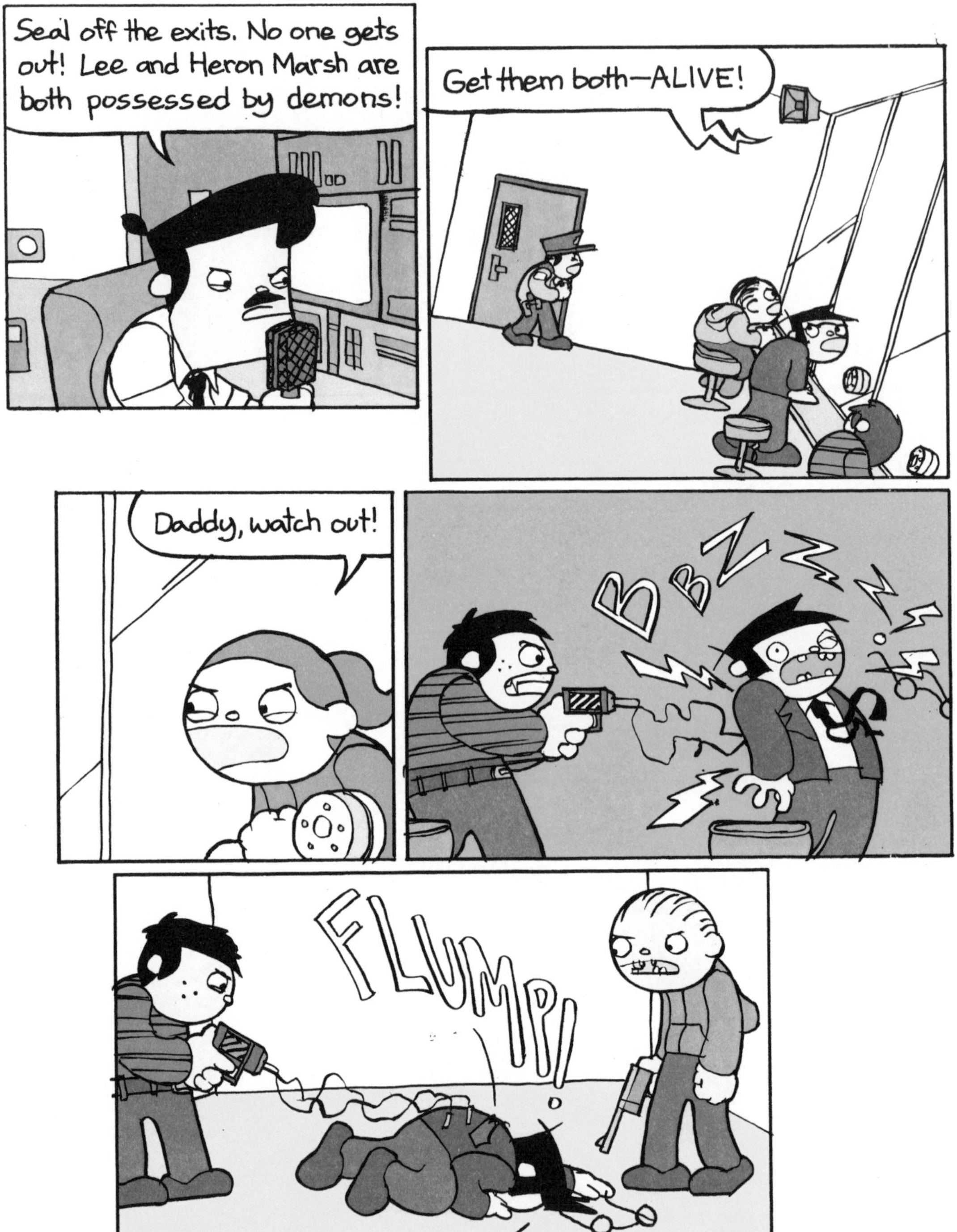
Seal off the exits. No one gets out! Lee and Heron Marsh are both possessed by demons!
Get them both—ALIVE!
Daddy, watch out!
BBZZZZ
FLUMP!

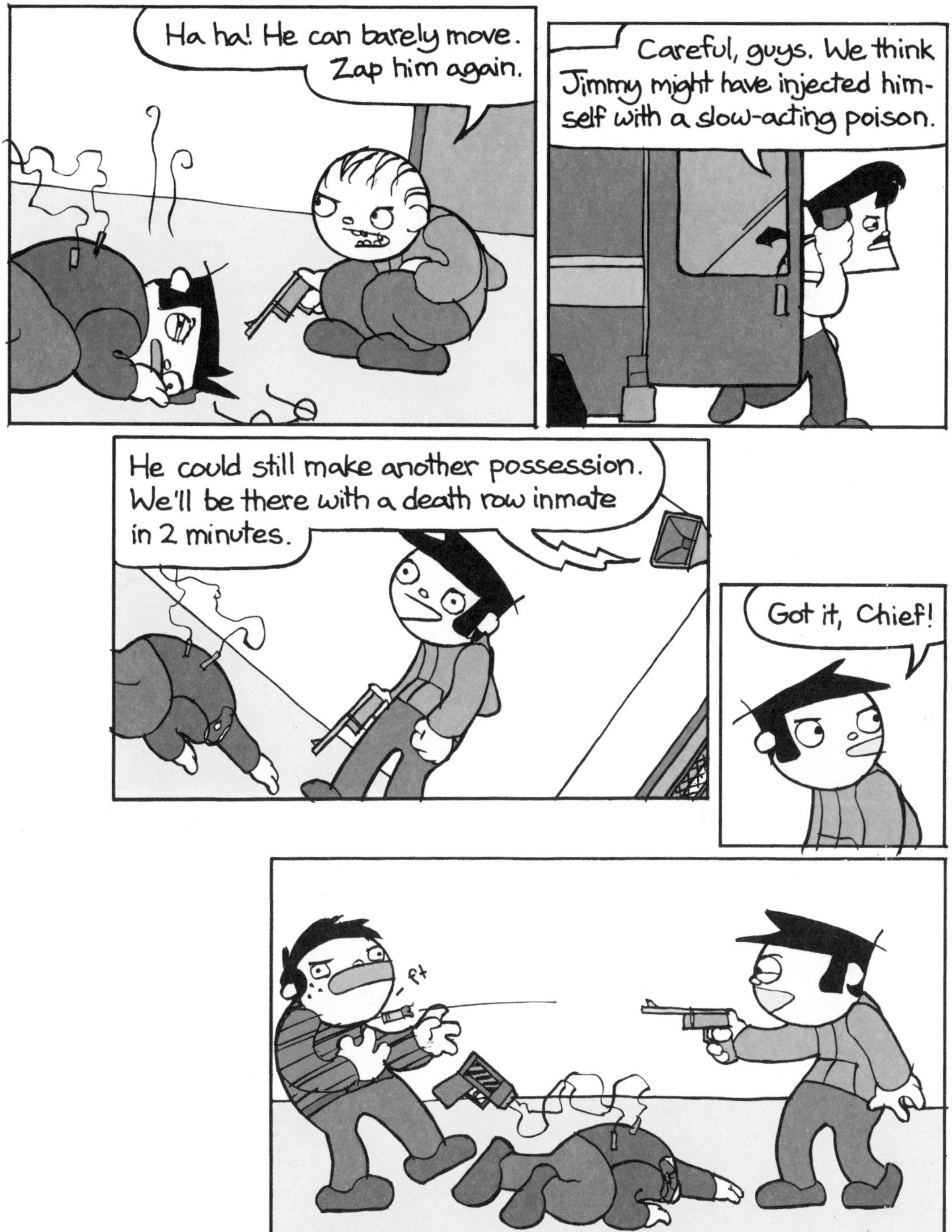
Ha ha! He can barely move. Zap him again.
Careful, guys. We think Jimmy might have injected himself with a slow-acting poison.
He could still make another possession. We'll be there with a death row inmate in 2 minutes.
Got it, Chief!
pt

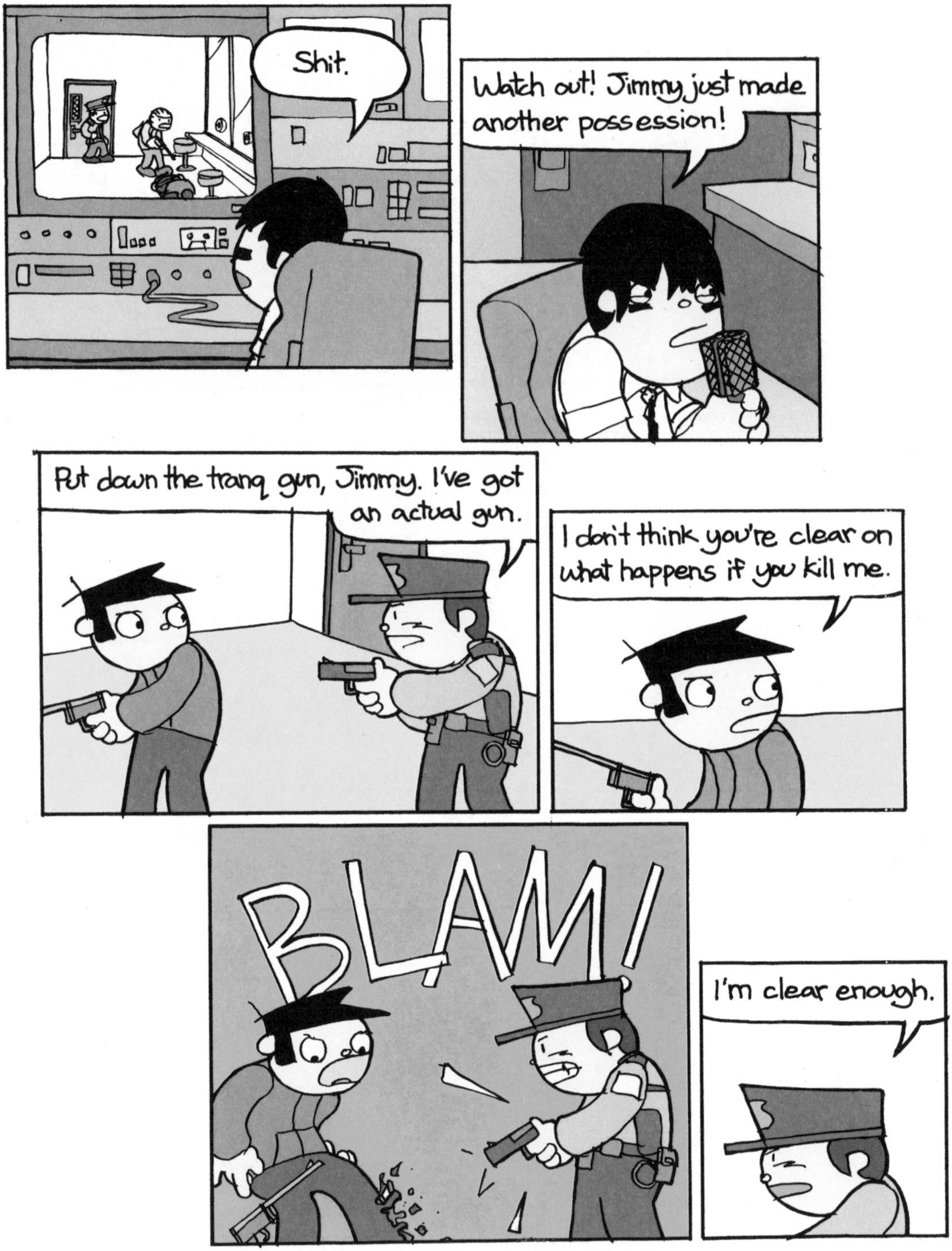
Shit.
Watch out! Jimmy just made another possession!
Put down the tranq gun, Jimmy. I've got an actual gun.
I don't think you're clear on what happens if you kill me.
BLAM!
I'm clear enough.

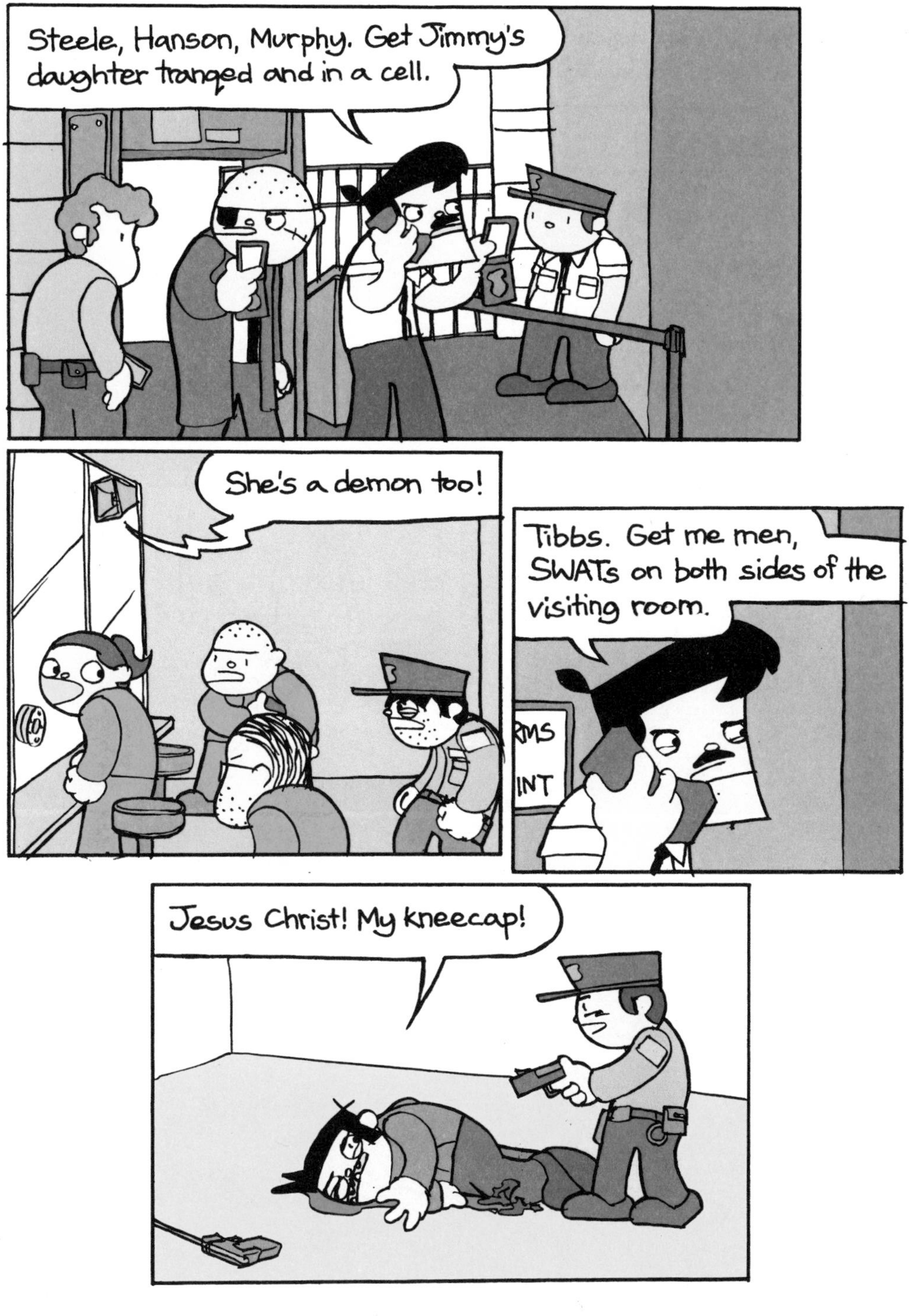
Steele, Hanson, Murphy. Get Jimmy's daughter tranqed and in a cell.
She's a demon too!
Tibbs. Get me men, SWATs on both sides of the visiting room.
RMS
INT
Jesus Christ! My kneecap!

Unless you want to lose your hand too, slowly move it away from the tranq gun.

GRAB!

SCOOP

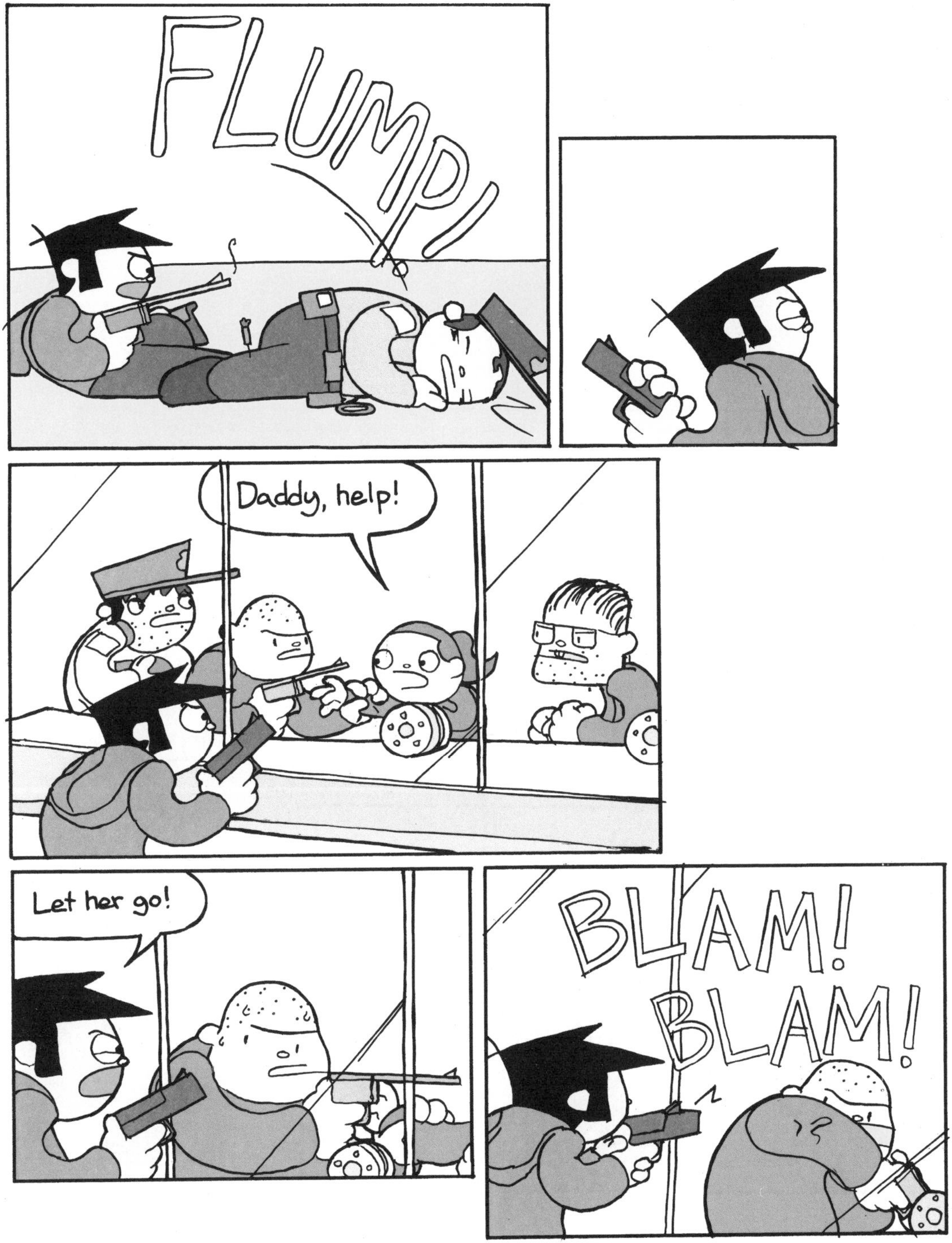
FLUMP!
Daddy, help!
Let her go!
BLAM!
BLAM!

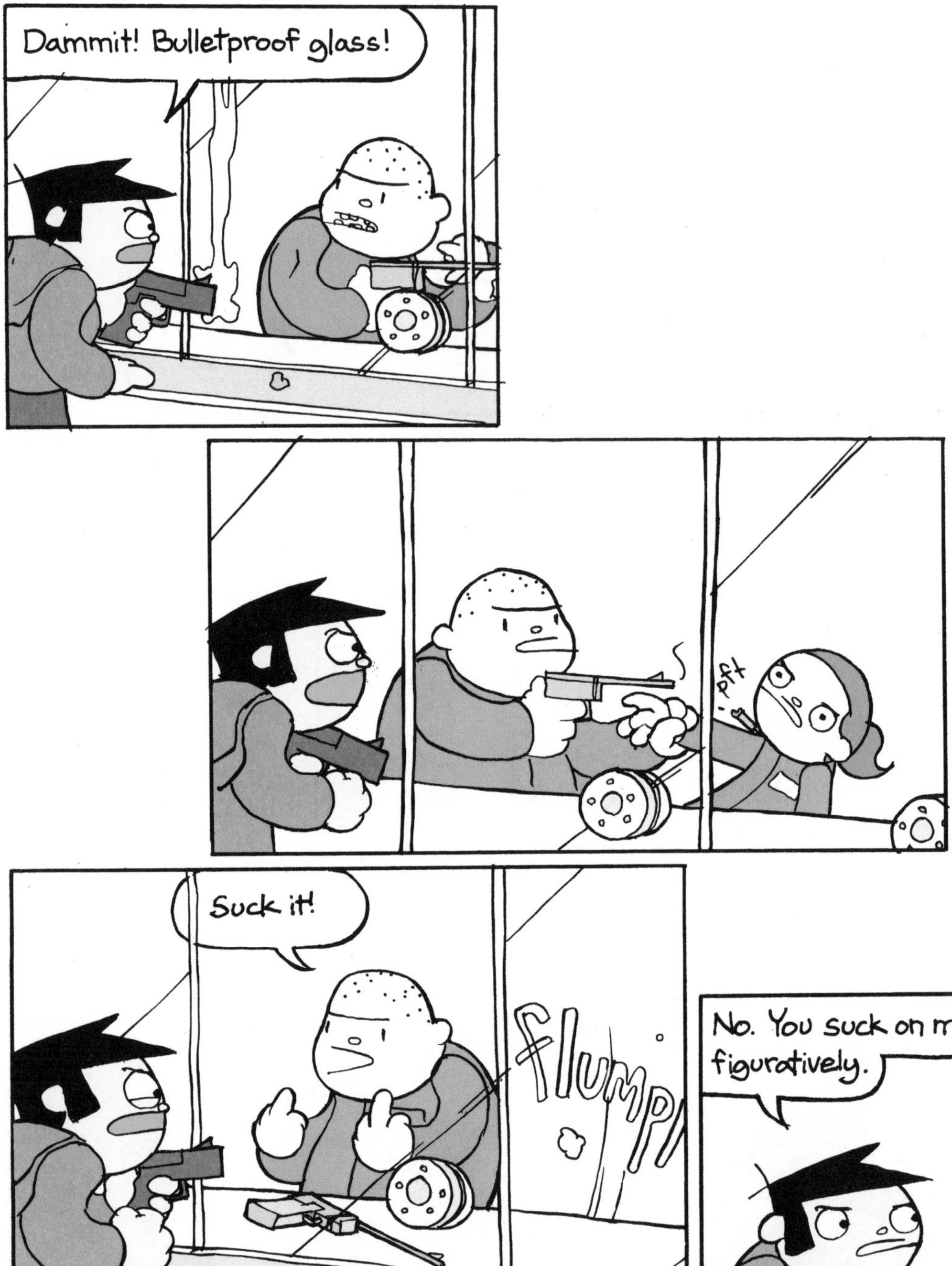
Dammit! Bulletproof glass!
pft
Suck it!
flump!
No. You suck on mine, figuratively.

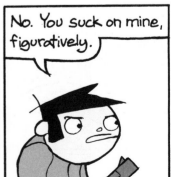

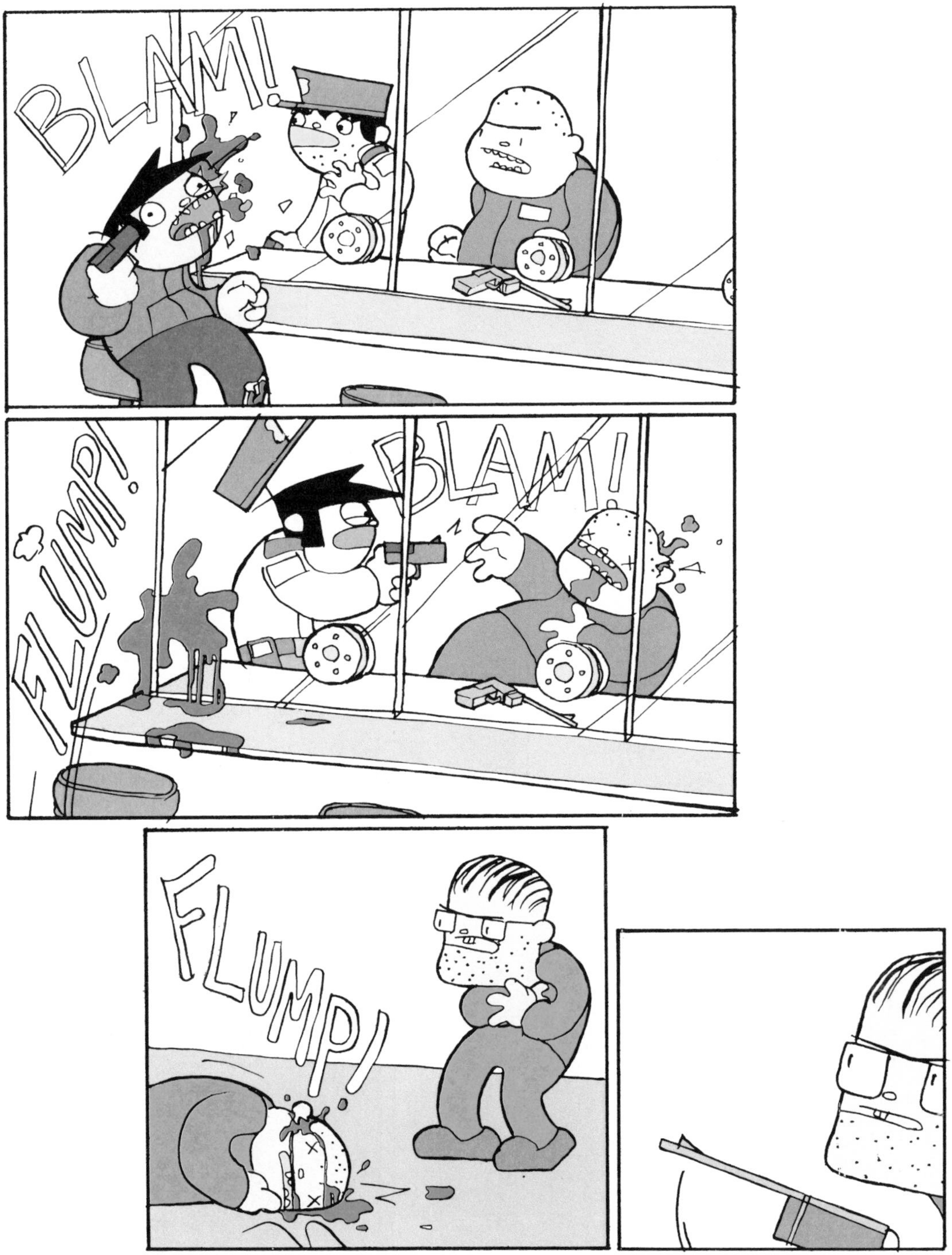
BLAM!
FLUMP!
BLAM!
FLUMP!

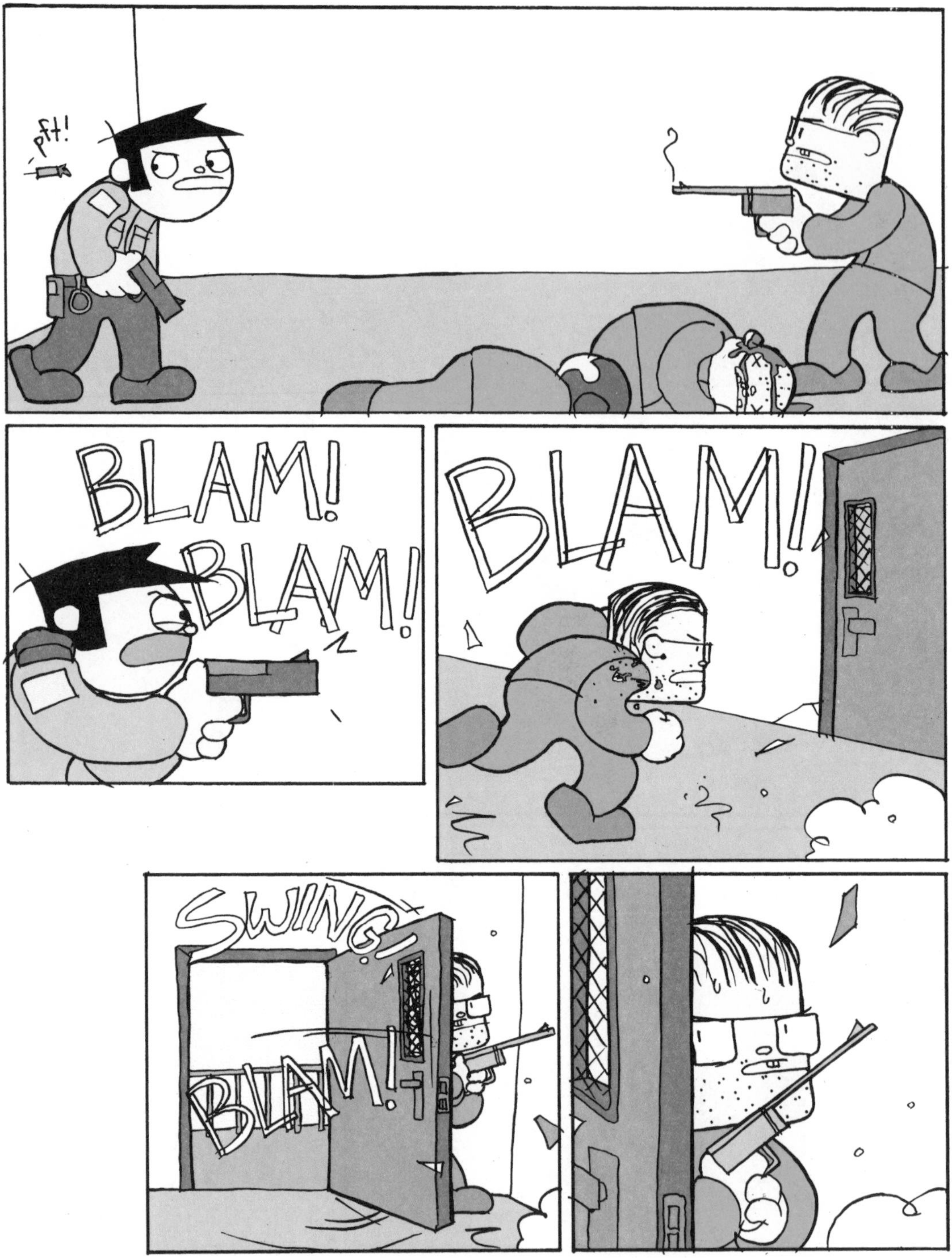
pft!
BLAM! BLAM!
BLAM!
SWING!
BLAM!

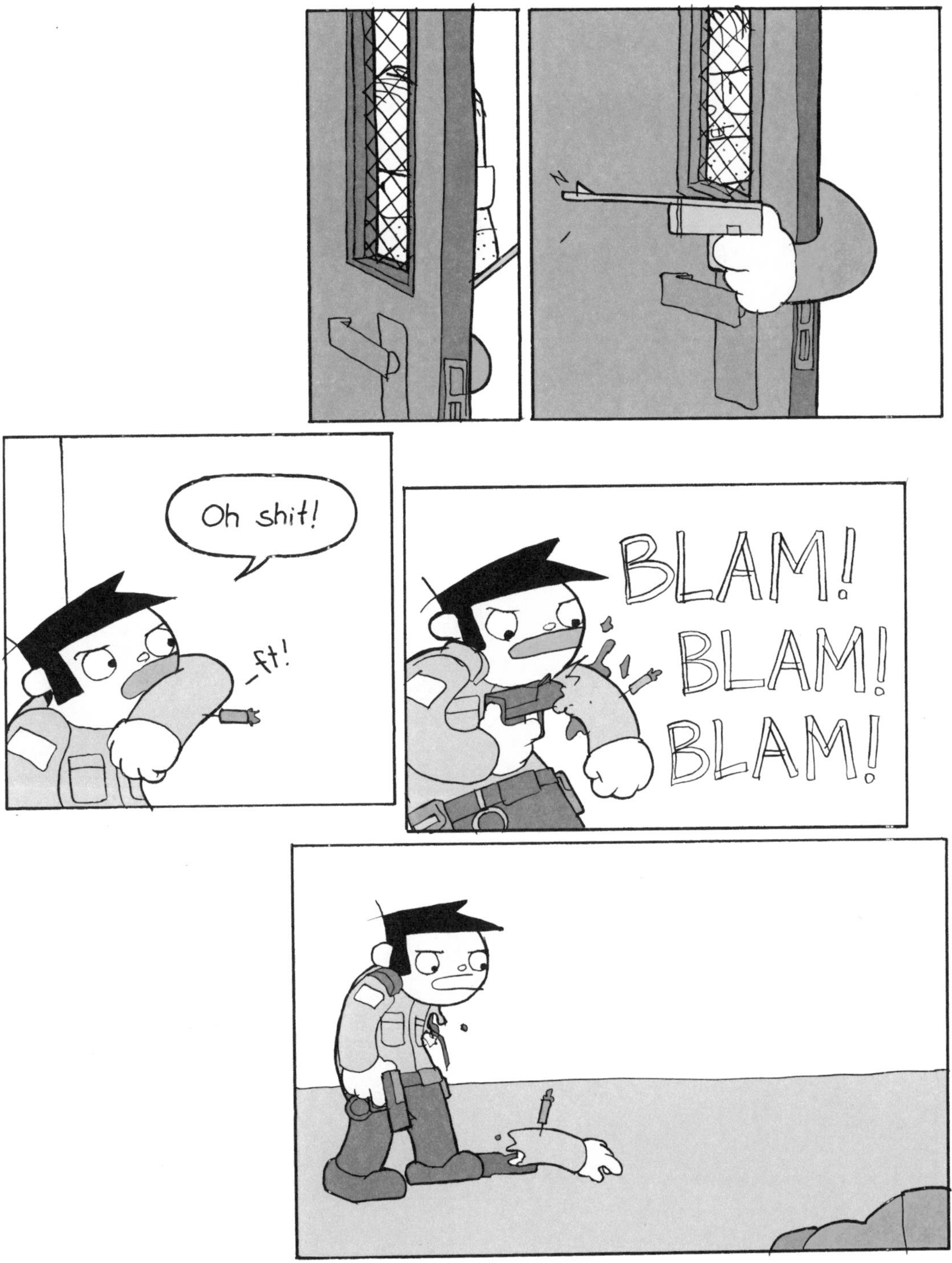
Oh shit!
ft!
BLAM!
BLAM!
BLAM!

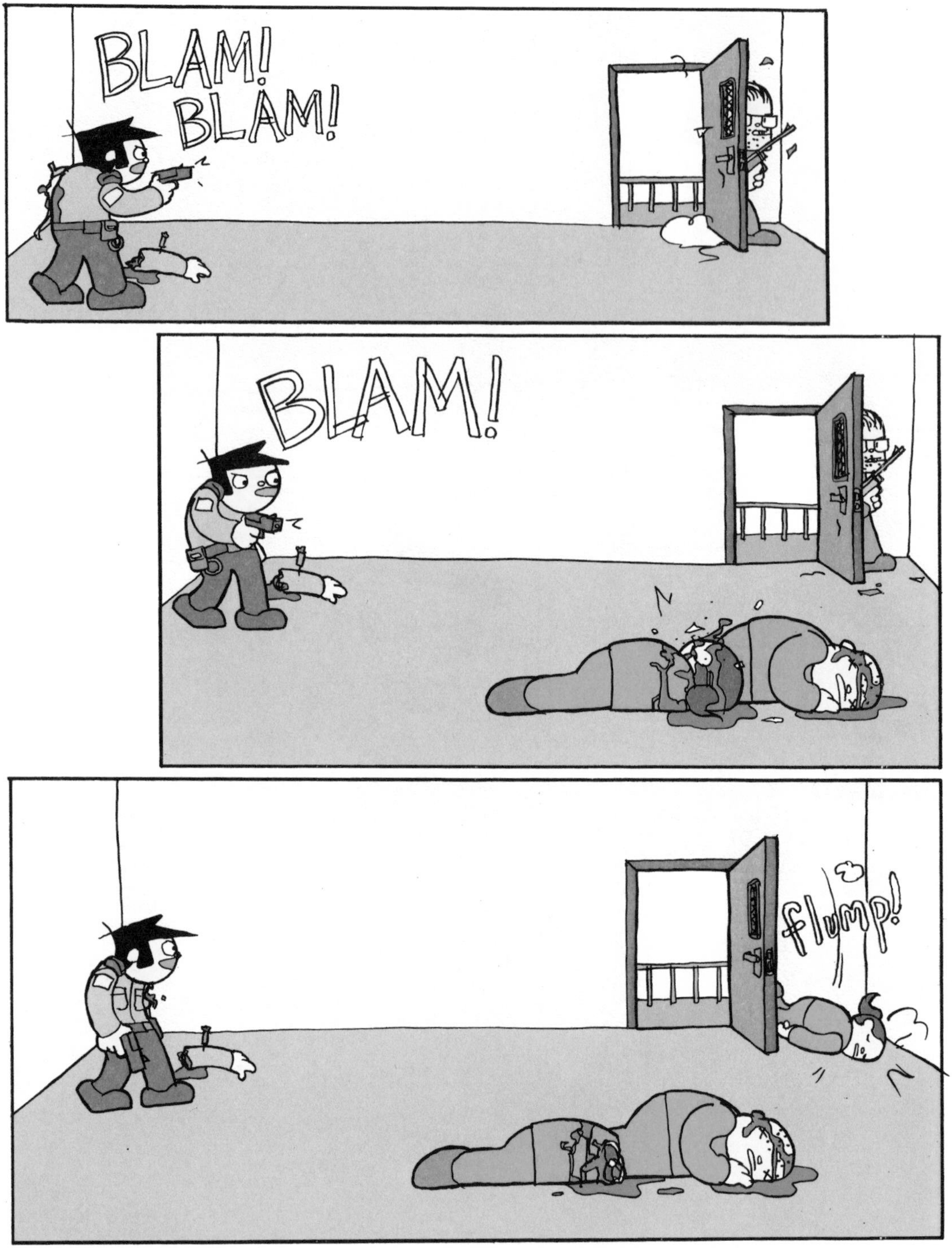
BLAM!
BLAM!
BLAM!
flump!

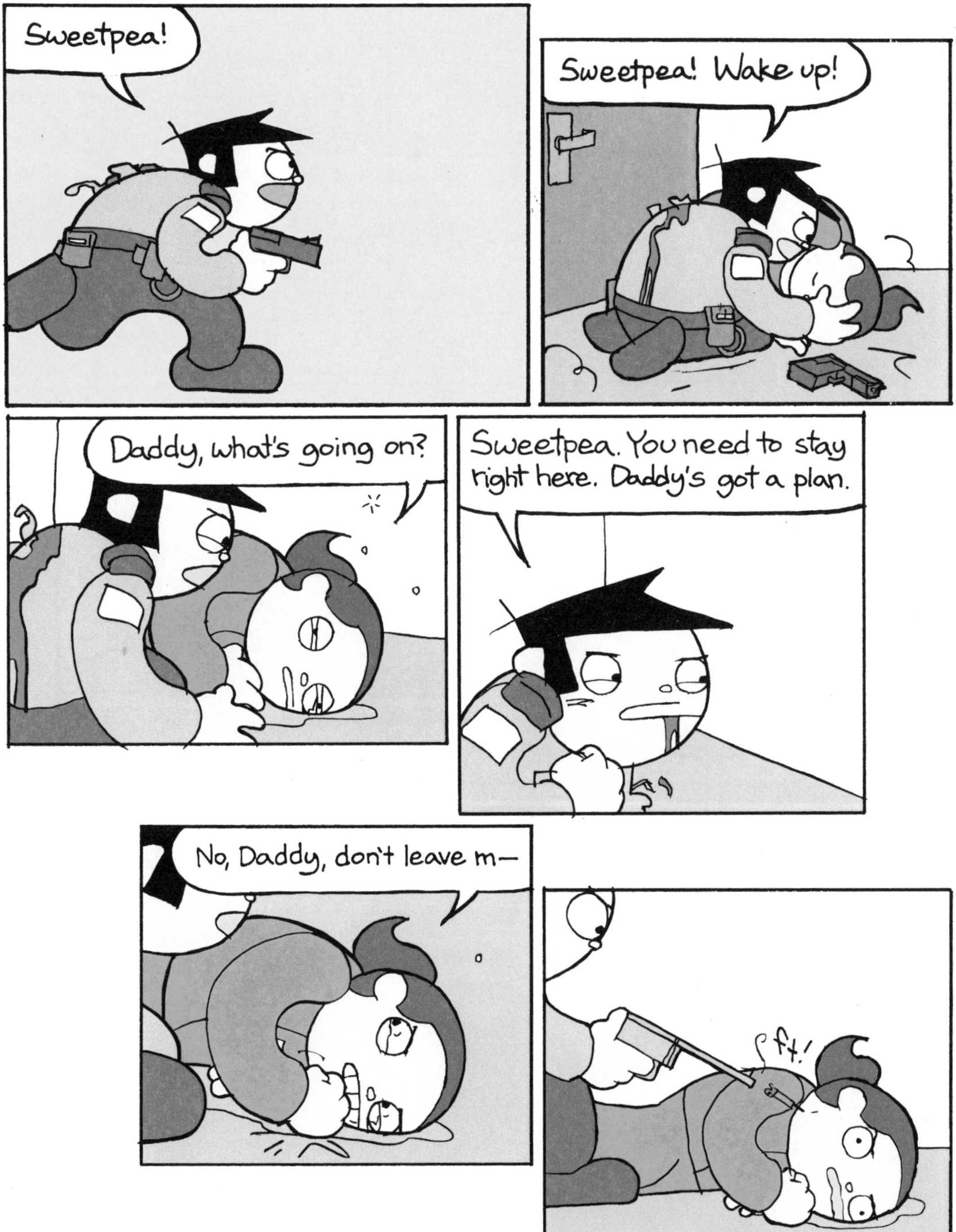
Sweetpea!
Sweetpea! Wake up!
Daddy, what's going on?
Sweetpea. You need to stay right here. Daddy's got a plan.
No, Daddy, don't leave m—
ft!

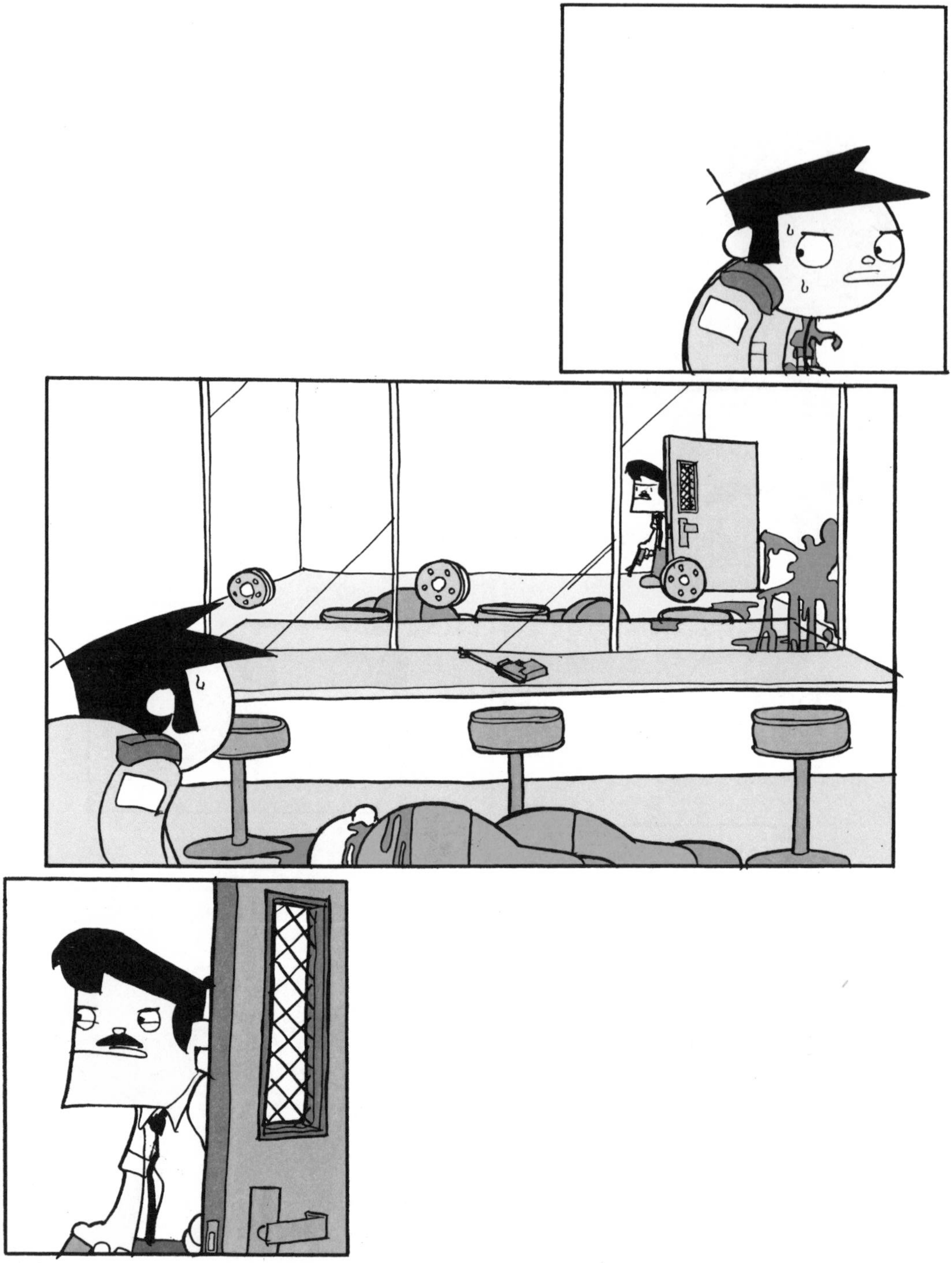

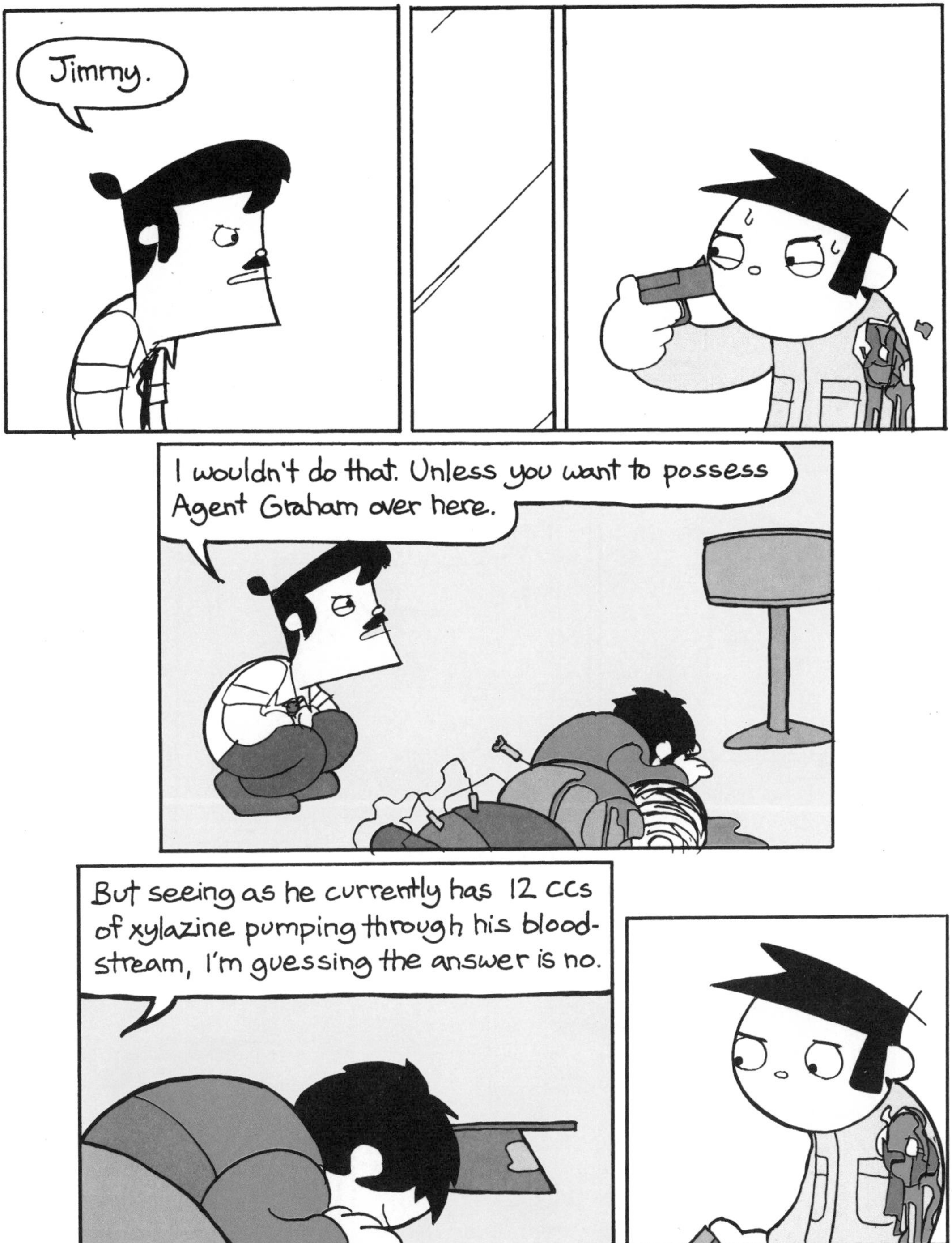
Jimmy.
I wouldn't do that. Unless you want to possess Agent Graham over here.
But seeing as he currently has 12 CCs of xylazine pumping through his bloodstream, I'm guessing the answer is no.

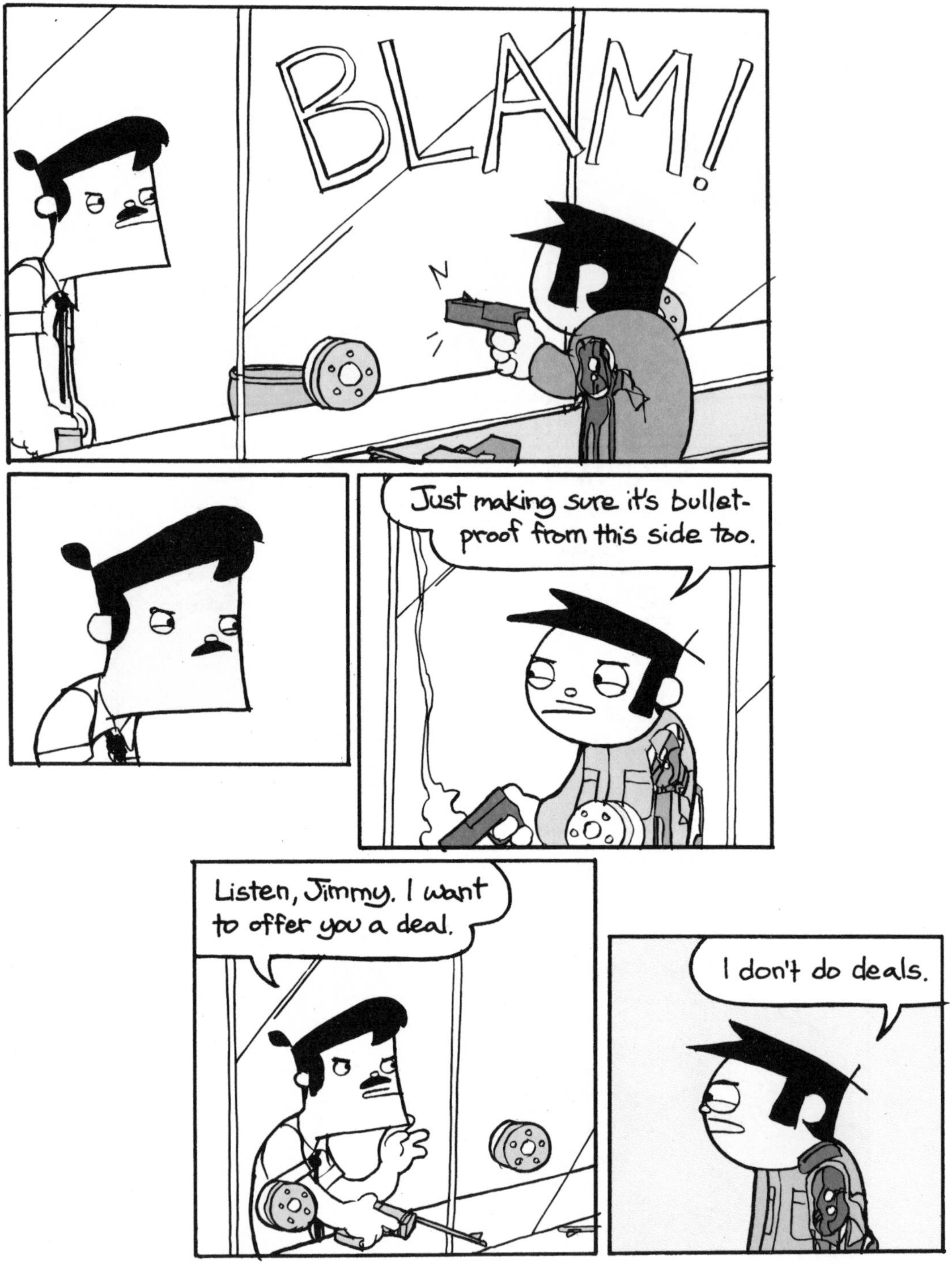
BLAM!
Just making sure it's bullet-proof from this side too.
Listen, Jimmy. I want to offer you a deal.
I don't do deals.

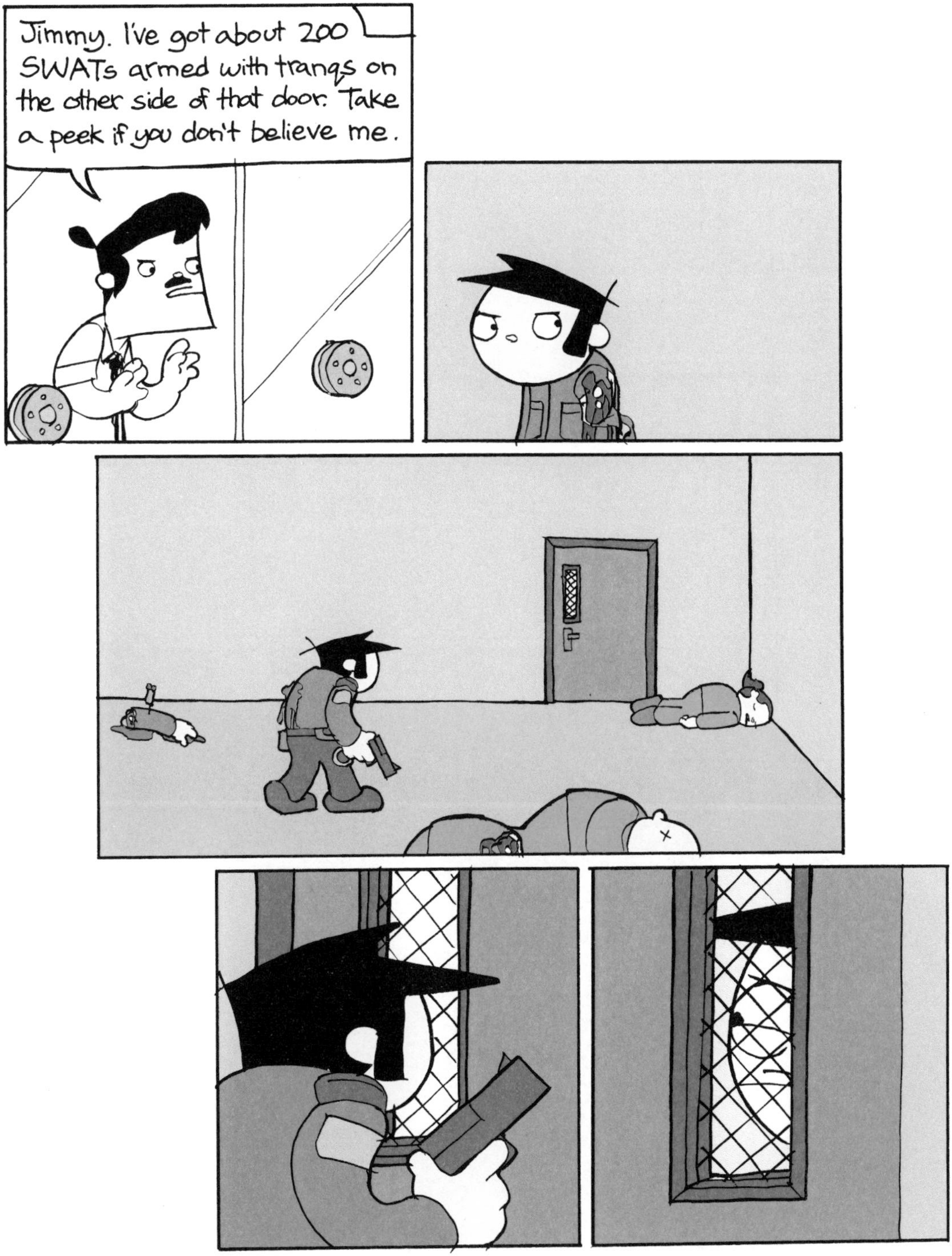
Jimmy. I've got about 200 SWATs armed with tranqs on the other side of that door. Take a peek if you don't believe me.

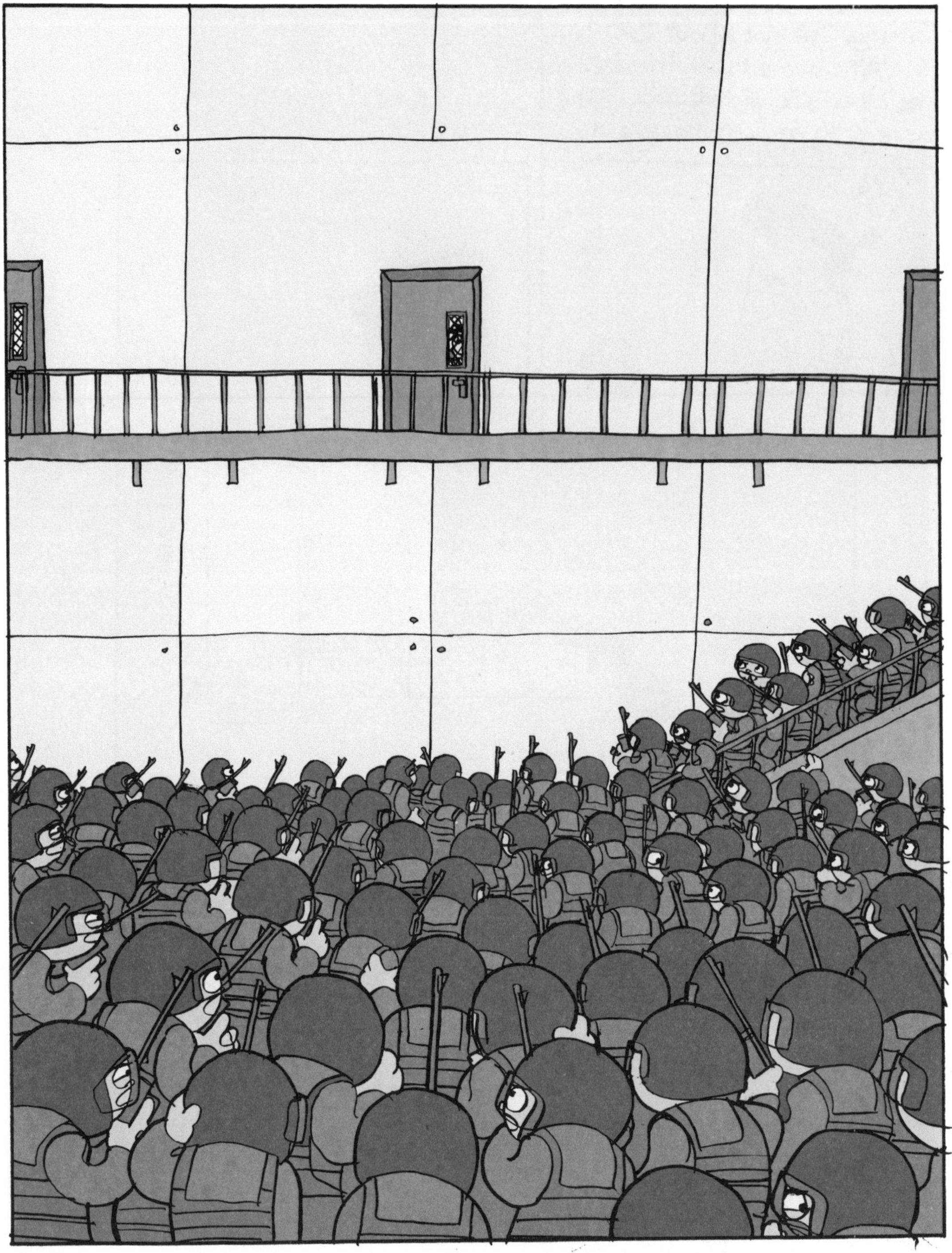

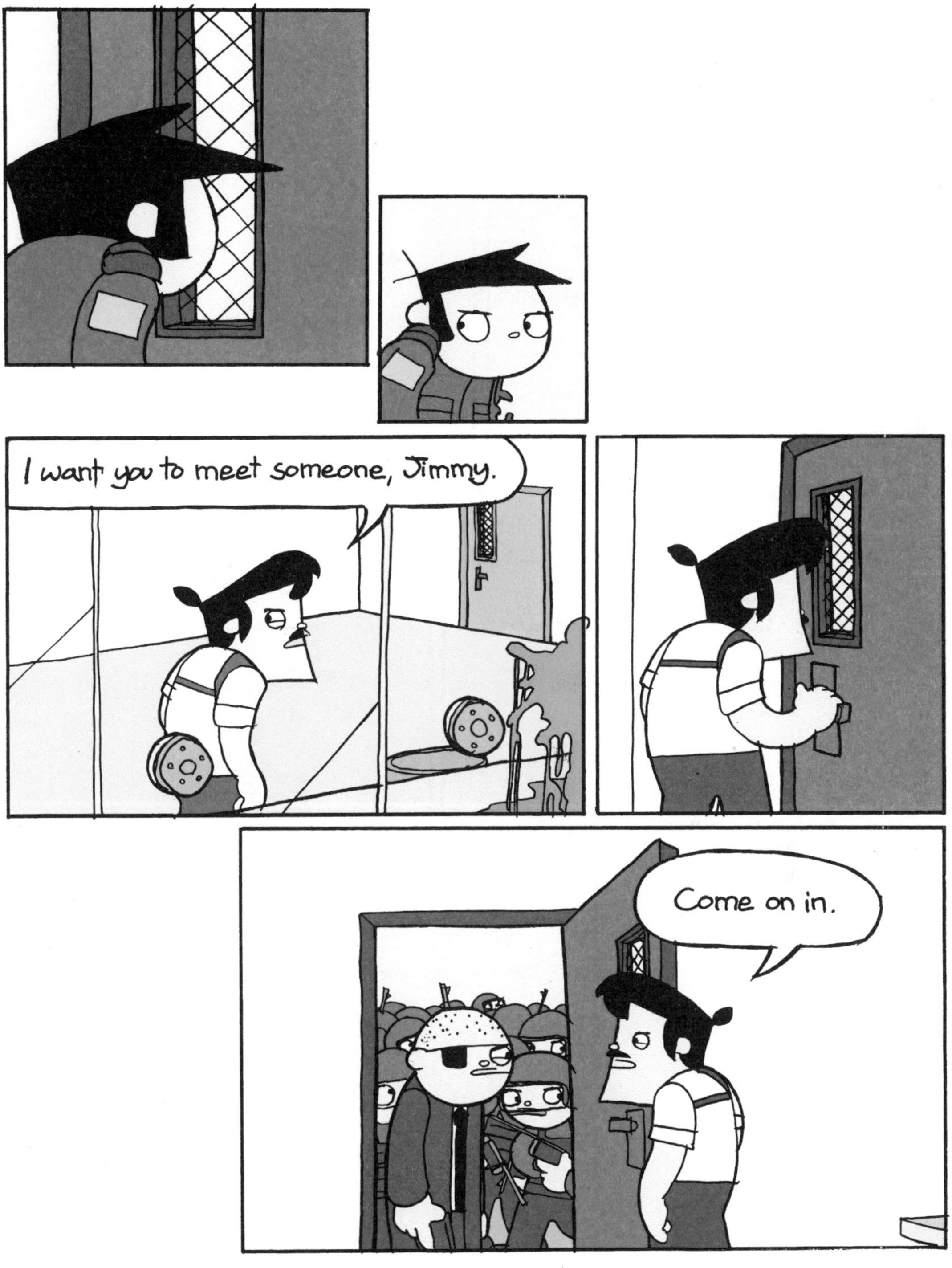
I want you to meet someone, Jimmy.
Come on in.

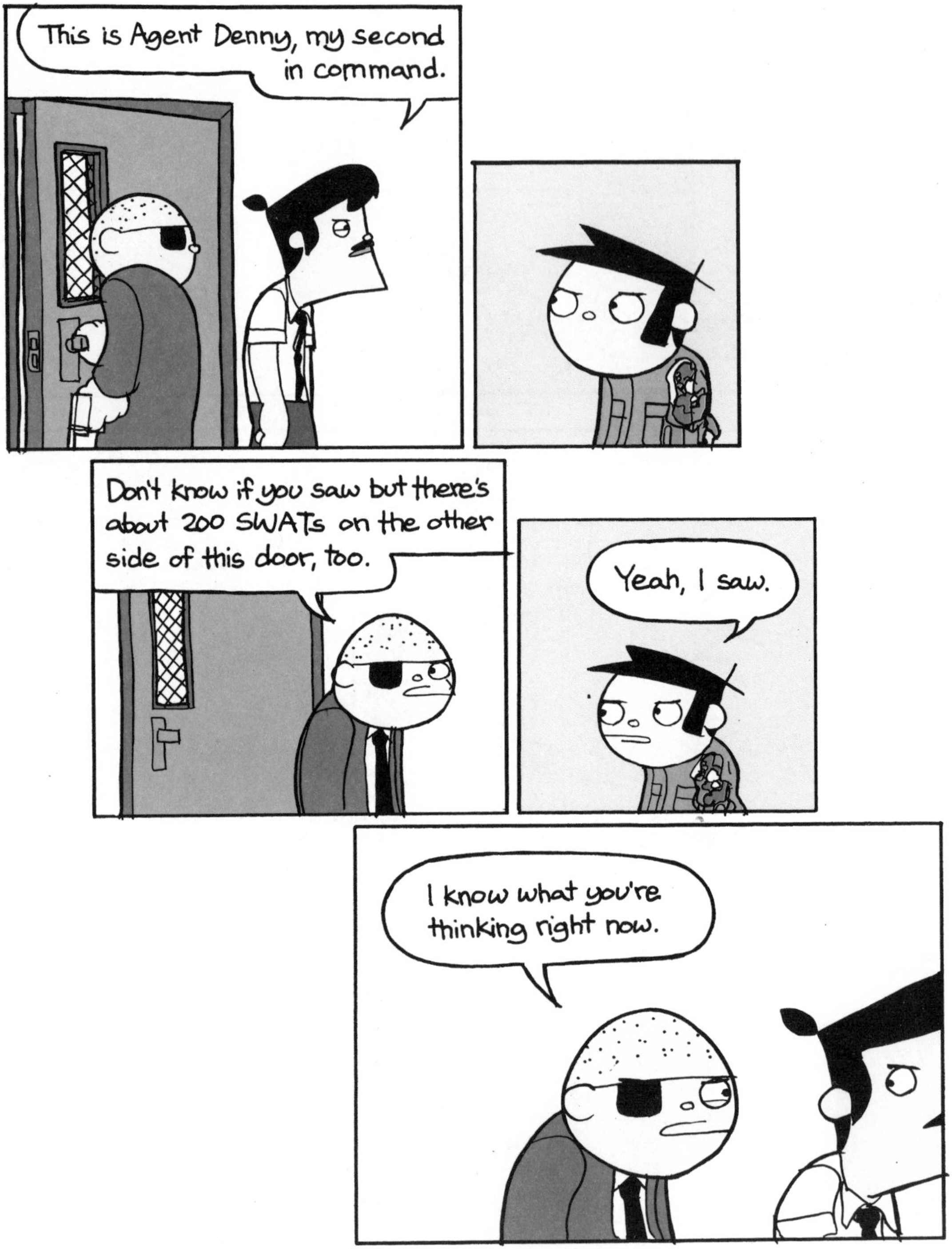
This is Agent Denny, my second in command.
Don't know if you saw but there's about 200 SWATs on the other side of this door, too.
Yeah, I saw.
I know what you're thinking right now.

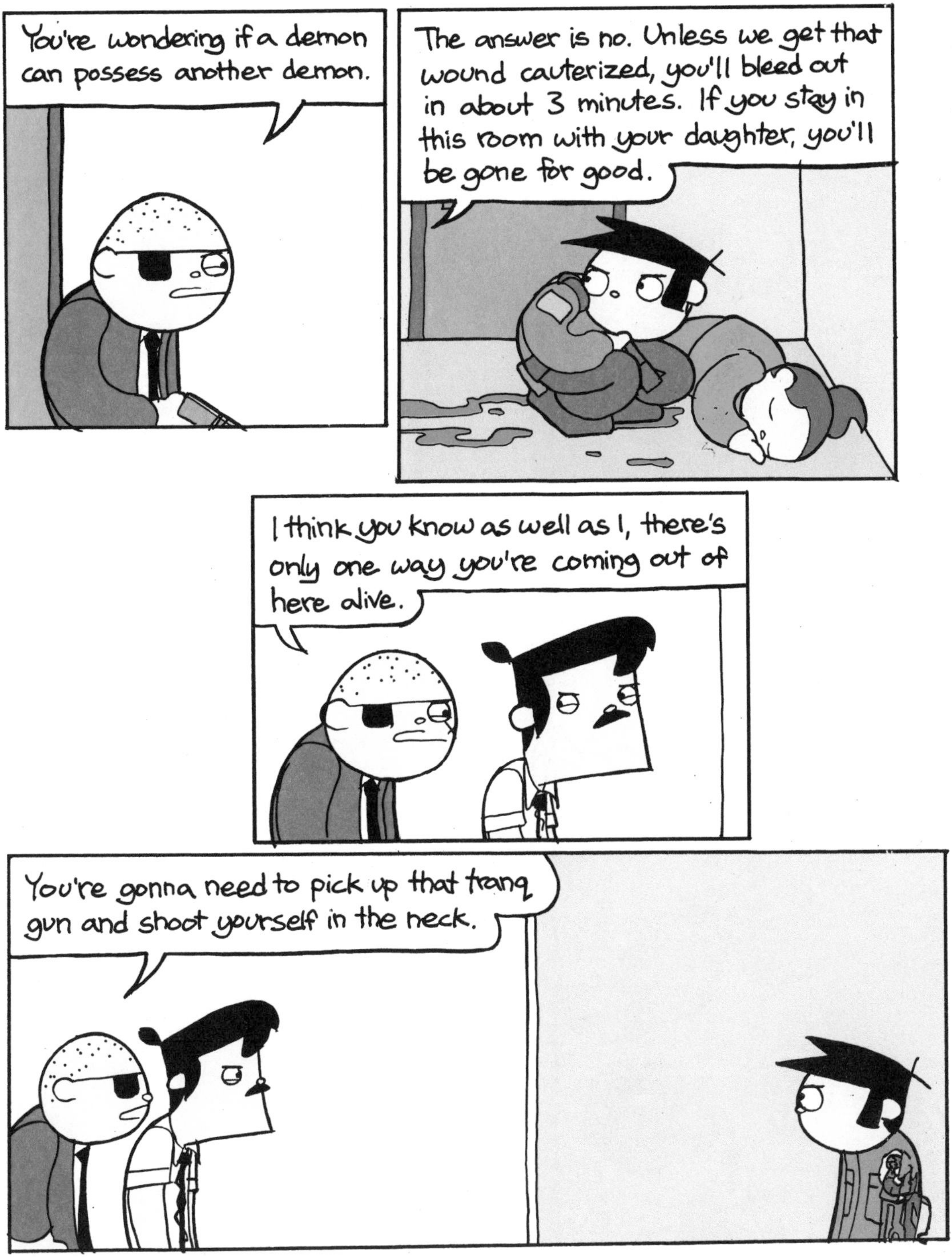
You're wondering if a demon can possess another demon.
The answer is no. Unless we get that wound cauterized, you'll bleed out in about 3 minutes. If you stay in this room with your daughter, you'll be gone for good.
I think you know as well as I, there's only one way you're coming out of here alive.
You're gonna need to pick up that tranq gun and shoot yourself in the neck.

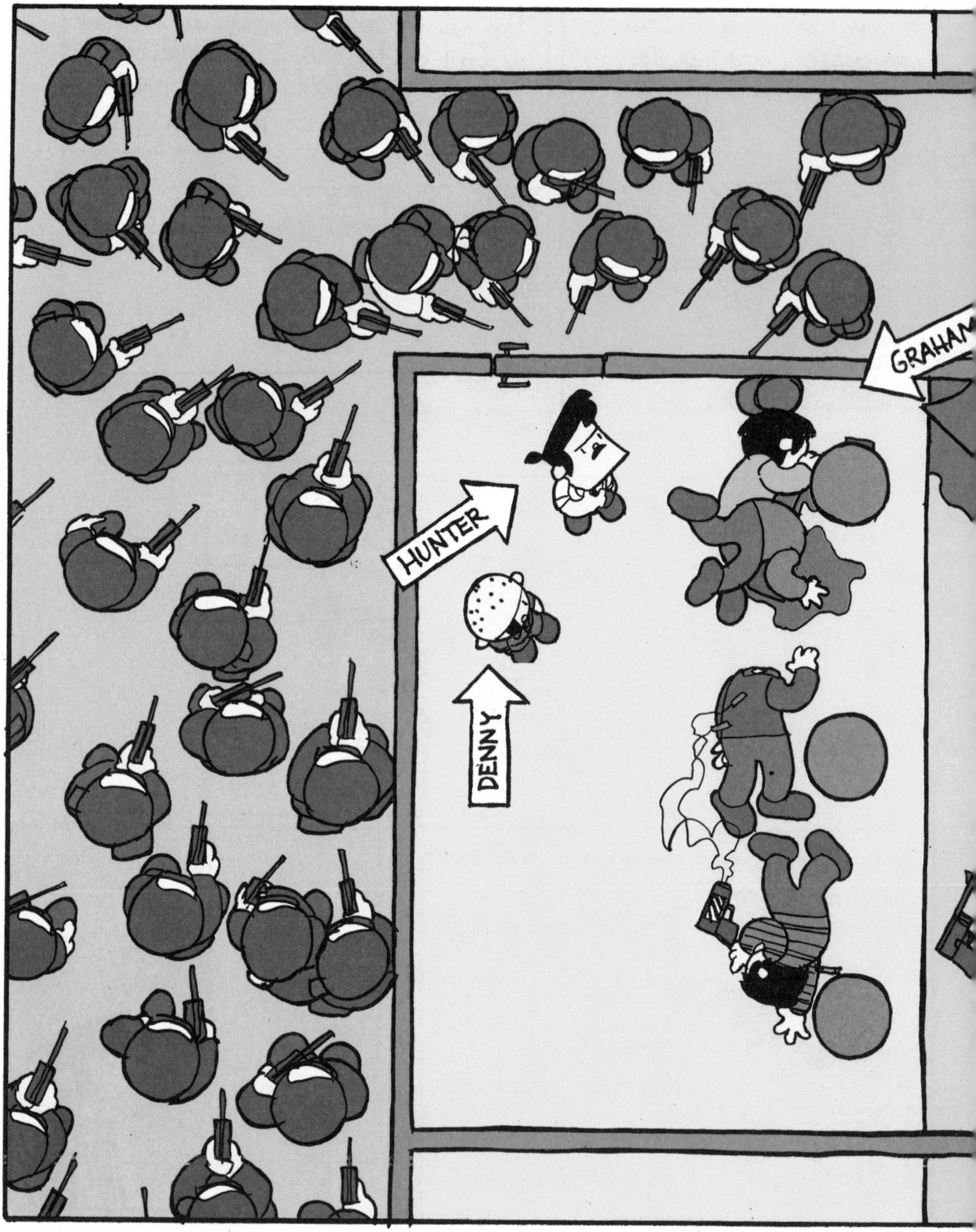

GRAHAM
HUNTER
DENNY

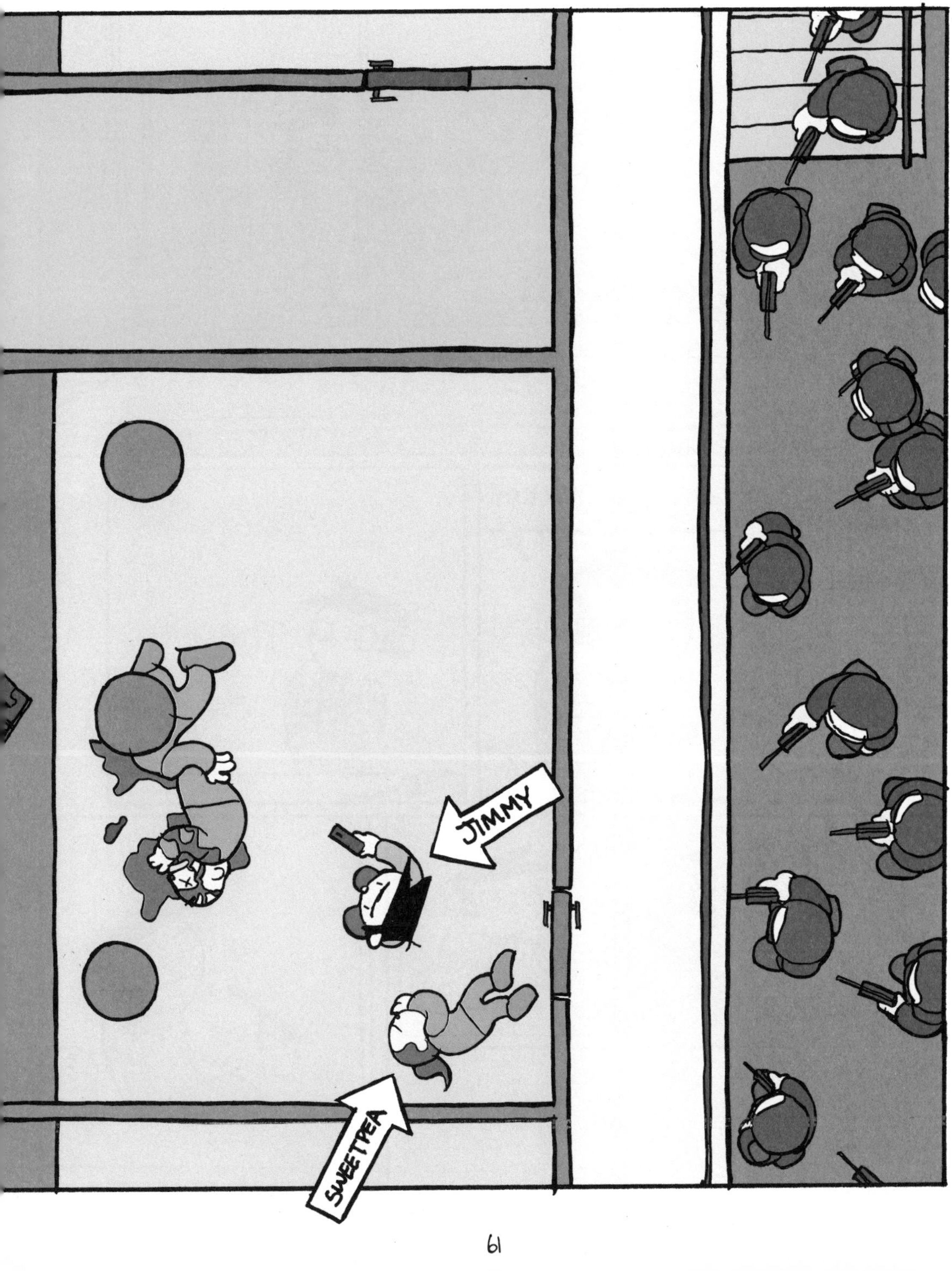
JIMMY
SWEETPEA

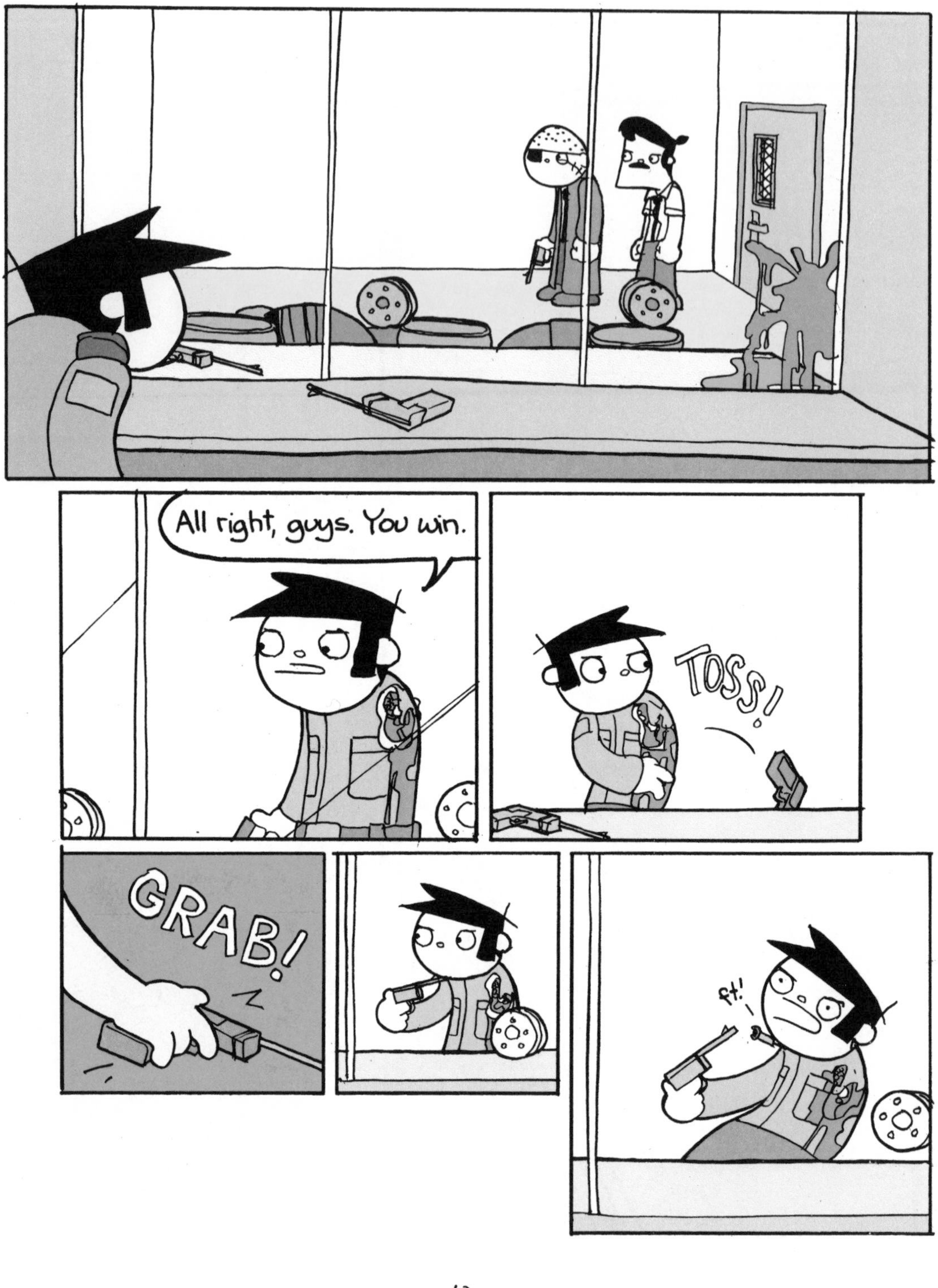
All right, guys. You win.
TOSS!
GRAB!
ft!

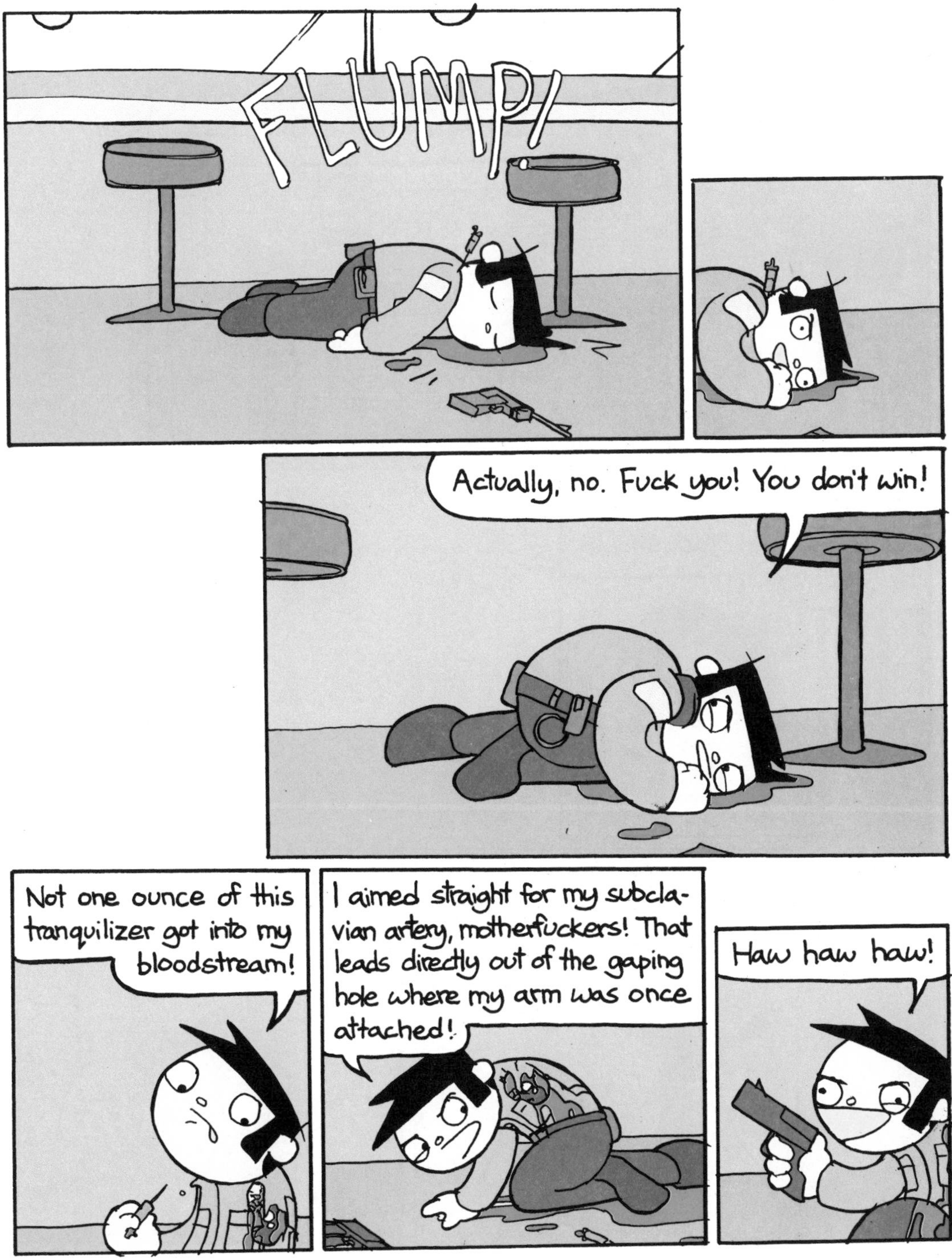
FLUMP!
Actually, no. Fuck you! You don't win!
Not one ounce of this tranquilizer got into my bloodstream!
I aimed straight for my subcla-vian artery, motherfuckers! That leads directly out of the gaping hole where my arm was once attached!
Haw haw haw!

You see where he fell?

Somewhere behind the left side of the counter. I don't want to get too close.

Just stay on this side of Agent Graham. You should be fine.

Alpha Team, where's my death row inmate?

Just arrived at security, sir. Should be there in less than a minute.

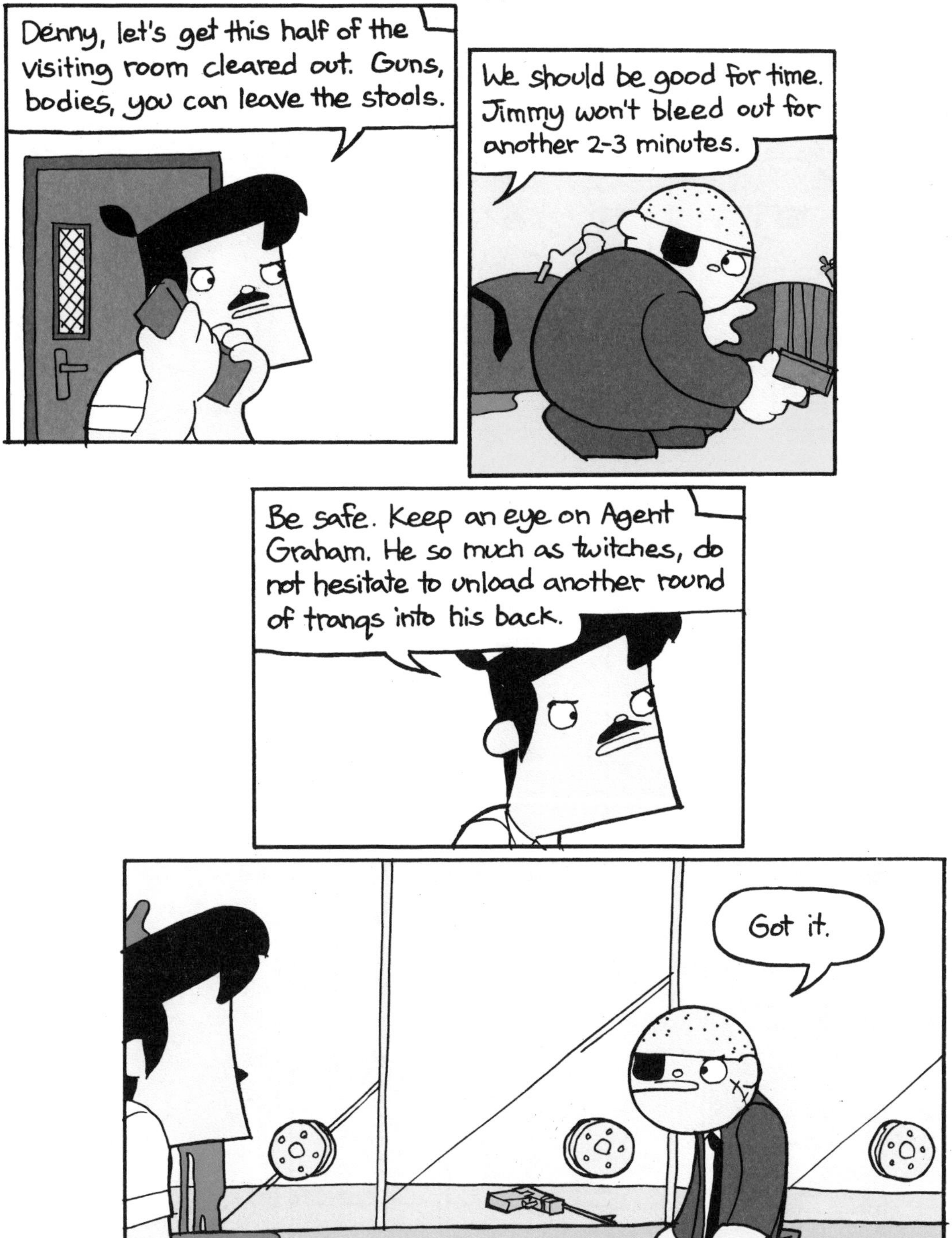
Denny, let's get this half of the visiting room cleared out. Guns, bodies, you can leave the stools.
We should be good for time. Jimmy won't bleed out for another 2-3 minutes.
Be safe. Keep an eye on Agent Graham. He so much as twitches, do not hesitate to unload another round of tranqs into his back.
Got it.

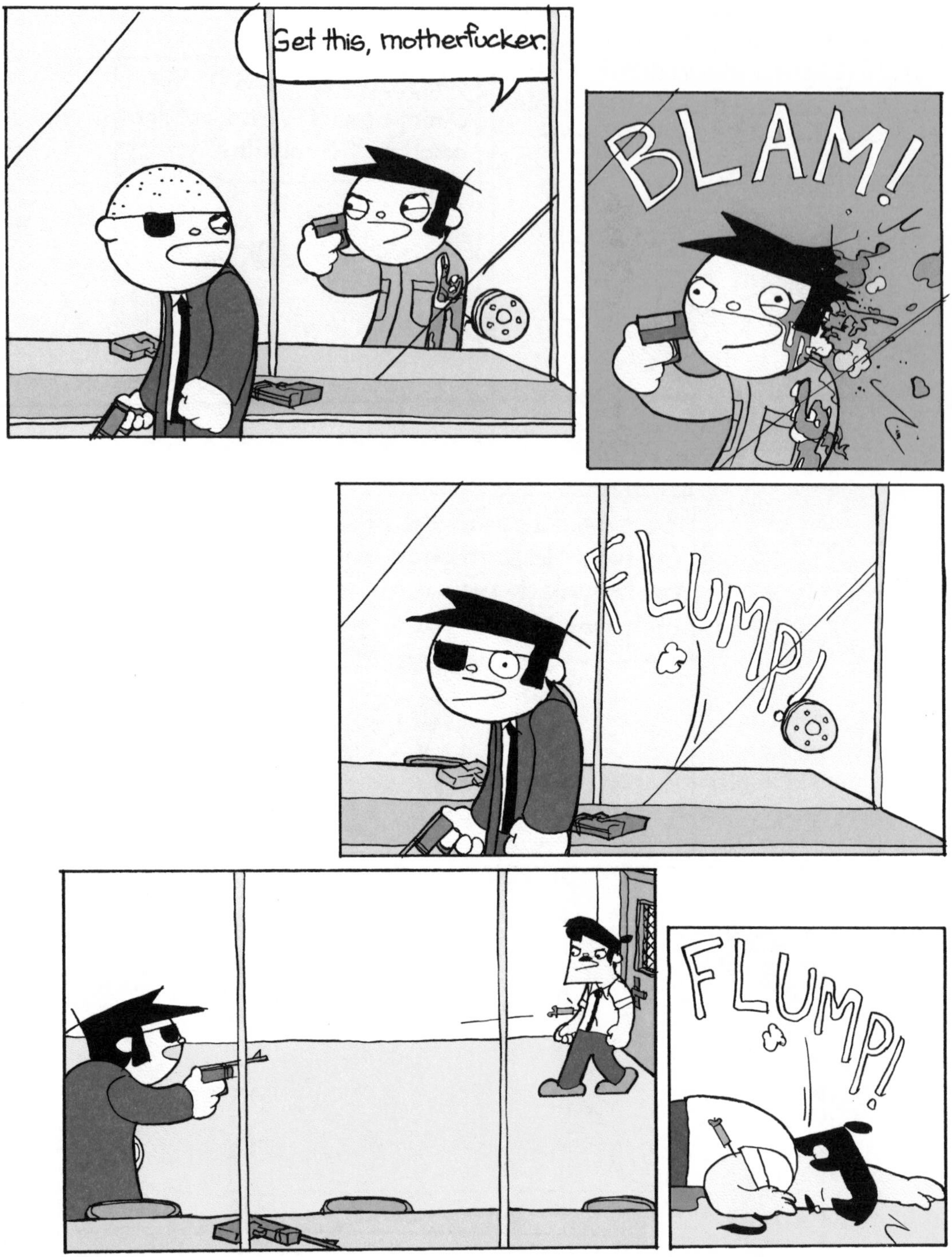
Get this, motherfucker.
BLAM!
FLUMP!
FLUMP!

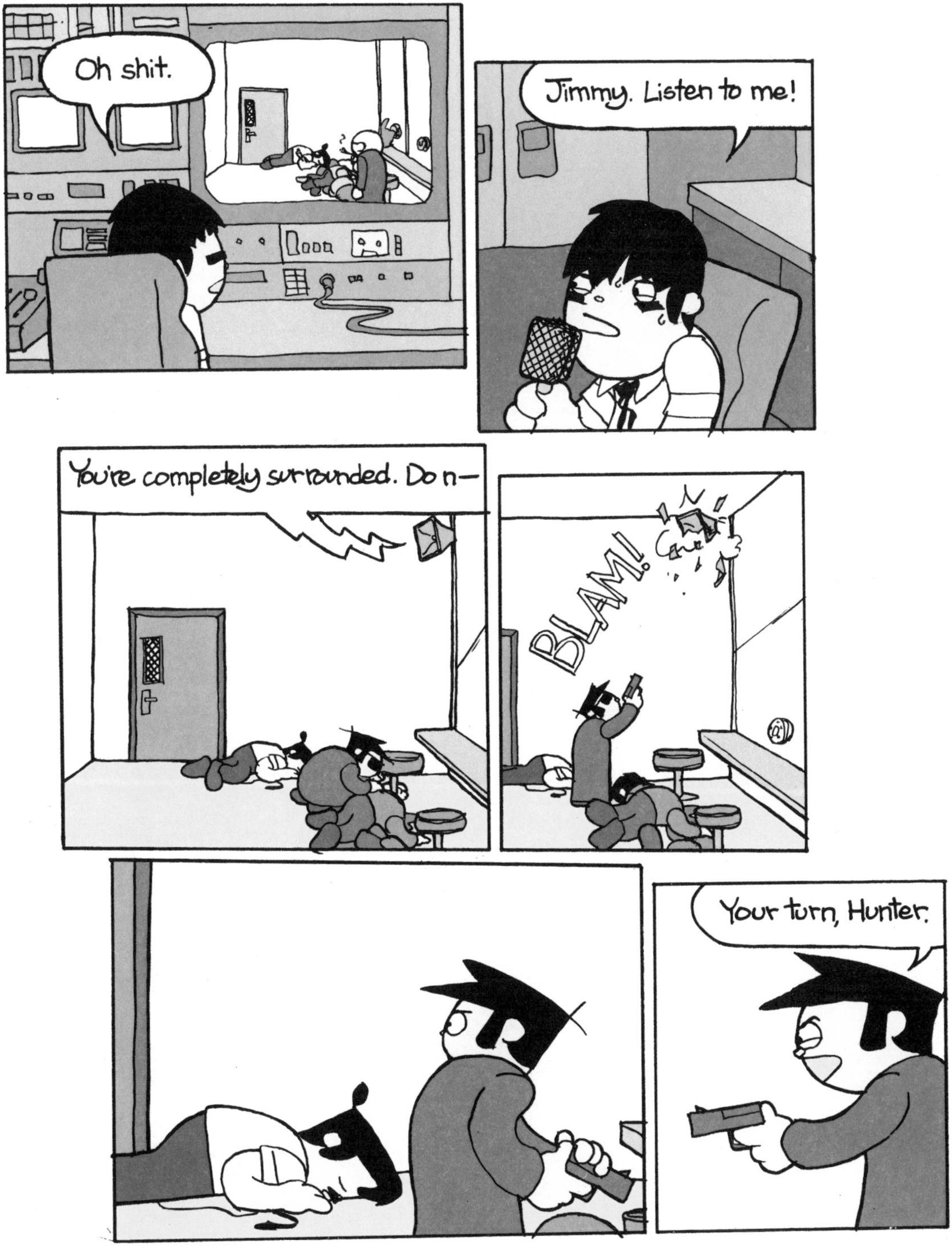
Oh shit.
Jimmy. Listen to me!
You're completely surrounded. Do n—
BLAM!
Your turn, Hunter.

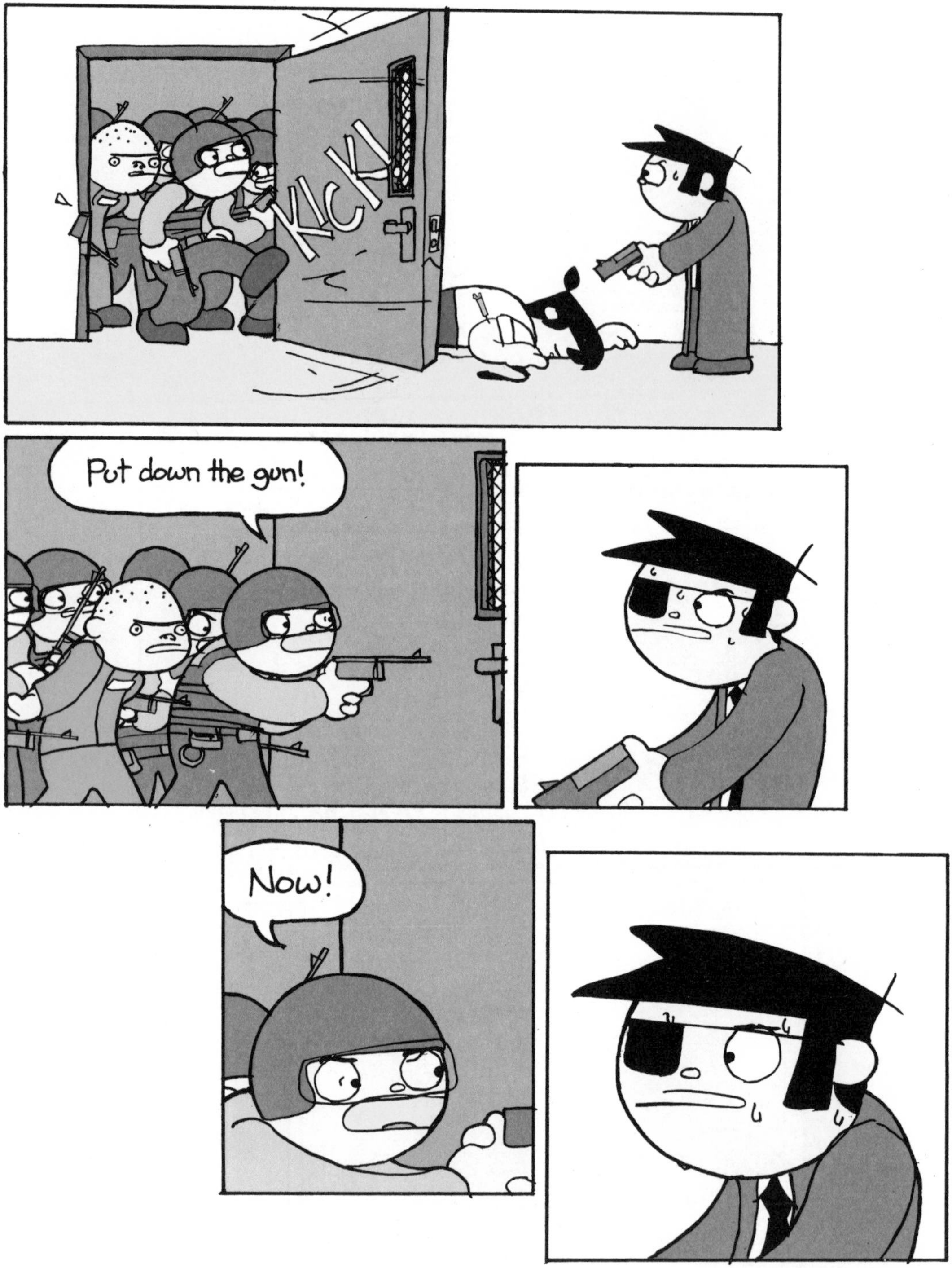
KICK!
Put down the gun!
Now!

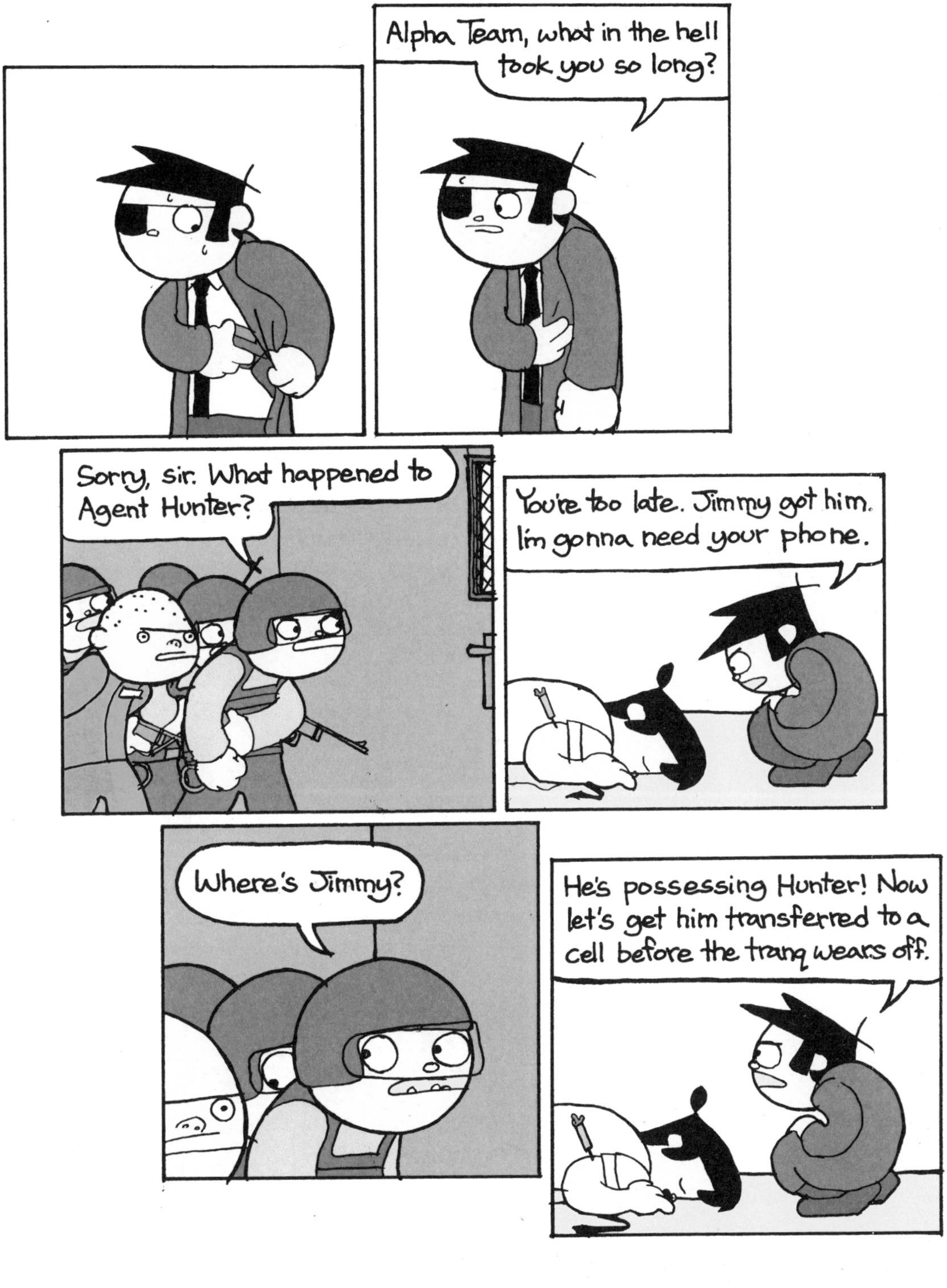
Alpha Team, what in the hell took you so long?
Sorry, sir. What happened to Agent Hunter?
You're too late. Jimmy got him. I'm gonna need your phone.
Where's Jimmy?
He's possessing Hunter! Now let's get him transferred to a cell before the tranq wears off.

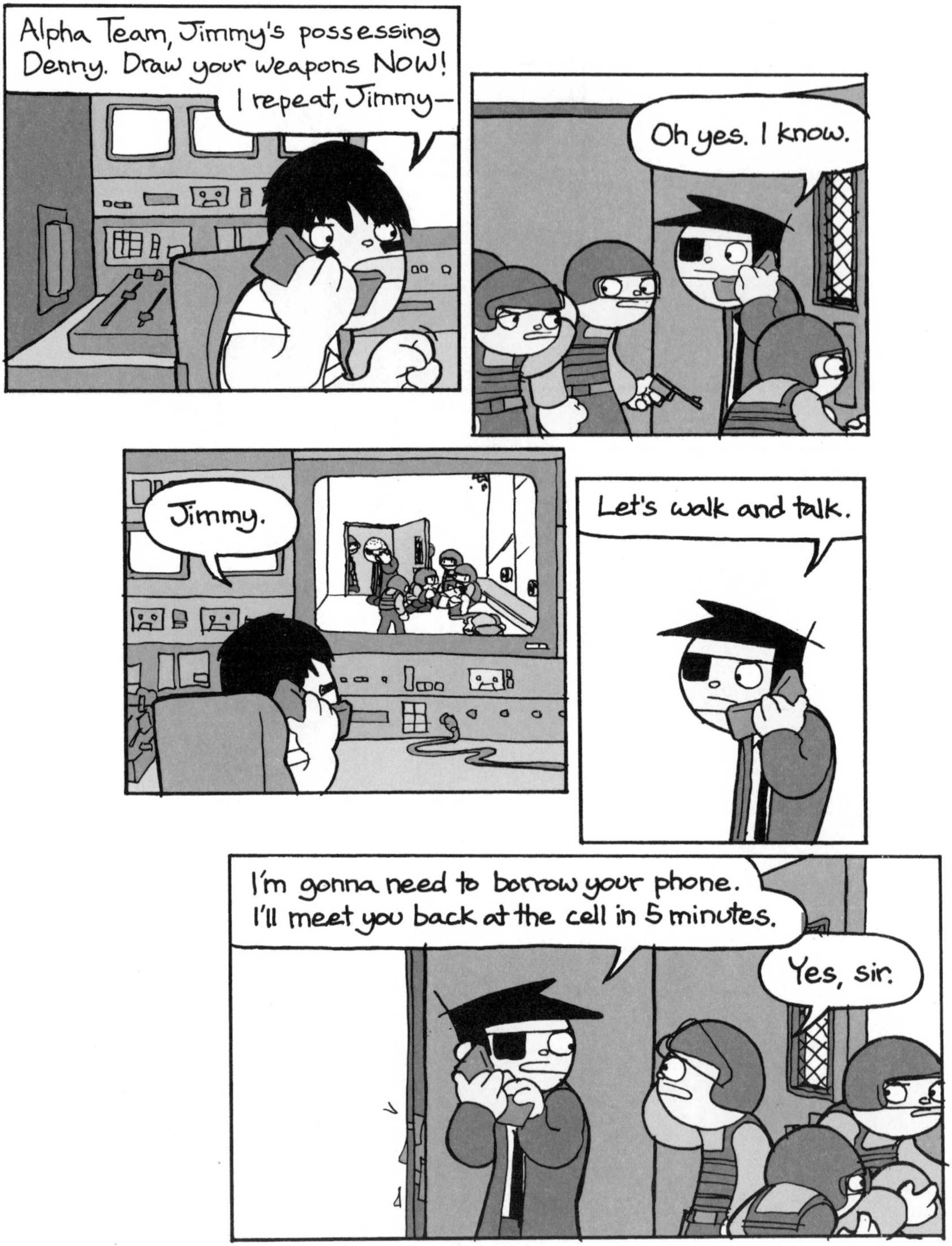
Alpha Team, Jimmy's possessing Denny. Draw your weapons NOW! I repeat, Jimmy—
Oh yes. I know.
Jimmy.
Let's walk and talk.
I'm gonna need to borrow your phone. I'll meet you back at the cell in 5 minutes.
Yes, sir.

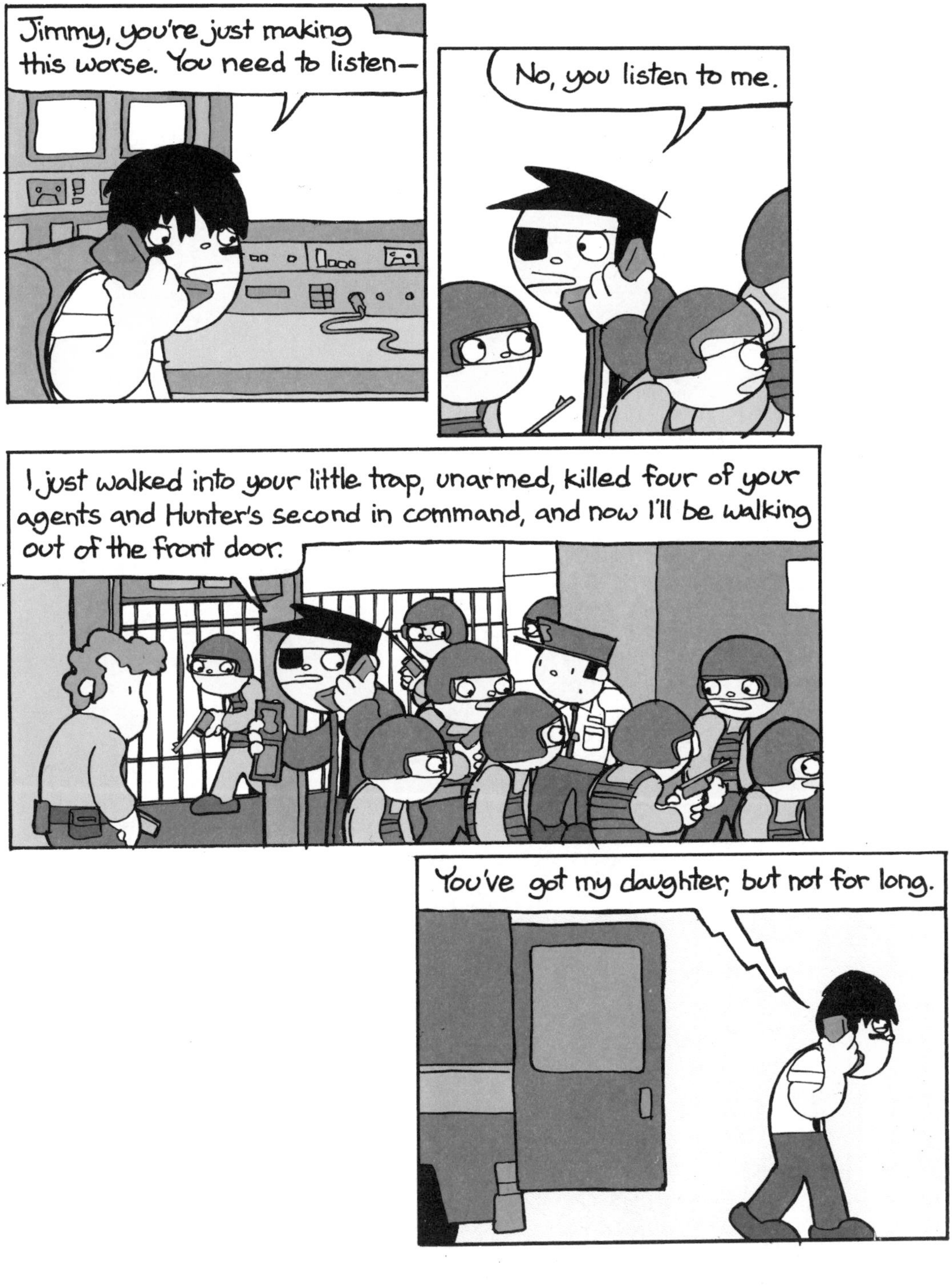
Jimmy, you're just making this worse. You need to listen—
No, you listen to me.
I just walked into your little trap, unarmed, killed four of your agents and Hunter's second in command, and now I'll be walking out of the front door.
You've got my daughter, but not for long.

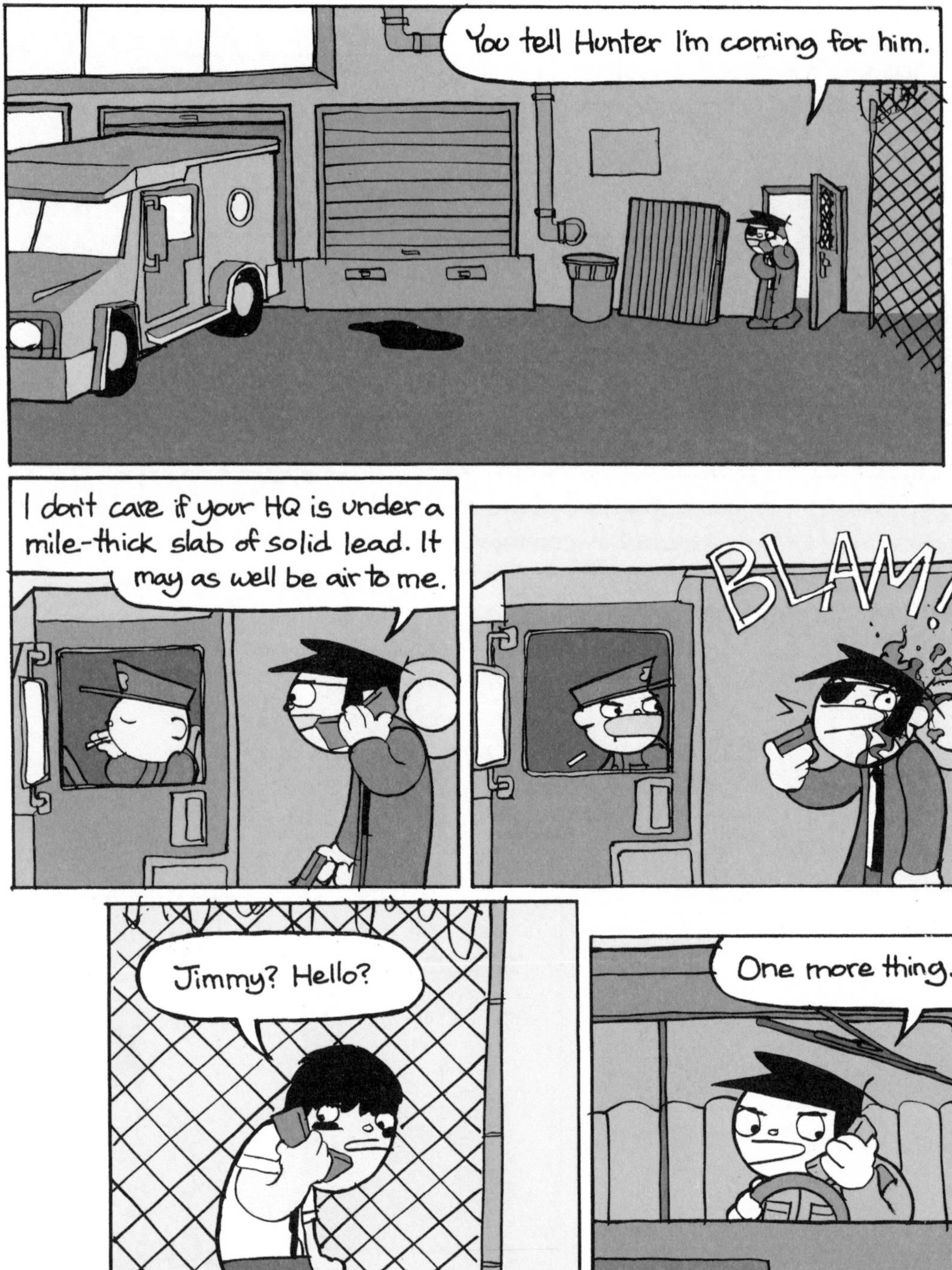
You tell Hunter I'm coming for him.
I don't care if your HQ is under a mile-thick slab of solid lead. It may as well be air to me.
BLAM!
Jimmy? Hello?
One more thing...

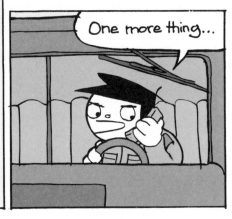

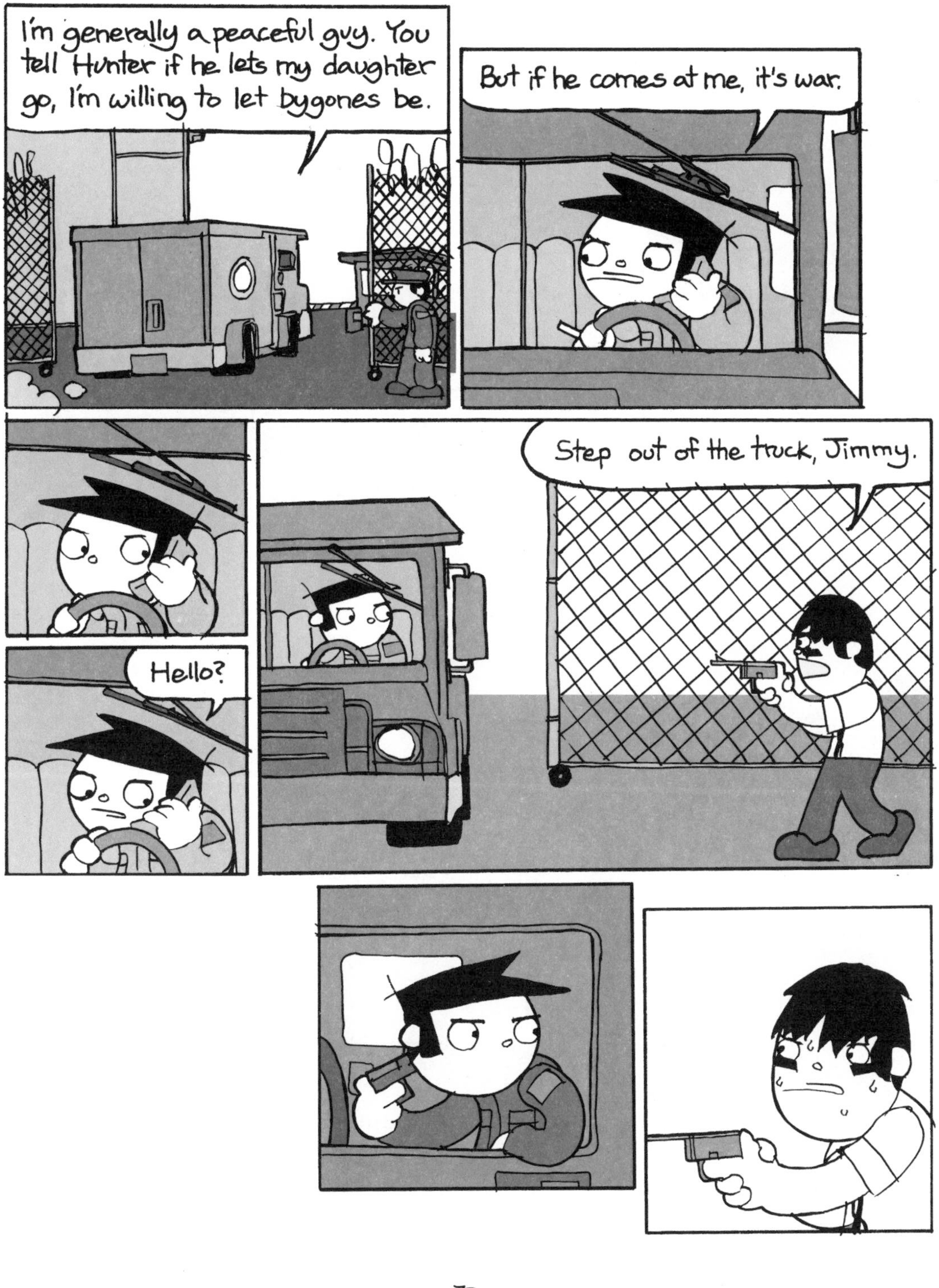
I'm generally a peaceful guy. You tell Hunter if he lets my daughter go, I'm willing to let bygones be.
But if he comes at me, it's war.
Hello?
Step out of the truck, Jimmy.

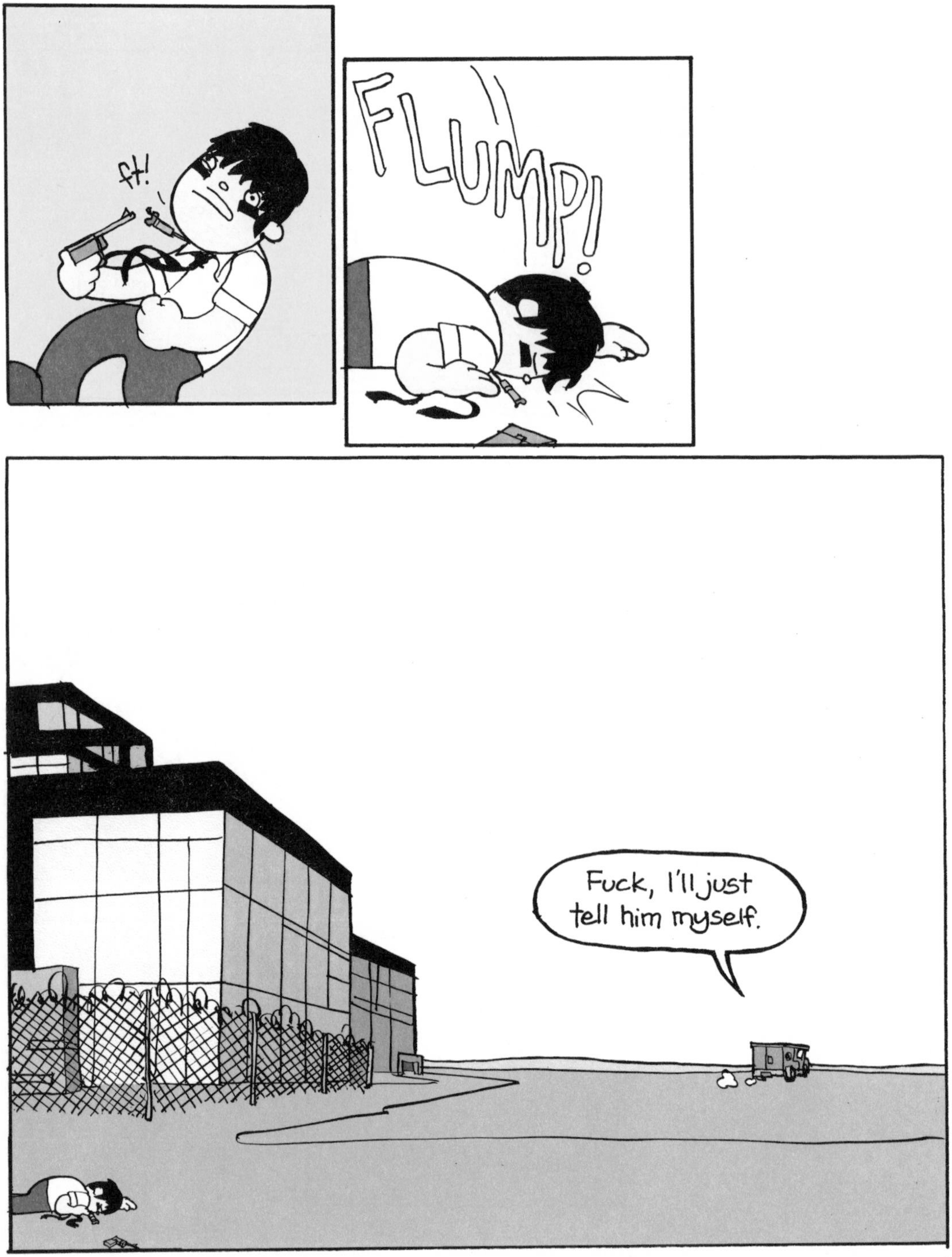
ft!
FLUMP!
Fuck, I'll just tell him myself.

# CHAPTER 9

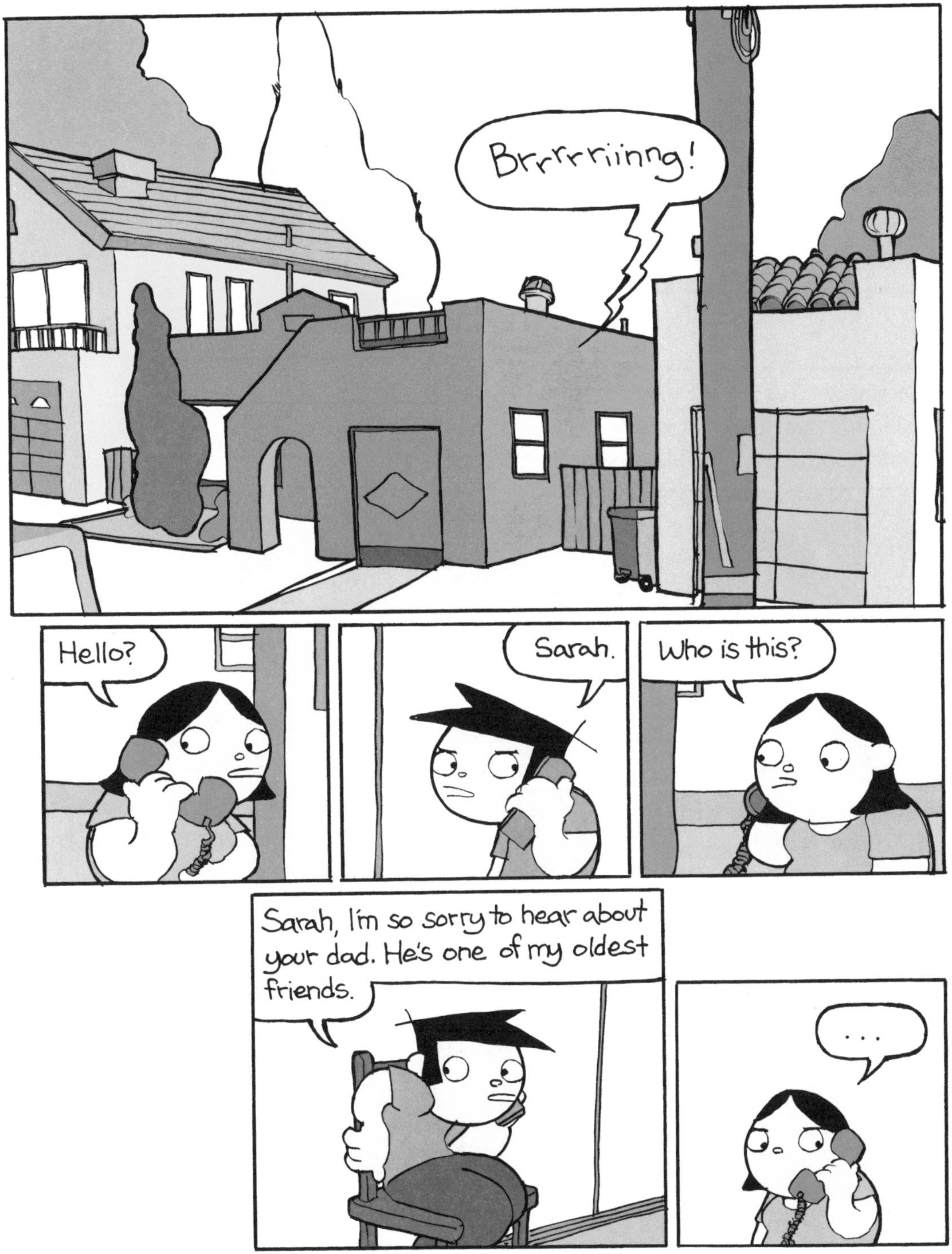
Brrrrriinng!
Hello?
Sarah.
Who is this?
Sarah, I'm so sorry to hear about your dad. He's one of my oldest friends.
. . .

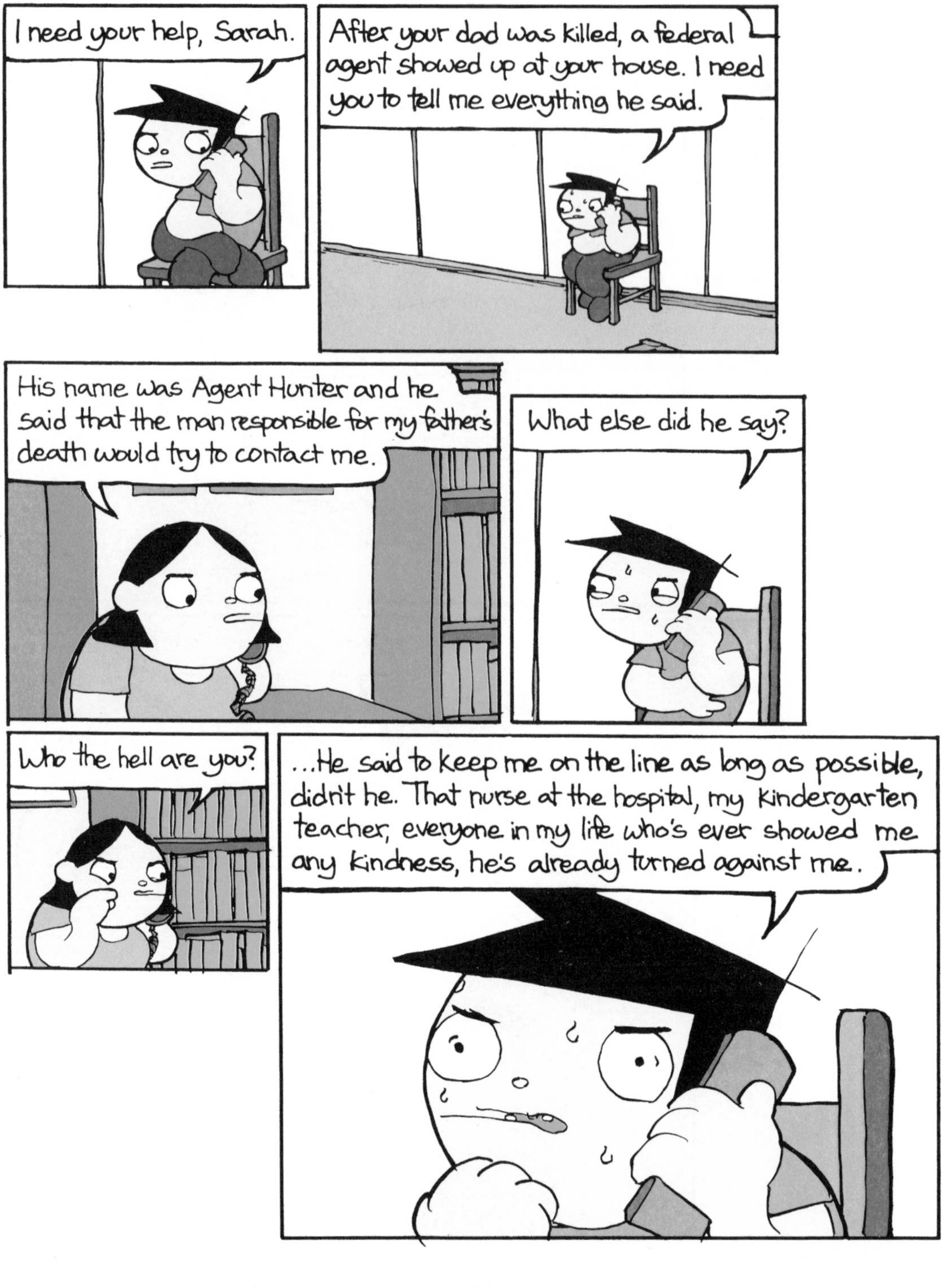
I need your help, Sarah.
After your dad was killed, a federal agent showed up at your house. I need you to tell me everything he said.
His name was Agent Hunter and he said that the man responsible for my father's death would try to contact me.
What else did he say?
Who the hell are you?
...He said to keep me on the line as long as possible, didn't he. That nurse at the hospital, my kindergarten teacher, everyone in my life who's ever showed me any kindness, he's already turned against me.

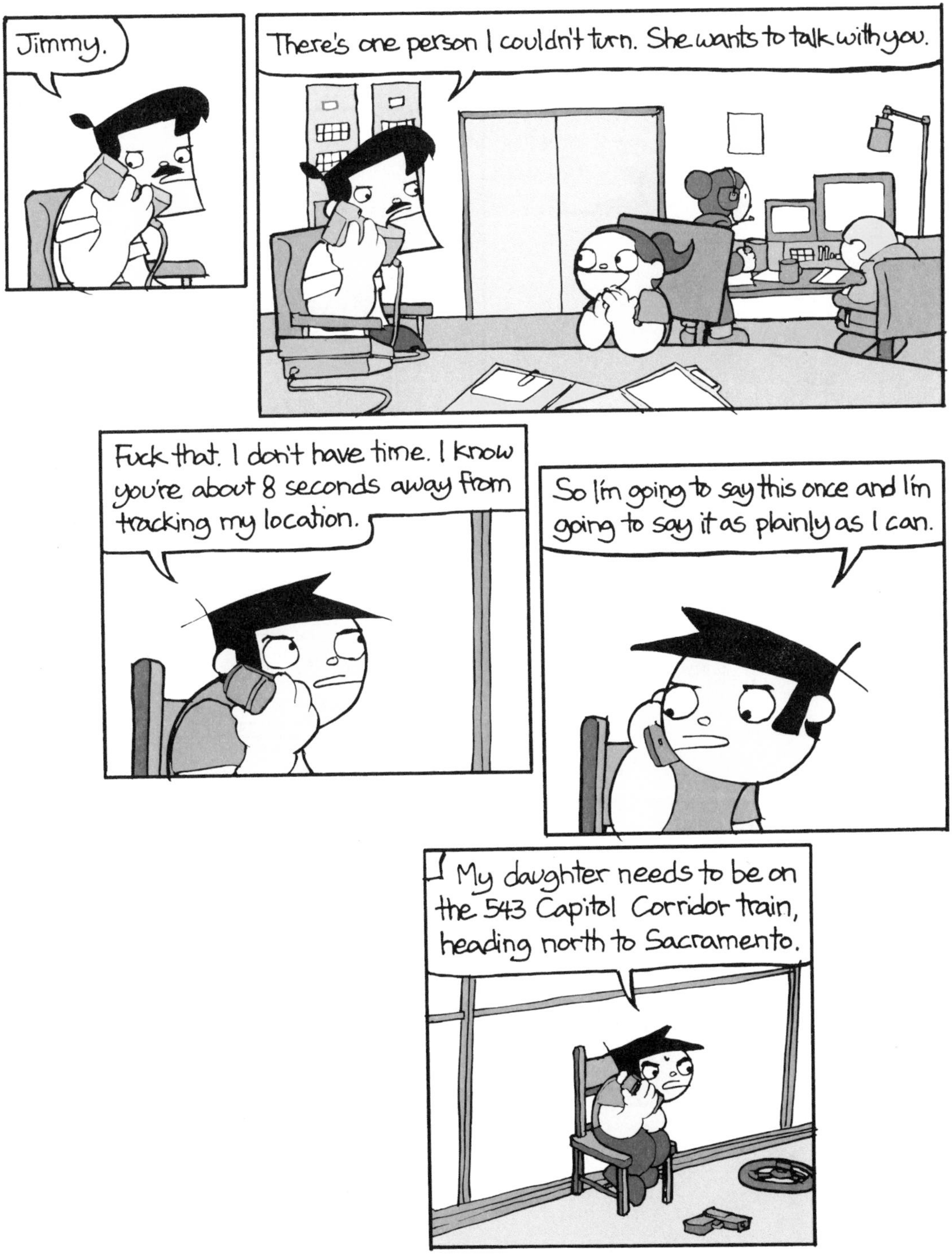

Jimmy.
There's one person I couldn't turn. She wants to talk with you.
Fuck that. I don't have time. I know you're about 8 seconds away from tracking my location.
So I'm going to say this once and I'm going to say it as plainly as I can.
My daughter needs to be on the 543 Capitol Corridor train, heading north to Sacramento.

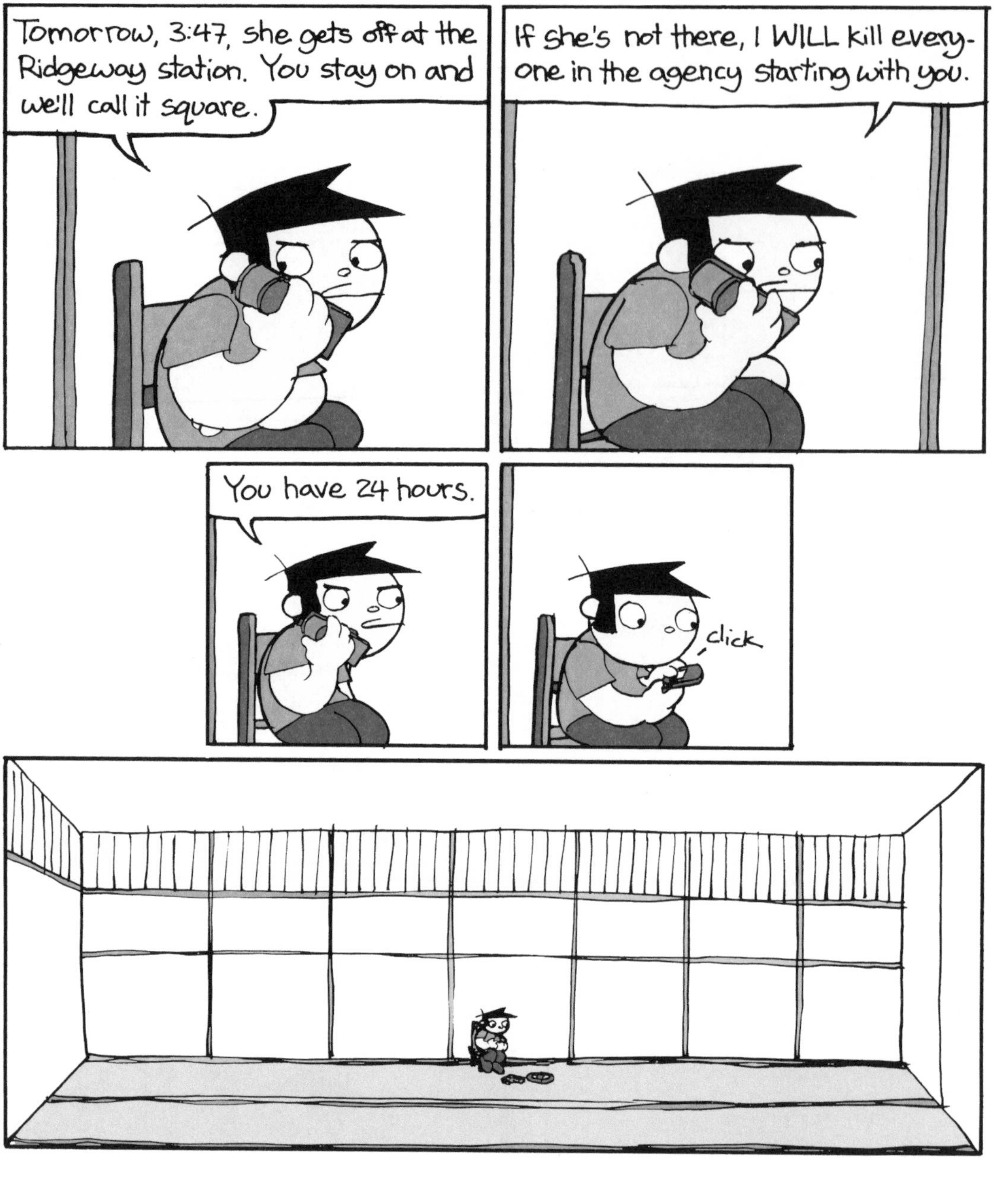

Tomorrow, 3:47, she gets off at the Ridgeway station. You stay on and we'll call it square.
If she's not there, I WILL kill every-one in the agency starting with you.
You have 24 hours.
click

What do you got for location?

The triangulation doesn't match up. Must be in a moving vehicle.

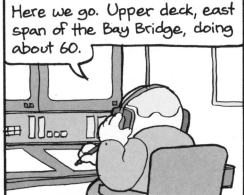

Here we go. Upper deck, east span of the Bay Bridge, doing about 60.

Tibbs, get that bridge blocked off. Seal the westbound exits and the eastbound entrance.

After 10 minutes, he'll jump off the side. I want death row inmates posted on the lower deck every 244 feet.

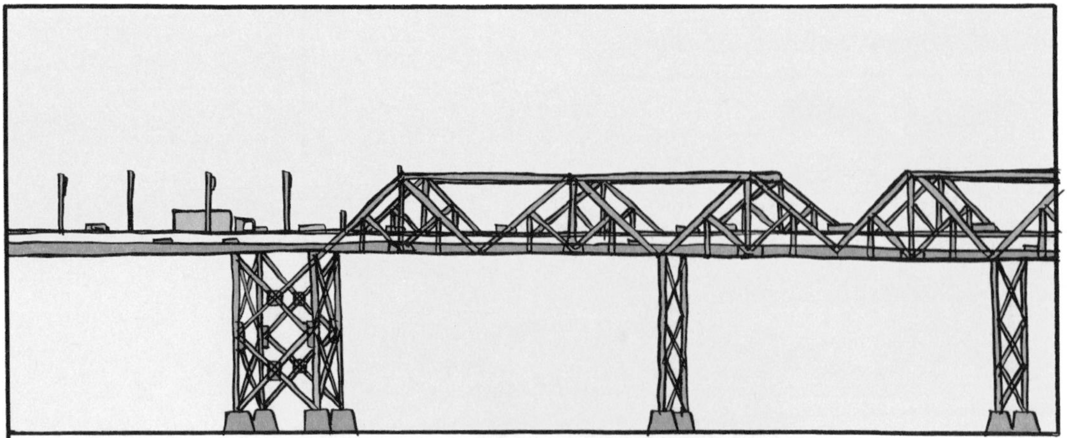
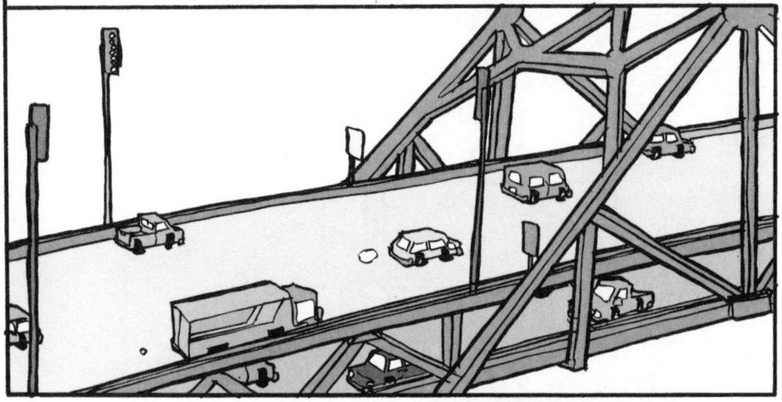
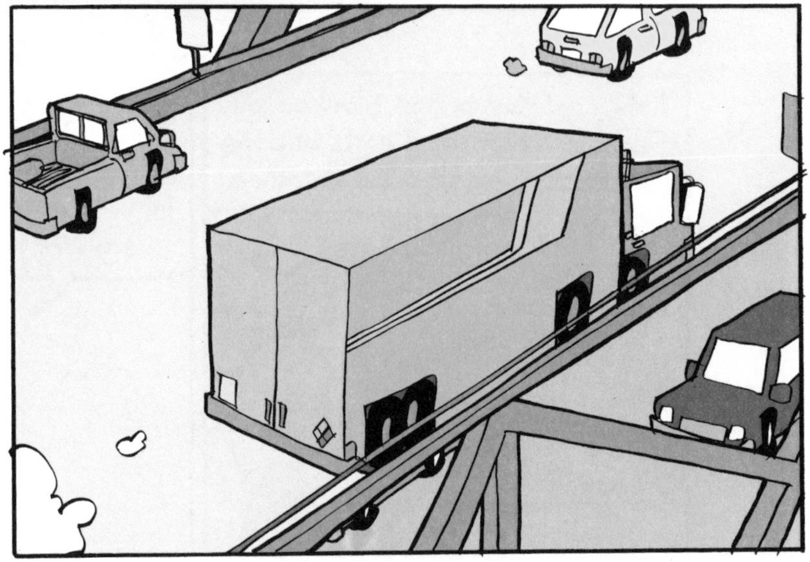

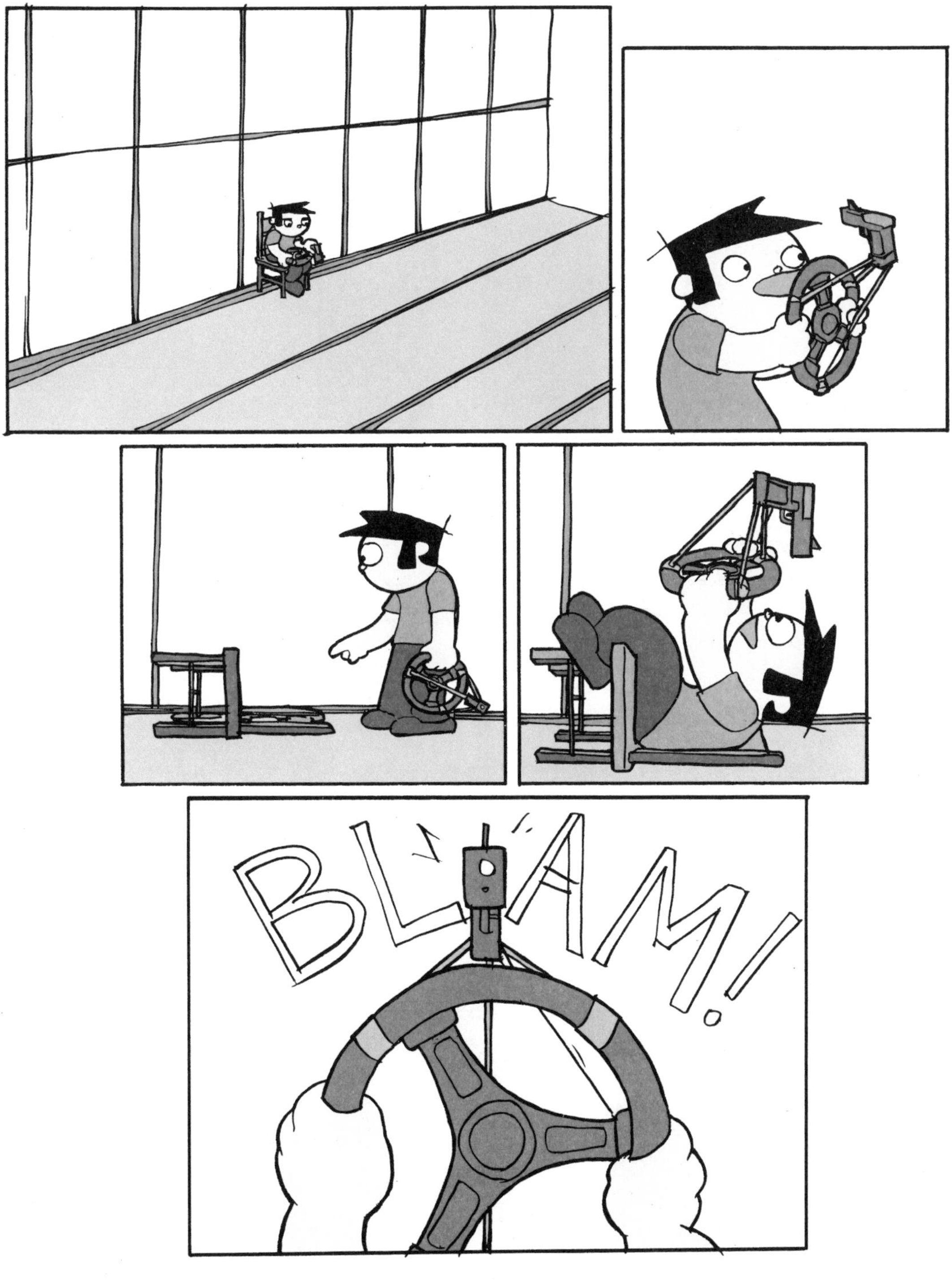
BLAM!

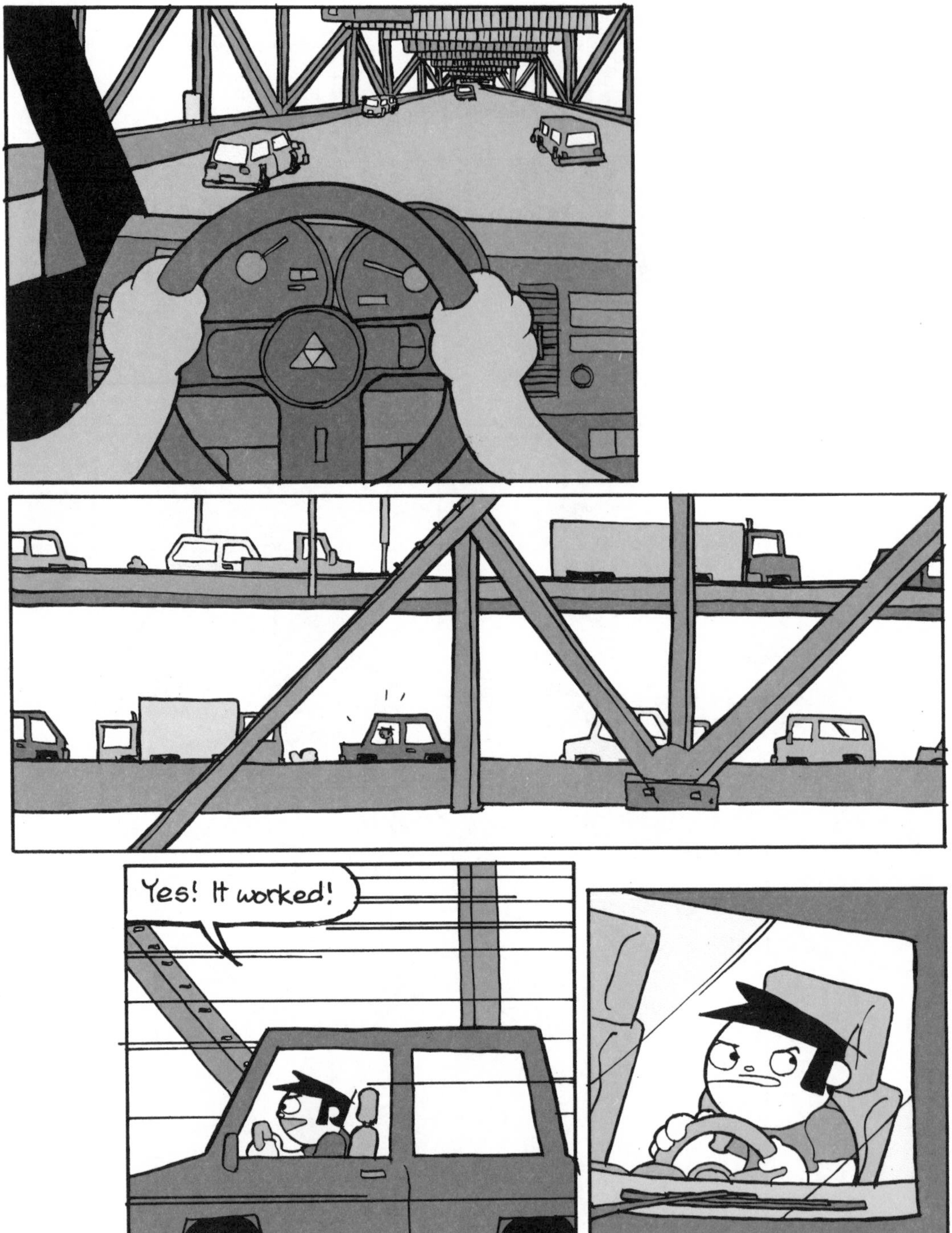
Yes! It worked!

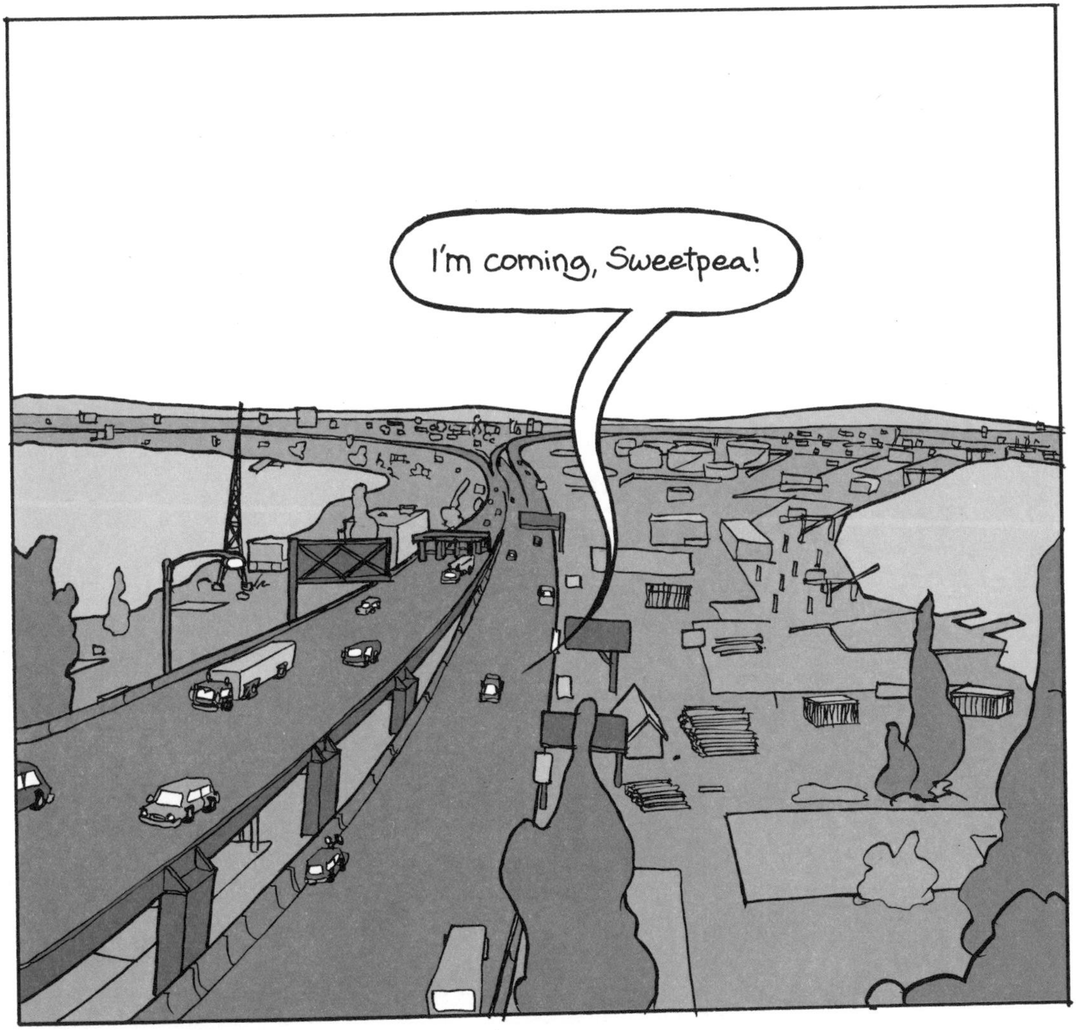
I'm coming, Sweetpea!

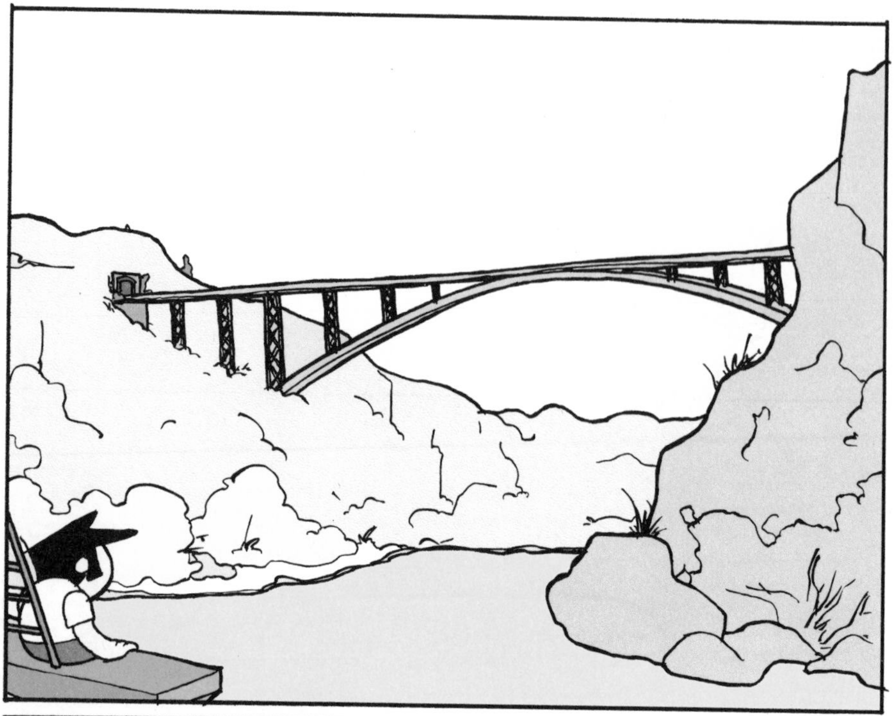

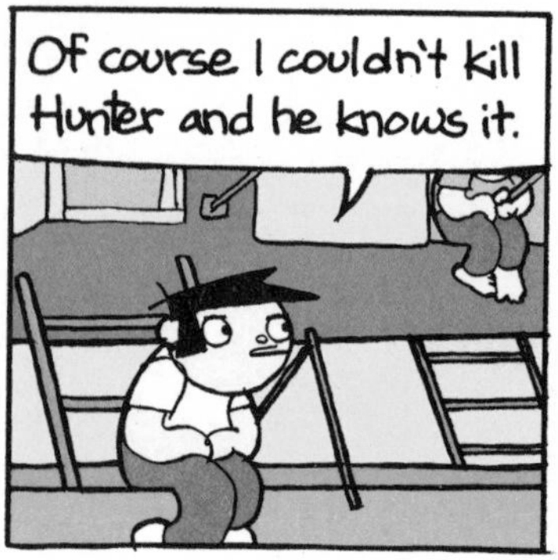
Of course I couldn't kill Hunter and he knows it.

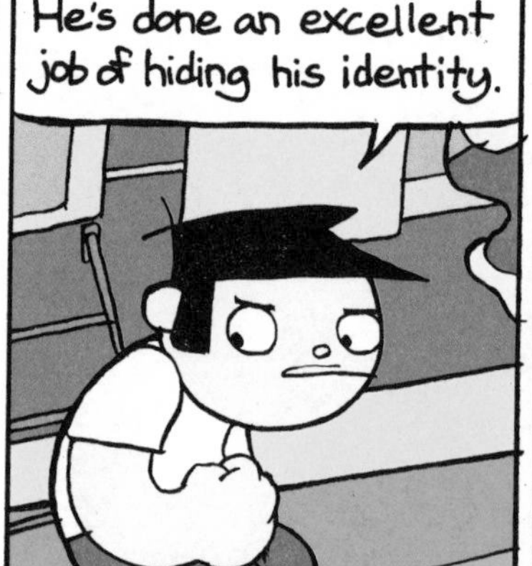
He's done an excellent job of hiding his identity.

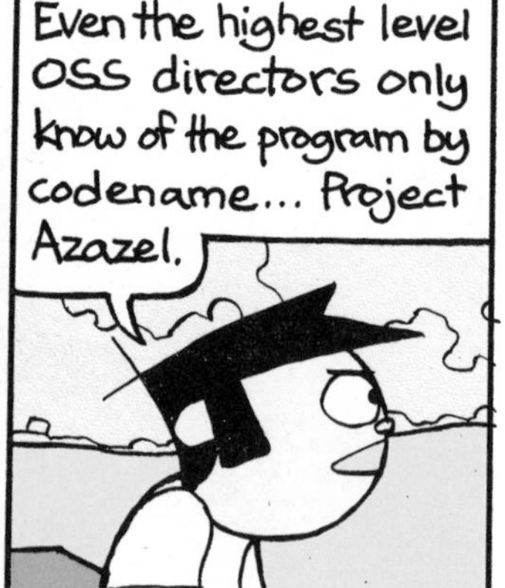
Even the highest level OSS directors only know of the program by codename... Project Azazel.

I don't blame them for the secrecy. If word ever got out, there'd be no end to the demon arms race that would follow.

On the plus side, I figure that makes fewer than 800 people who know of my existence.

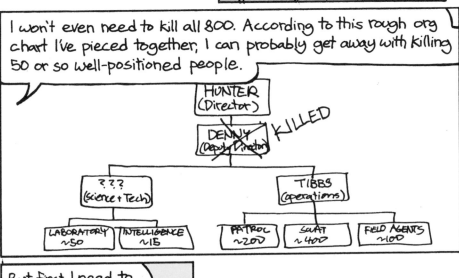

I won't even need to kill all 800. According to this rough org chart I've pieced together, I can probably get away with killing 50 or so well-positioned people.

HUNTER
(Director)

DENNY
(Deputy Director) KILLED

???
(Science + Tech)

TIBBS
(operations)

LABORATORY
~50

INTELLIGENCE
~15

PATROL
~200

SWAT
~400

FIELD AGENTS
~100

But first I need to get my baby back.

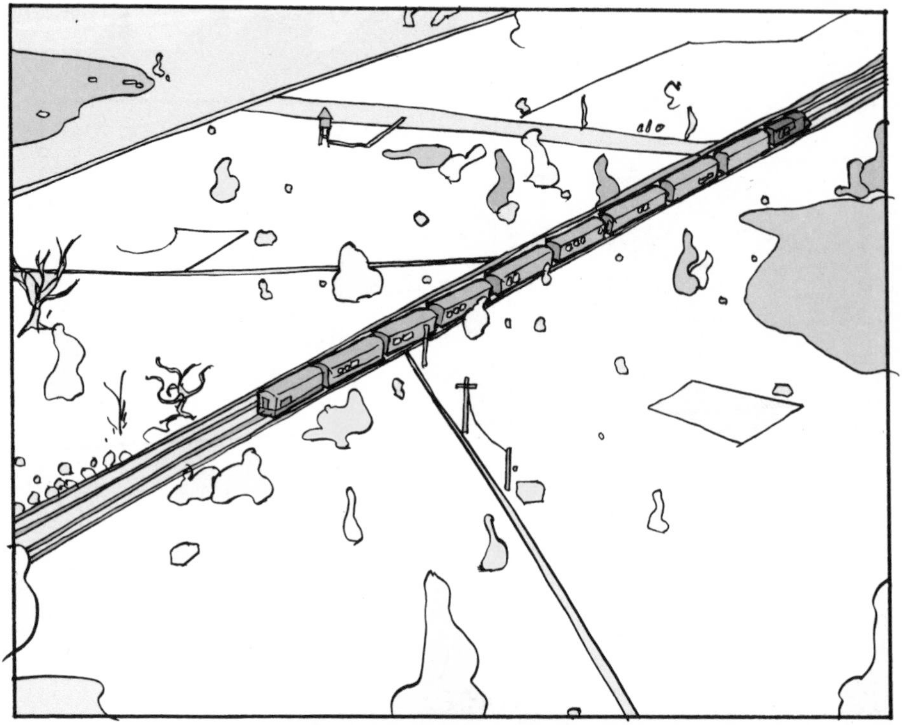

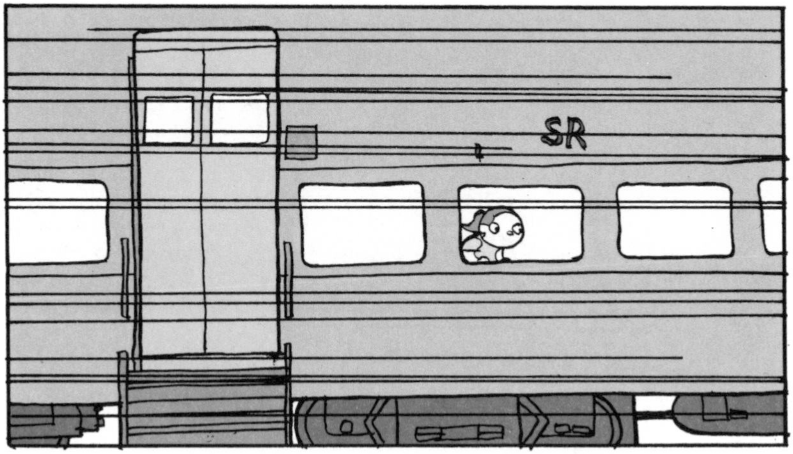
SR

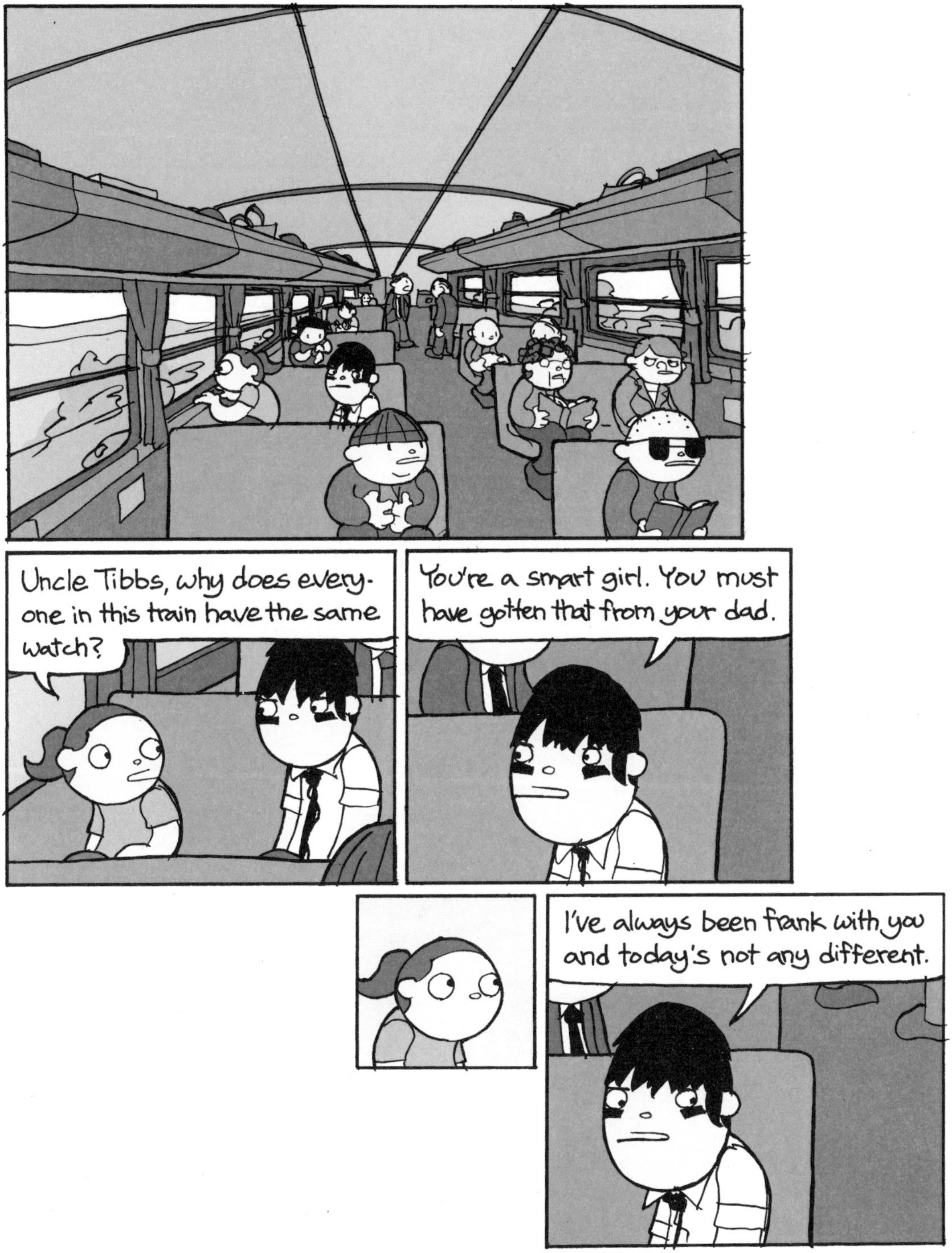
Uncle Tibbs, why does every-one in this train have the same watch?
You're a smart girl. You must have gotten that from your dad.
I've always been frank with you and today's not any different.

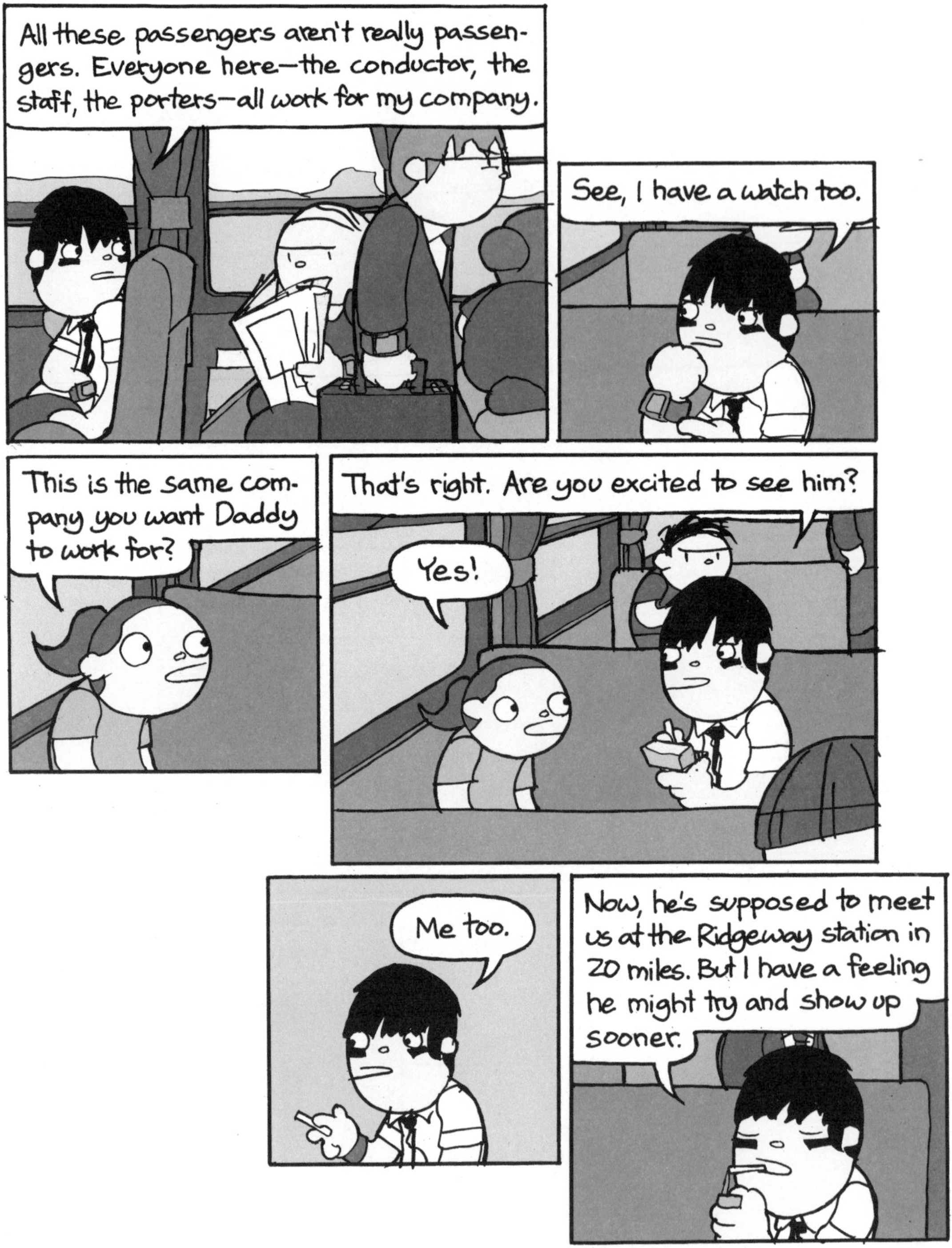
All these passengers aren't really passengers. Everyone here—the conductor, the staff, the porters—all work for my company.
See, I have a watch too.
This is the same company you want Daddy to work for?
That's right. Are you excited to see him?
Yes!
Me too.
Now, he's supposed to meet us at the Ridgeway station in 20 miles. But I have a feeling he might try and show up sooner.

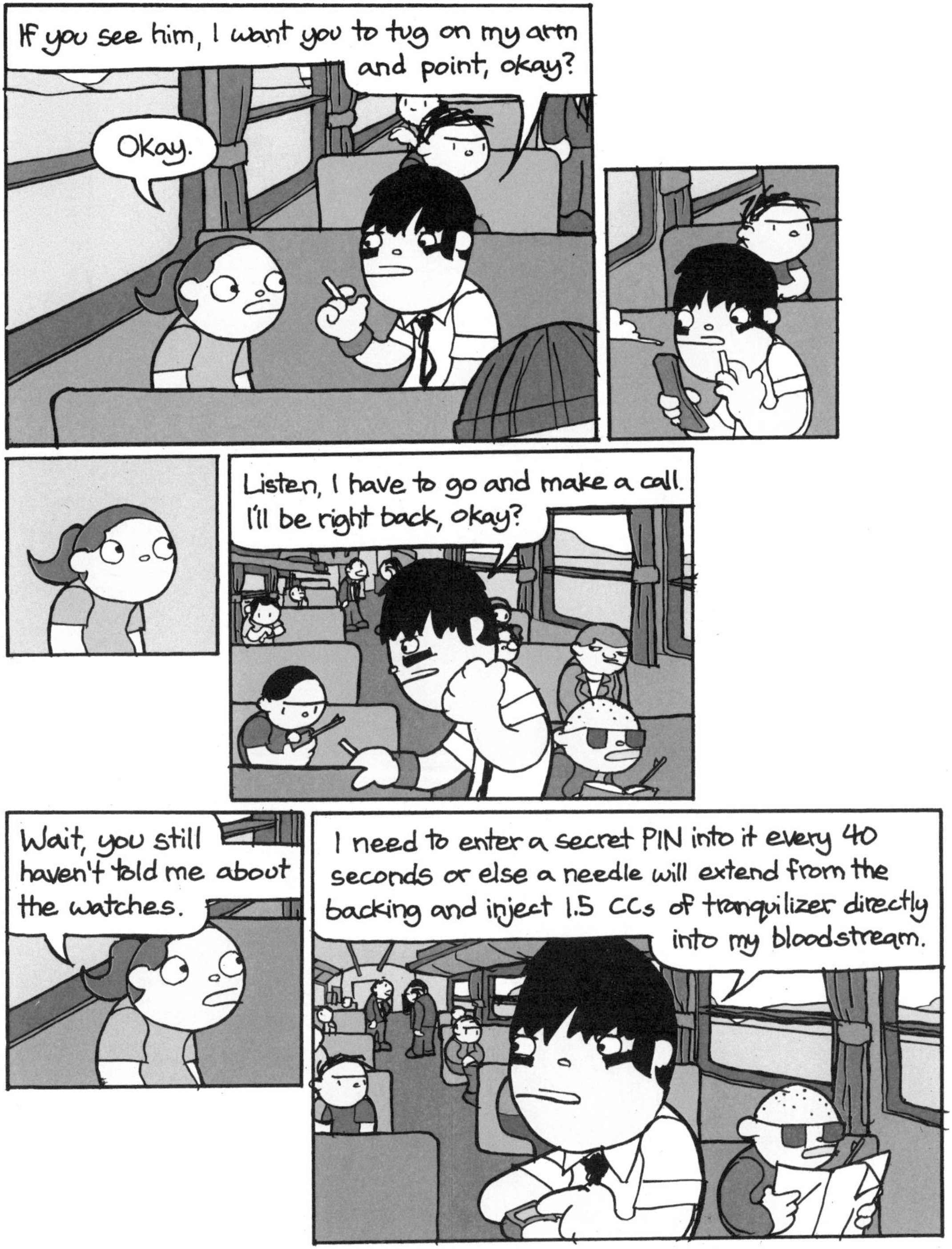
If you see him, I want you to tug on my arm and point, okay?
Okay.
Listen, I have to go and make a call. I'll be right back, okay?
Wait, you still haven't told me about the watches.
I need to enter a secret PIN into it every 40 seconds or else a needle will extend from the backing and inject 1.5 CCs of tranquilizer directly into my bloodstream.

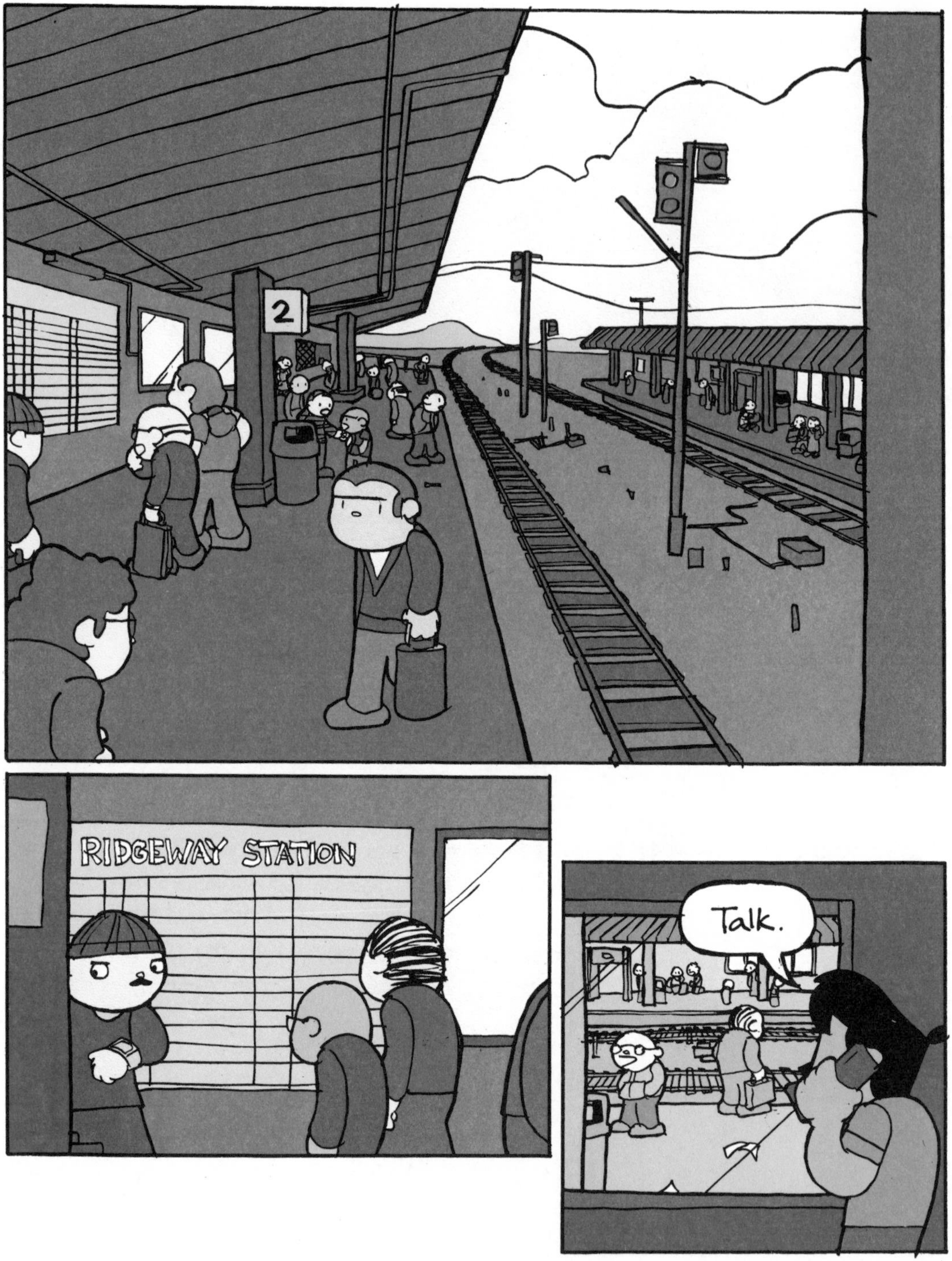
2
RIDGEWAY STATION
Talk.

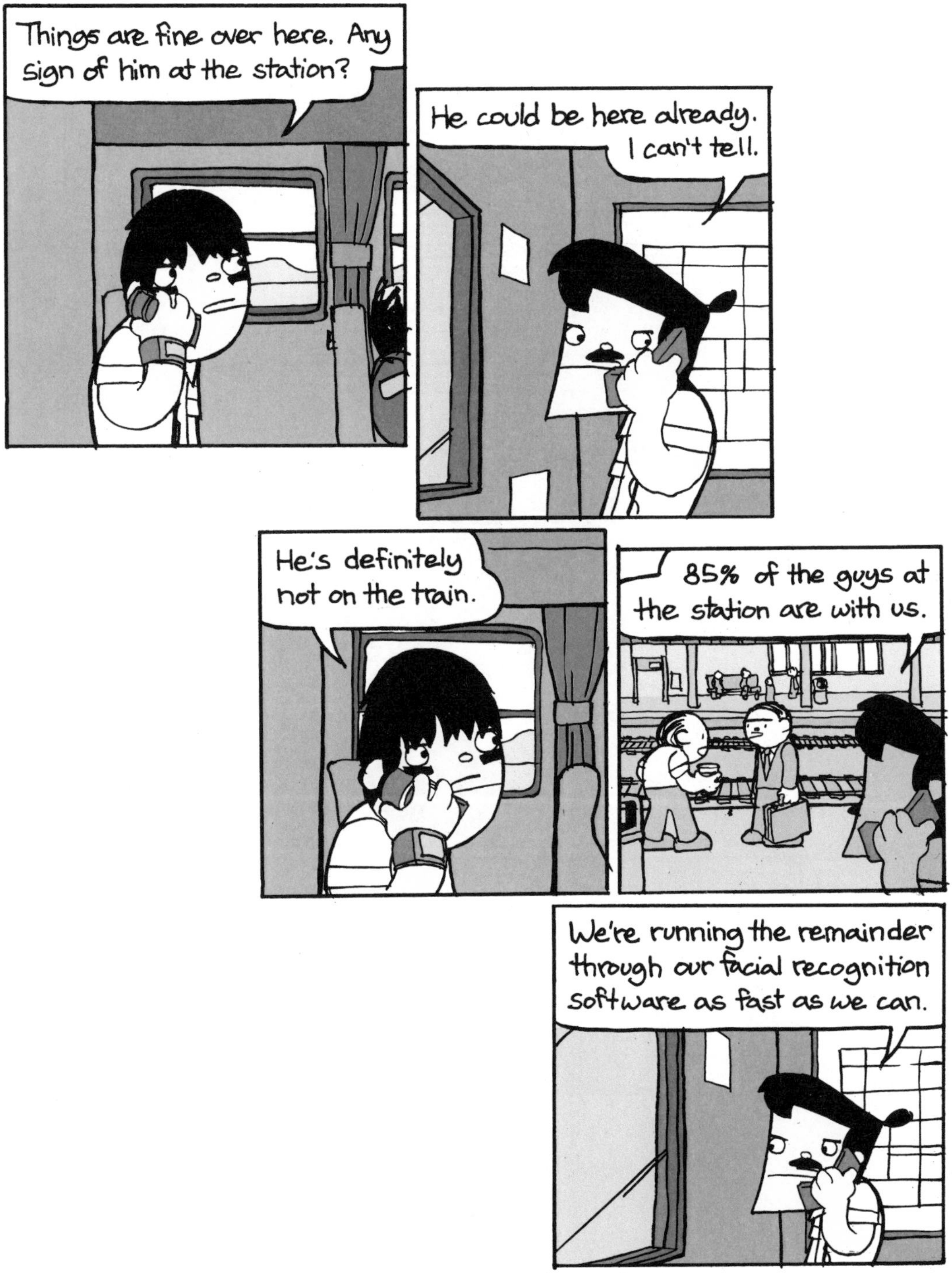
Things are fine over here. Any sign of him at the station?
He could be here already. I can't tell.
He's definitely not on the train.
85% of the guys at the station are with us.
We're running the remainder through our facial recognition software as fast as we can.

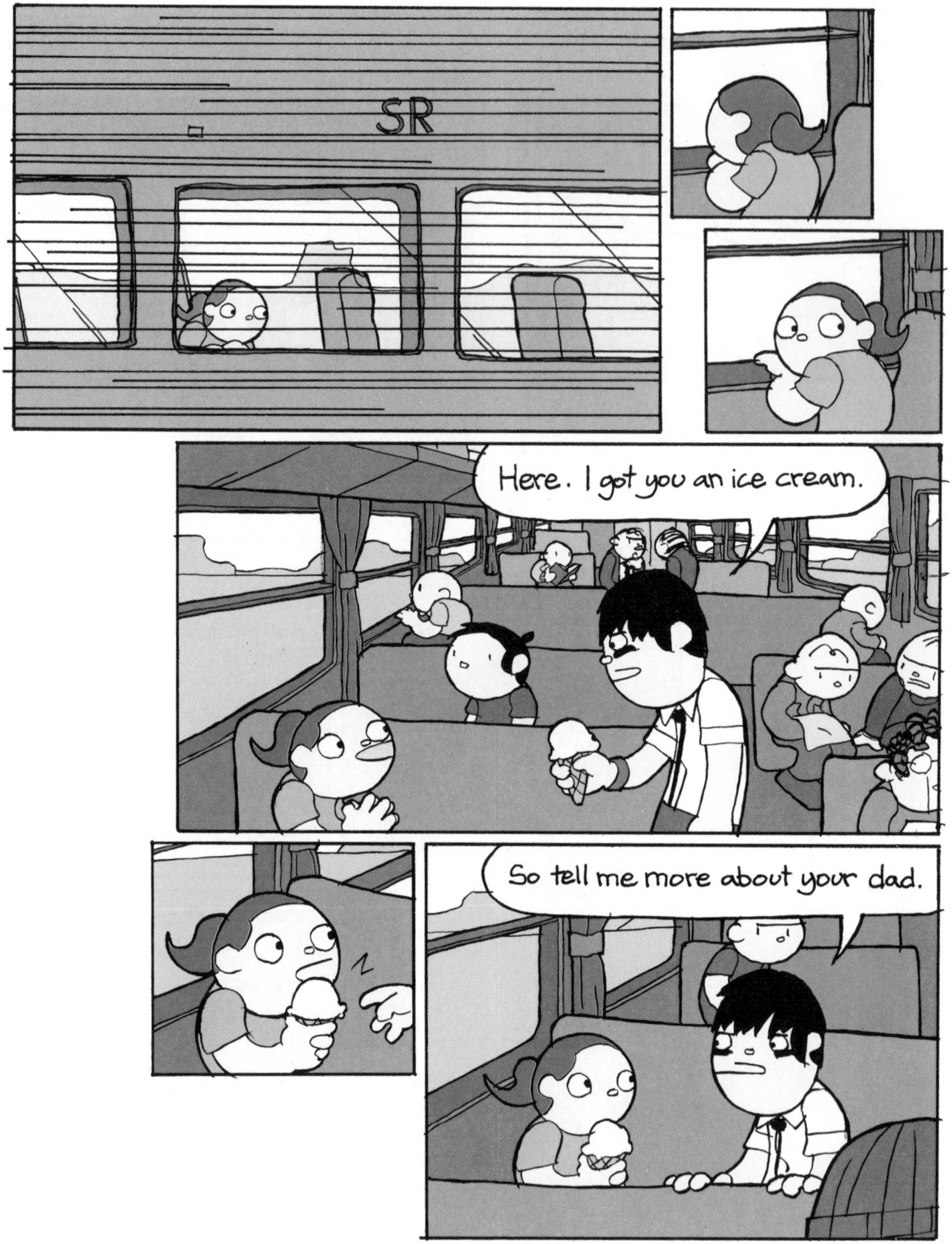
SR
Here. I got you an ice cream.
So tell me more about your dad.

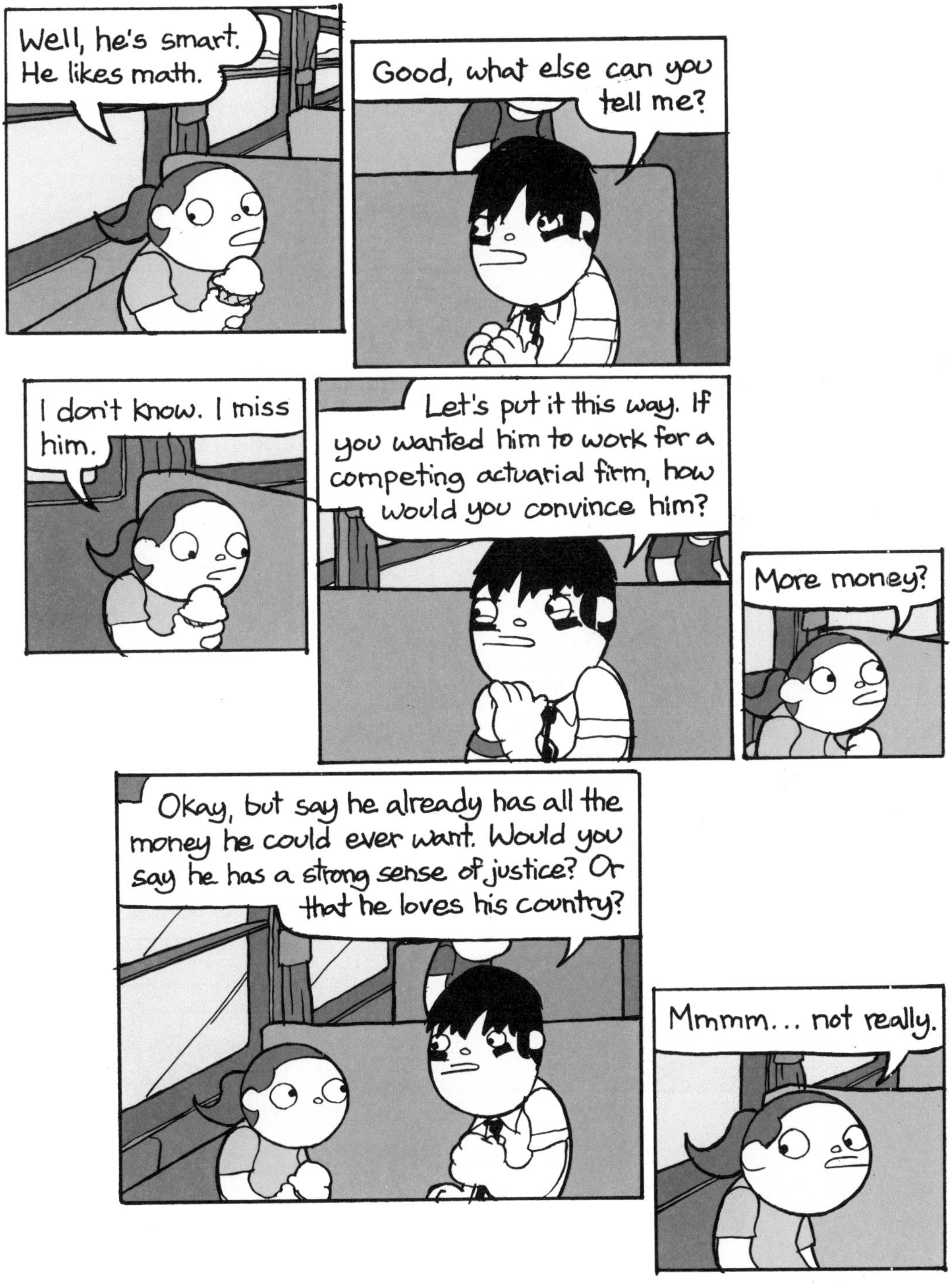
Well, he's smart. He likes math.
Good, what else can you tell me?
I don't know. I miss him.
Let's put it this way. If you wanted him to work for a competing actuarial firm, how would you convince him?
More money?
Okay, but say he already has all the money he could ever want. Would you say he has a strong sense of justice? Or that he loves his country?
Mmmm... not really.

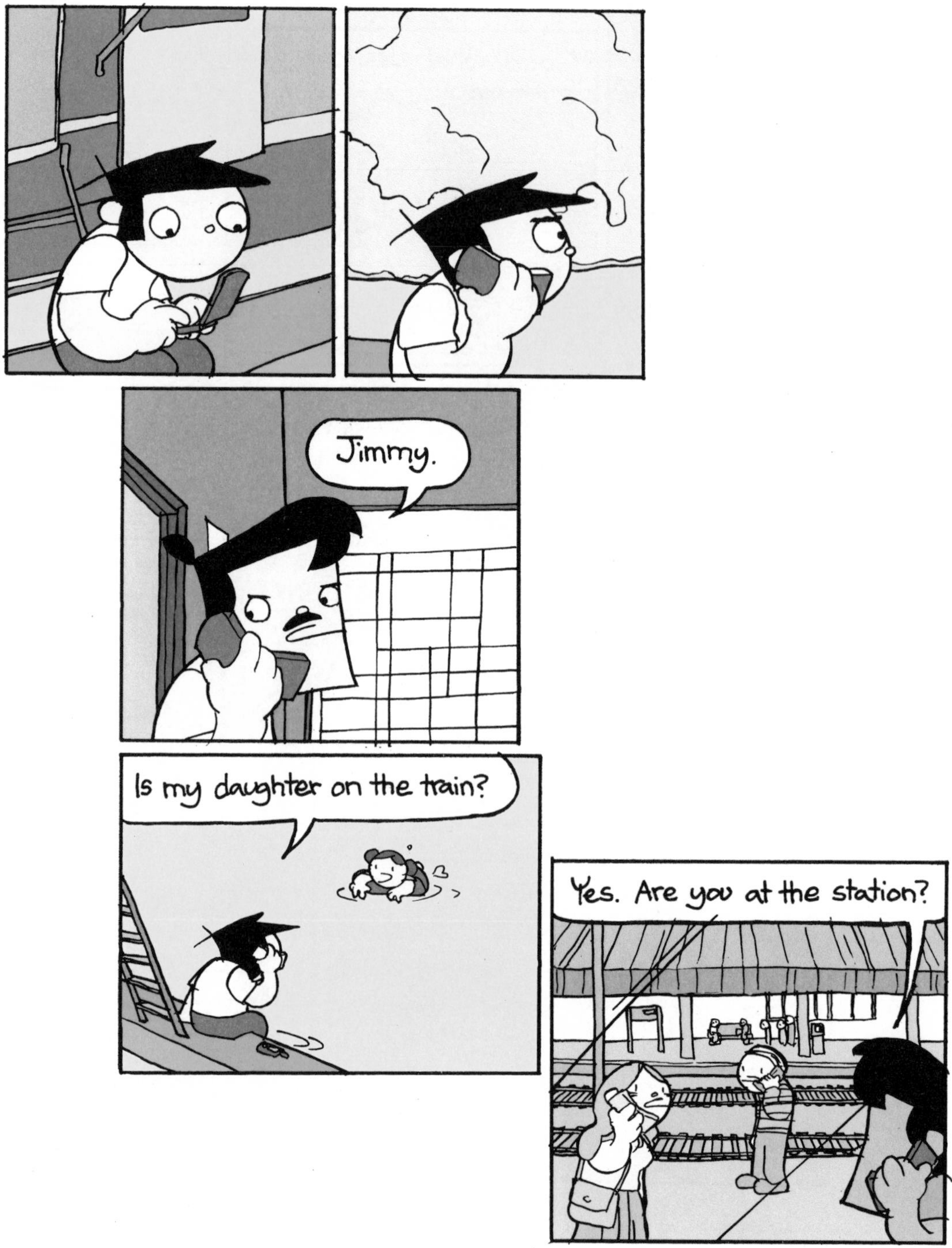
Jimmy.
Is my daughter on the train?
Yes. Are you at the station?

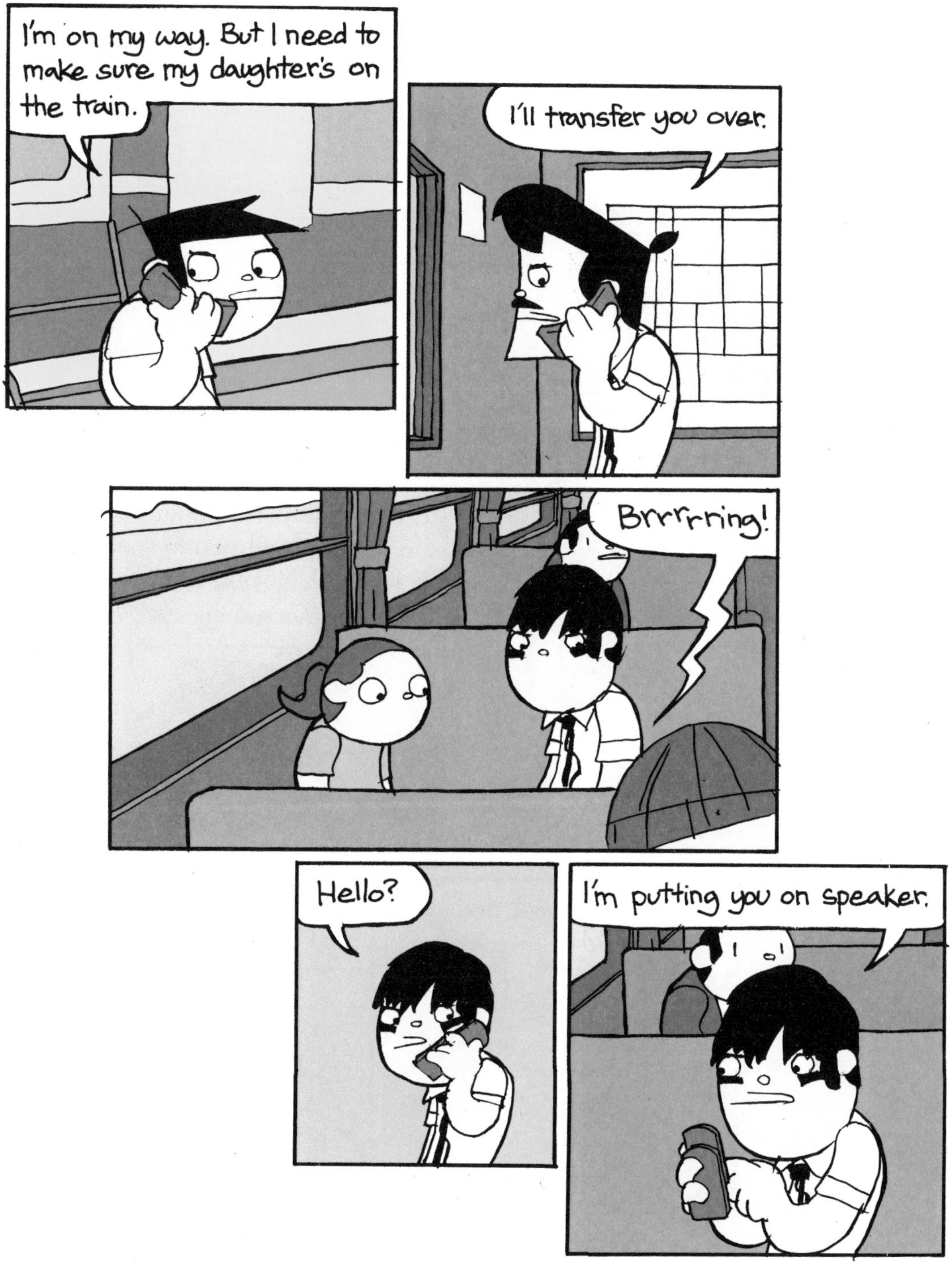
I'm on my way. But I need to make sure my daughter's on the train.
I'll transfer you over.
Brrrrring!
Hello?
I'm putting you on speaker.

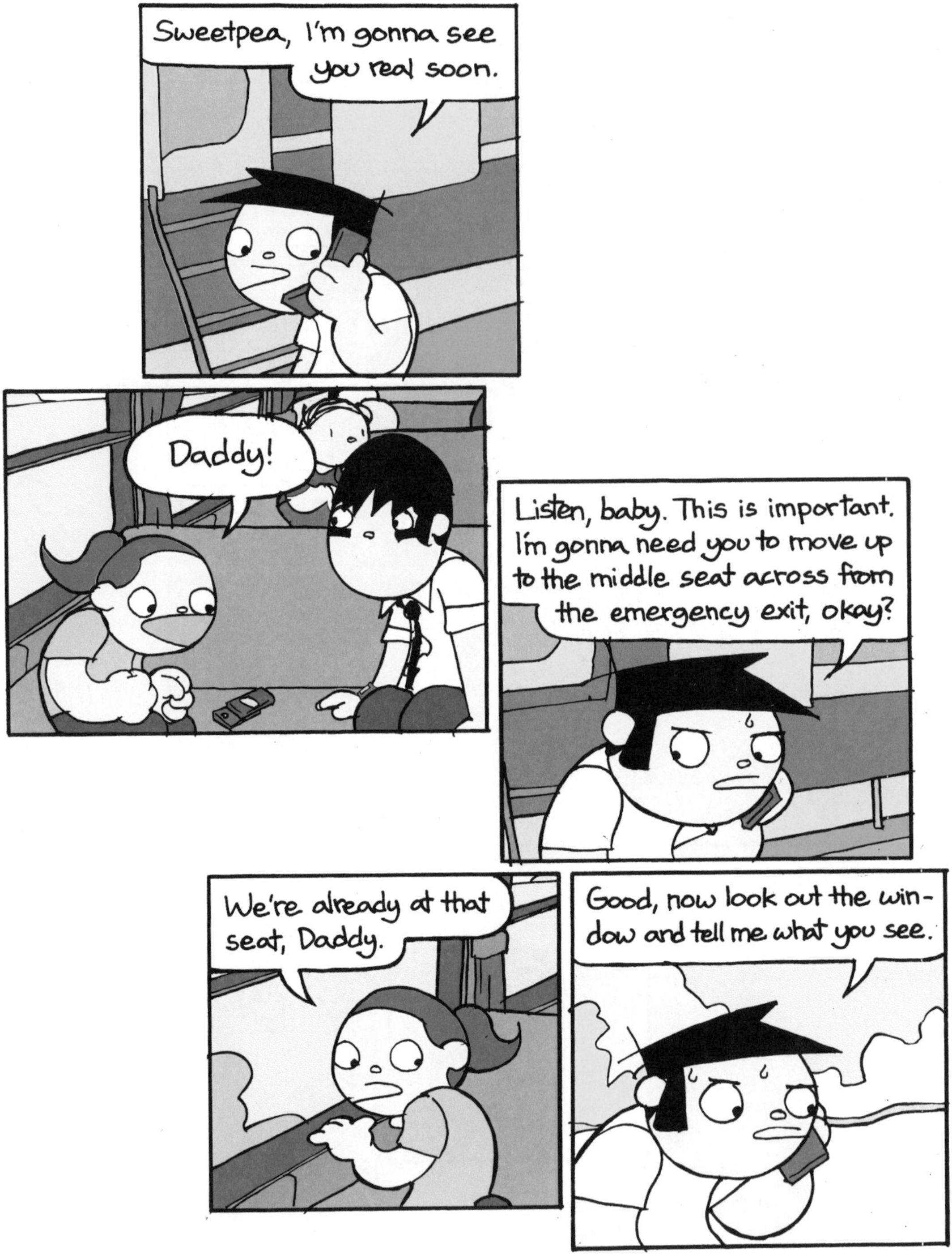
Sweetpea, I'm gonna see you real soon.
Daddy!
Listen, baby. This is important. I'm gonna need you to move up to the middle seat across from the emergency exit, okay?
We're already at that seat, Daddy.
Good, now look out the window and tell me what you see.

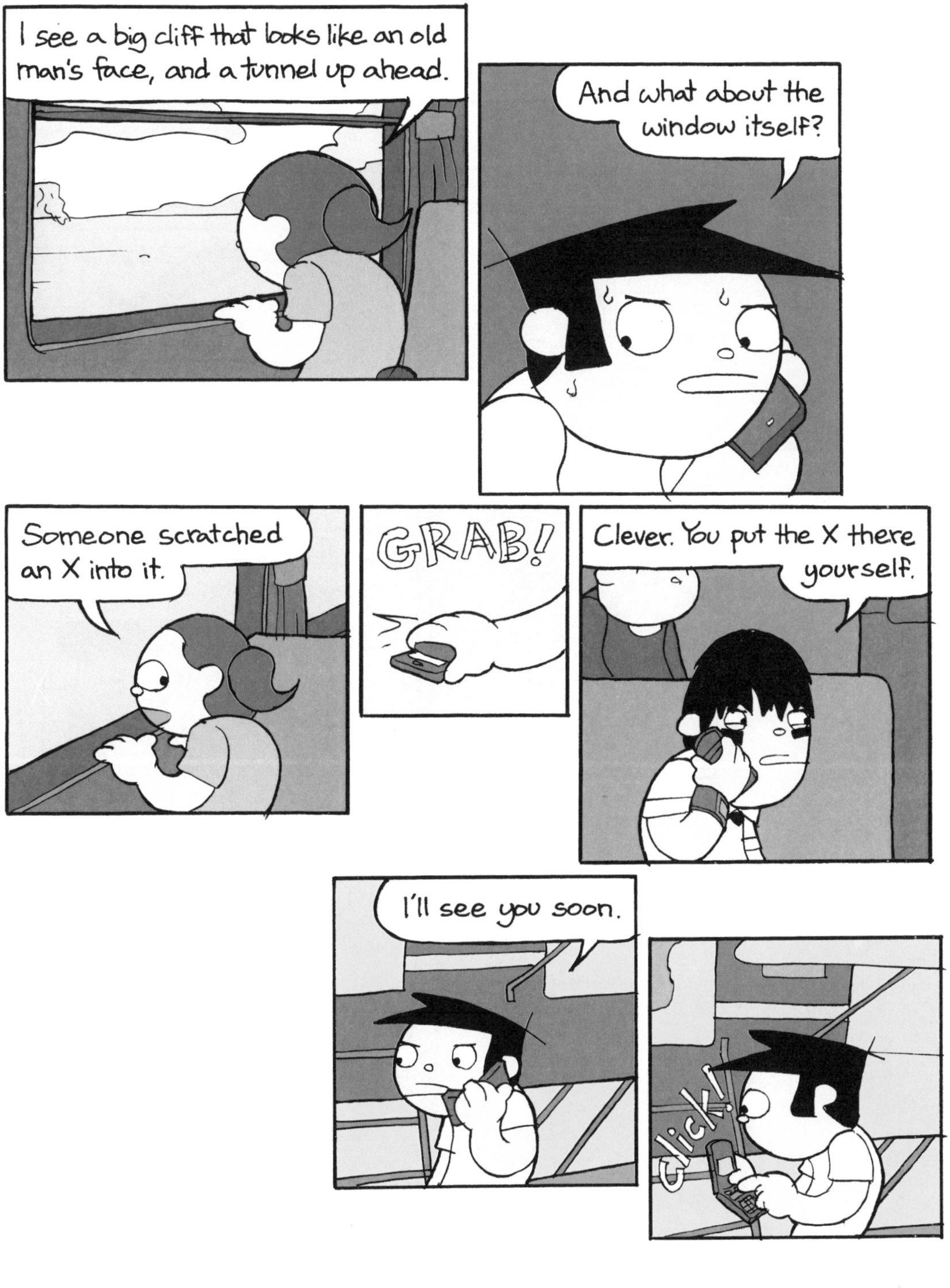
I see a big cliff that looks like an old man's face, and a tunnel up ahead.
And what about the window itself?
Someone scratched an X into it.
GRAB!
Clever. You put the X there yourself.
I'll see you soon.
Click!

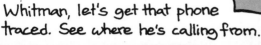

Whitman, let's get that phone traced. See where he's calling from.

Tibbs, get your men to see if he's scratched an X in every window. Could be some kinda code.

Yes, sir.

While you're at it, move Jimmy's daughter as far away from the emergency exits as you can.

Are you okay, Uncle Tibbs?

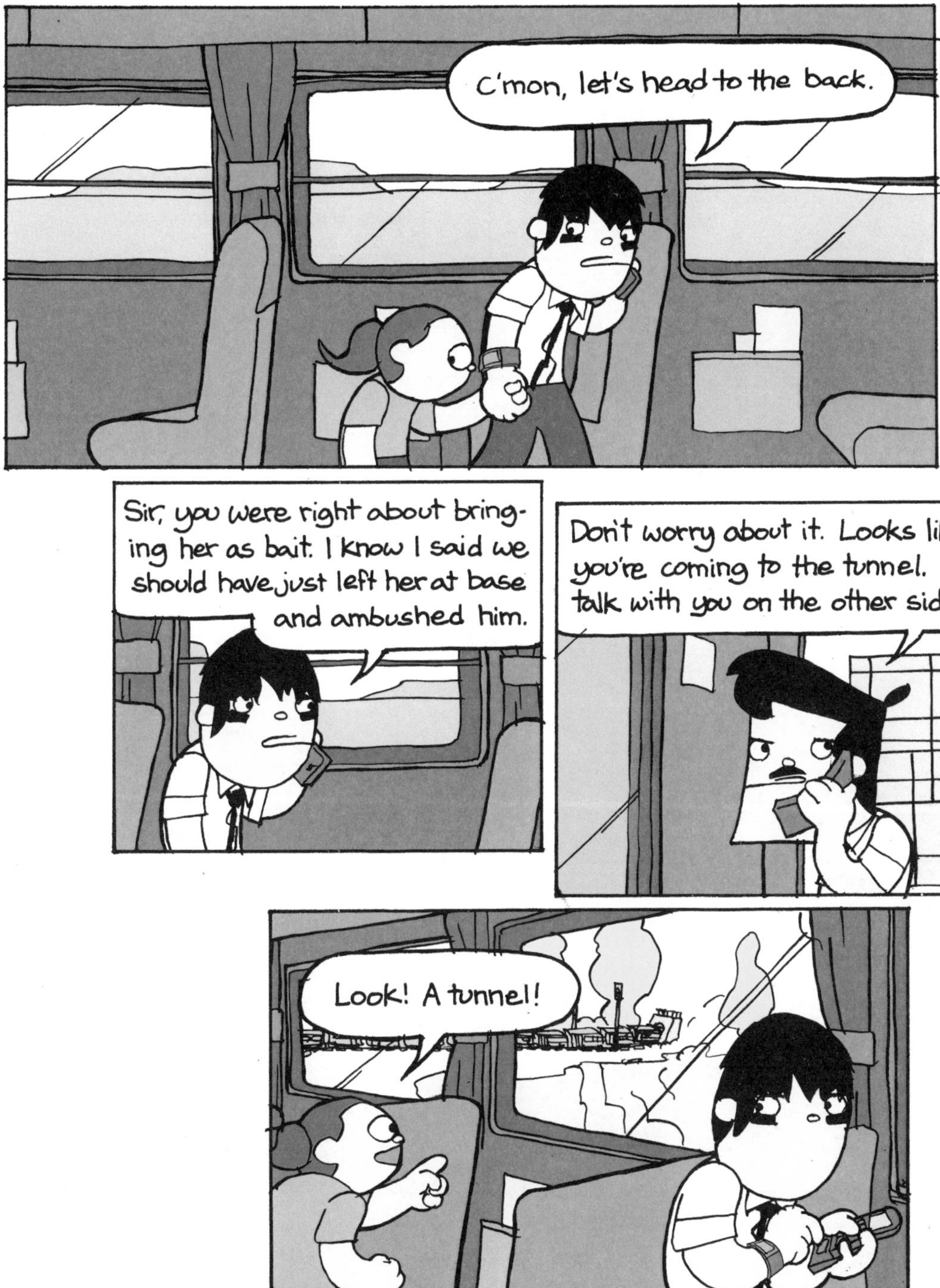
C'mon, let's head to the back.
Sir, you were right about bringing her as bait. I know I said we should have just left her at base and ambushed him.
Don't worry about it. Looks like you're coming to the tunnel. I'll talk with you on the other side.
Look! A tunnel!

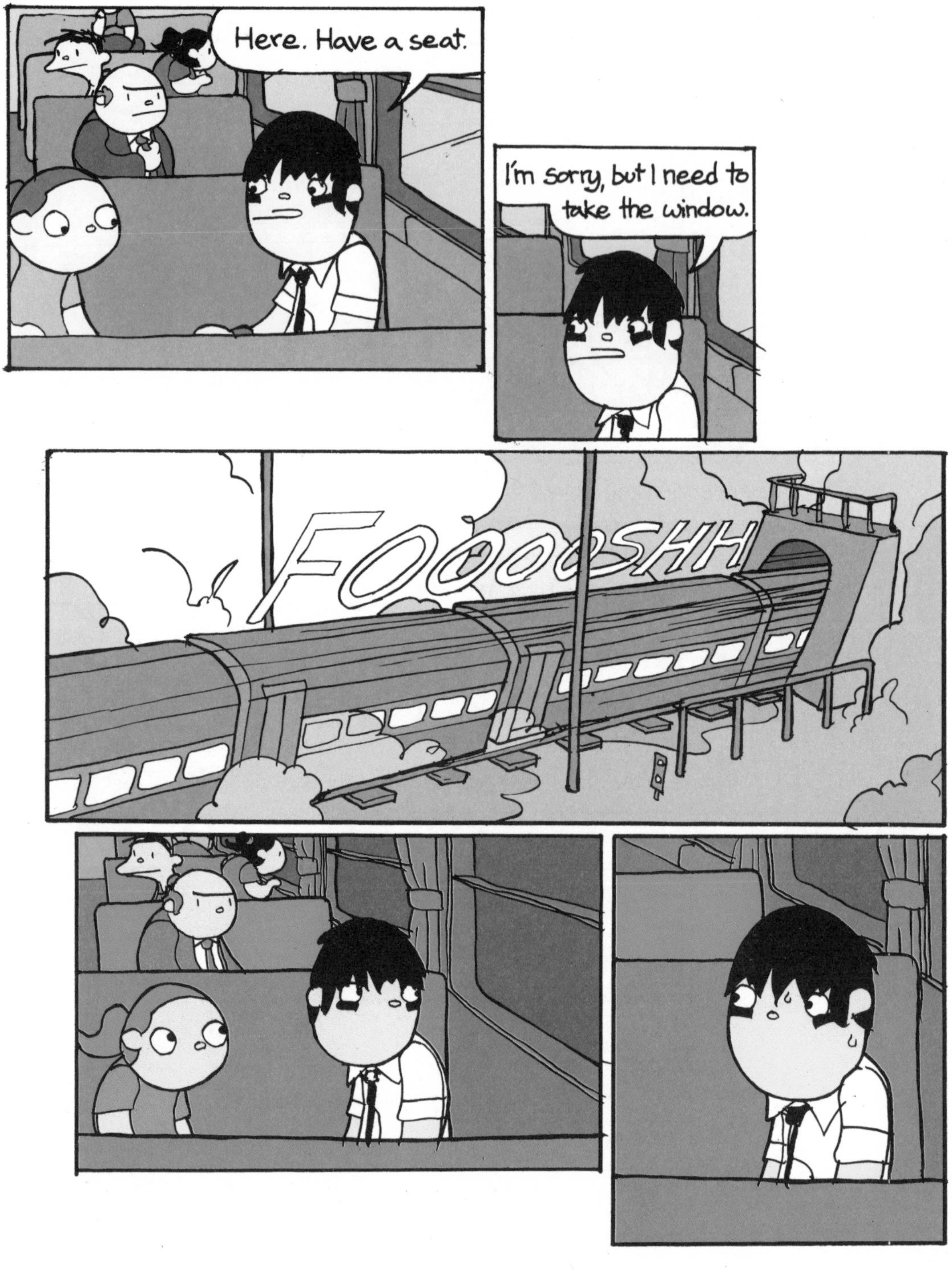
Here. Have a seat.
I'm sorry, but I need to take the window.
FOOOOSHH

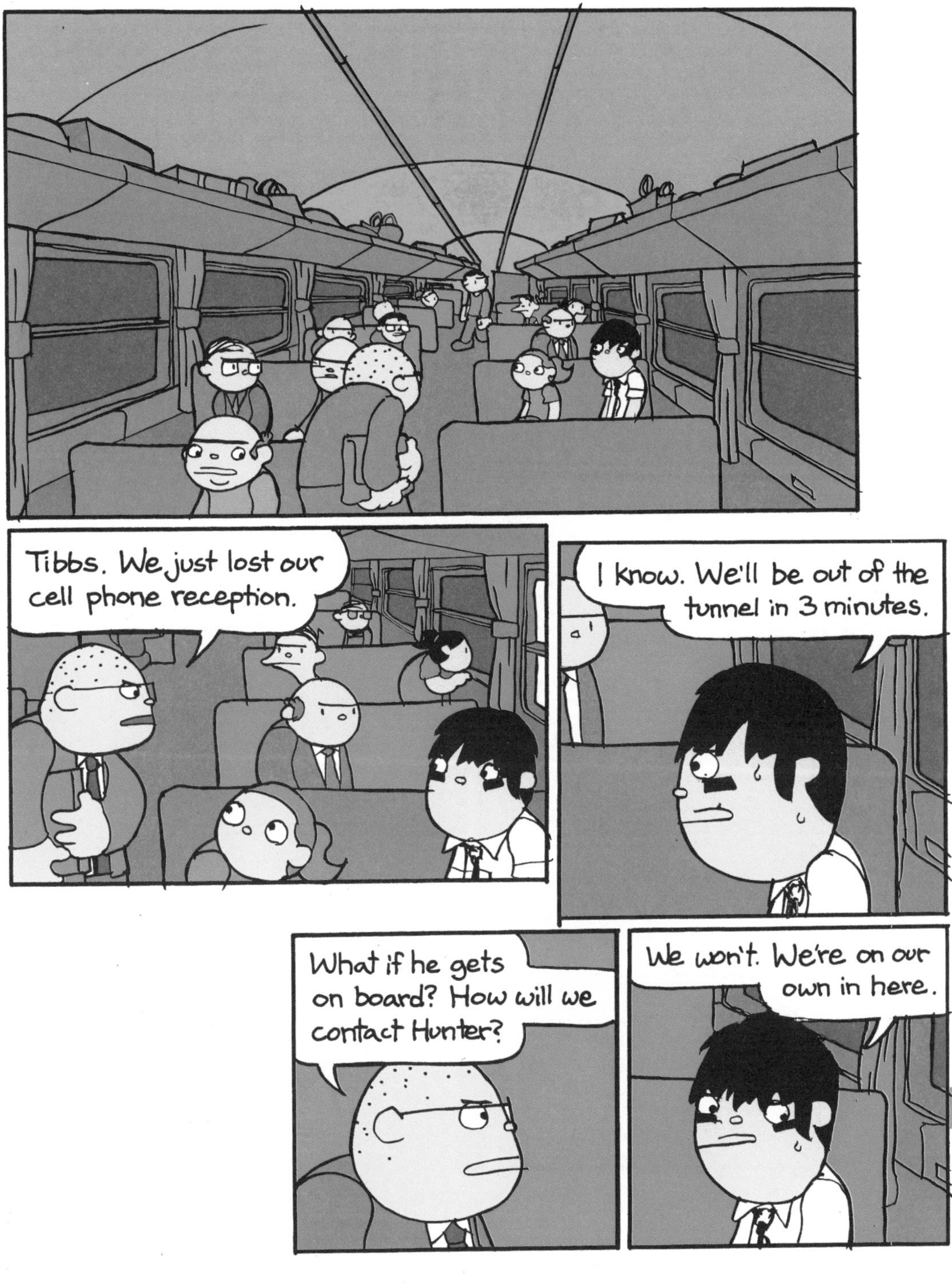
Tibbs. We just lost our cell phone reception.
I know. We'll be out of the tunnel in 3 minutes.
What if he gets on board? How will we contact Hunter?
We won't. We're on our own in here.

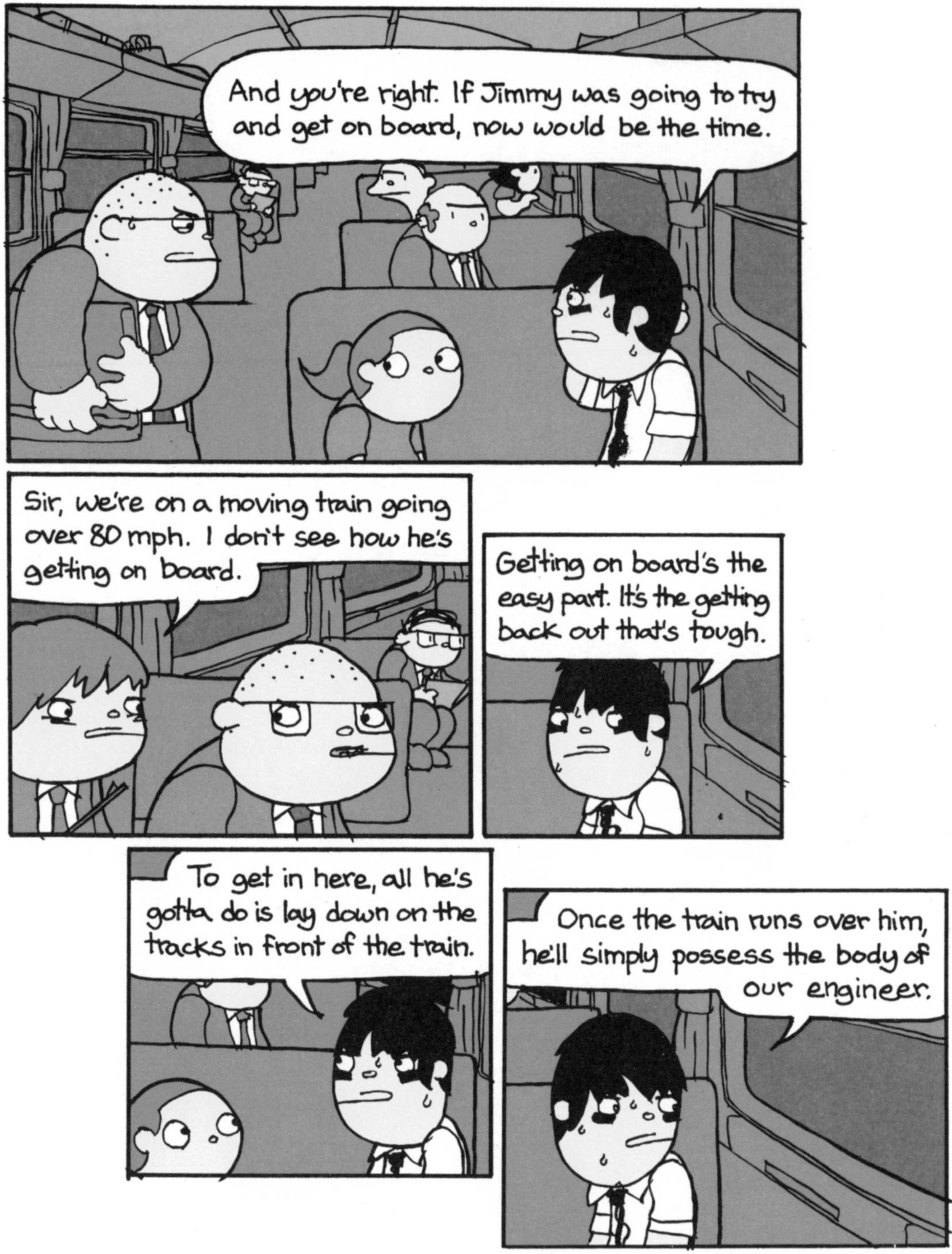
And you're right. If Jimmy was going to try and get on board, now would be the time.
Sir, we're on a moving train going over 80 mph. I don't see how he's getting on board.
Getting on board's the easy part. It's the getting back out that's tough.
To get in here, all he's gotta do is lay down on the tracks in front of the train.
Once the train runs over him, he'll simply possess the body of our engineer.

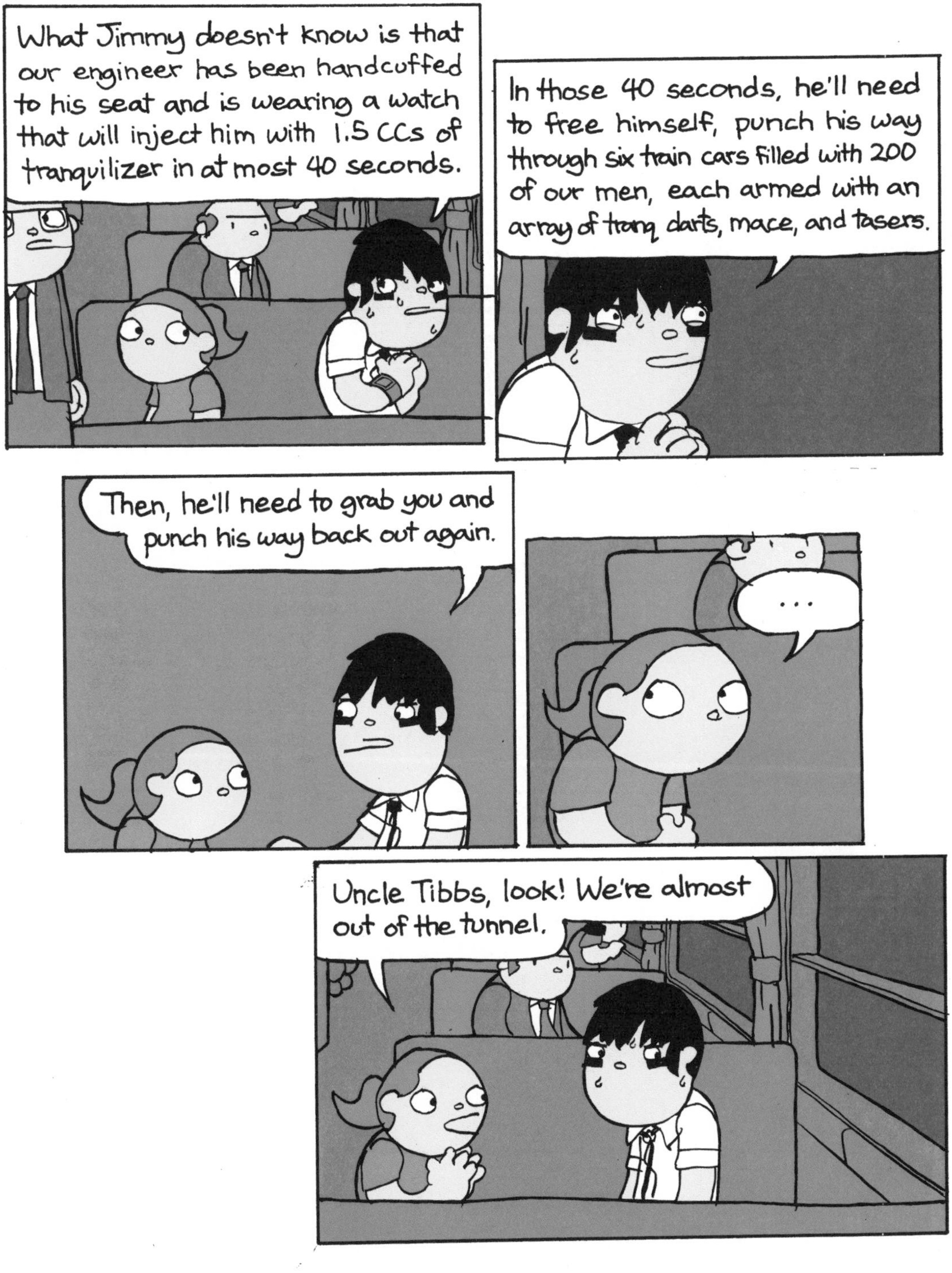
What Jimmy doesn't know is that our engineer has been handcuffed to his seat and is wearing a watch that will inject him with 1.5 CCs of tranquilizer in at most 40 seconds.
In those 40 seconds, he'll need to free himself, punch his way through six train cars filled with 200 of our men, each armed with an array of tranq darts, mace, and tasers.
Then, he'll need to grab you and punch his way back out again.
...
Uncle Tibbs, look! We're almost out of the tunnel.

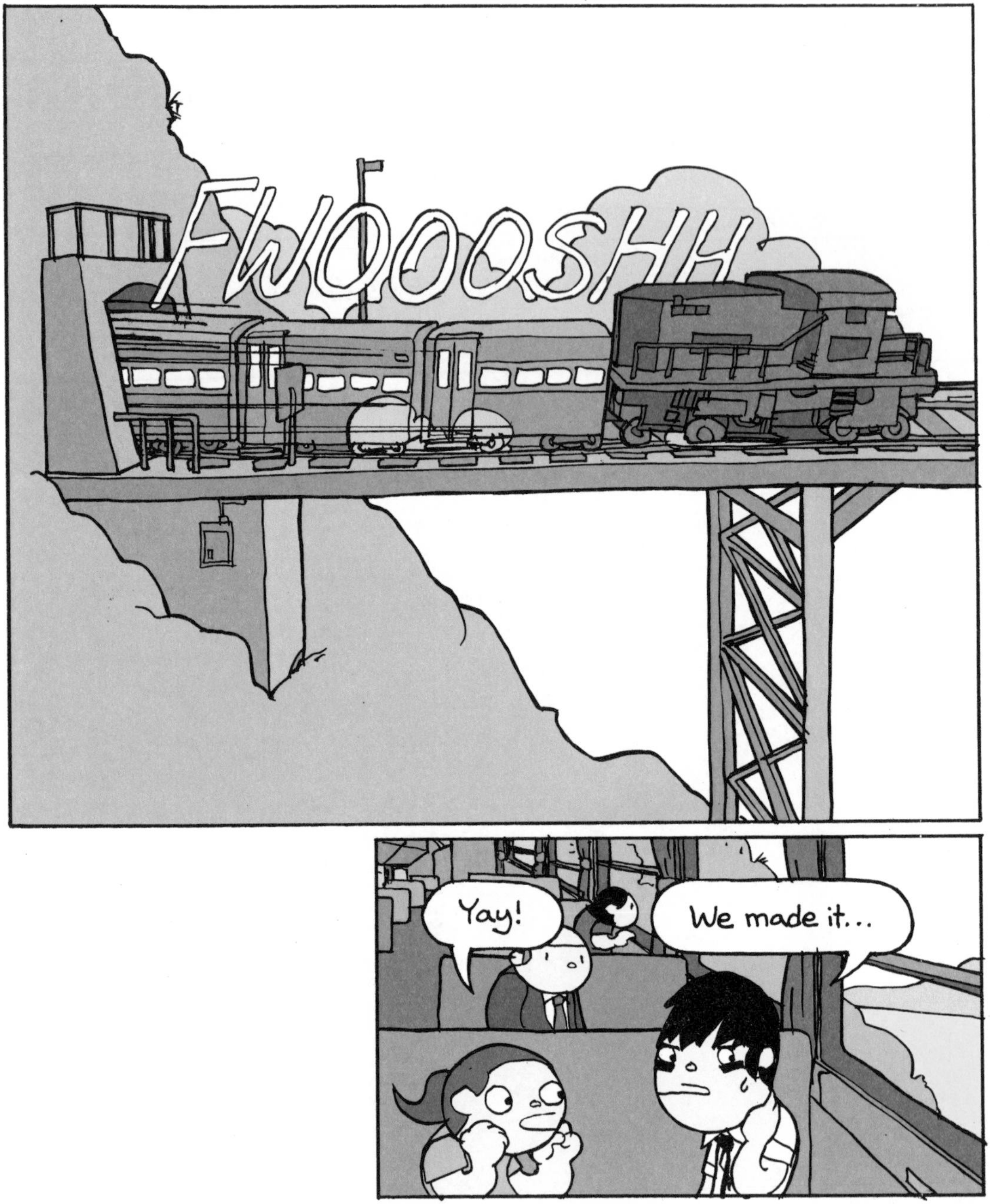
FWOOOSHH
Yay!
We made it...

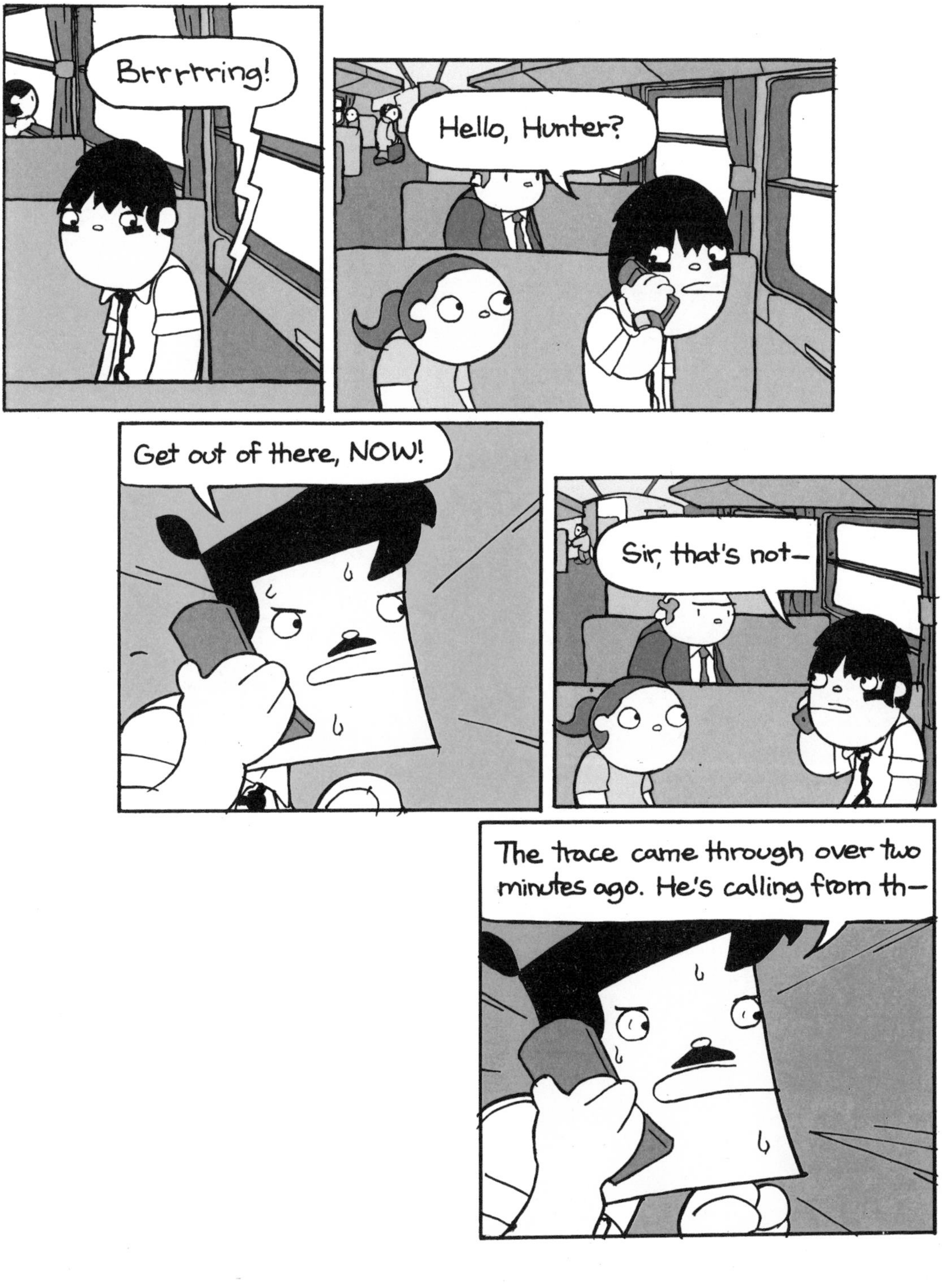
Brrrrring!
Hello, Hunter?
Get out of there, NOW!
Sir, that's not—
The trace came through over two minutes ago. He's calling from th—

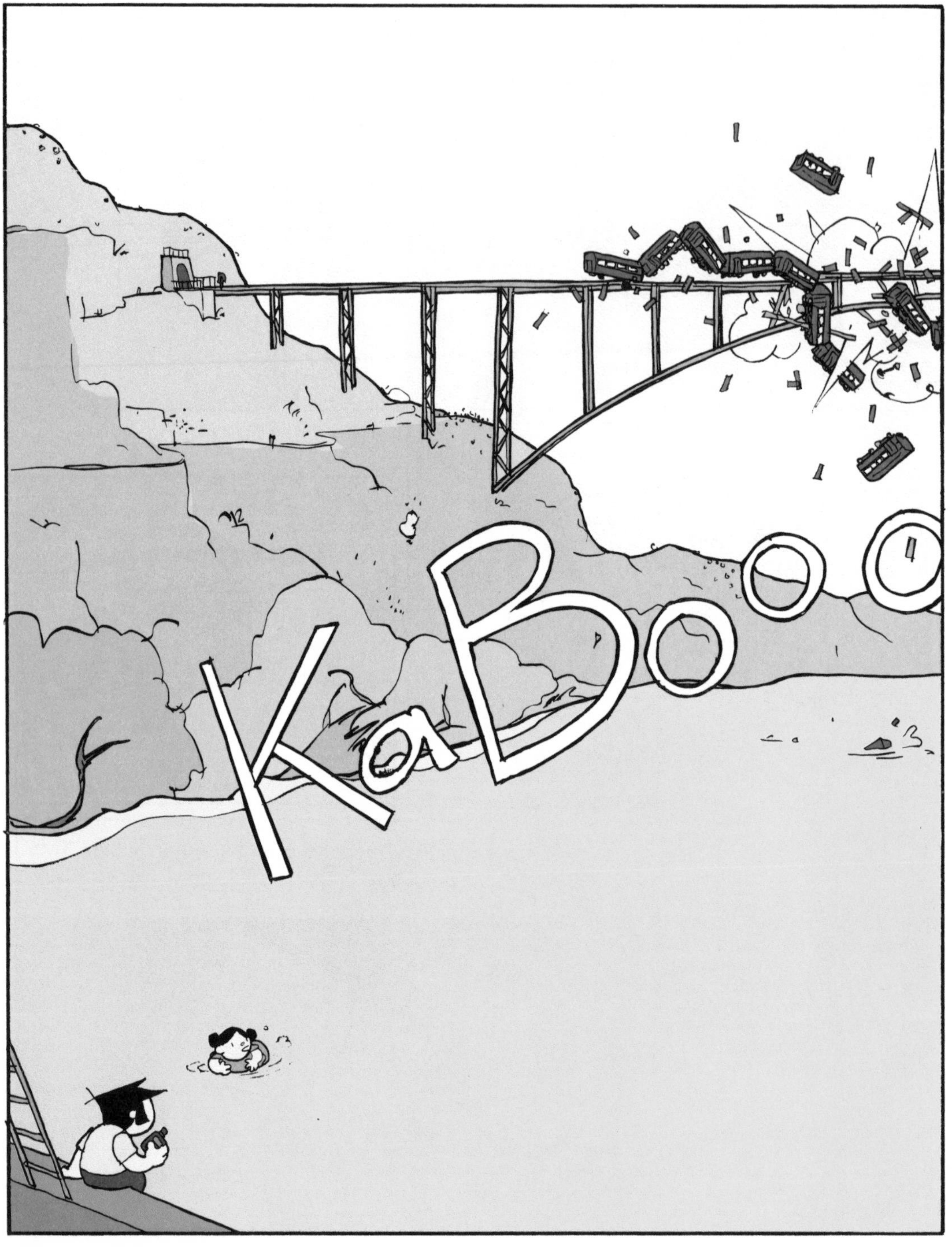
KaBooo

# CHAPTER 10

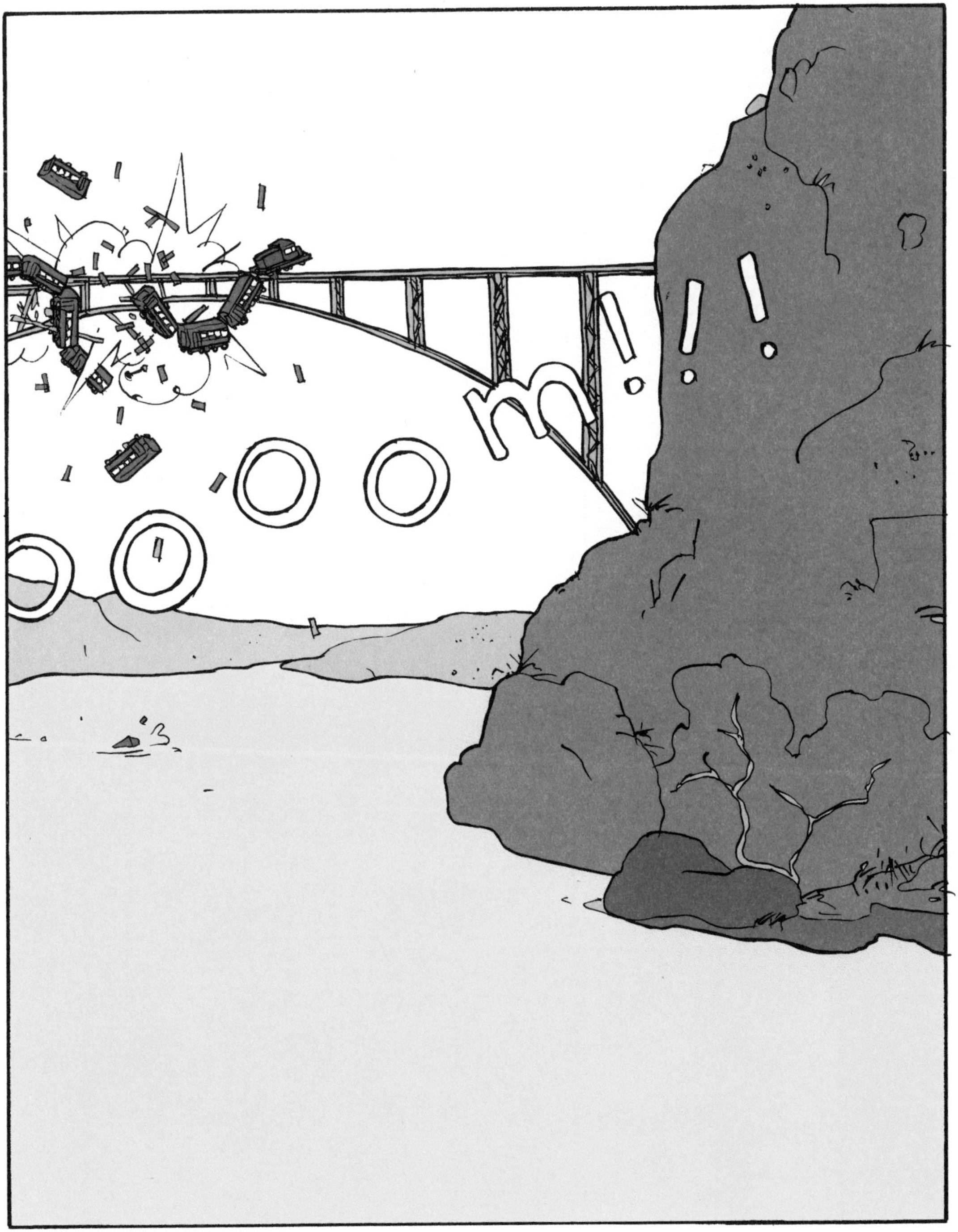
OOOOm!!!

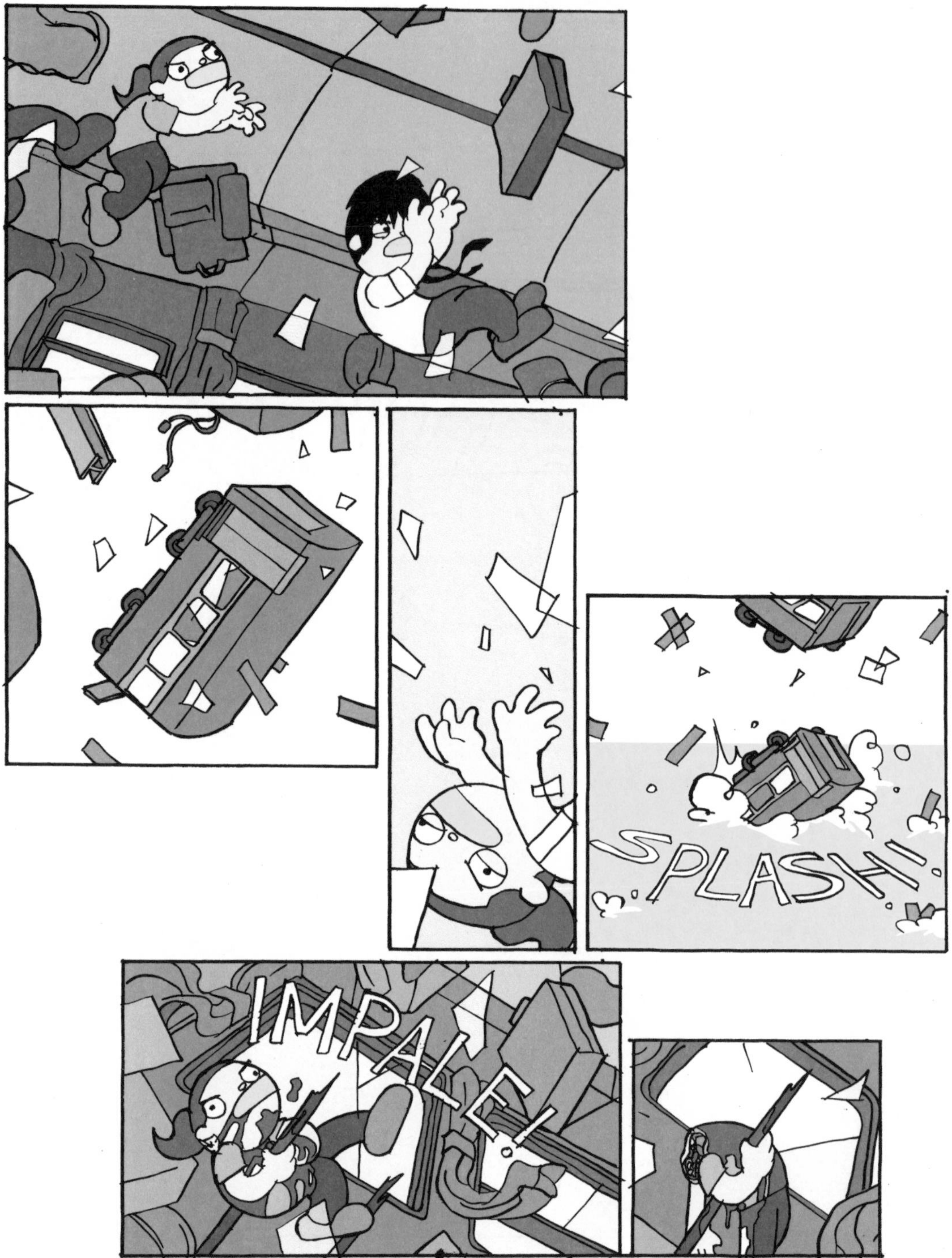
SPLASH!
IMPALE!

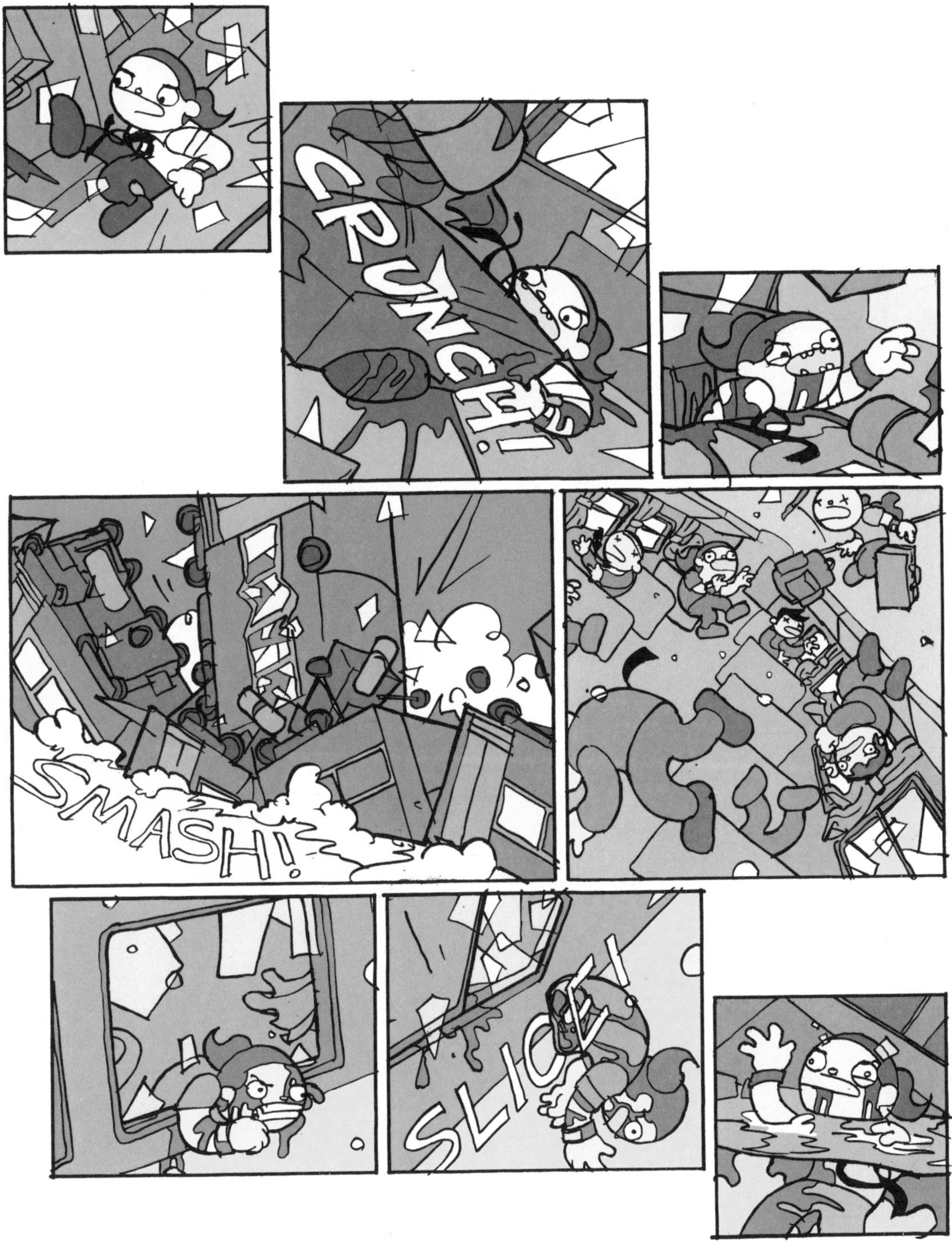
CRUNCH!
SMASH!
SLICE!

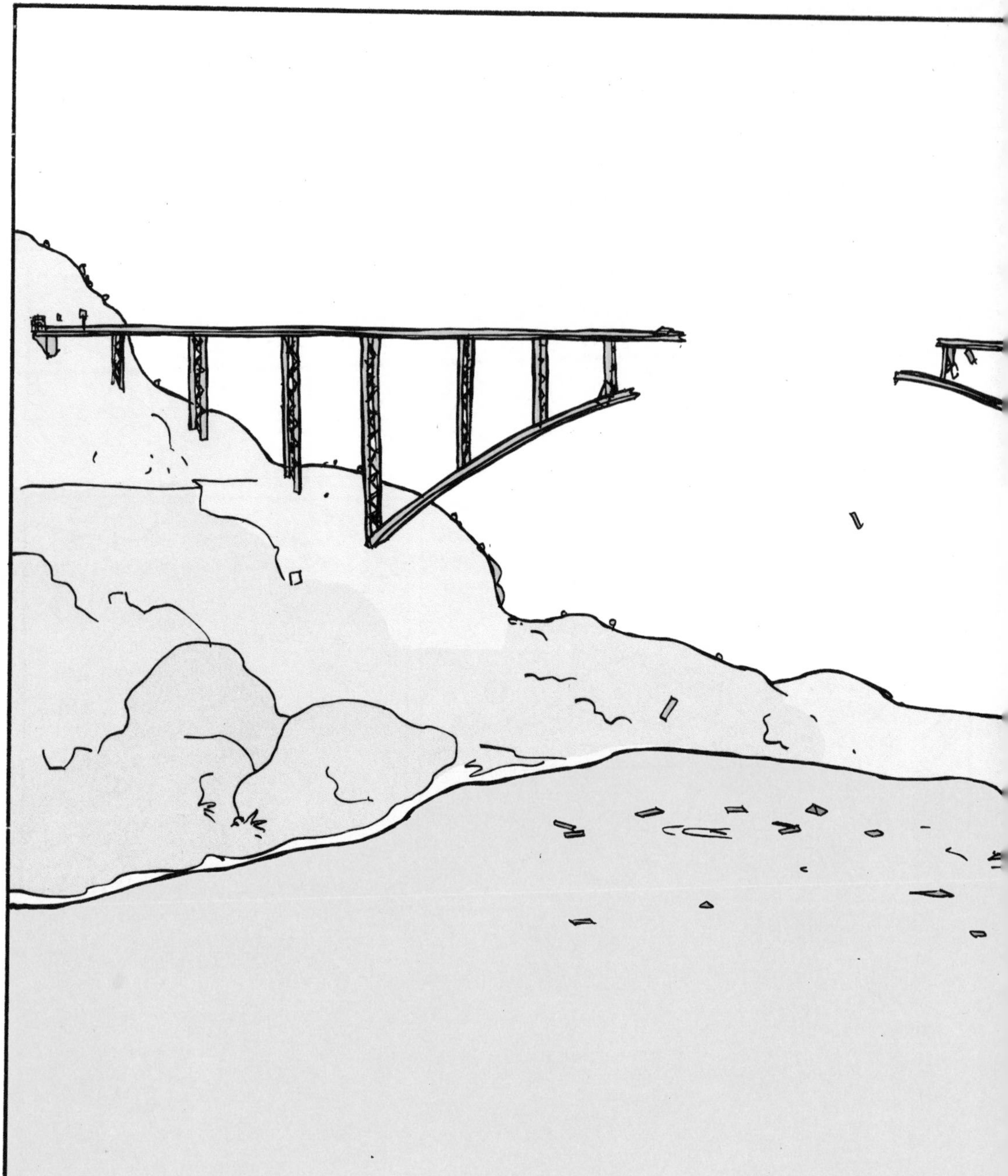

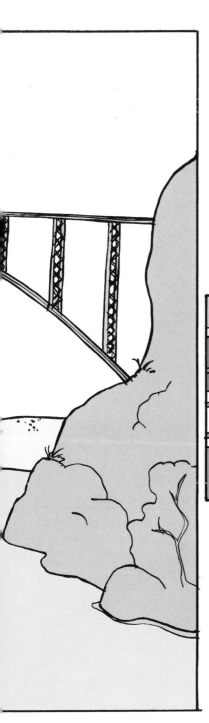

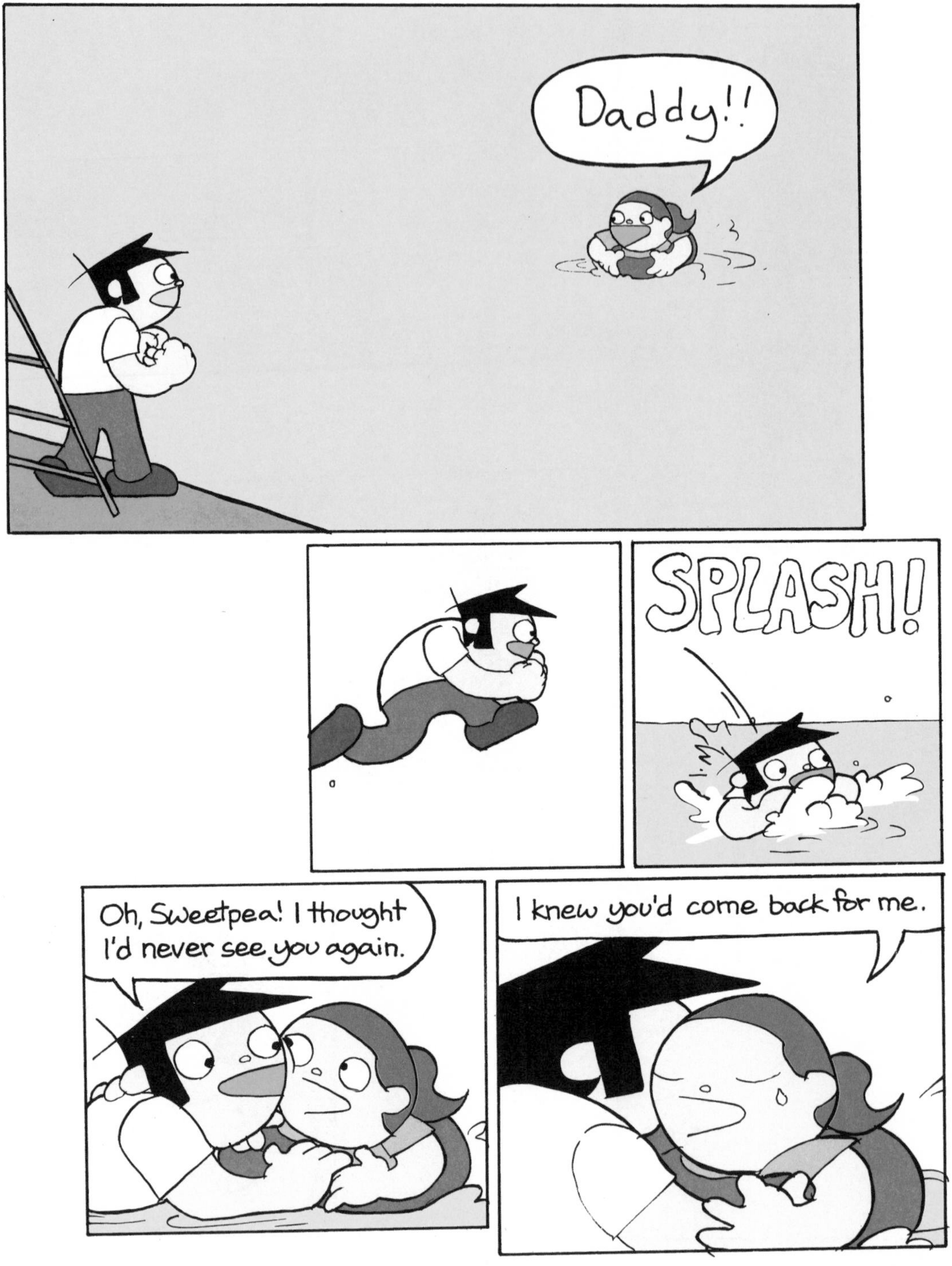
Daddy!!
SPLASH!
Oh, Sweetpea! I thought I'd never see you again.
I knew you'd come back for me.

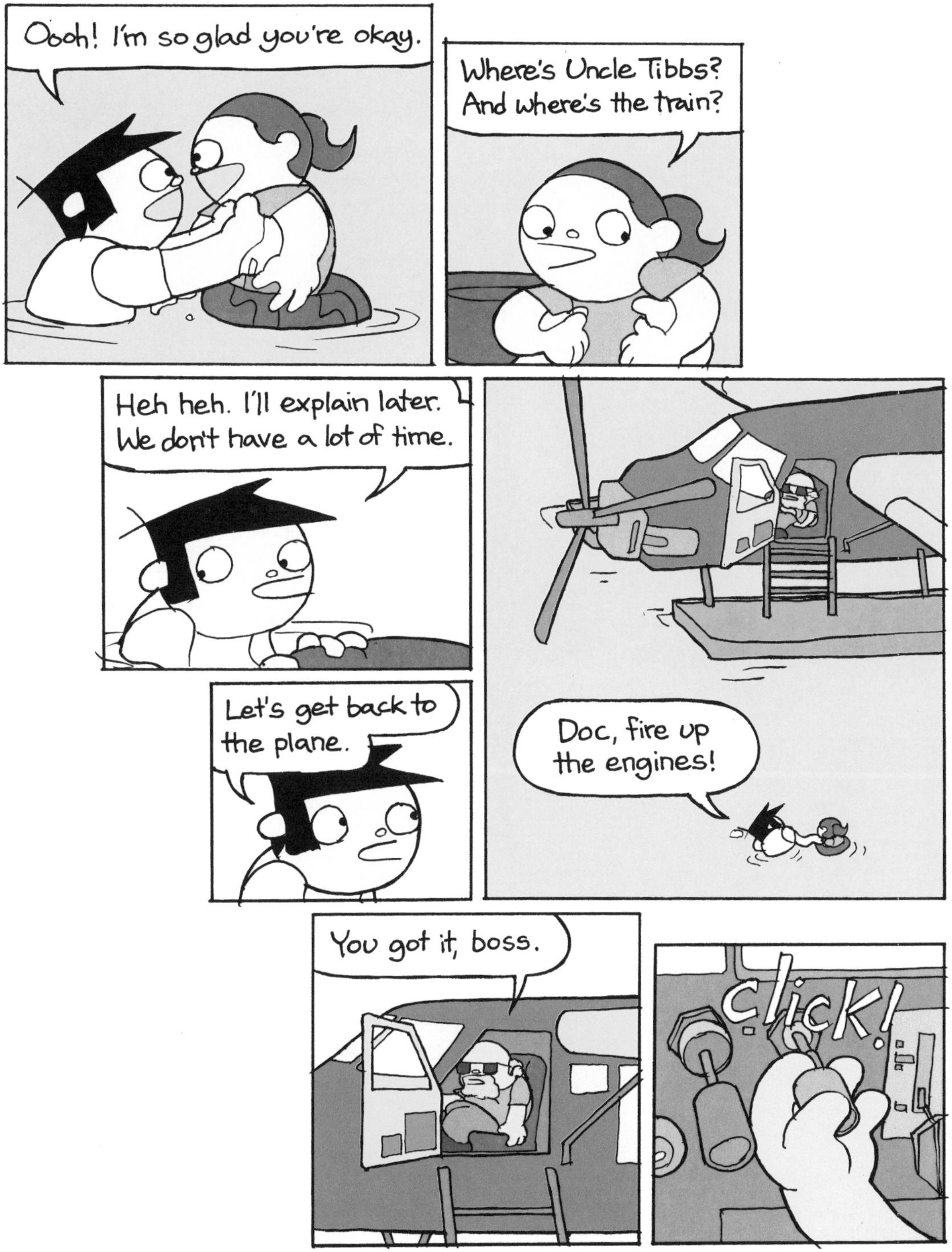
Oooh! I'm so glad you're okay.
Where's Uncle Tibbs? And where's the train?
Heh heh. I'll explain later. We don't have a lot of time.
Let's get back to the plane.
Doc, fire up the engines!
You got it, boss.
click!

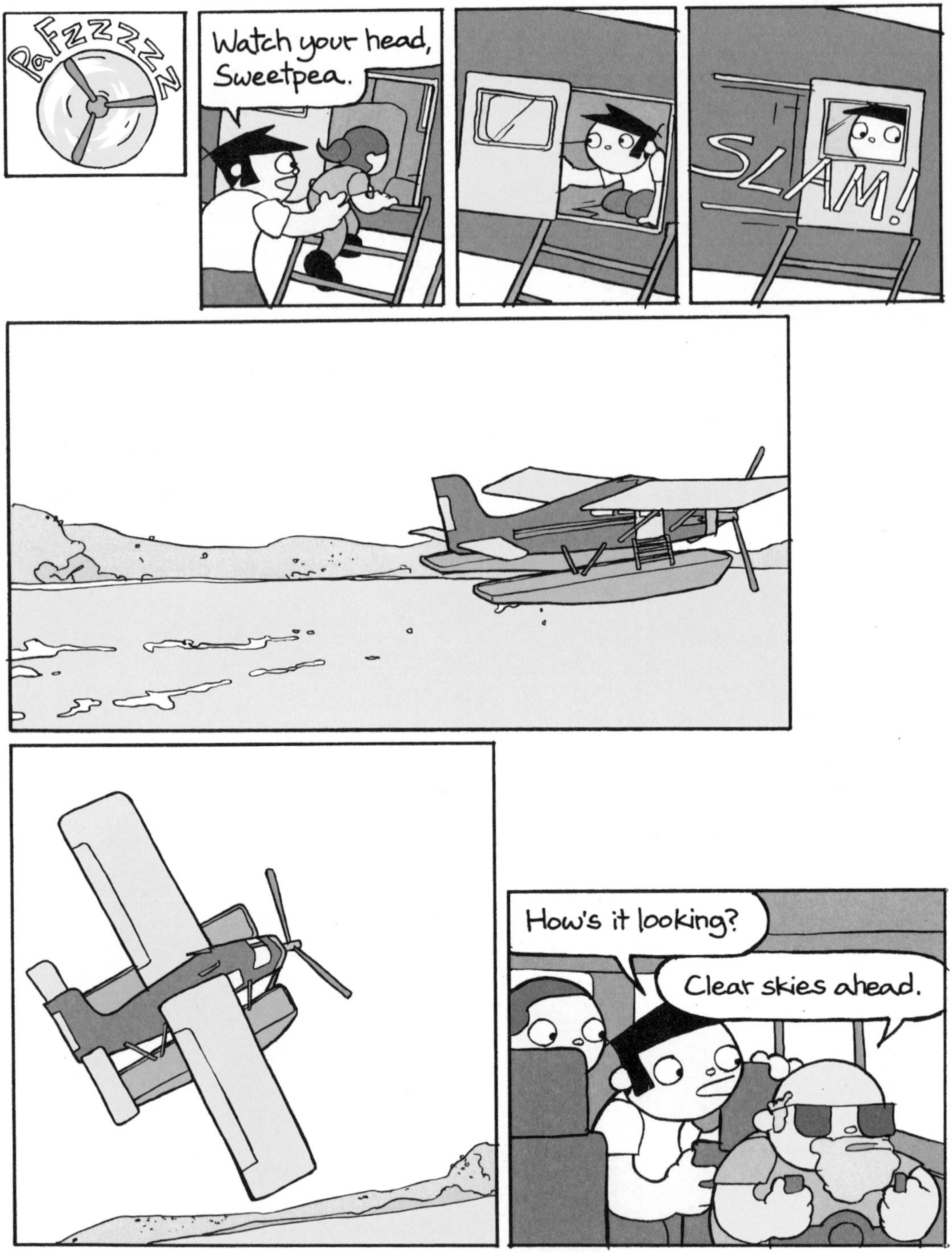
PaFzzzzzz
Watch your head, Sweetpea.
SLAM!
How's it looking?
Clear skies ahead.

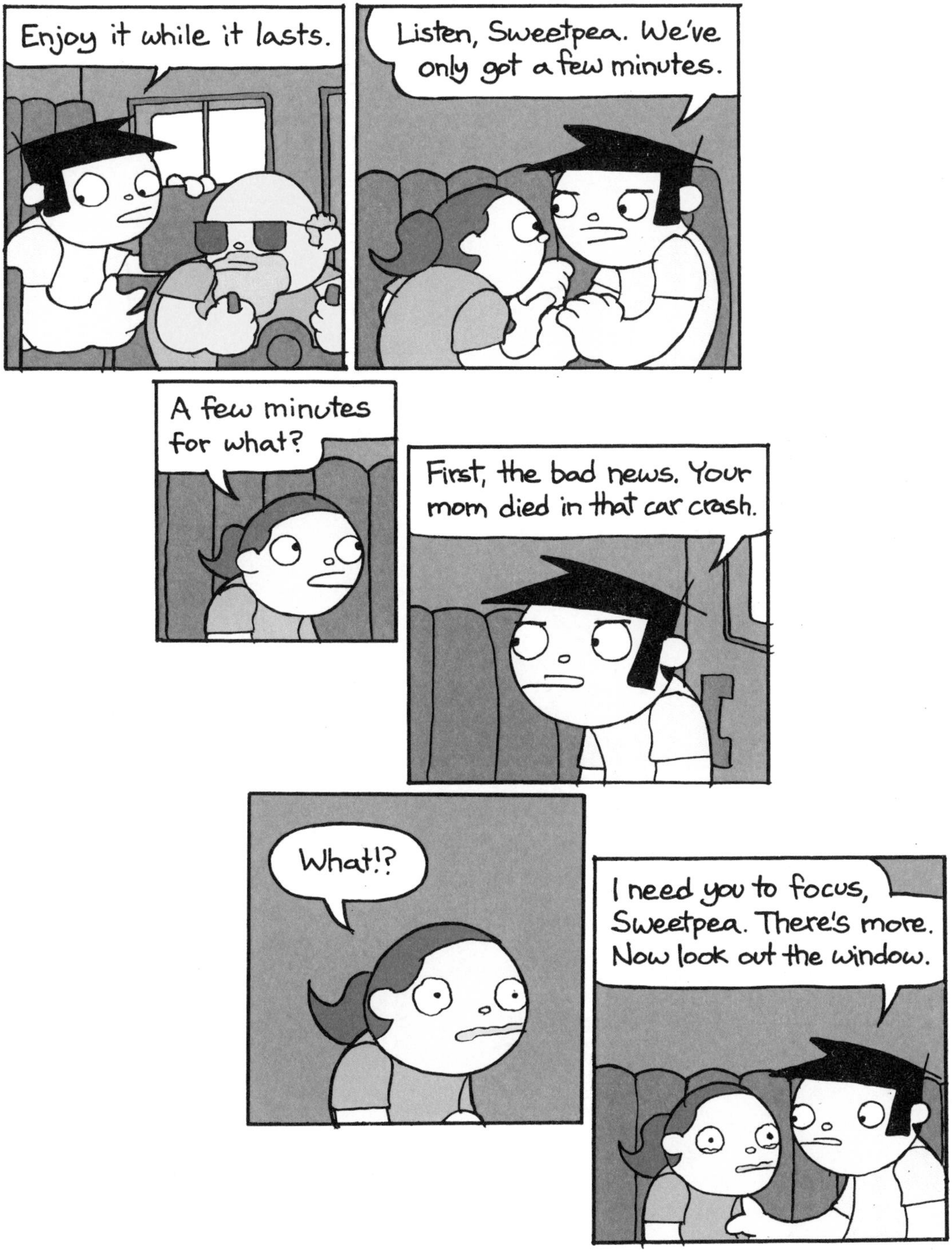
Enjoy it while it lasts.
Listen, Sweetpea. We've only got a few minutes.
A few minutes for what?
First, the bad news. Your mom died in that car crash.
What!?
I need you to focus, Sweetpea. There's more. Now look out the window.

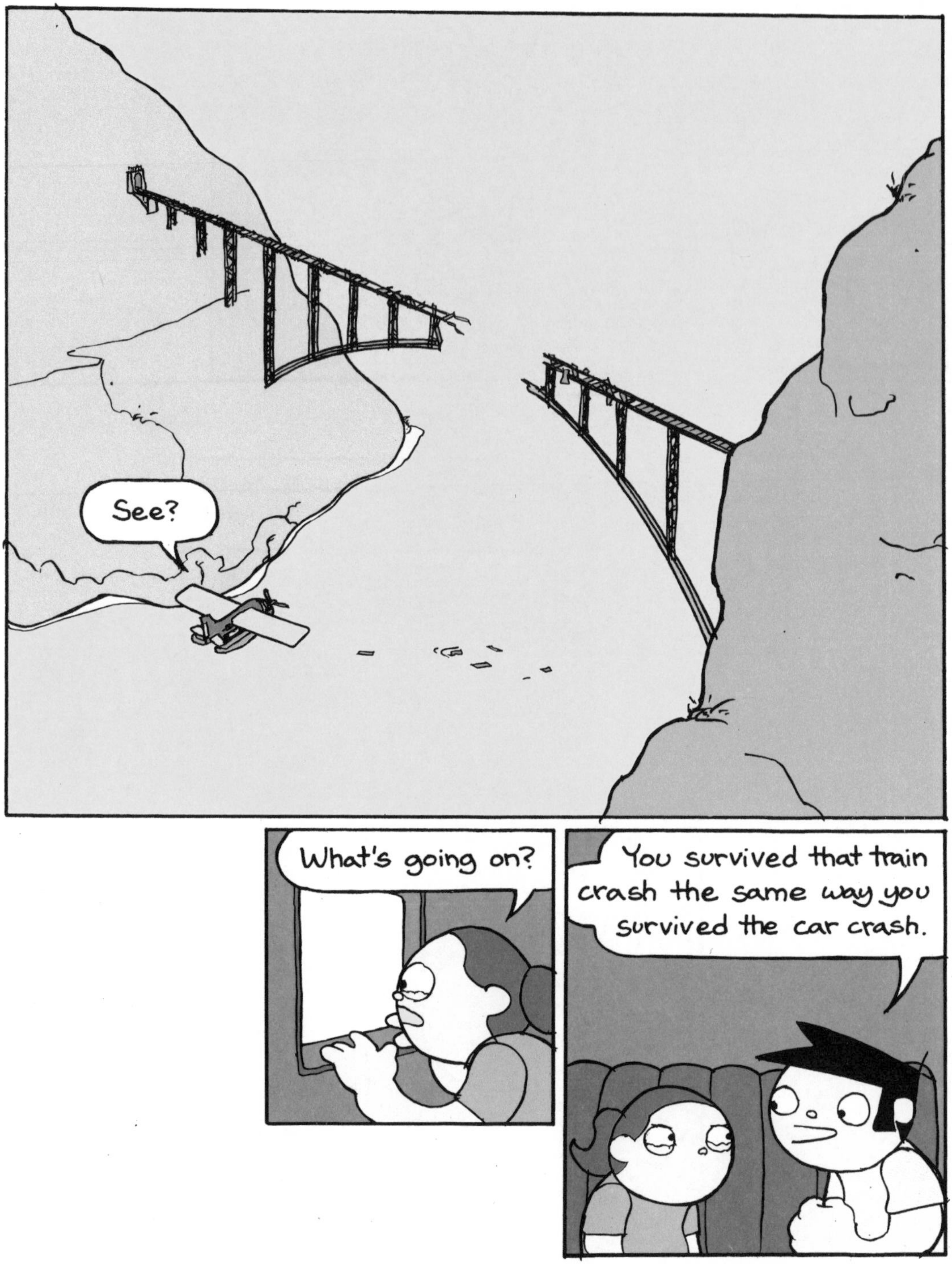
See?
What's going on?
You survived that train crash the same way you survived the car crash.

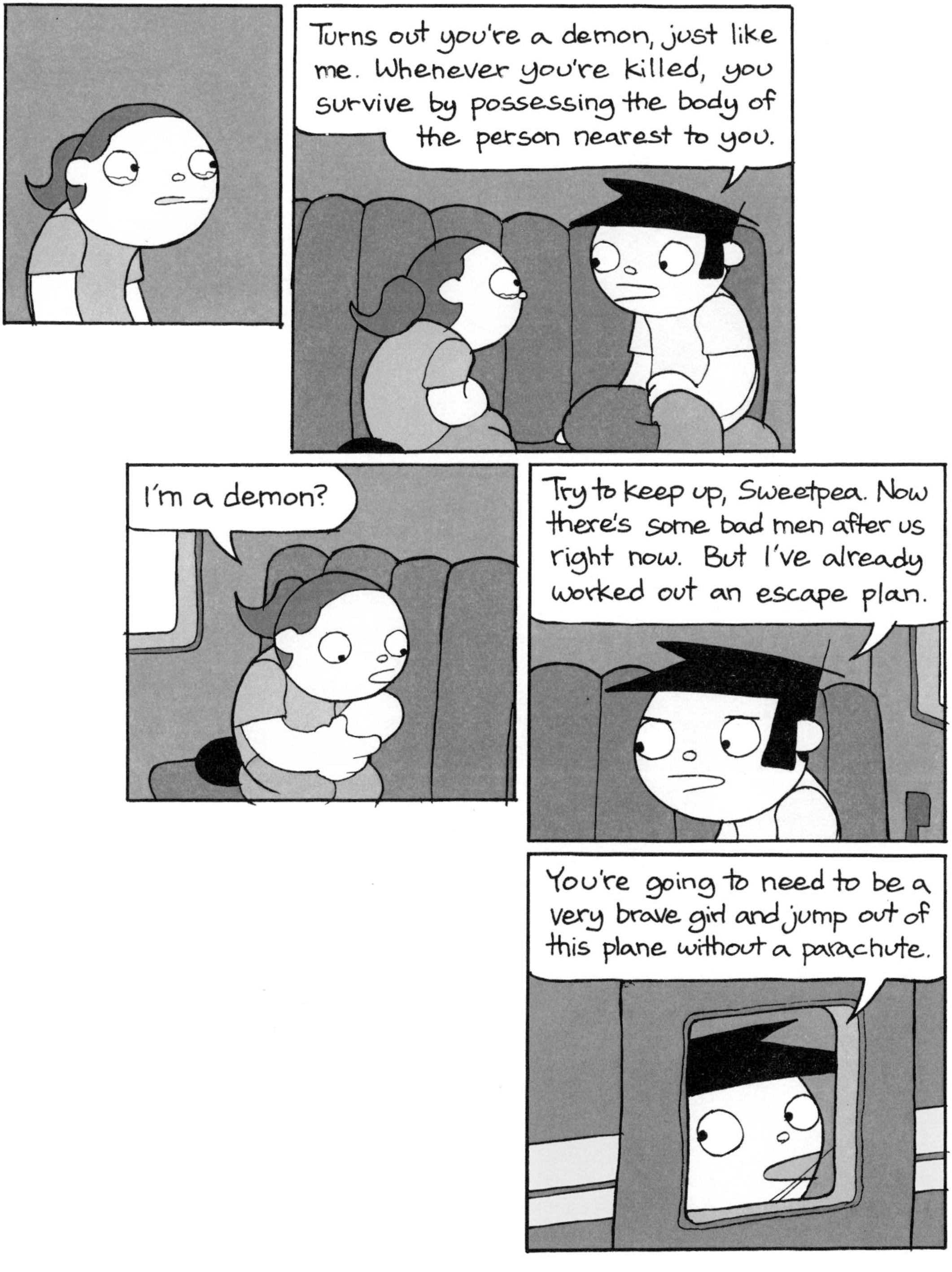
Turns out you're a demon, just like me. Whenever you're killed, you survive by possessing the body of the person nearest to you.
I'm a demon?
Try to keep up, Sweetpea. Now there's some bad men after us right now. But I've already worked out an escape plan.
You're going to need to be a very brave girl and jump out of this plane without a parachute.

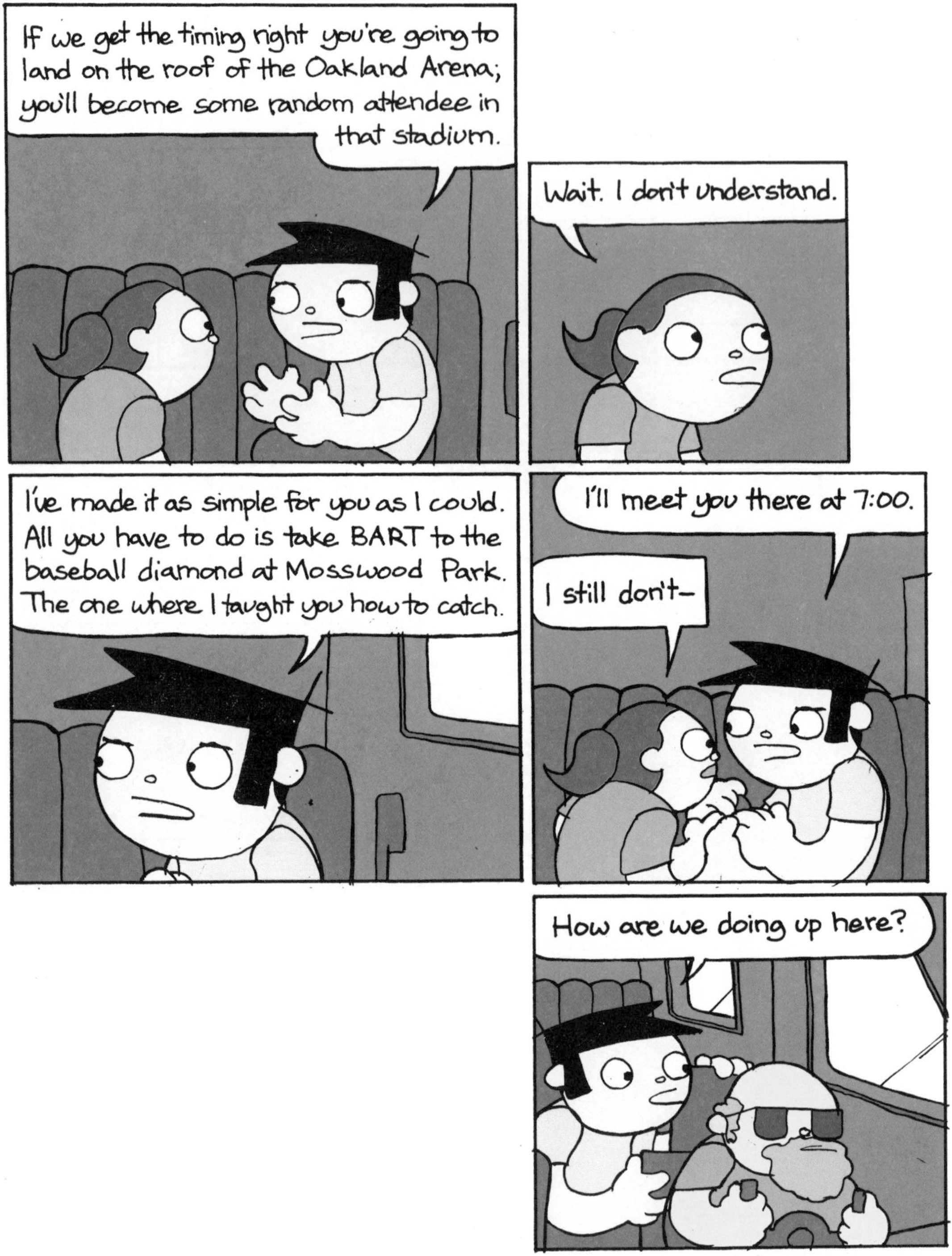
If we get the timing right you're going to land on the roof of the Oakland Arena; you'll become some random attendee in that stadium.
Wait. I don't understand.
I've made it as simple for you as I could. All you have to do is take BART to the baseball diamond at Mosswood Park. The one where I taught you how to catch.
I'll meet you there at 7:00.
I still don't–
How are we doing up here?

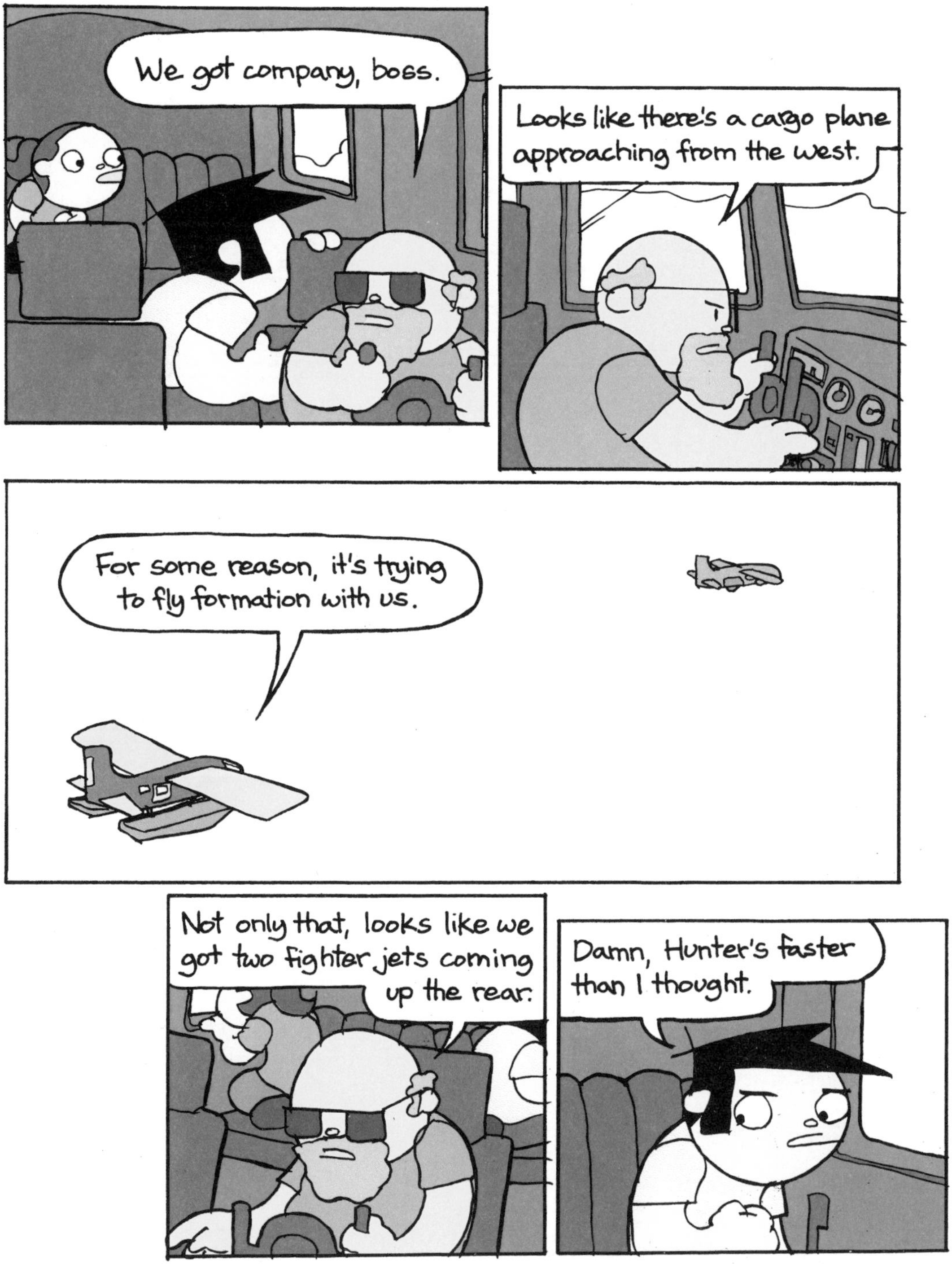
We got company, boss.
Looks like there's a cargo plane approaching from the west.
For some reason, it's trying to fly formation with us.
Not only that, looks like we got two fighter jets coming up the rear.
Damn, Hunter's faster than I thought.

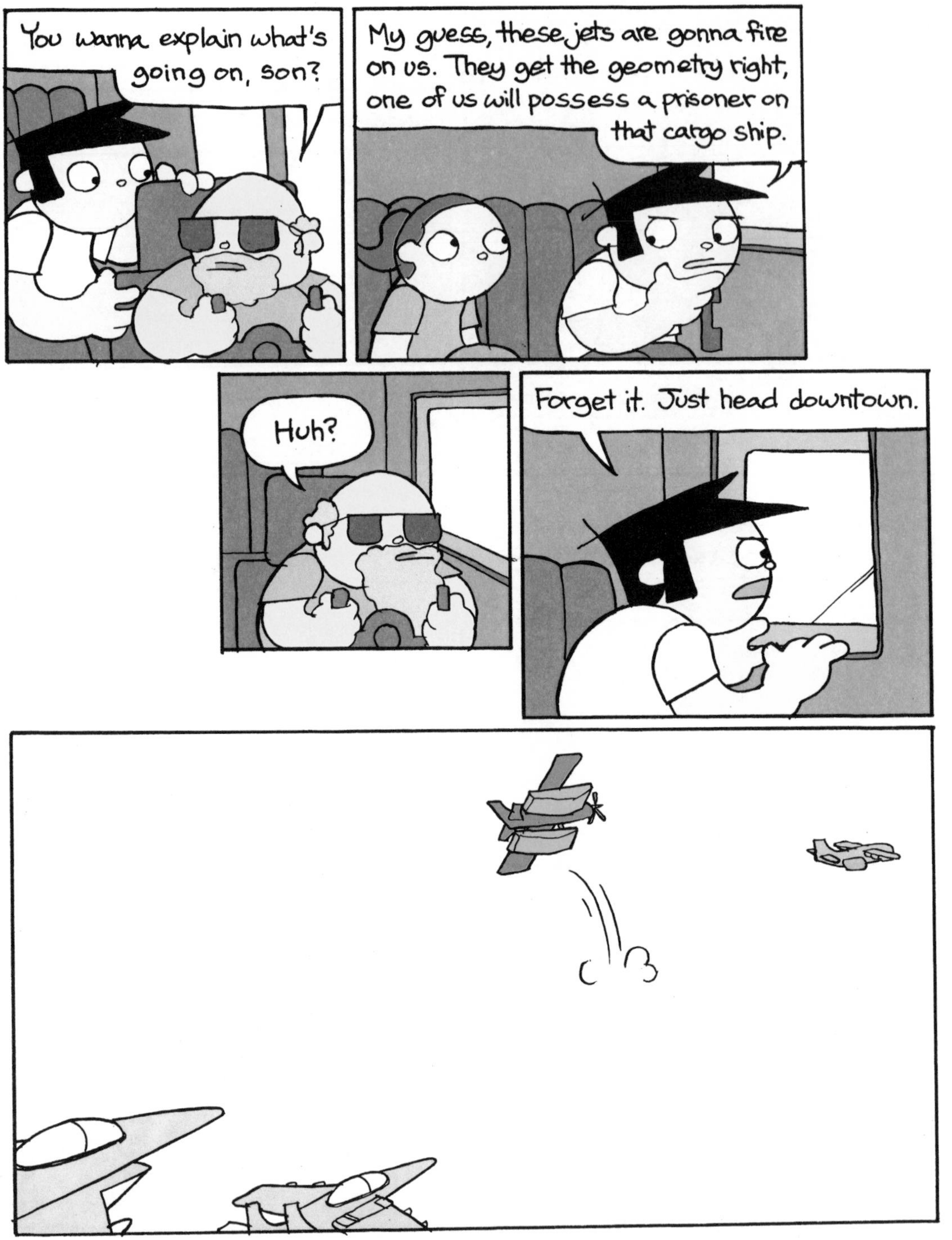
You wanna explain what's going on, son?
My guess, these jets are gonna fire on us. They get the geometry right, one of us will possess a prisoner on that cargo ship.
Huh?
Forget it. Just head downtown.

Change of plans, Sweetpea. We gotta get going, now.

I don't—

BLAM!

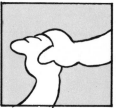

c'mon.

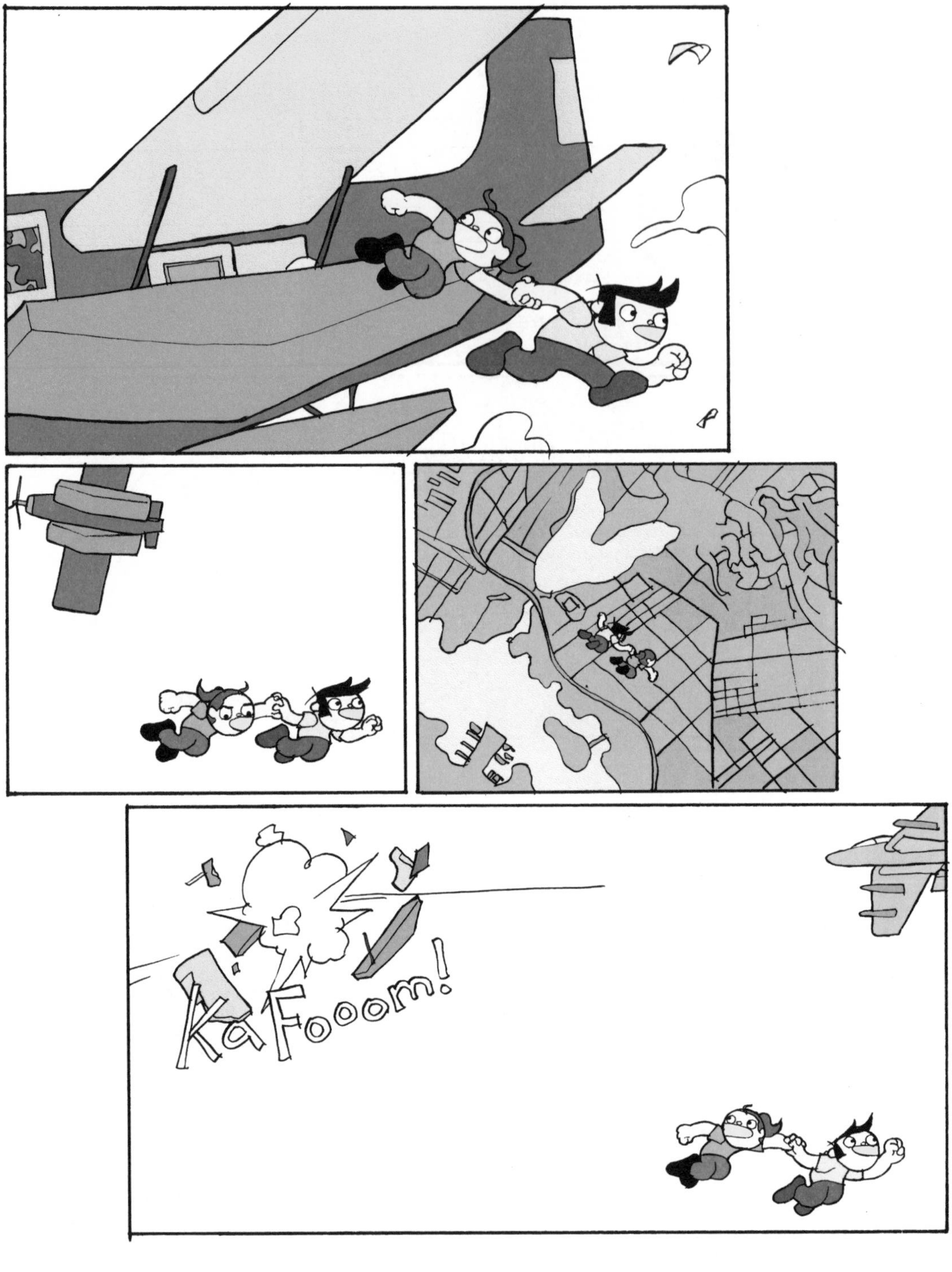
KaFooom!

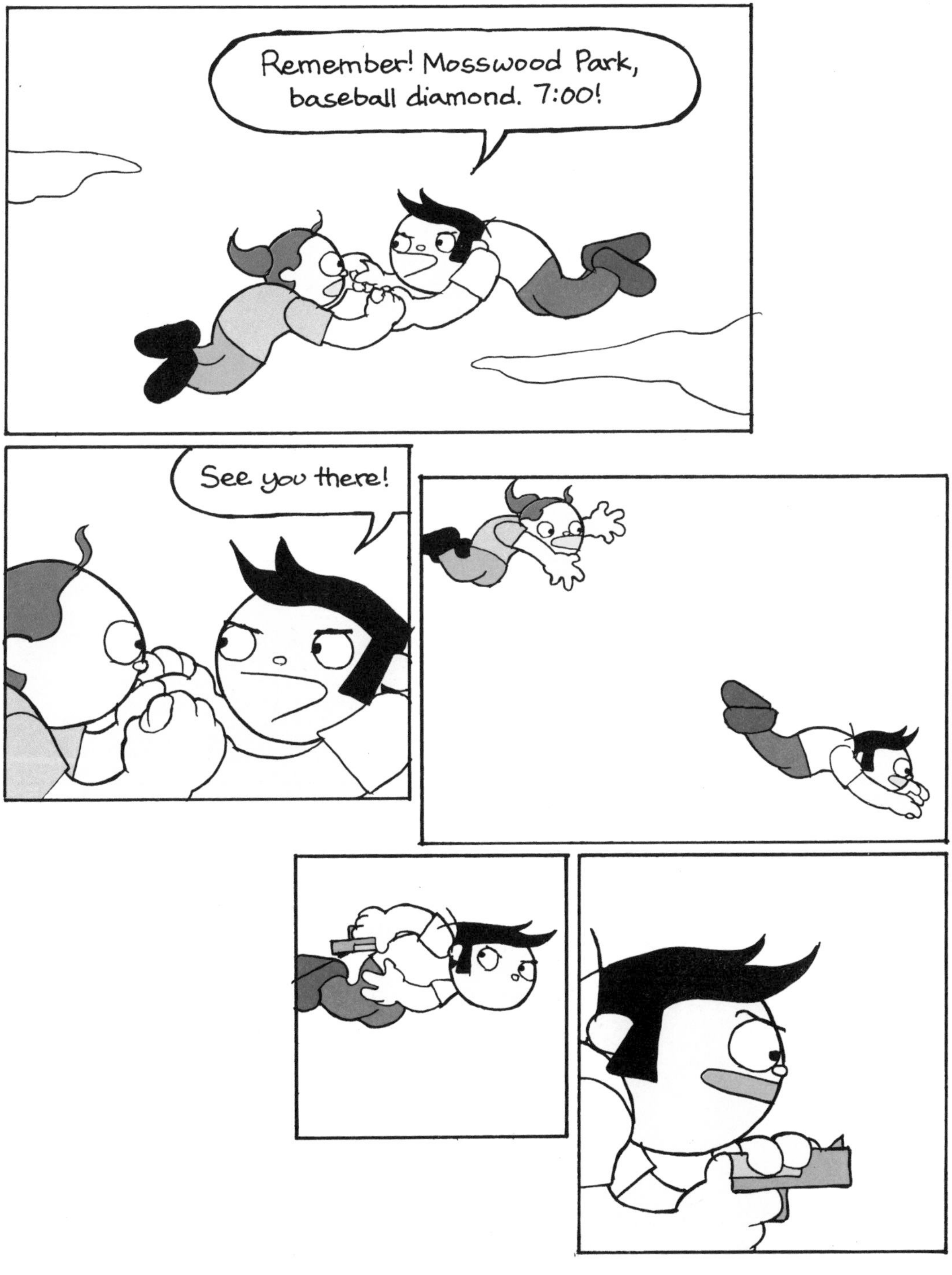
Remember! Mosswood Park, baseball diamond. 7:00!
See you there!

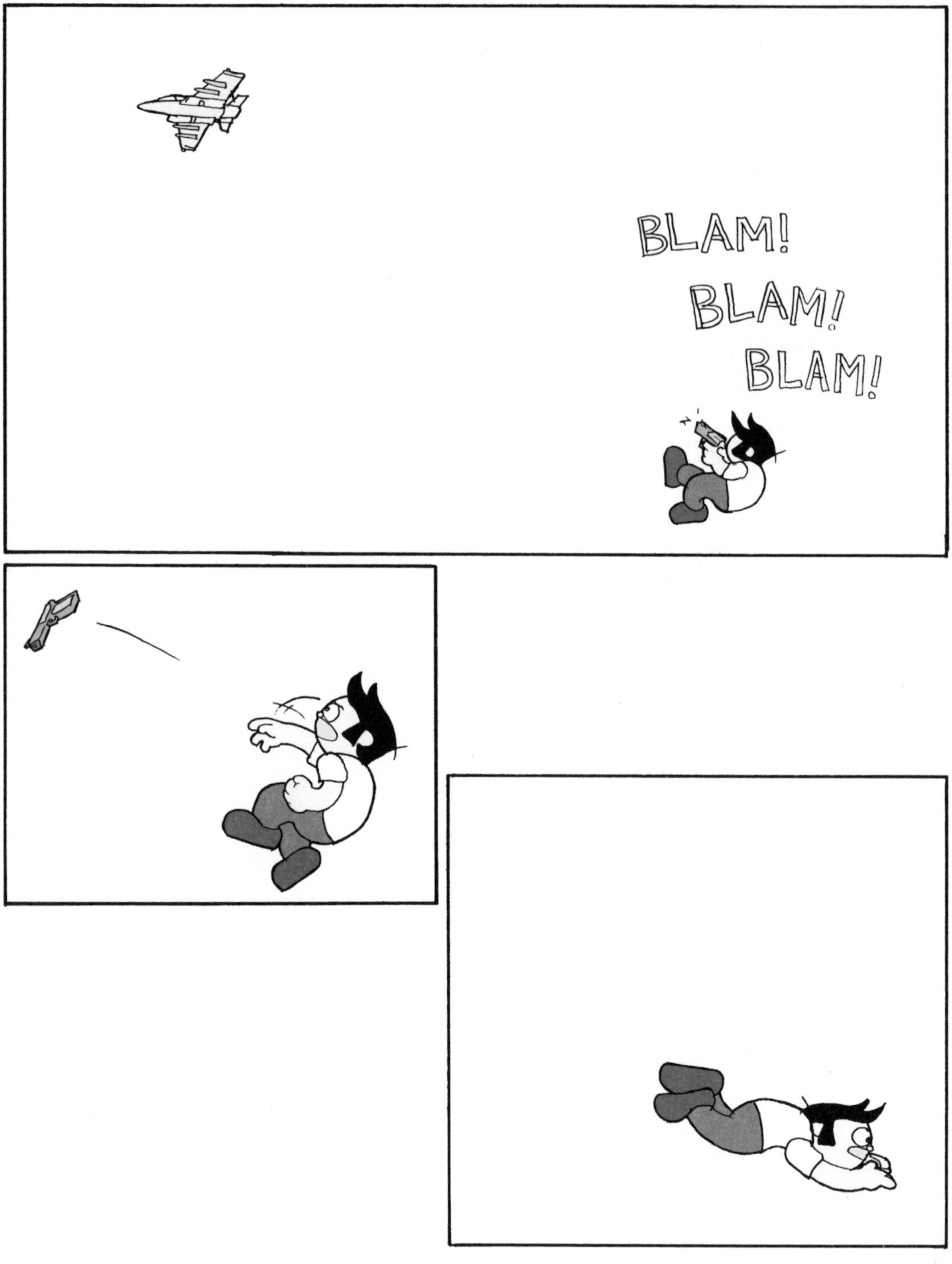
BLAM!
BLAM!
BLAM!

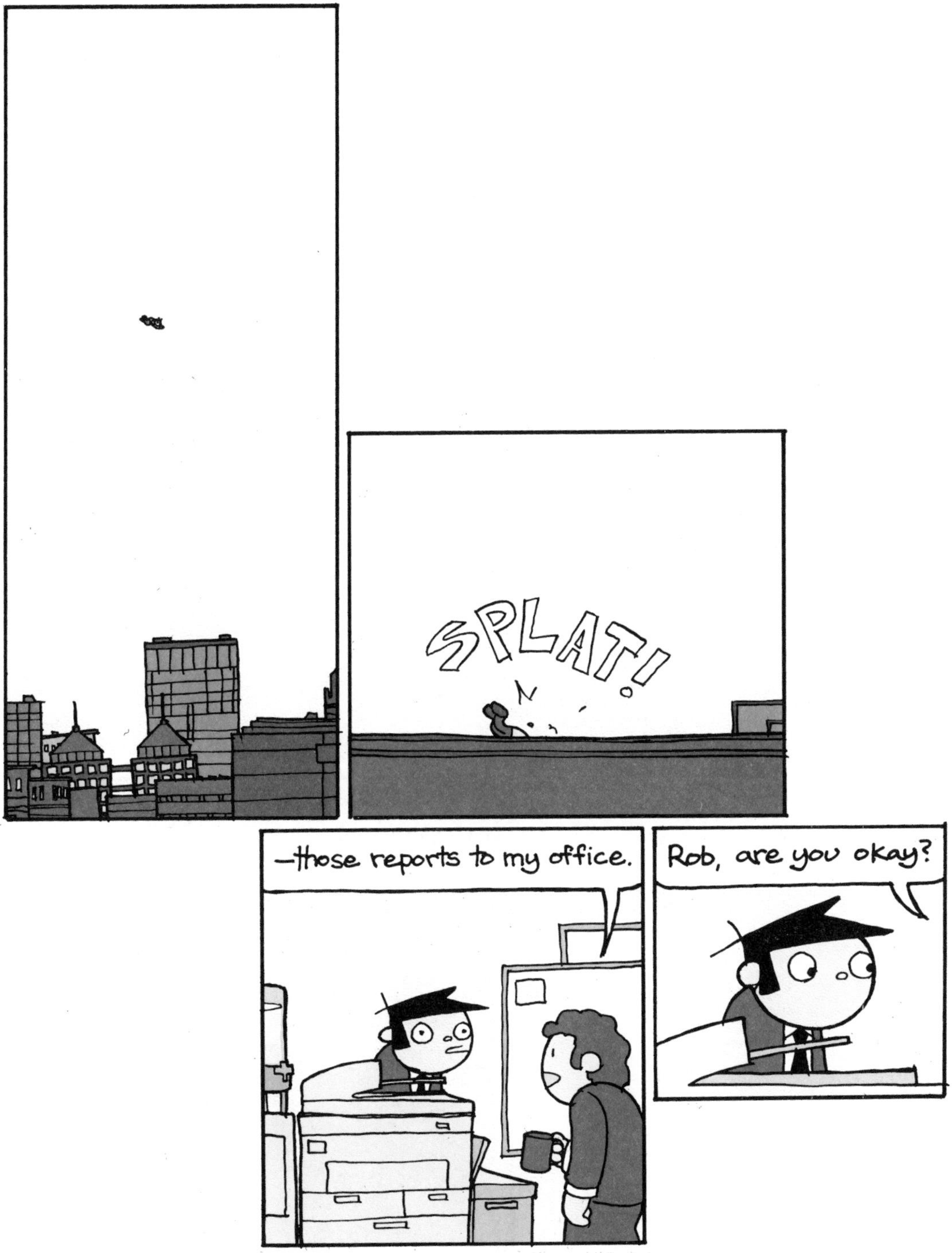
SPLAT!
—those reports to my office.
Rob, are you okay?

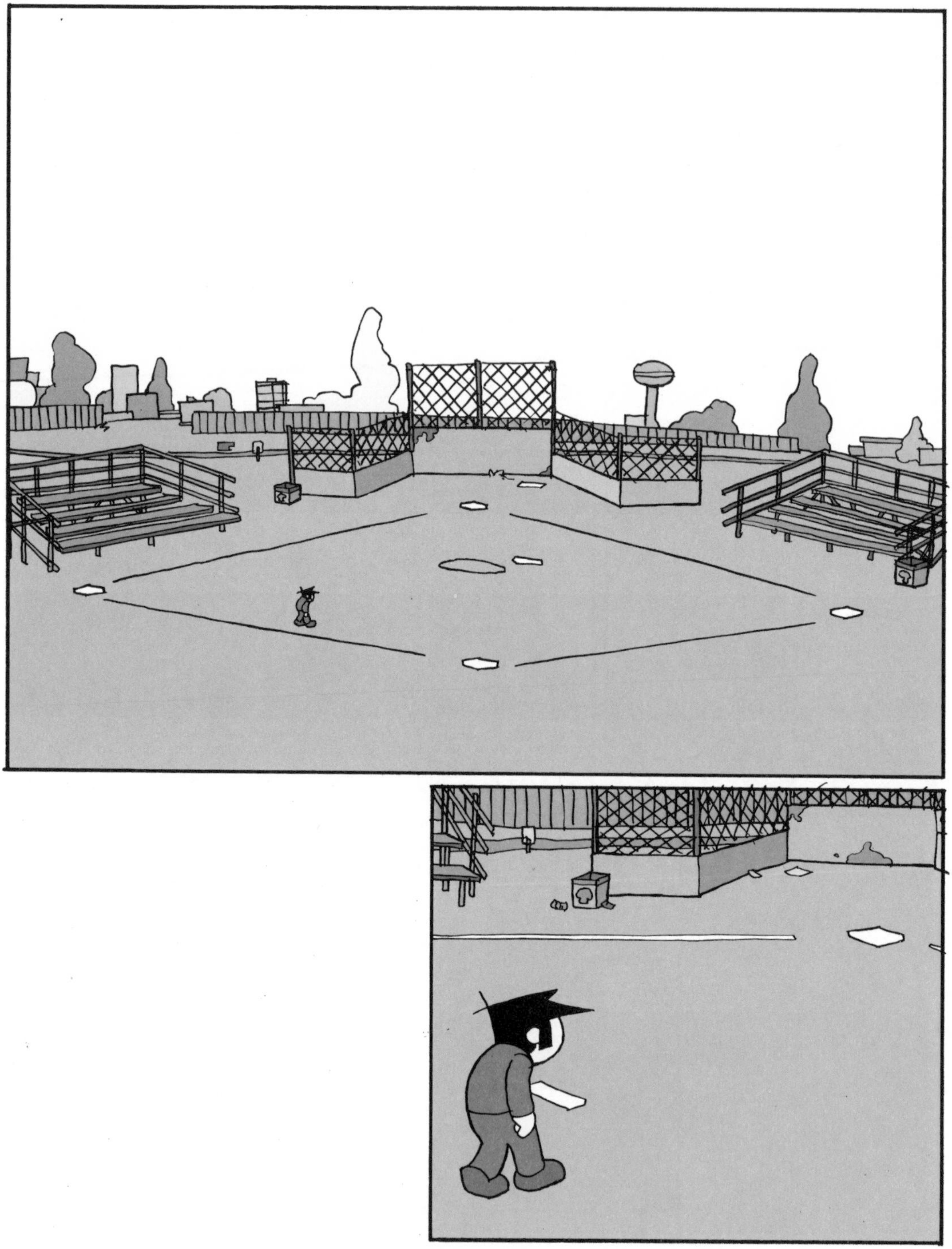

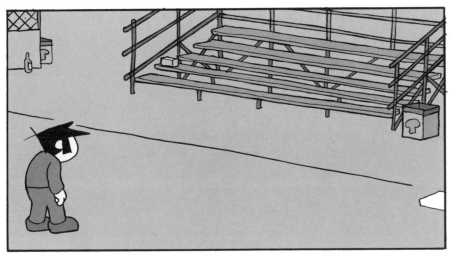

Jimmy!

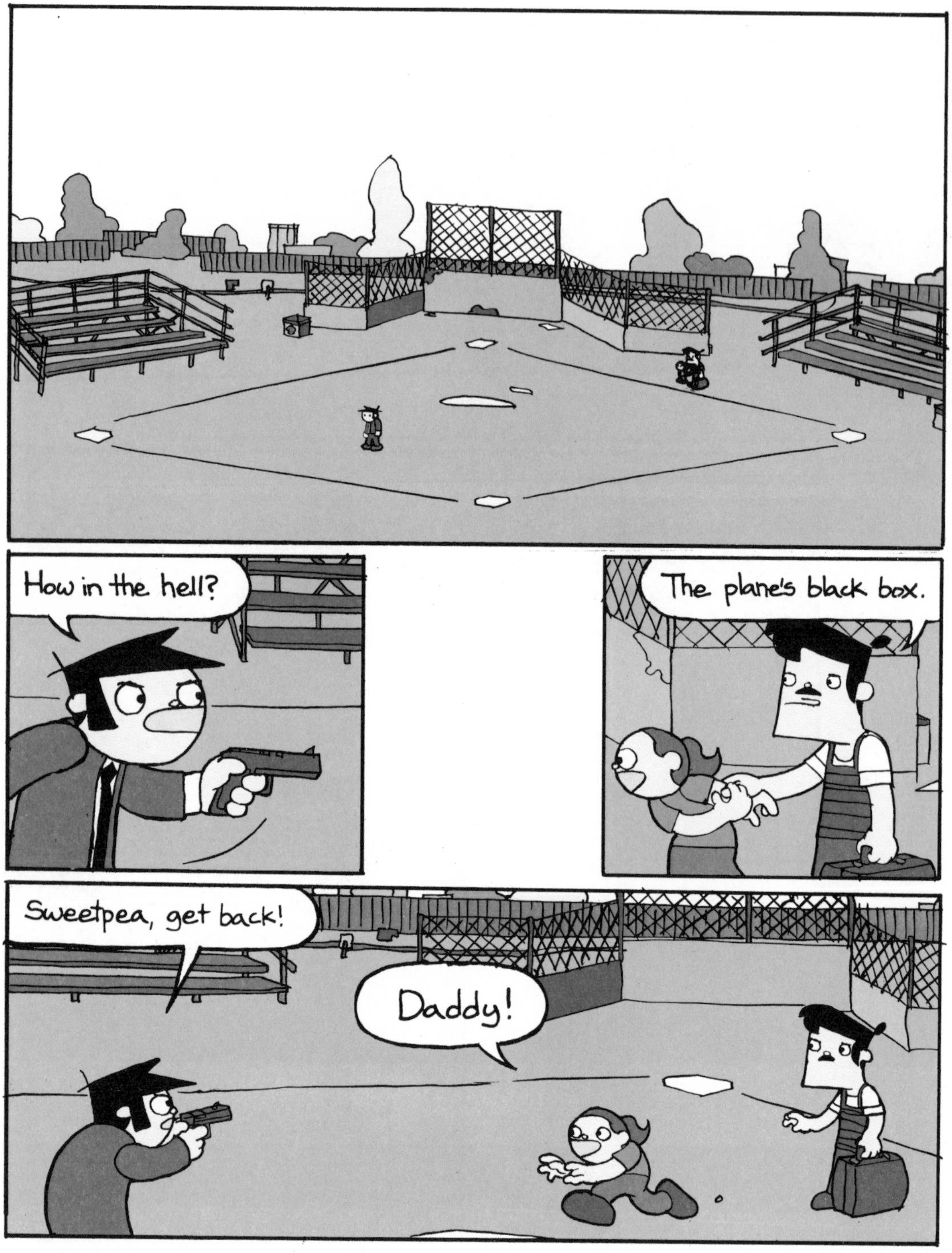
How in the hell?
The plane's black box.
Sweetpea, get back!
Daddy!

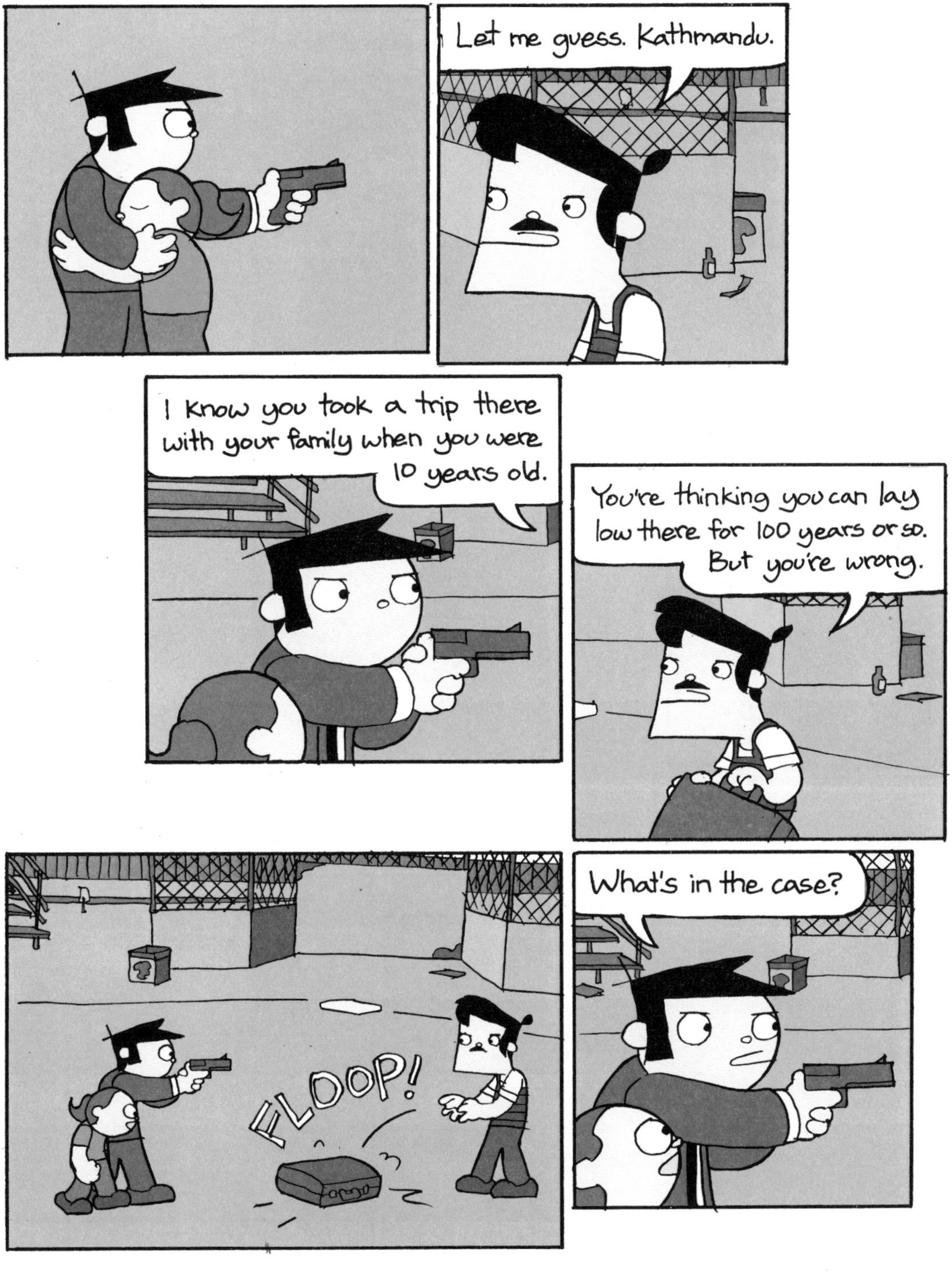
Let me guess. Kathmandu.
I know you took a trip there with your family when you were 10 years old.
You're thinking you can lay low there for 100 years or so. But you're wrong.
FLOOP!
What's in the case?

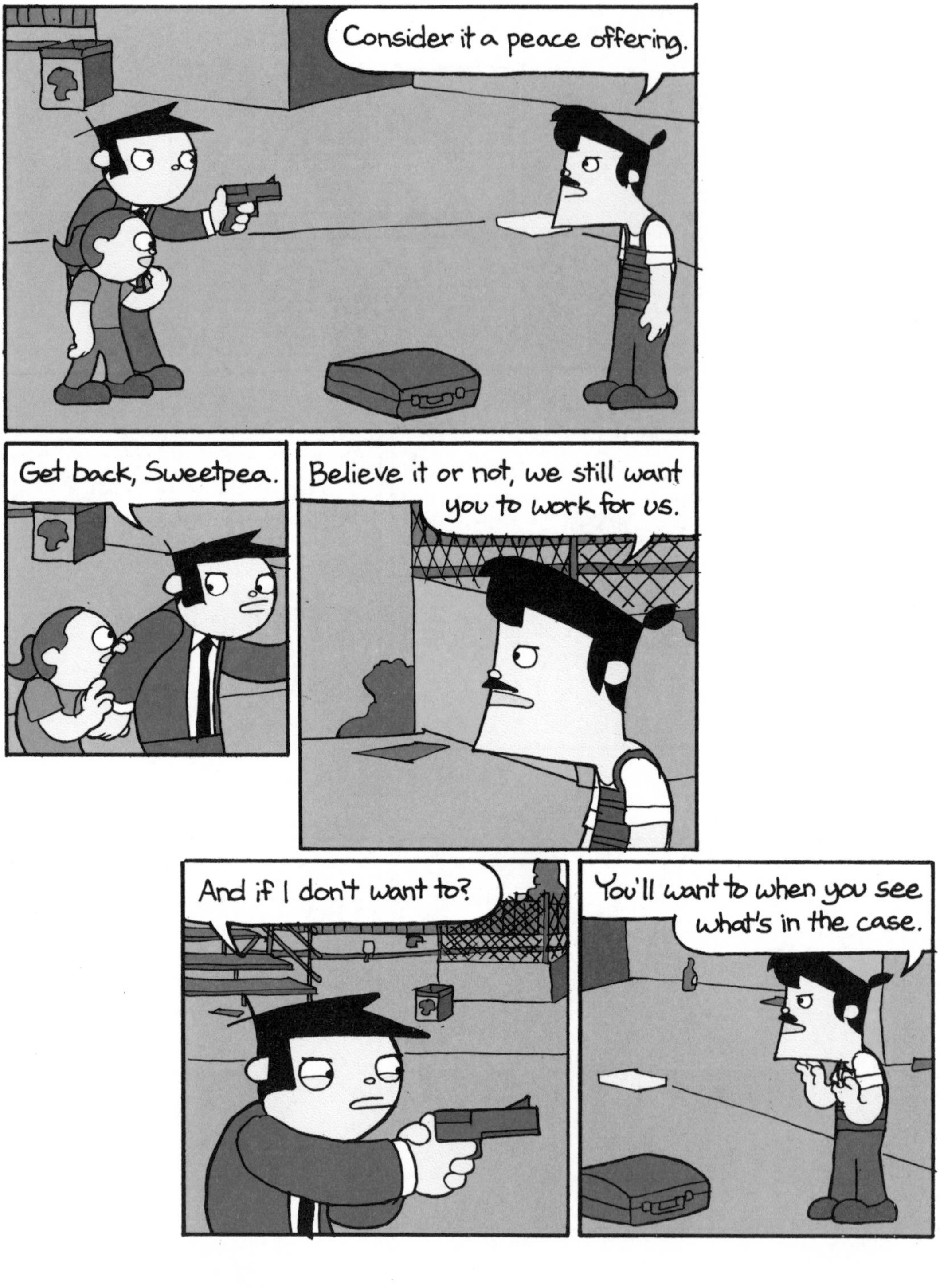
Consider it a peace offering.
Get back, Sweetpea.
Believe it or not, we still want you to work for us.
And if I don't want to?
You'll want to when you see what's in the case.

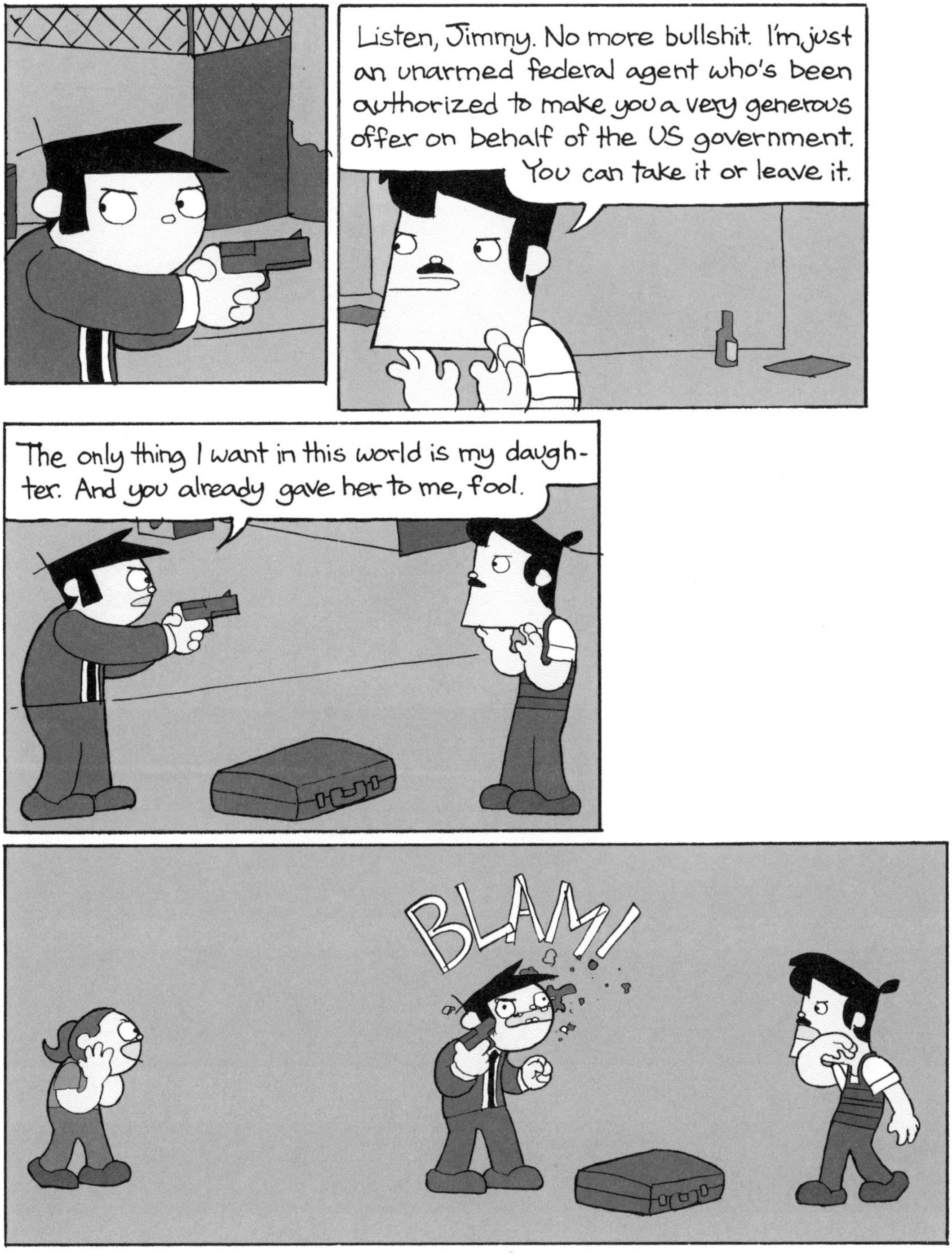
Listen, Jimmy. No more bullshit. I'm just an unarmed federal agent who's been authorized to make you a very generous offer on behalf of the US government. You can take it or leave it.
The only thing I want in this world is my daughter. And you already gave her to me, fool.
BLAM!

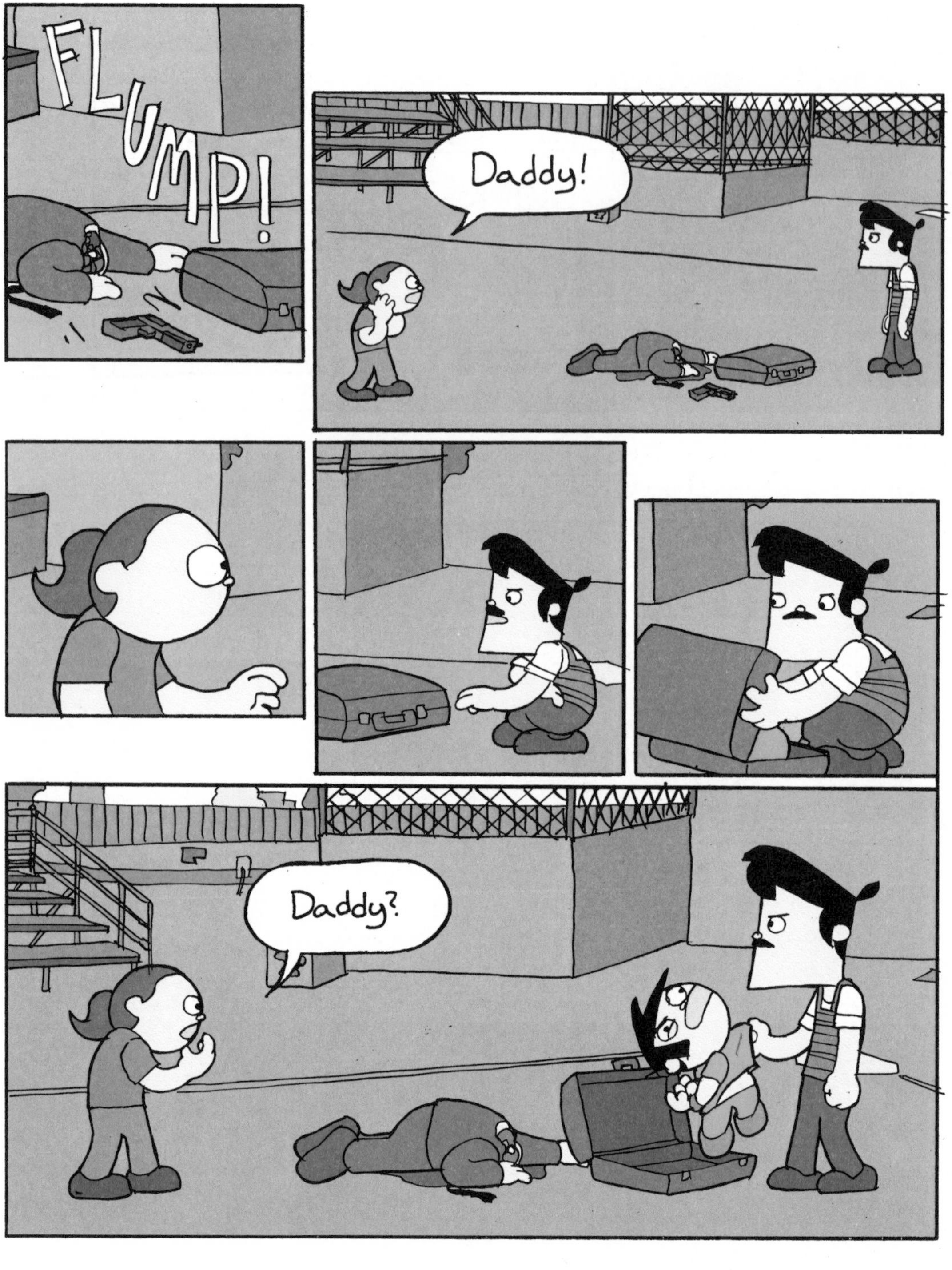
FLUMP!
Daddy!
Daddy?

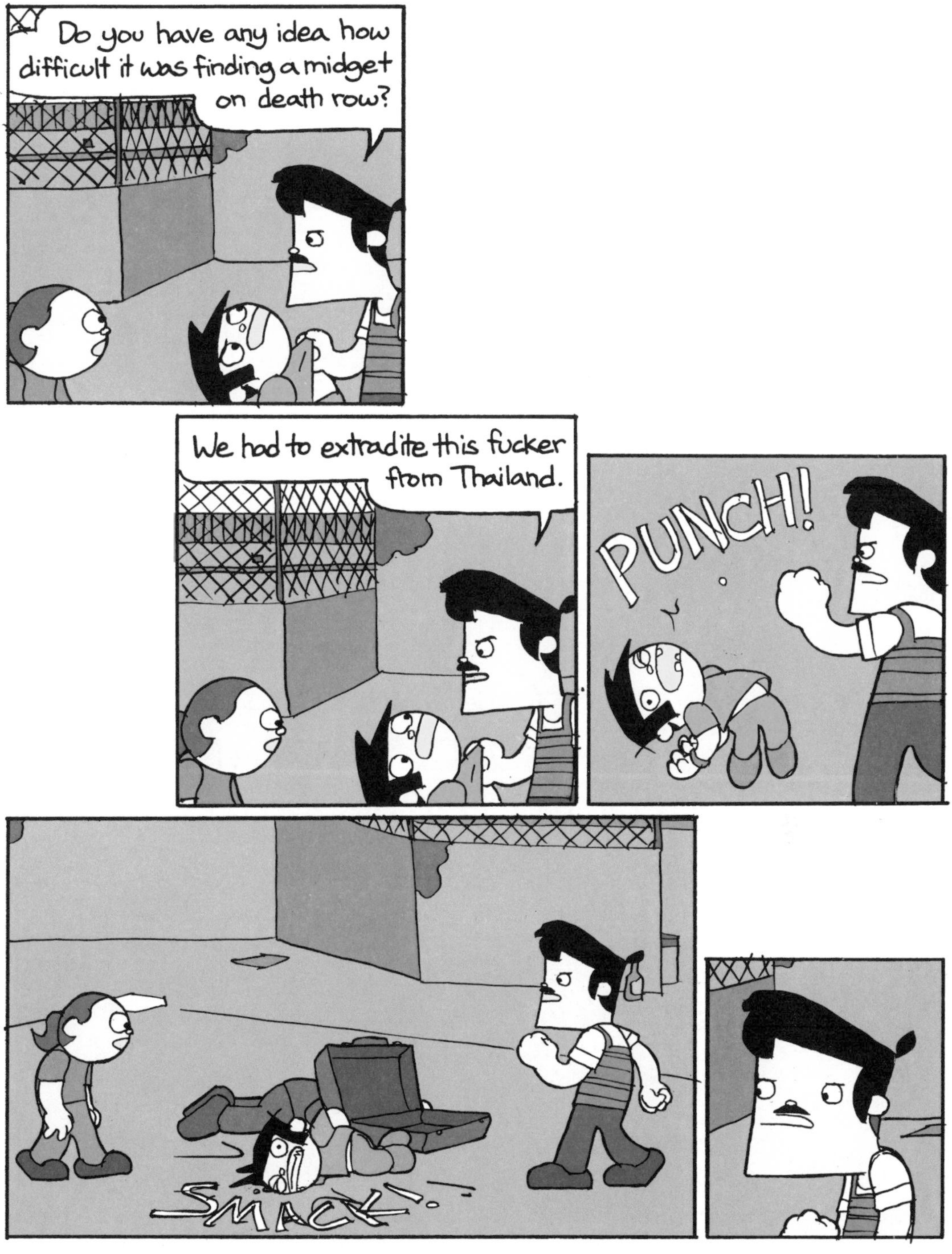
Do you have any idea how difficult it was finding a midget on death row?
We had to extradite this fucker from Thailand.
PUNCH!
SMACK!

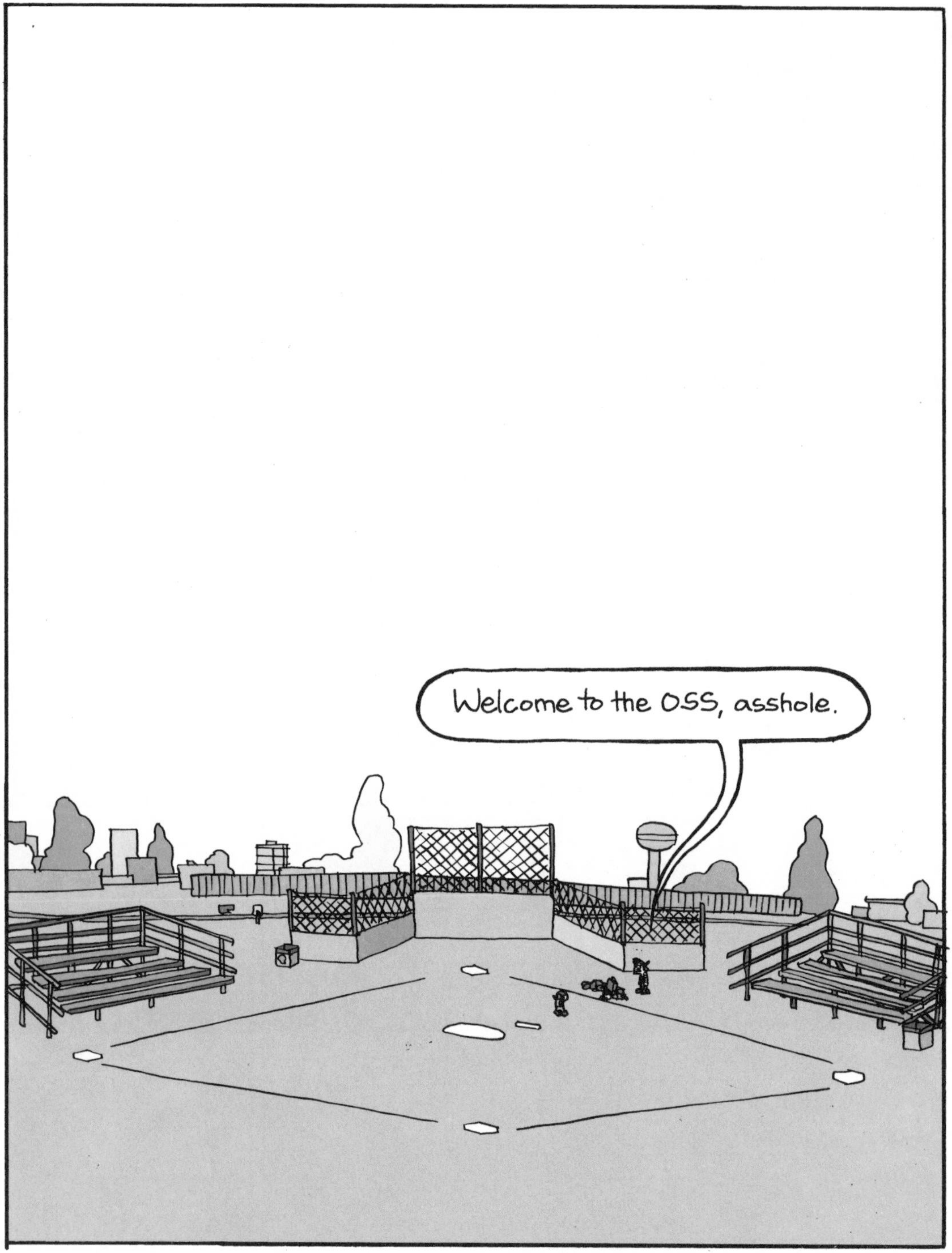
Welcome to the OSS, asshole.

# CHAPTER 11

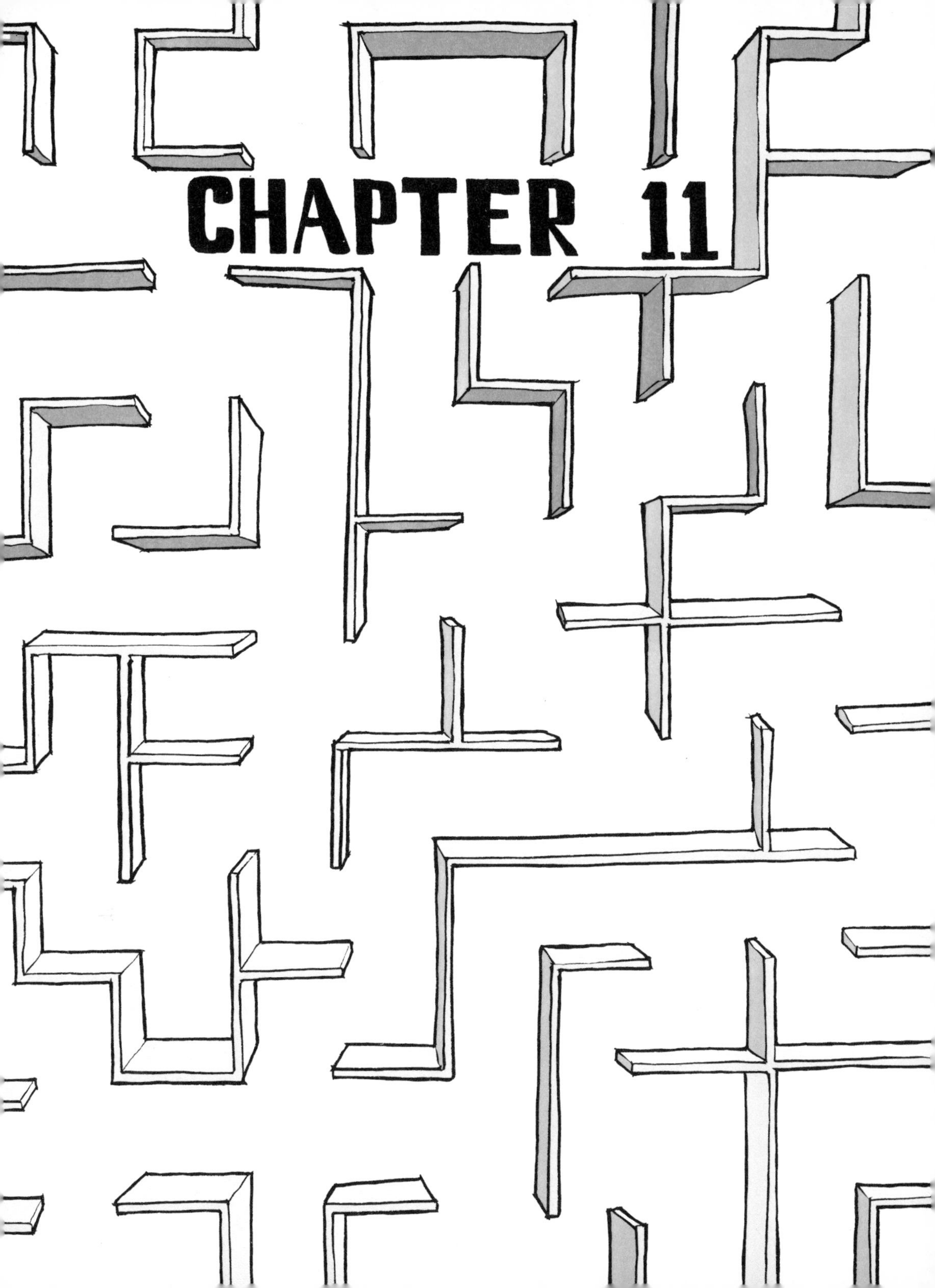

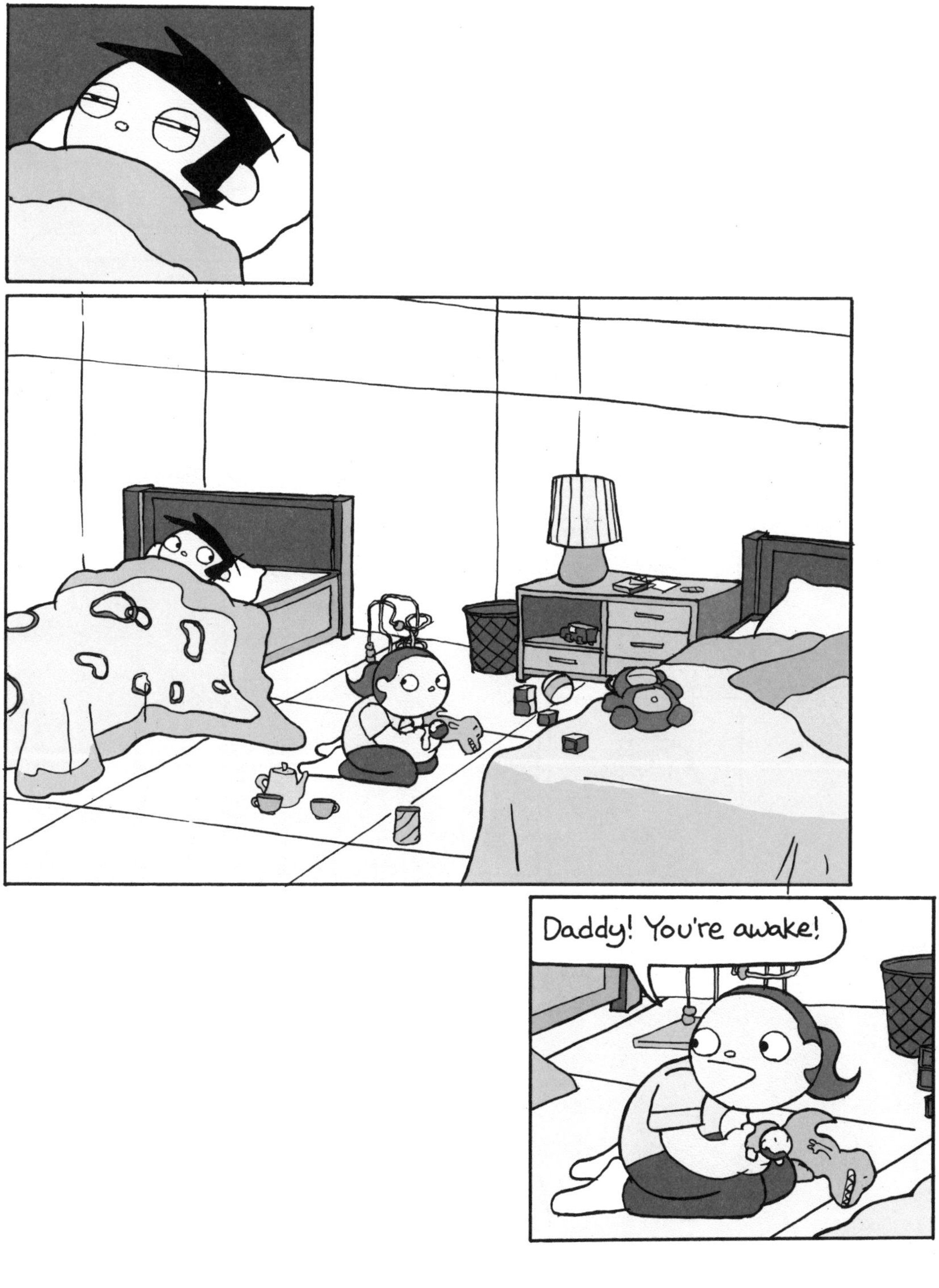
Daddy! You're awake!

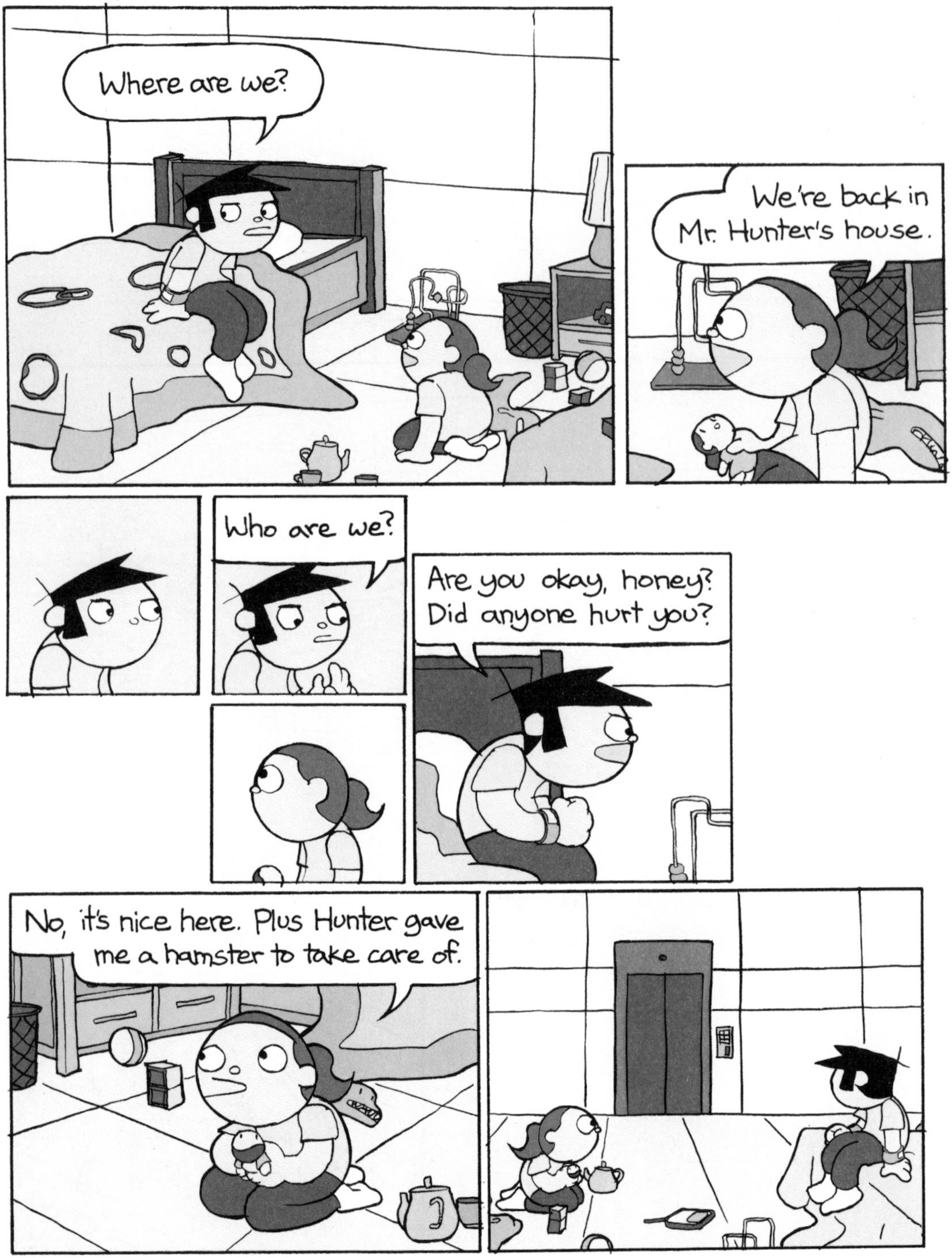

Where are we?
We're back in Mr. Hunter's house.
Who are we?
Are you okay, honey? Did anyone hurt you?
No, it's nice here. Plus Hunter gave me a hamster to take care of.

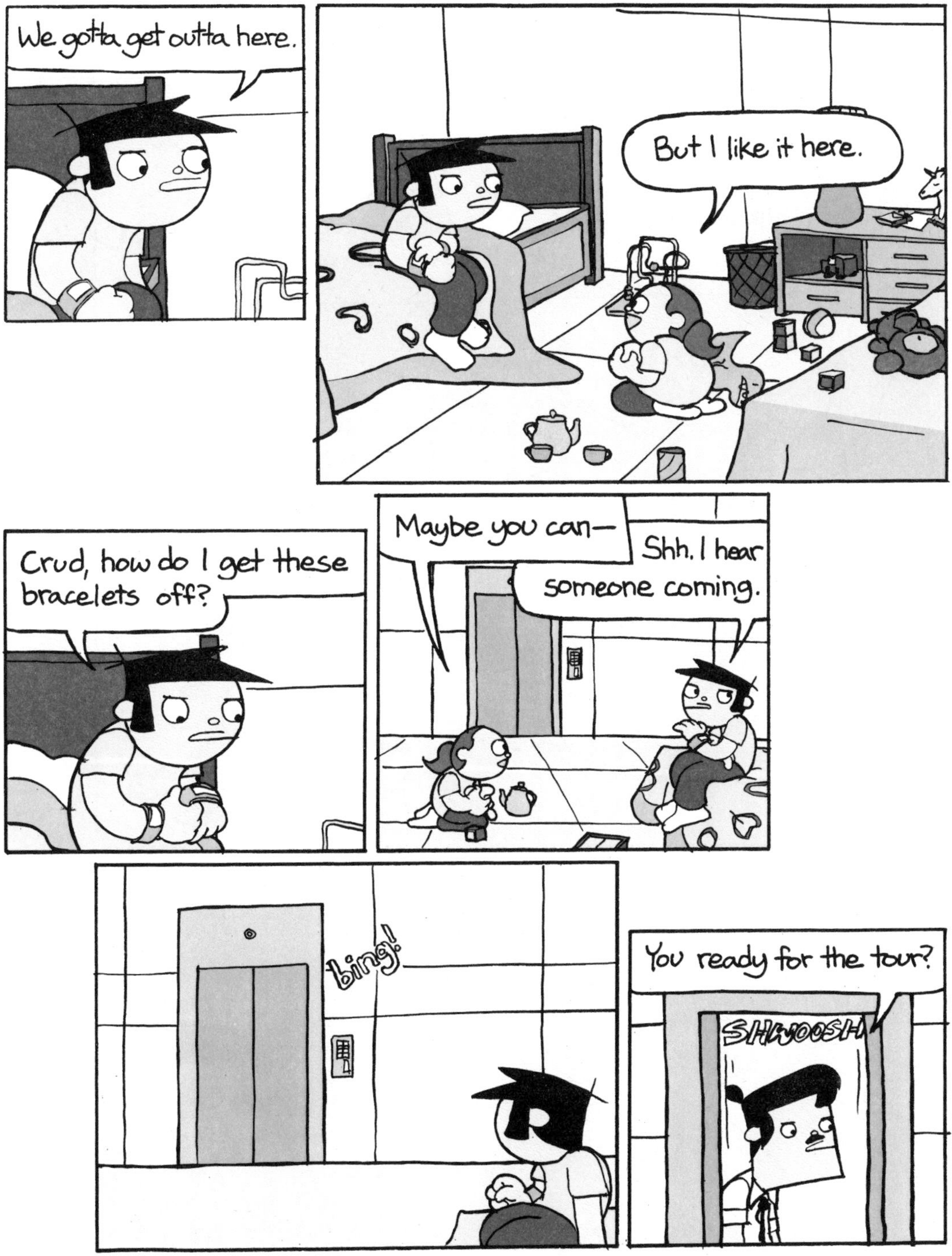

We gotta get outta here.
But I like it here.
Crud, how do I get these bracelets off?
Maybe you can—
Shh. I hear someone coming.
bing!
You ready for the tour?
SHWOOSH

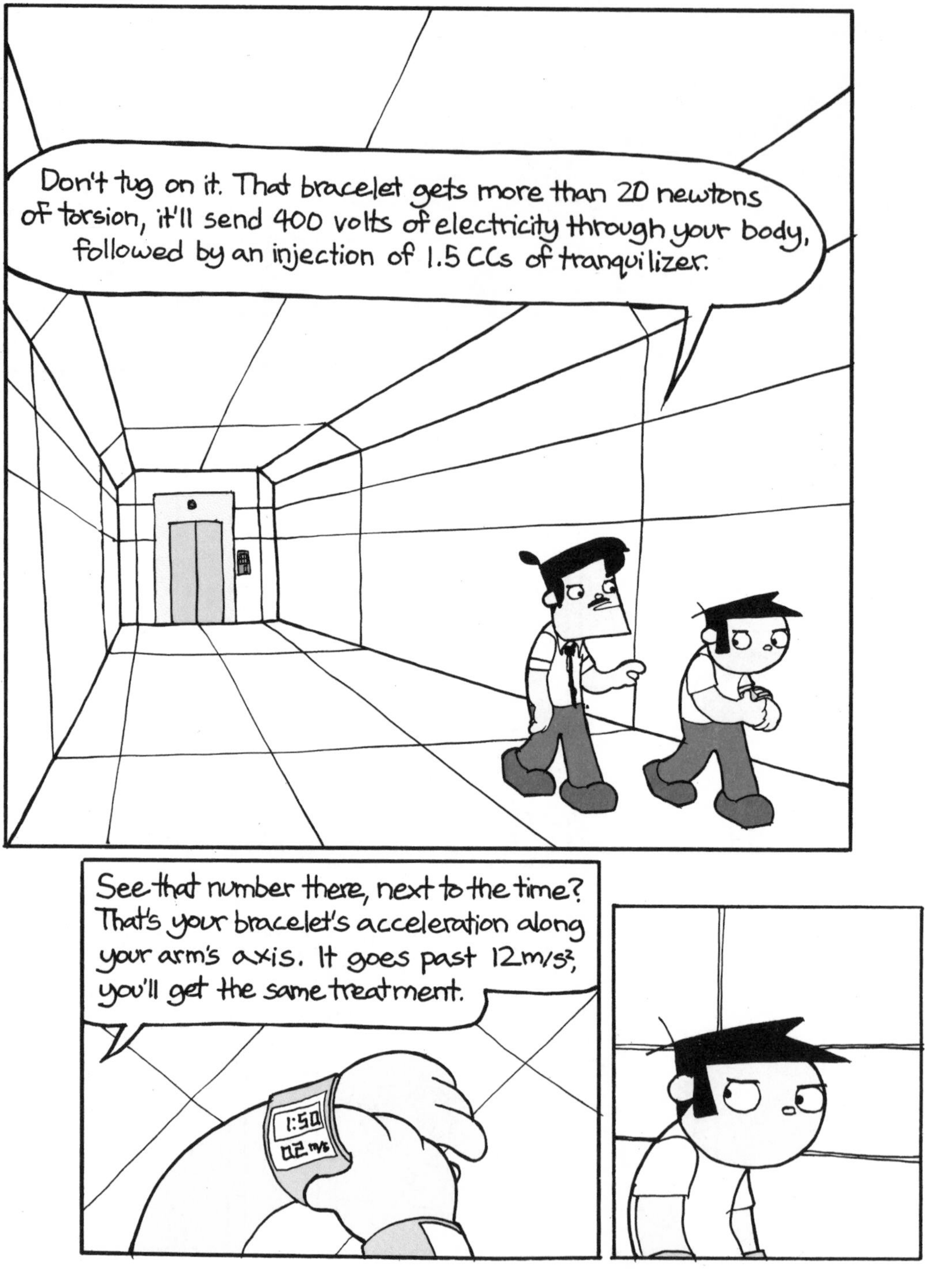
Don't tug on it. That bracelet gets more than 20 newtons of torsion, it'll send 400 volts of electricity through your body, followed by an injection of 1.5 CCs of tranquilizer.
See that number there, next to the time? That's your bracelet's acceleration along your arm's axis. It goes past 12 m/s², you'll get the same treatment.
1:50
0.2 m/s

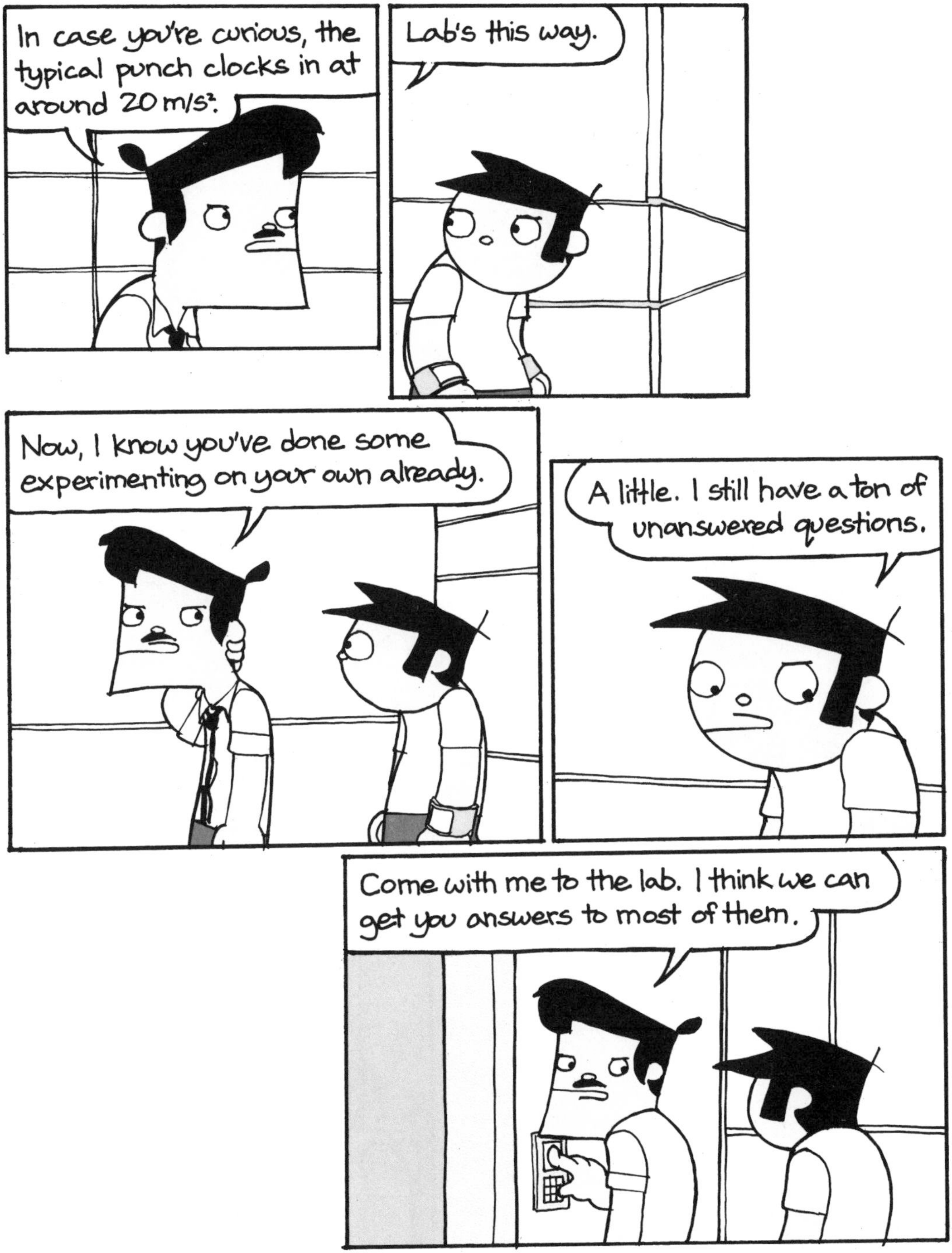
In case you're curious, the typical punch clocks in at around 20 m/s².
Lab's this way.
Now, I know you've done some experimenting on your own already.
A little. I still have a ton of unanswered questions.
Come with me to the lab. I think we can get you answers to most of them.

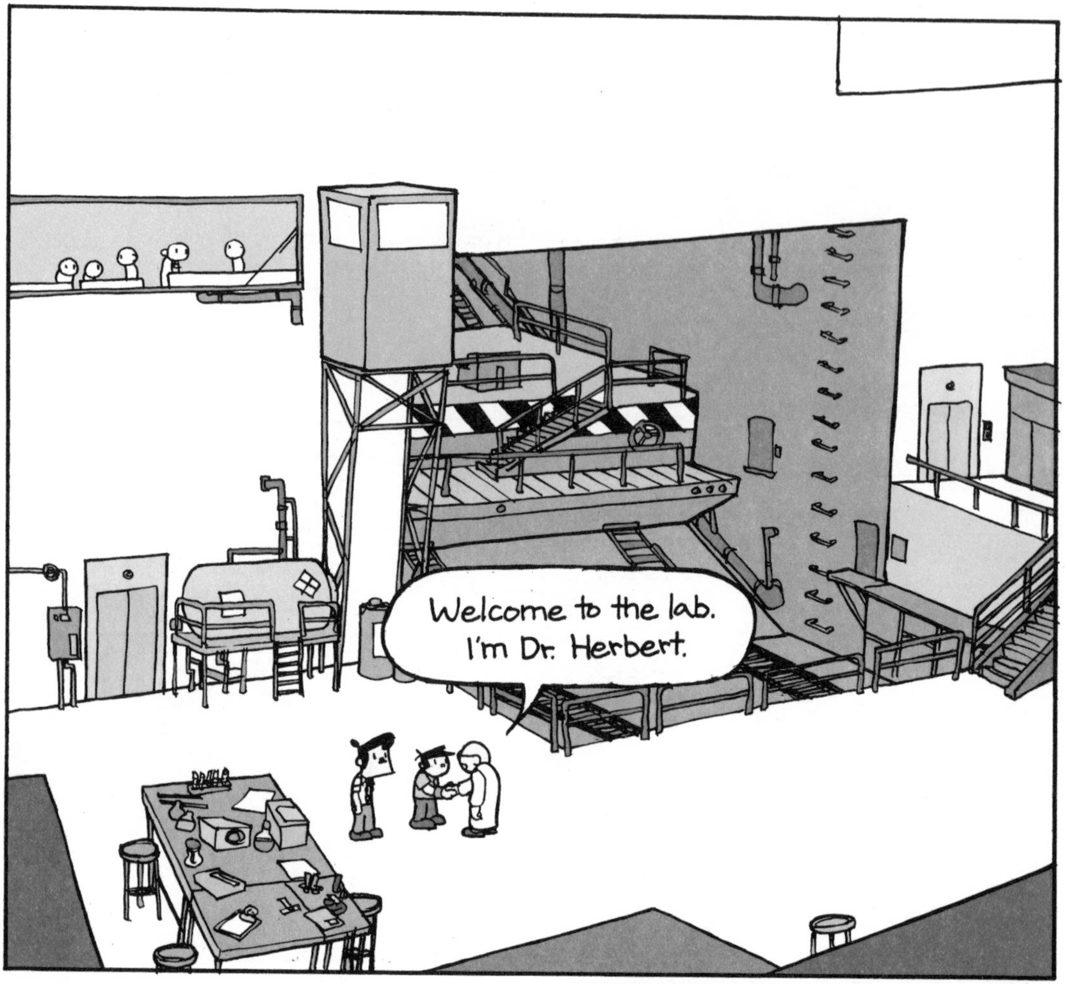
Welcome to the lab.
I'm Dr. Herbert.

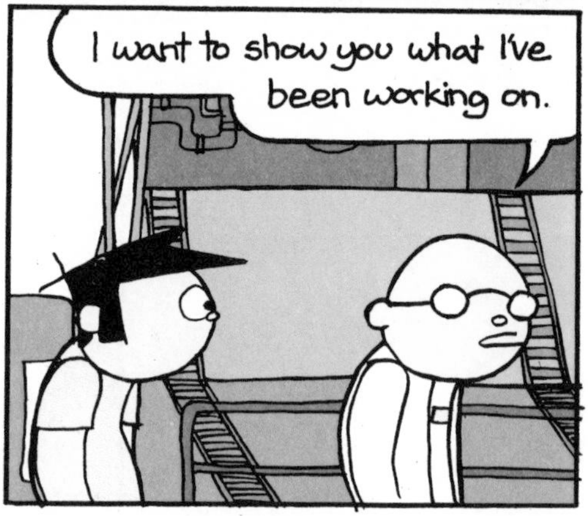
I want to show you what I've been working on.

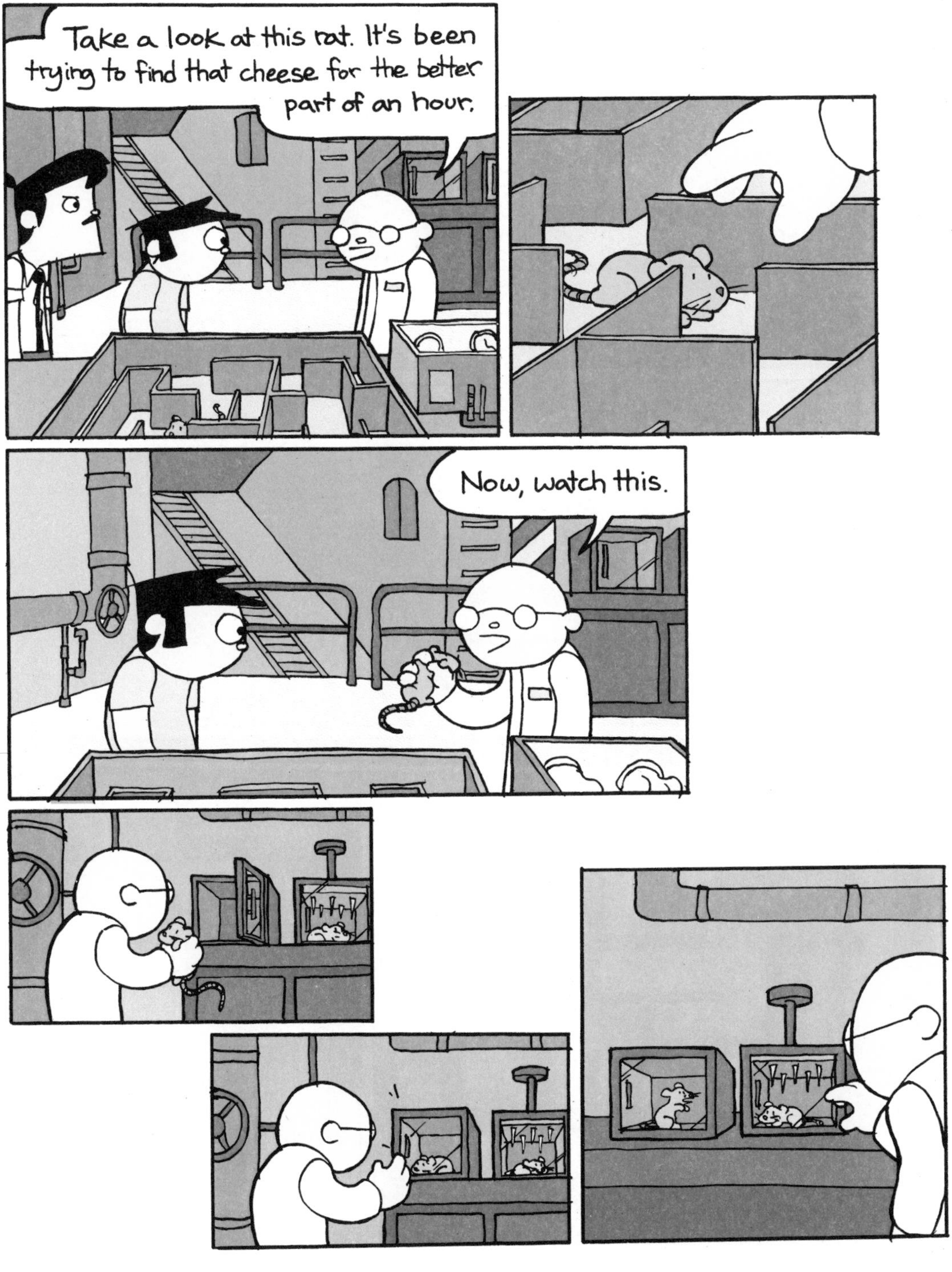

Take a look at this rat. It's been trying to find that cheese for the better part of an hour.
Now, watch this.

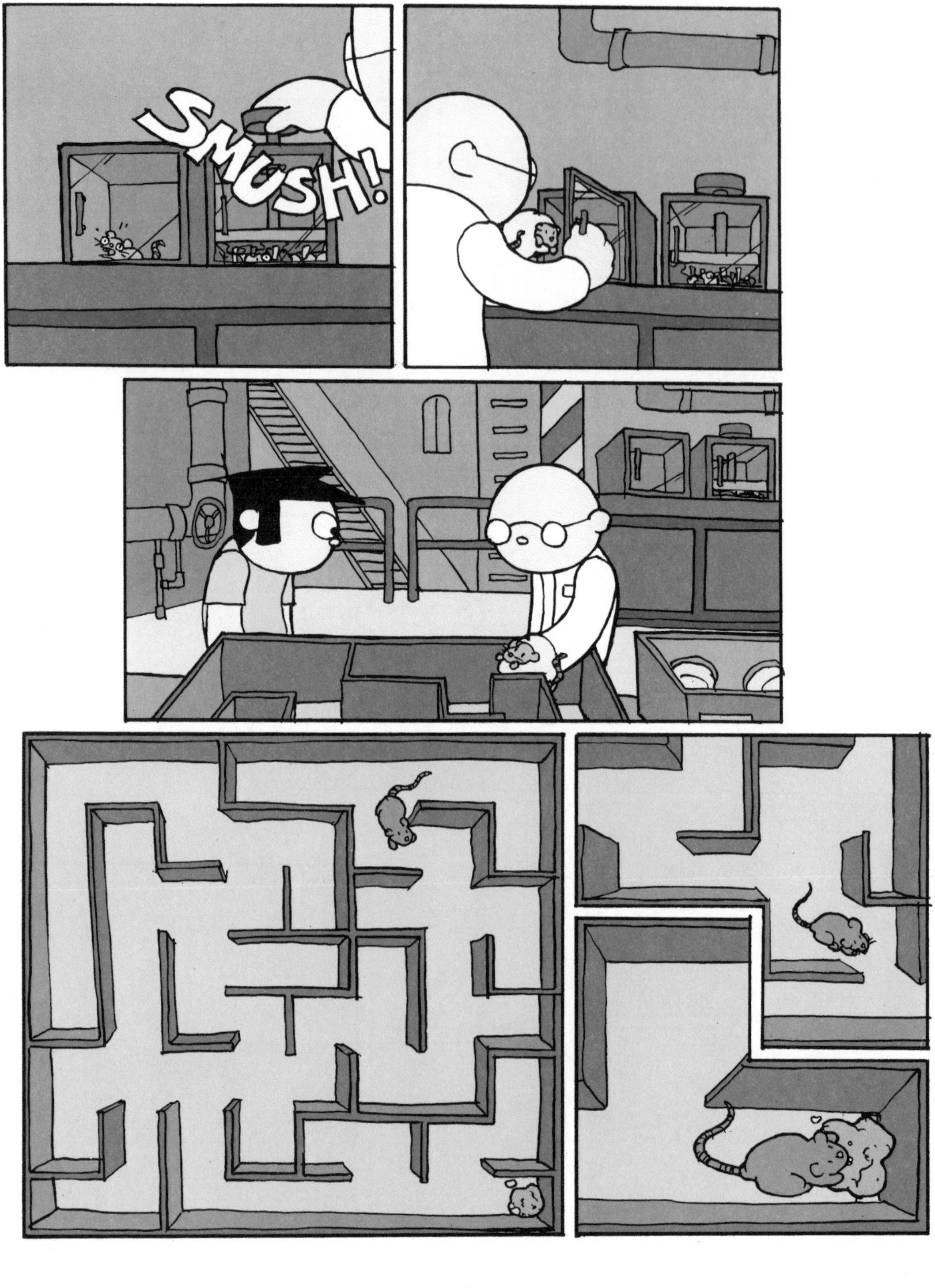
SMUSH!

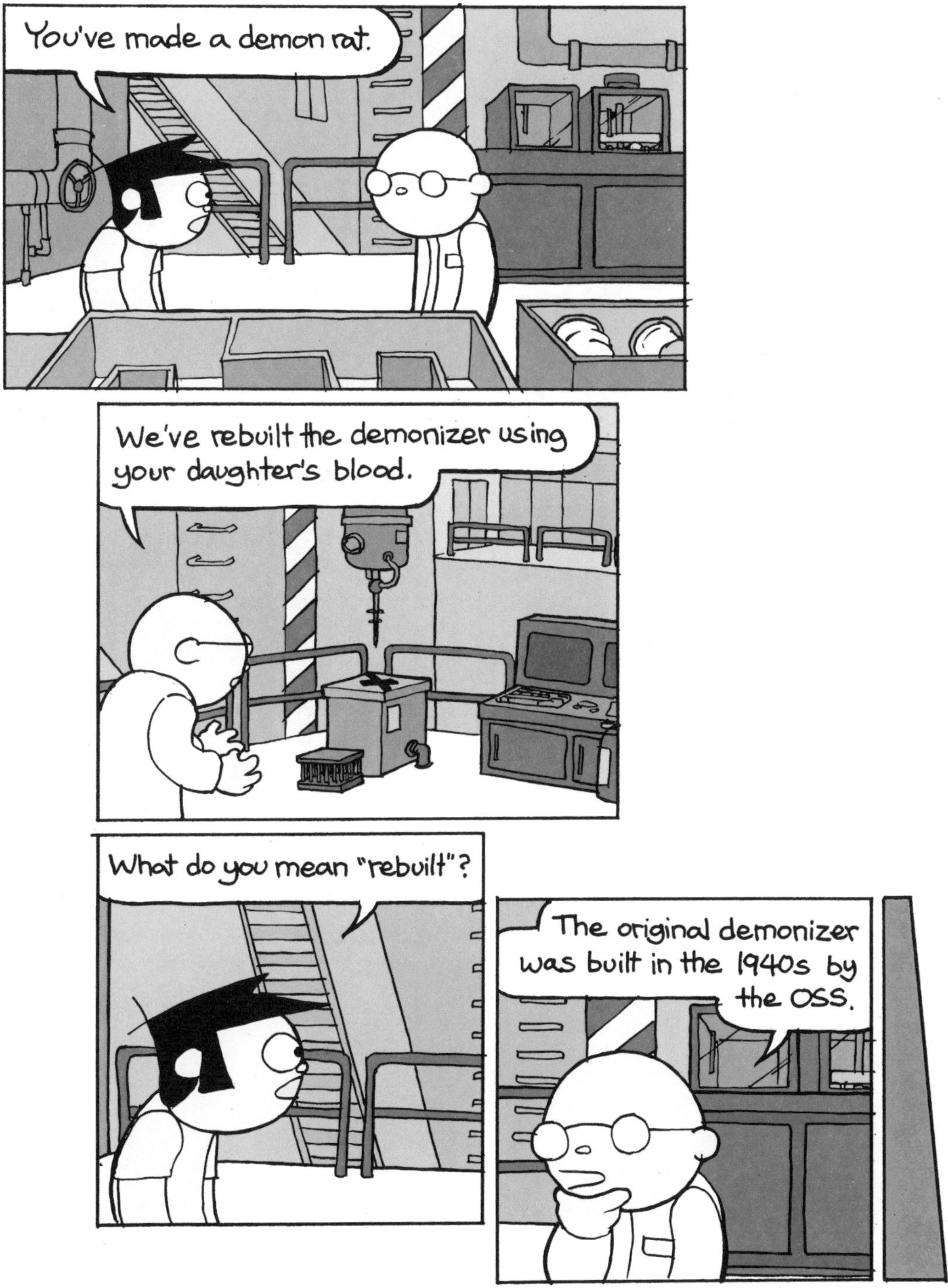
You've made a demon rat.
We've rebuilt the demonizer using your daughter's blood.
What do you mean "rebuilt"?
The original demonizer was built in the 1940s by the OSS.

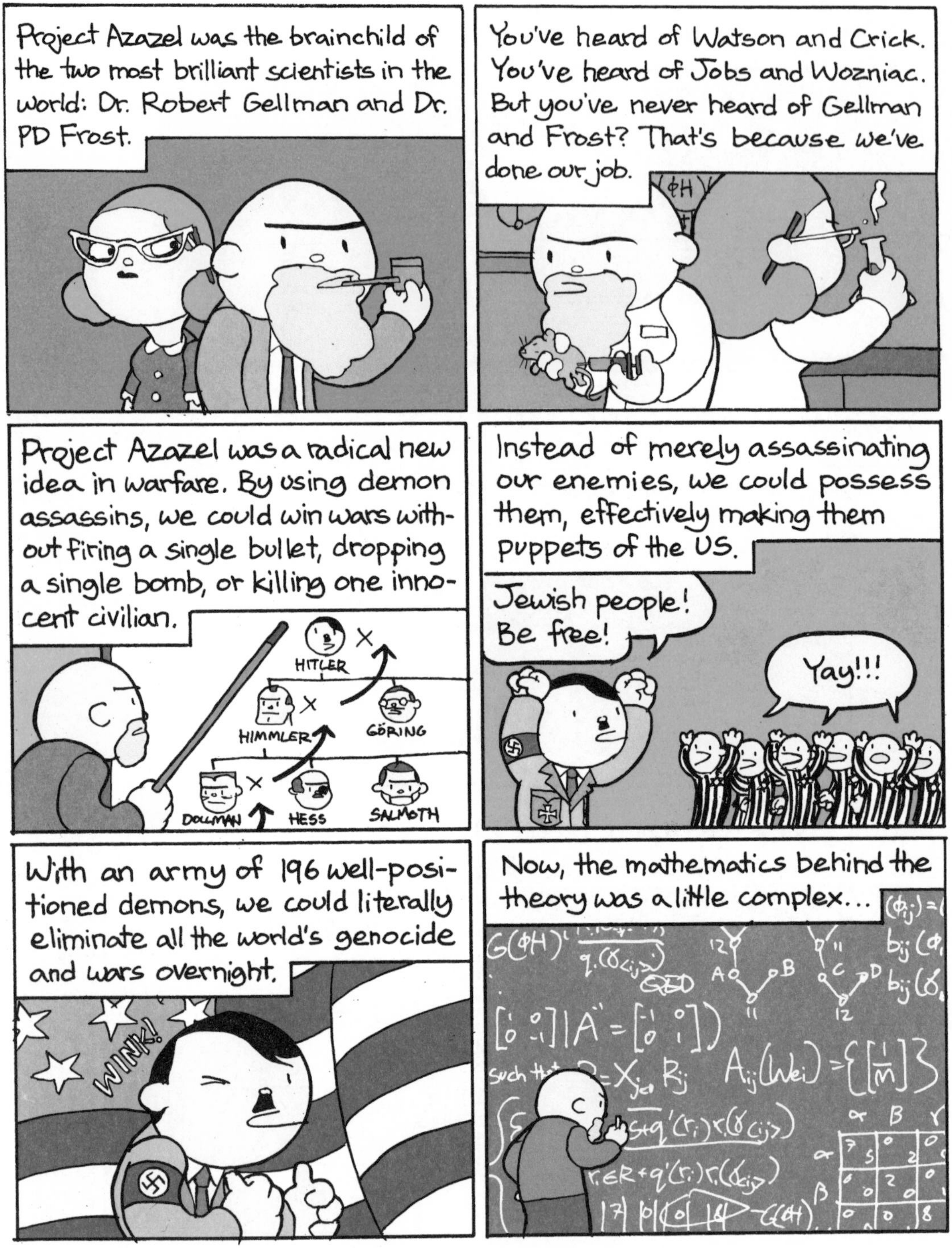

Project Azazel was the brainchild of the two most brilliant scientists in the world: Dr. Robert Gellman and Dr. PD Frost.
You've heard of Watson and Crick. You've heard of Jobs and Wozniac. But you've never heard of Gellman and Frost? That's because we've done our job.
Project Azazel was a radical new idea in warfare. By using demon assassins, we could win wars without firing a single bullet, dropping a single bomb, or killing one innocent civilian.
HITLER
HIMMLER
GÖRING
DOLLMAN
HESS
SALMOTH
Instead of merely assassinating our enemies, we could possess them, effectively making them puppets of the US.
Jewish people! Be free!
Yay!!!
With an army of 196 well-positioned demons, we could literally eliminate all the world's genocide and wars overnight.
WINK!
Now, the mathematics behind the theory was a little complex...

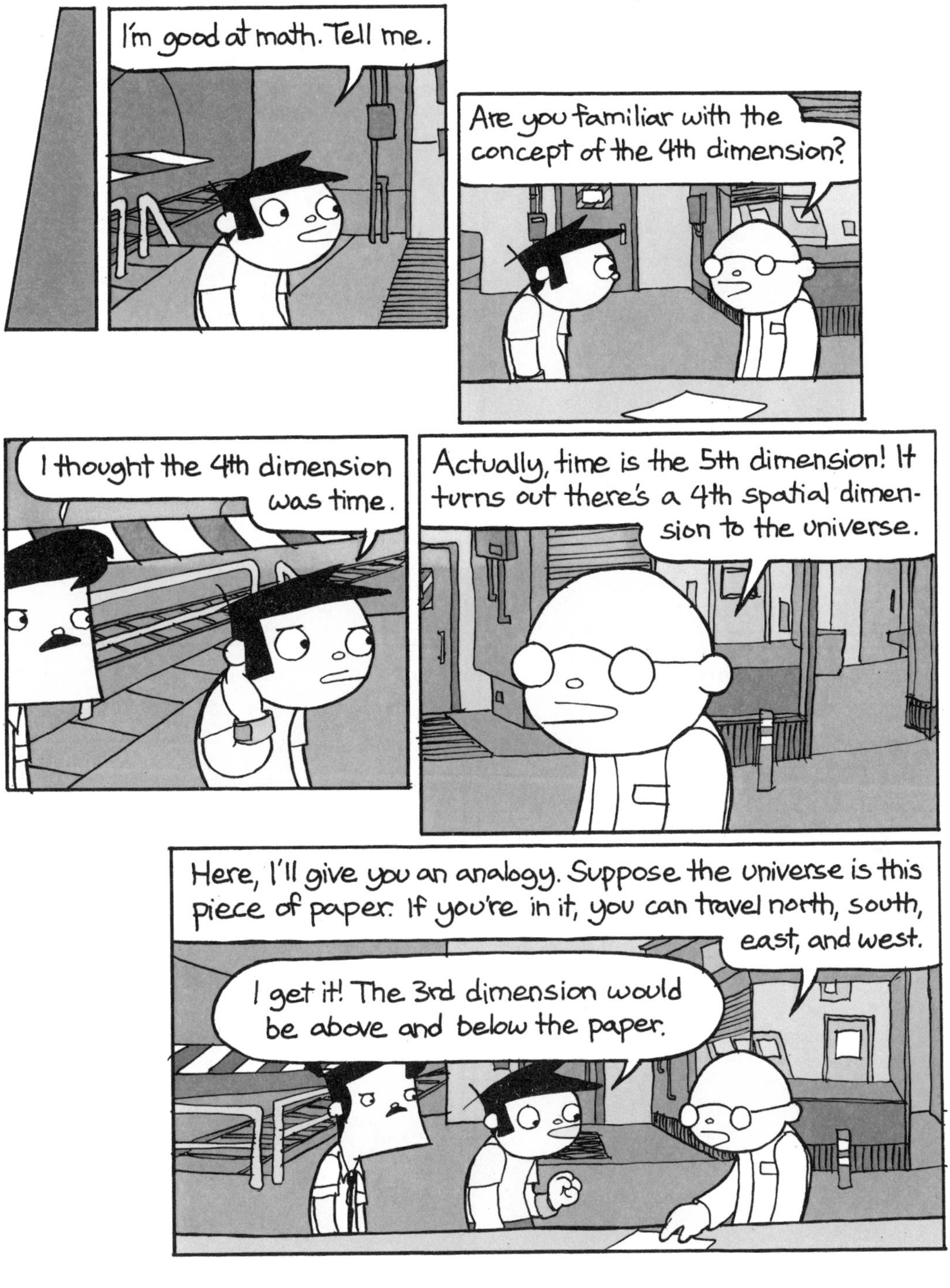
I'm good at math. Tell me.
Are you familiar with the concept of the 4th dimension?
I thought the 4th dimension was time.
Actually, time is the 5th dimension! It turns out there's a 4th spatial dimension to the universe.
Here, I'll give you an analogy. Suppose the universe is this piece of paper. If you're in it, you can travel north, south, east, and west.
I get it! The 3rd dimension would be above and below the paper.

Exactly! Now, according to our research, people's memories are not actually stored in their brains.

Rather, they're stored in an organ called the flastical, which rests "above" the brain in the 4th dimension.

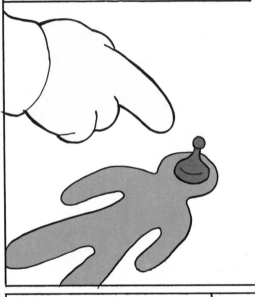

Normally you don't have to worry about your flastical drifting off; it's connected to your brain via the pineal gland.

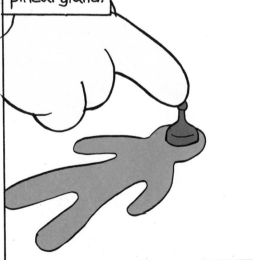

Even when you die, your flastical usually just sits there and withers away.

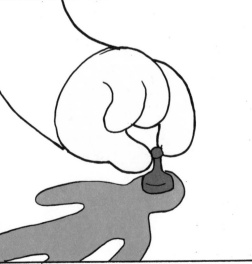

Demons, it turns out, have parasitic flasticals.

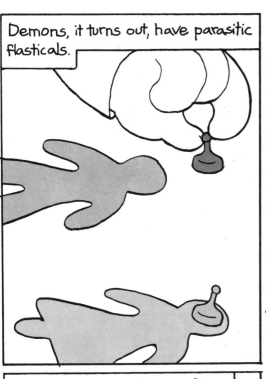

When a demon dies, its flastical finds the nearest one and takes its host body.

From the point of view of an observer, it looks like a demon possession.

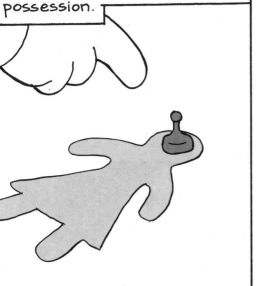

In fact, it's just the flastical being passed from one host to another.

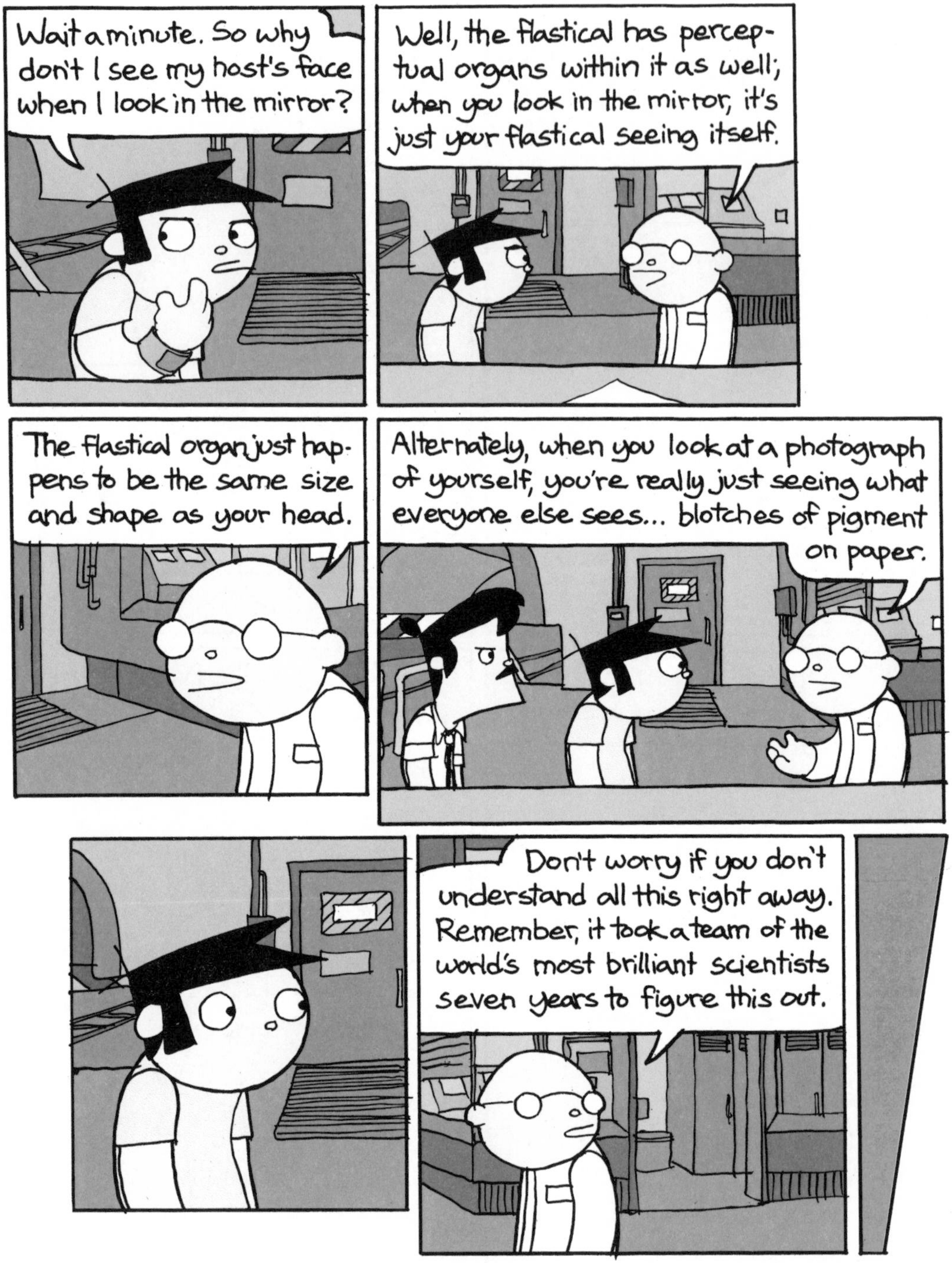

Wait a minute. So why don't I see my host's face when I look in the mirror?
Well, the flastical has perceptual organs within it as well; when you look in the mirror, it's just your flastical seeing itself.
The flastical organ just happens to be the same size and shape as your head.
Alternately, when you look at a photograph of yourself, you're really just seeing what everyone else sees... blotches of pigment on paper.
Don't worry if you don't understand all this right away. Remember, it took a team of the world's most brilliant scientists seven years to figure this out.

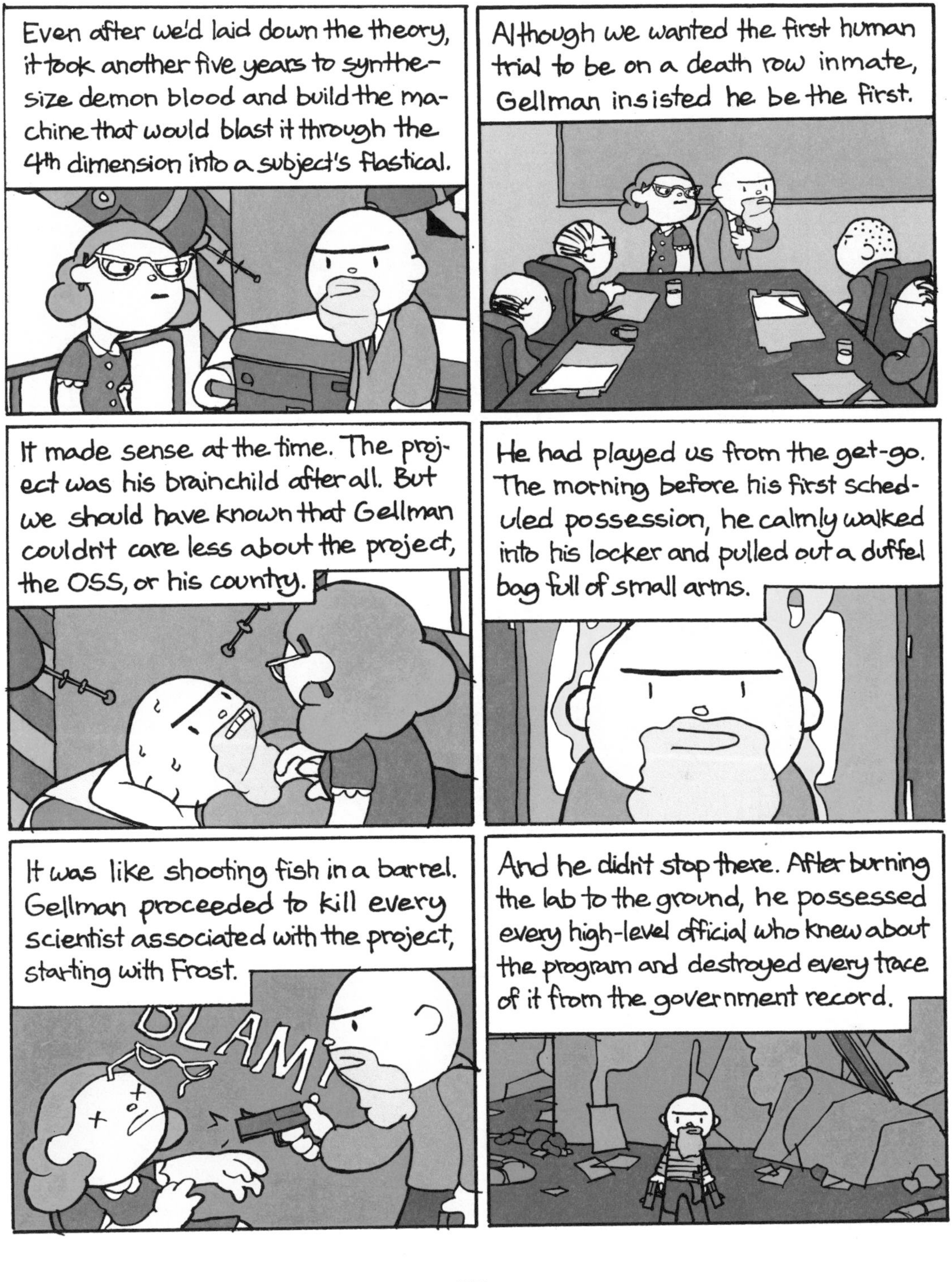
Even after we'd laid down the theory, it took another five years to synthesize demon blood and build the machine that would blast it through the 4th dimension into a subject's flastical.
Although we wanted the first human trial to be on a death row inmate, Gellman insisted he be the first.
It made sense at the time. The project was his brainchild after all. But we should have known that Gellman couldn't care less about the project, the OSS, or his country.
He had played us from the get-go. The morning before his first scheduled possession, he calmly walked into his locker and pulled out a duffel bag full of small arms.
It was like shooting fish in a barrel. Gellman proceeded to kill every scientist associated with the project, starting with Frost.
BLAM!
And he didn't stop there. After burning the lab to the ground, he possessed every high-level official who knew about the program and destroyed every trace of it from the government record.

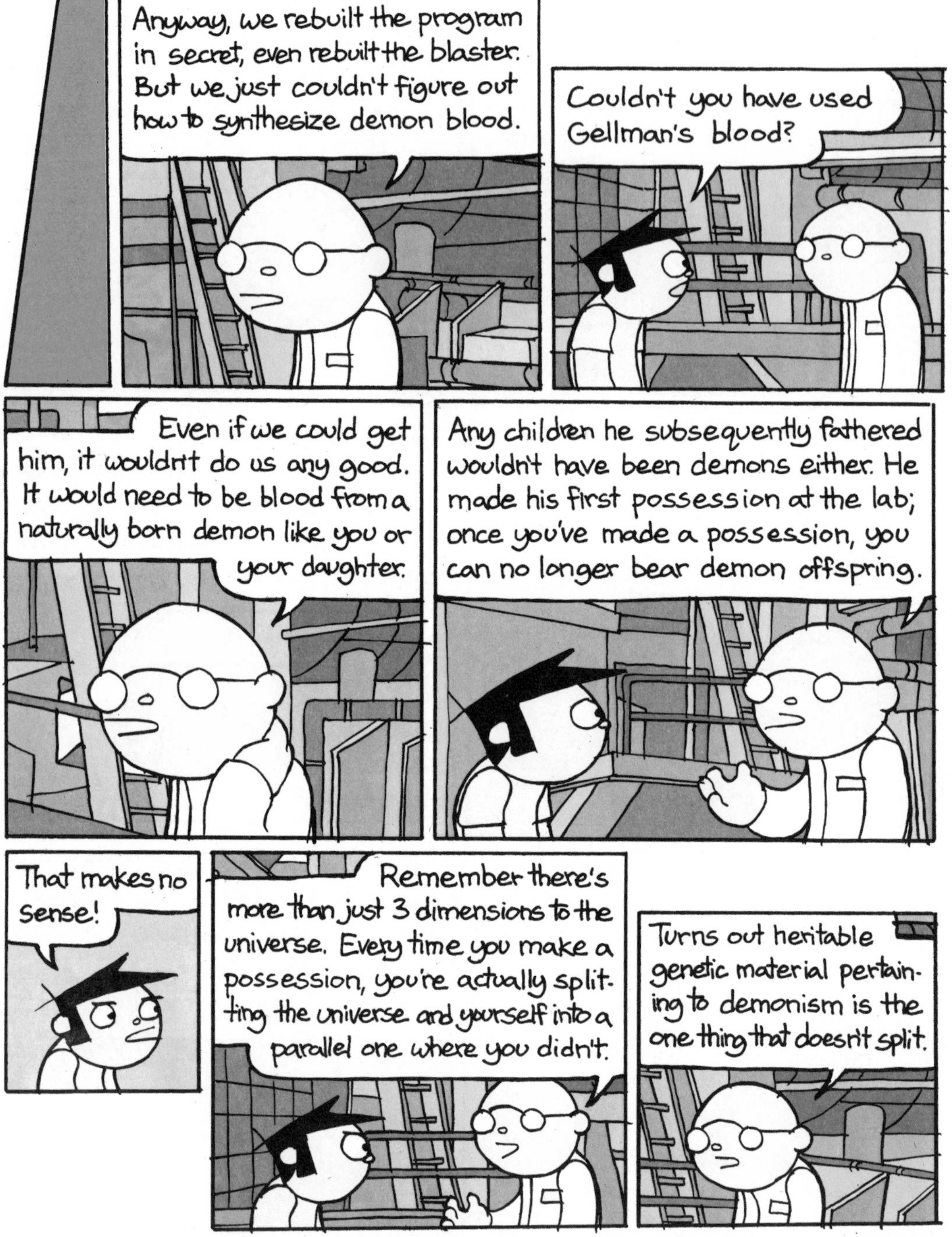
Anyway, we rebuilt the program in secret, even rebuilt the blaster. But we just couldn't figure out how to synthesize demon blood.
Couldn't you have used Gellman's blood?
Even if we could get him, it wouldn't do us any good. It would need to be blood from a naturally born demon like you or your daughter.
Any children he subsequently fathered wouldn't have been demons either. He made his first possession at the lab; once you've made a possession, you can no longer bear demon offspring.
That makes no sense!
Remember there's more than just 3 dimensions to the universe. Every time you make a possession, you're actually splitting the universe and yourself into a parallel one where you didn't.
Turns out heritable genetic material pertaining to demonism is the one thing that doesn't split.

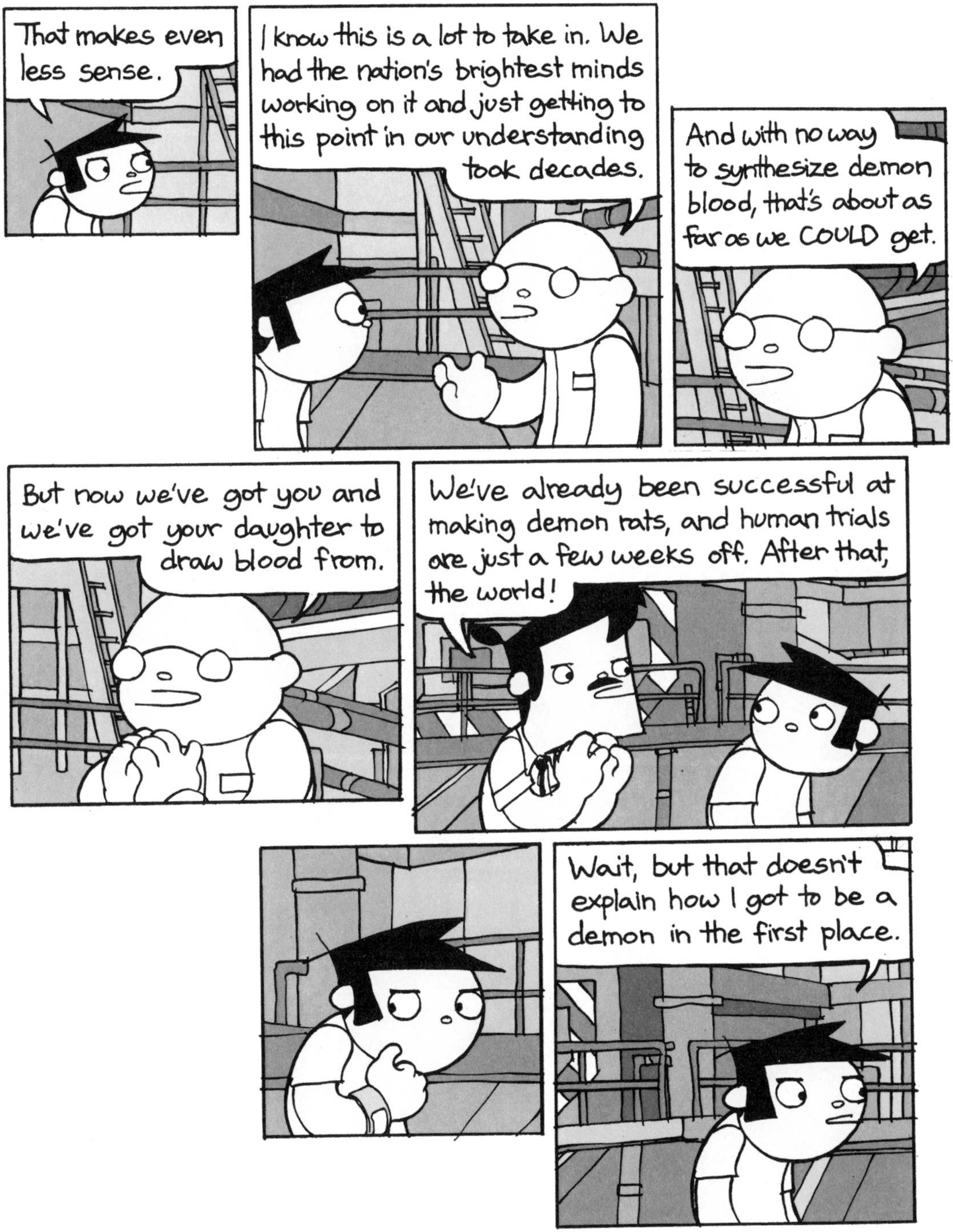
That makes even less sense.
I know this is a lot to take in. We had the nation's brightest minds working on it and just getting to this point in our understanding took decades.
And with no way to synthesize demon blood, that's about as far as we COULD get.
But now we've got you and we've got your daughter to draw blood from.
We've already been successful at making demon rats, and human trials are just a few weeks off. After that, the world!
Wait, but that doesn't explain how I got to be a demon in the first place.

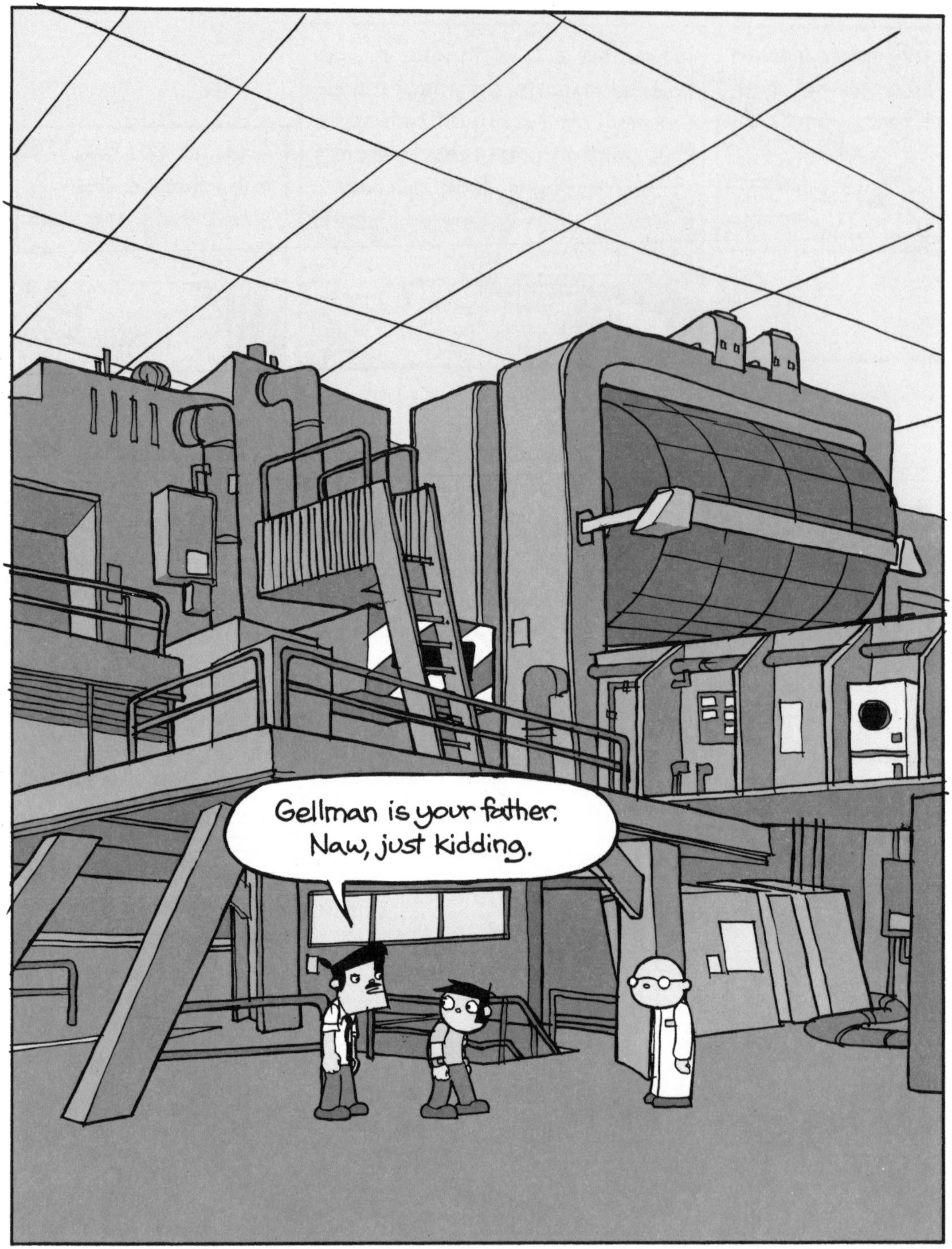
Gellman is your father. Naw, just kidding.

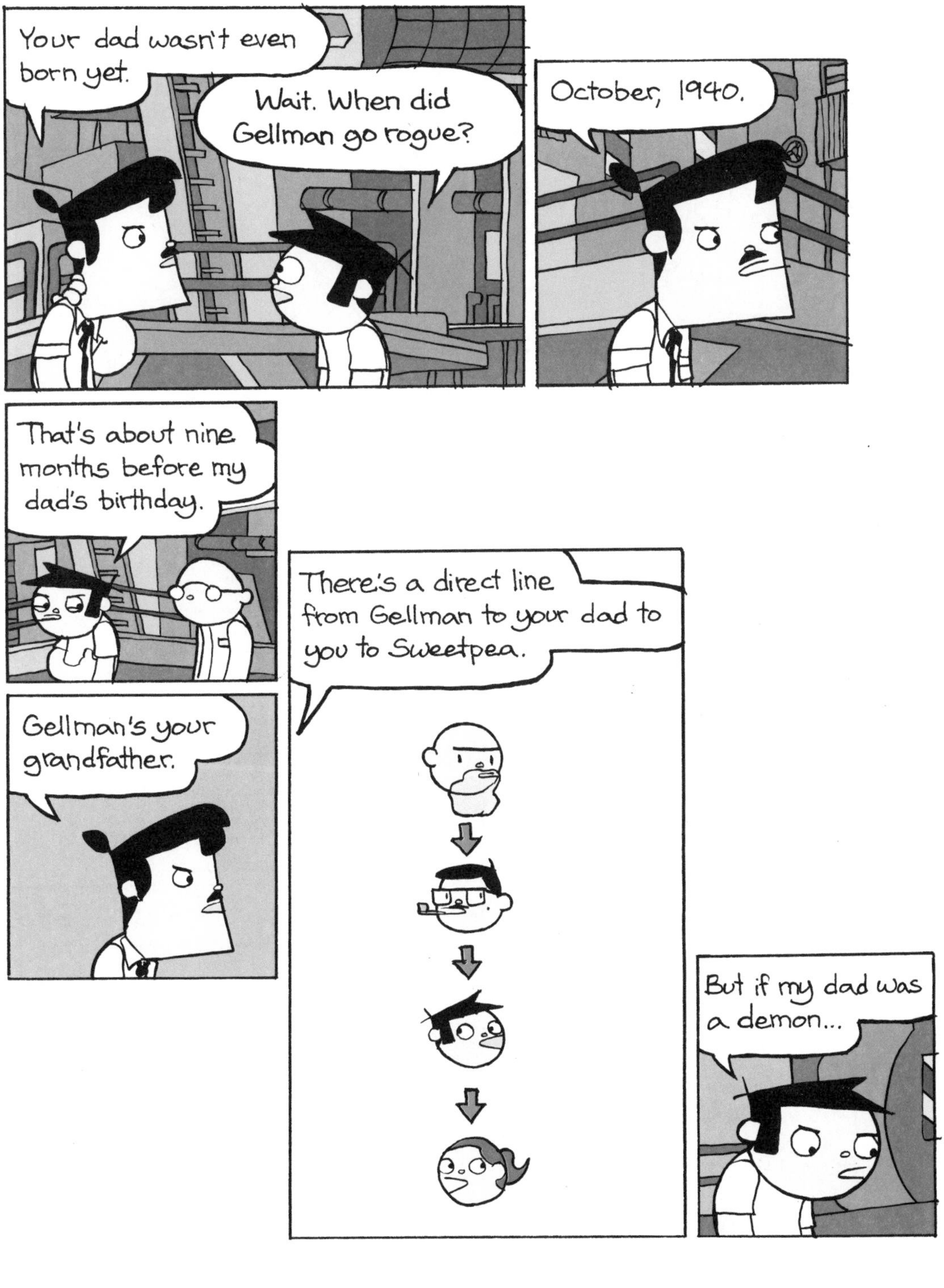

Your dad wasn't even born yet.
Wait. When did Gellman go rogue?
October, 1940.
That's about nine months before my dad's birthday.
Gellman's your grandfather.
There's a direct line from Gellman to your dad to you to Sweetpea.
But if my dad was a demon...

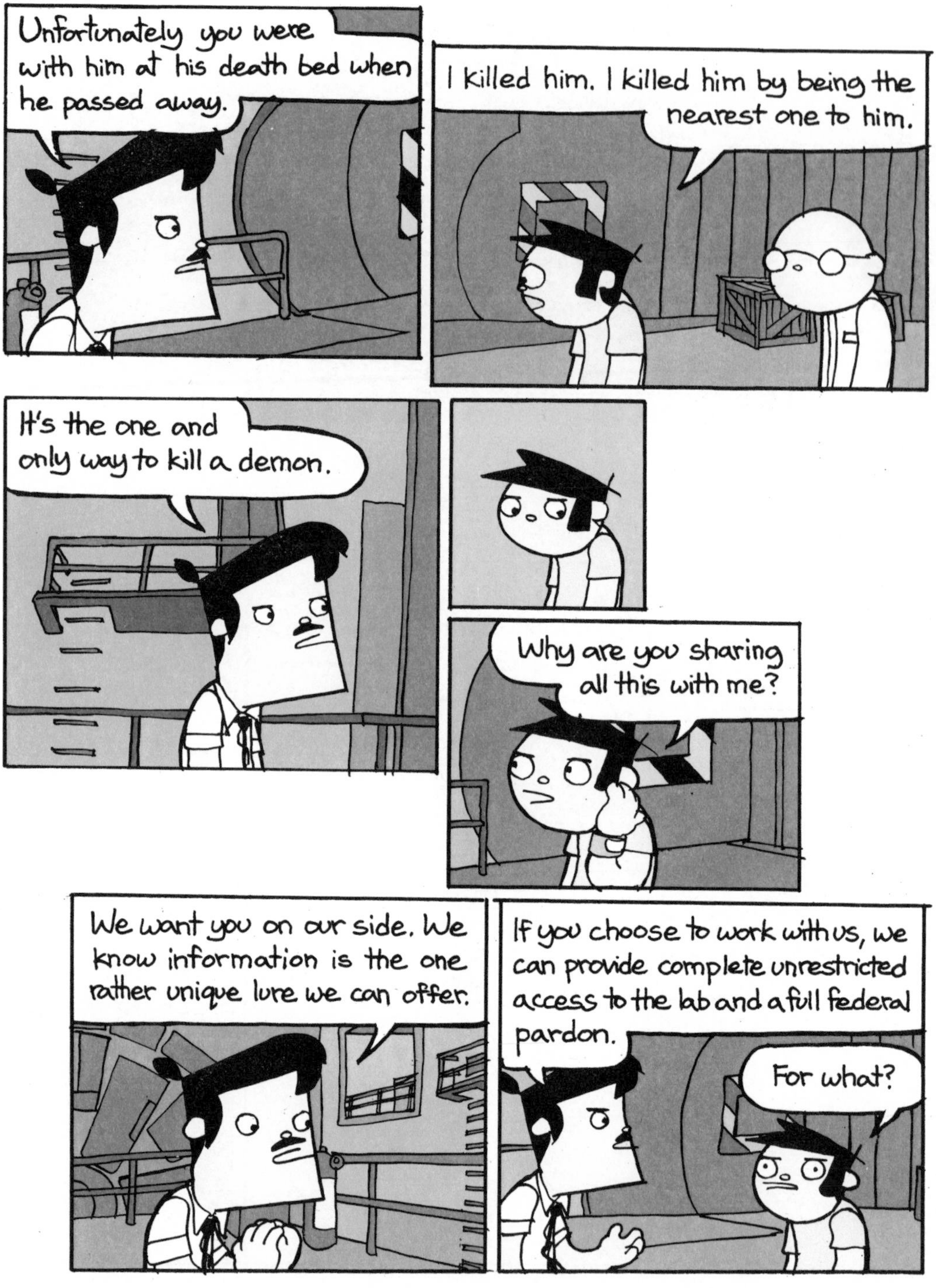
Unfortunately you were with him at his death bed when he passed away.
I killed him. I killed him by being the nearest one to him.
It's the one and only way to kill a demon.
Why are you sharing all this with me?
We want you on our side. We know information is the one rather unique lure we can offer.
If you choose to work with us, we can provide complete unrestricted access to the lab and a full federal pardon.
For what?

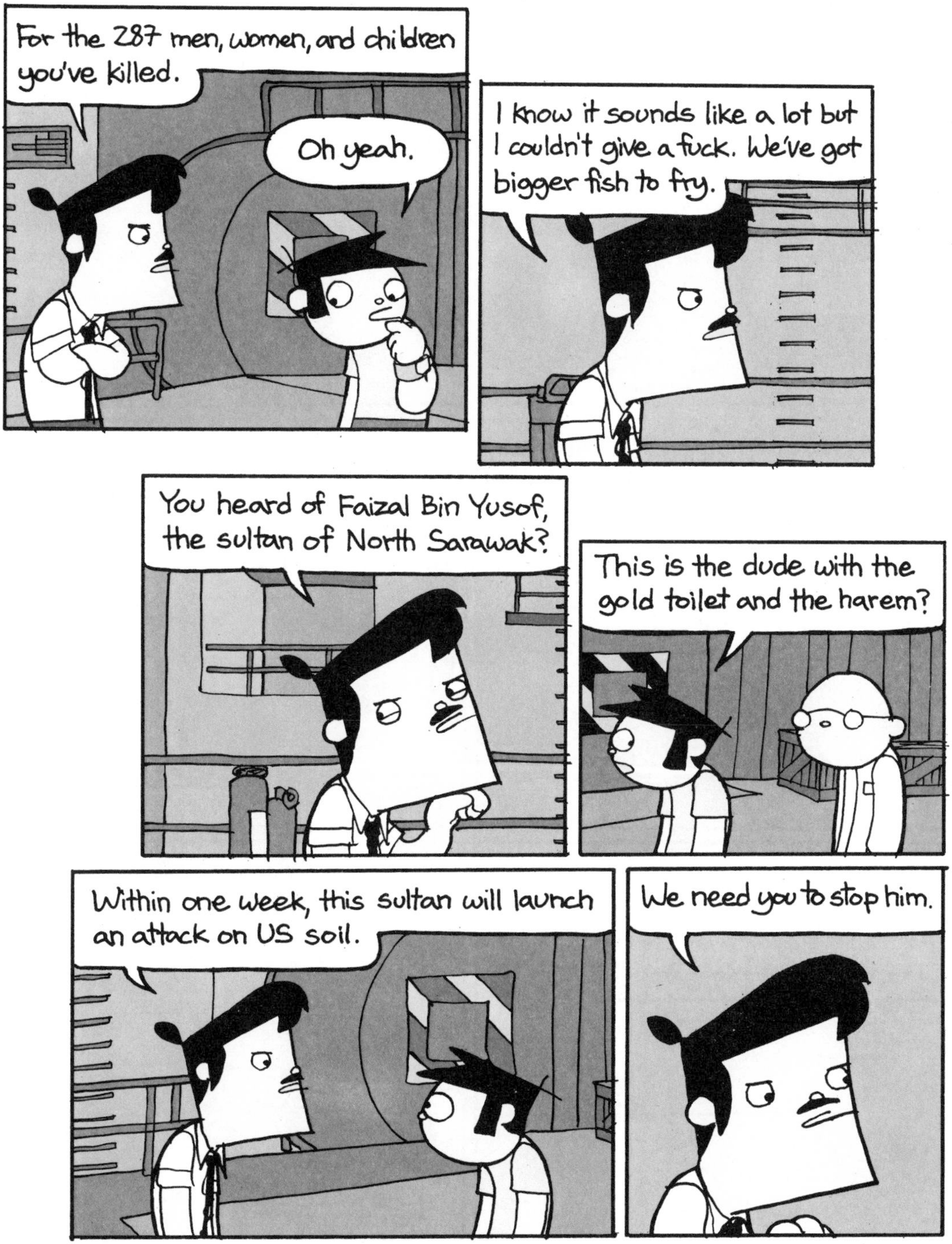
For the 287 men, women, and children you've killed.
Oh yeah.
I know it sounds like a lot but I couldn't give a fuck. We've got bigger fish to fry.
You heard of Faizal Bin Yusof, the sultan of North Sarawak?
This is the dude with the gold toilet and the harem?
Within one week, this sultan will launch an attack on US soil.
We need you to stop him.

The OSS was founded on the premise that through a radical application of intelligence gathering and technology, we could achieve in minutes what militaries accomplish in years.

We've already made our demon rats, and human trials are less than a week off. Once we've trained our demon army, the world will be ours for the remaking.

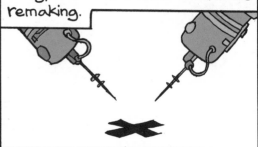

Imagine a world with no Hitler or Stalin or Pol Pot.

No corruption, no political instability, no genocide.

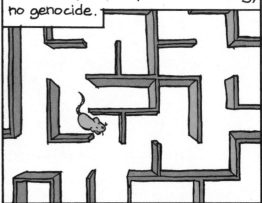

Imagine a world with no wars or conflicts. Every nation's military budget diverted to social and environmental programs and lower taxes.

Imagine a utopia on earth not in 1,000 years, but by late September.

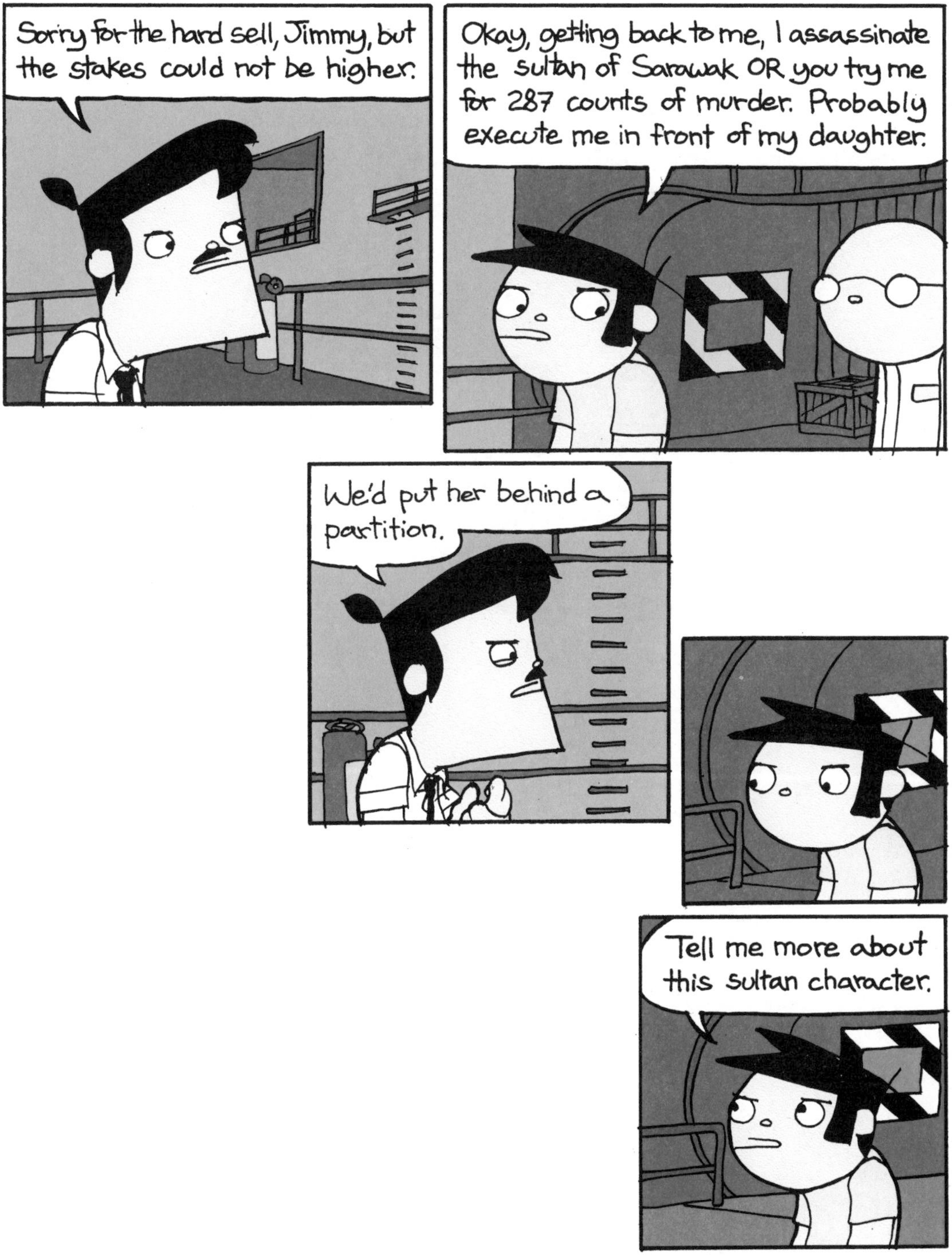
Sorry for the hard sell, Jimmy, but the stakes could not be higher.
Okay, getting back to me, I assassinate the sultan of Sarawak OR you try me for 287 counts of murder. Probably execute me in front of my daughter.
We'd put her behind a partition.
Tell me more about this sultan character.

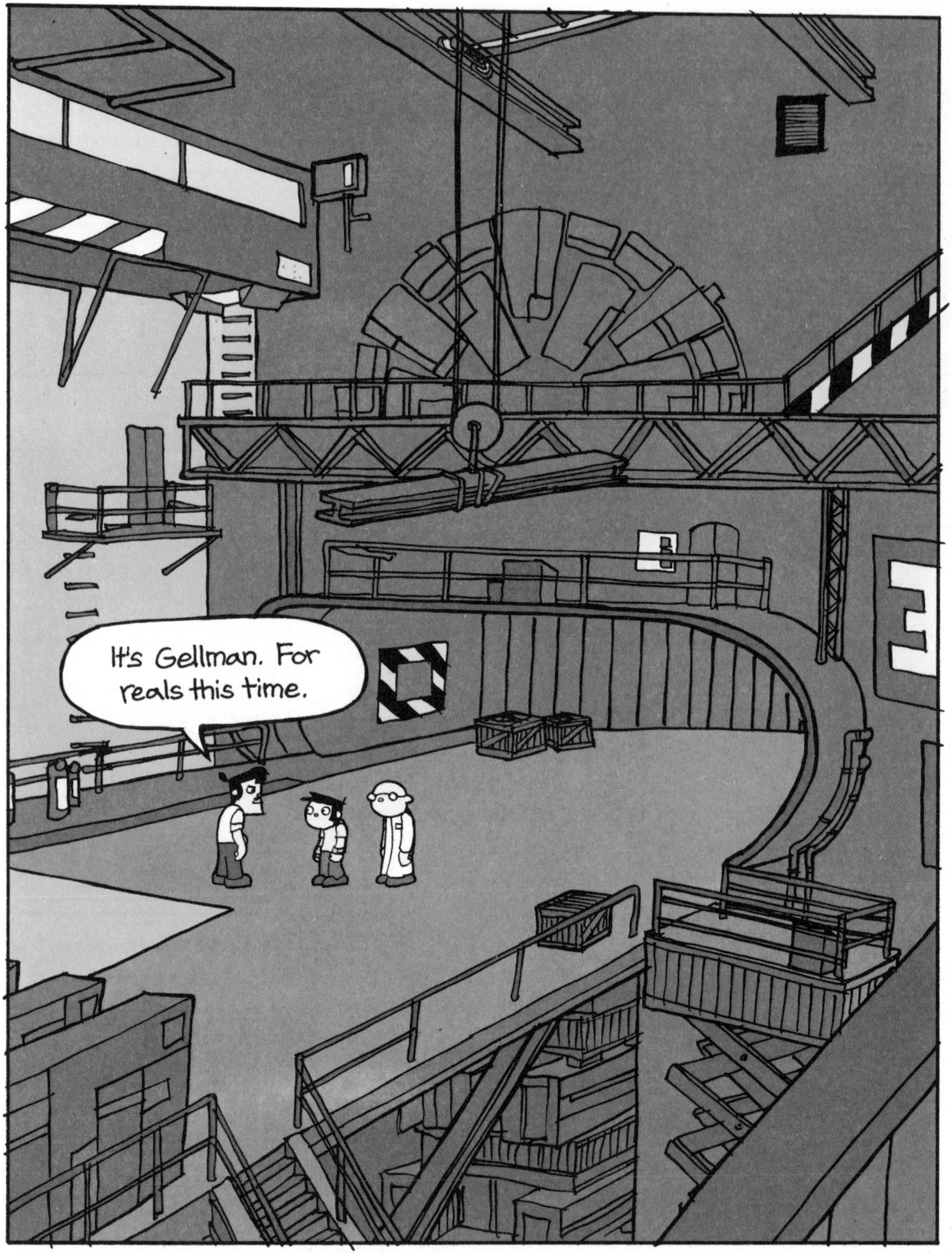
It's Gellman. For reals this time.

# CHAPTER 12

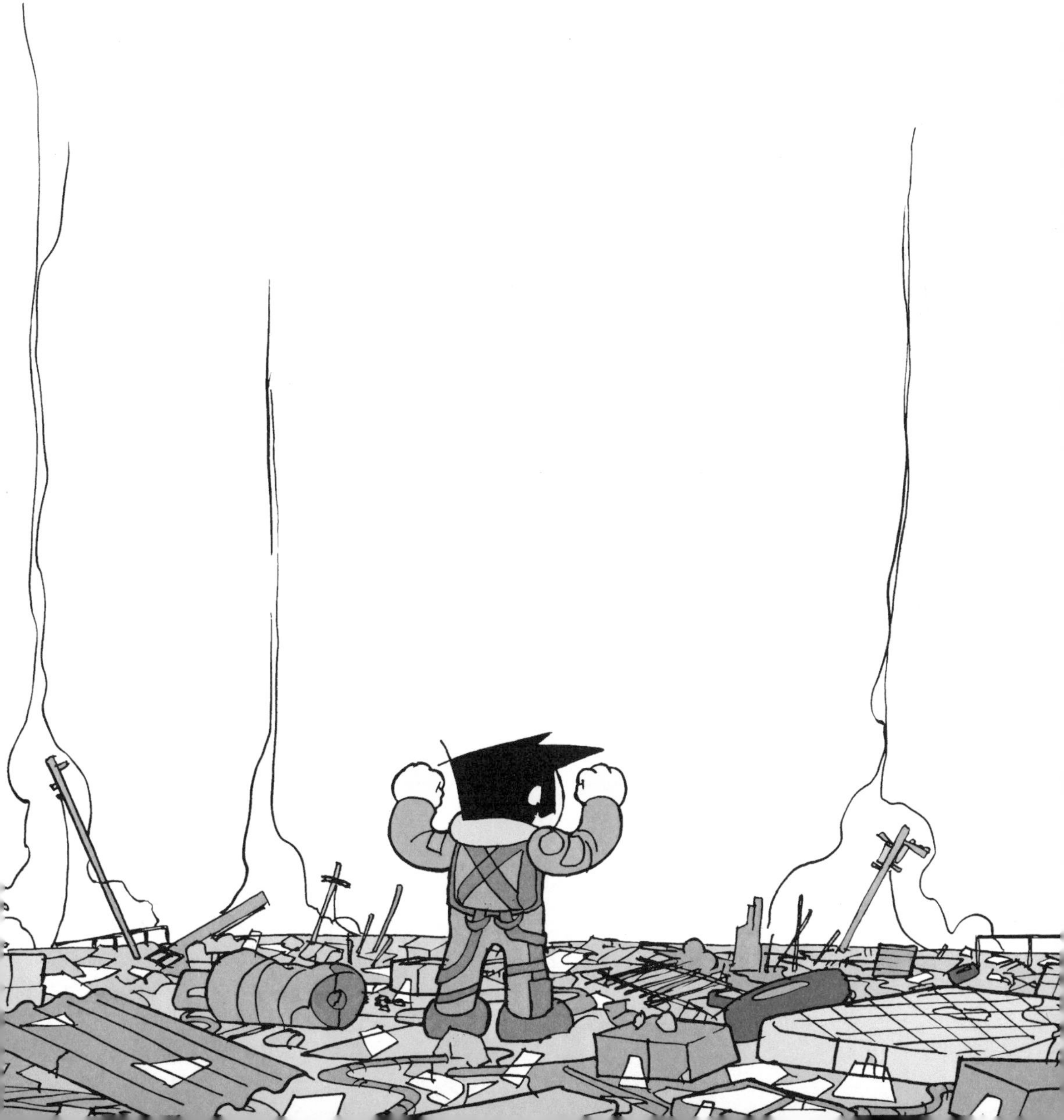

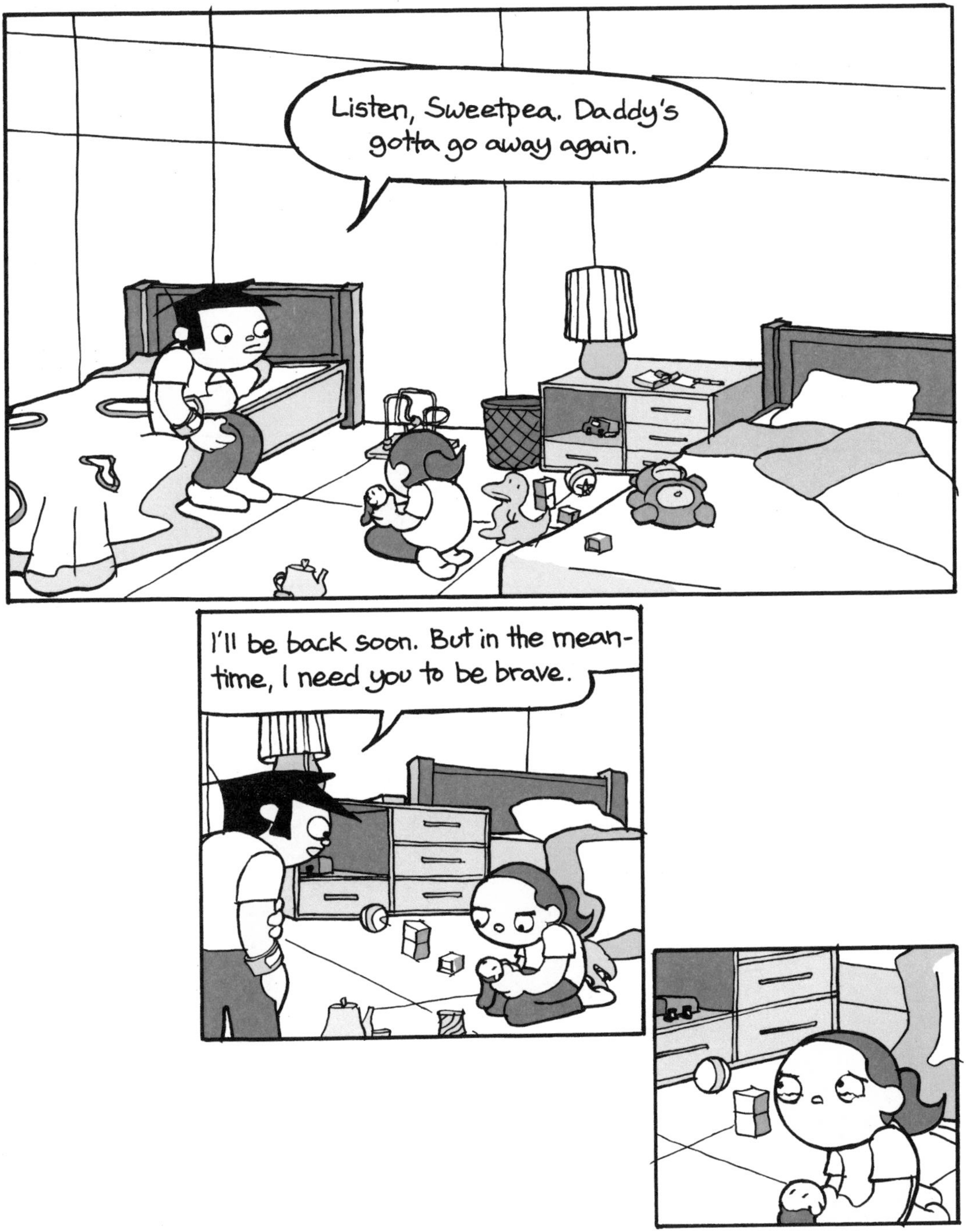
Listen, Sweetpea. Daddy's gotta go away again.
I'll be back soon. But in the mean-time, I need you to be brave.

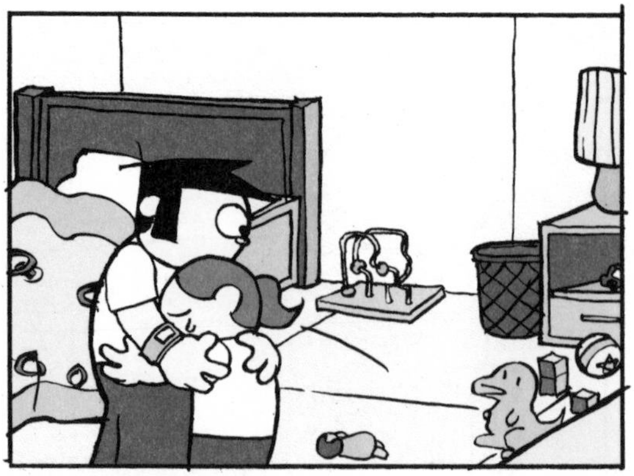

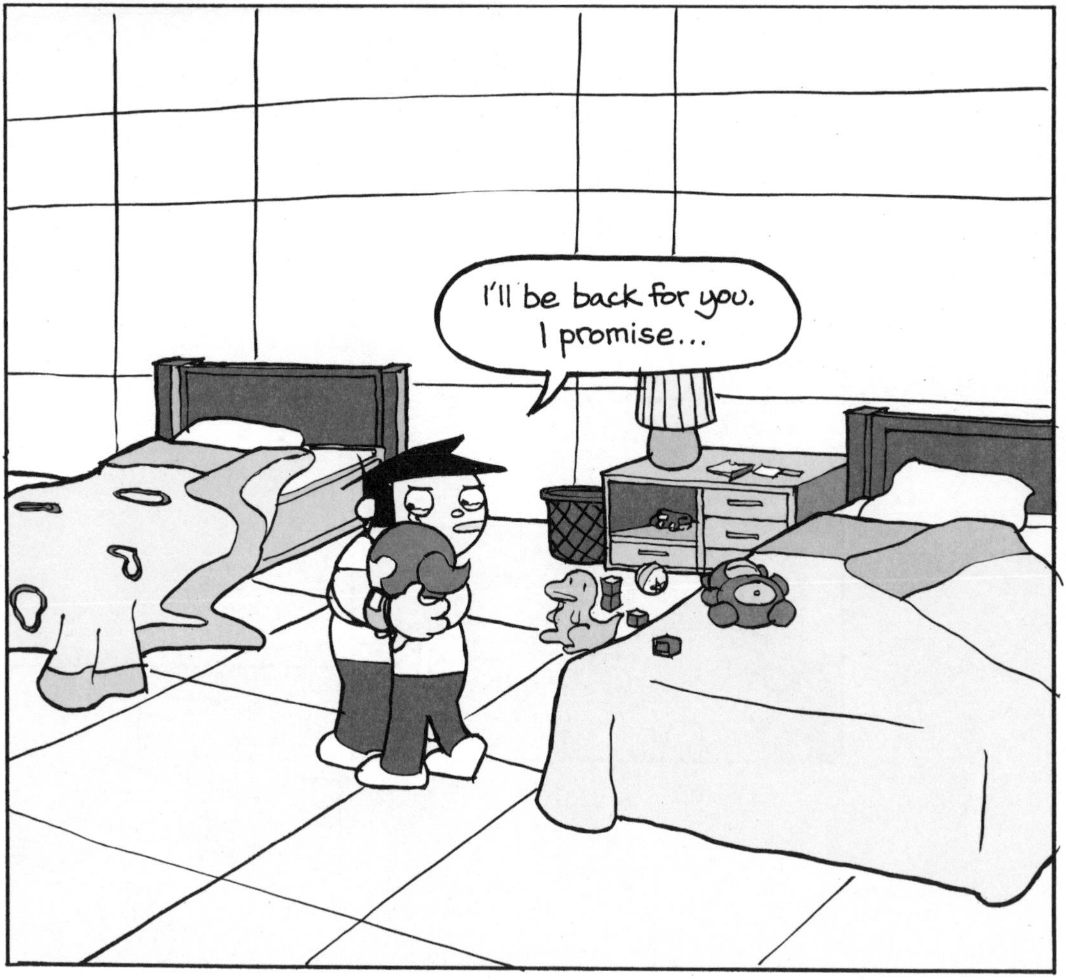
I'll be back for you. I promise...

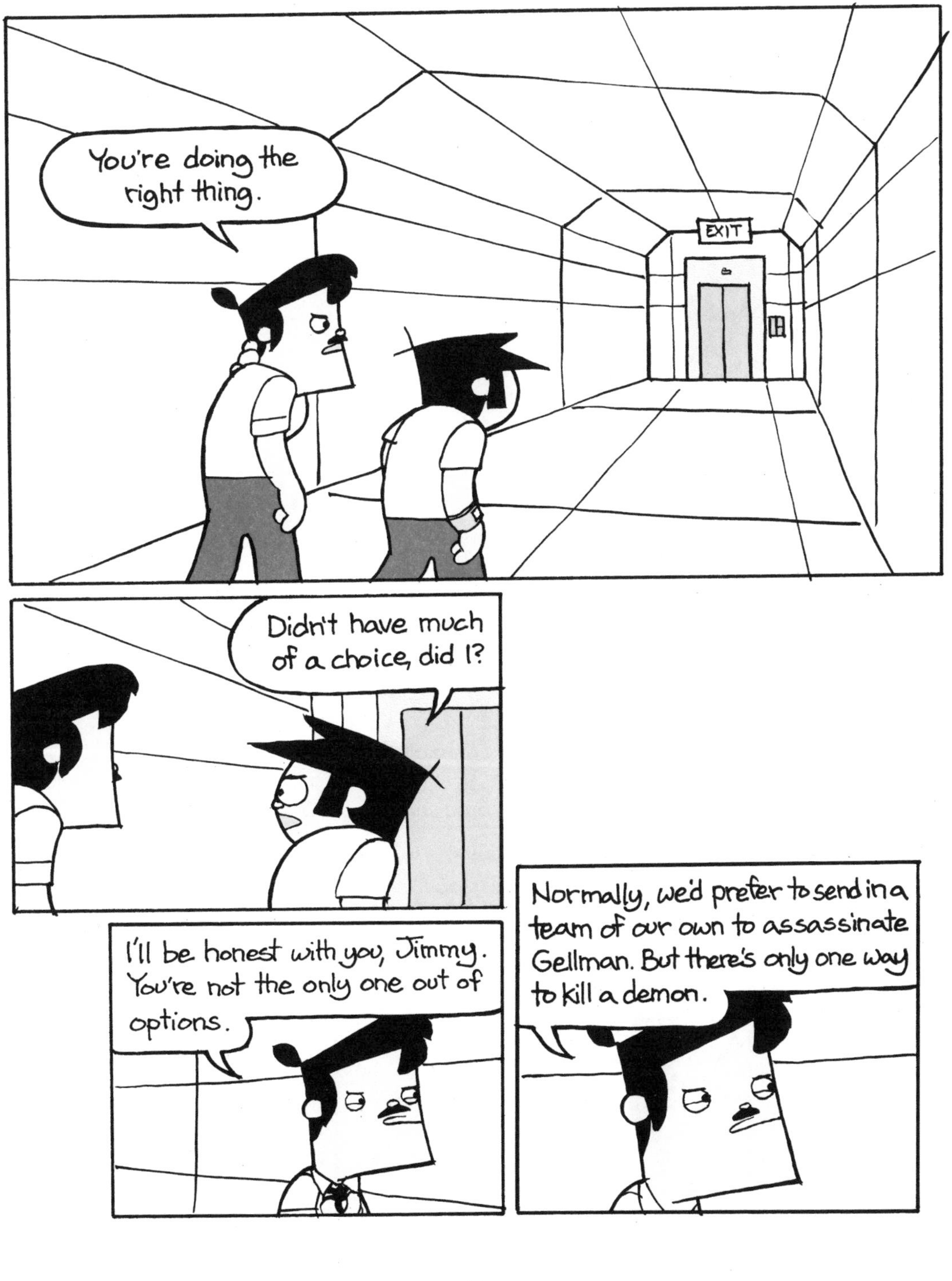
You're doing the right thing.
EXIT
Didn't have much of a choice, did I?
I'll be honest with you, Jimmy. You're not the only one out of options.
Normally, we'd prefer to send in a team of our own to assassinate Gellman. But there's only one way to kill a demon.

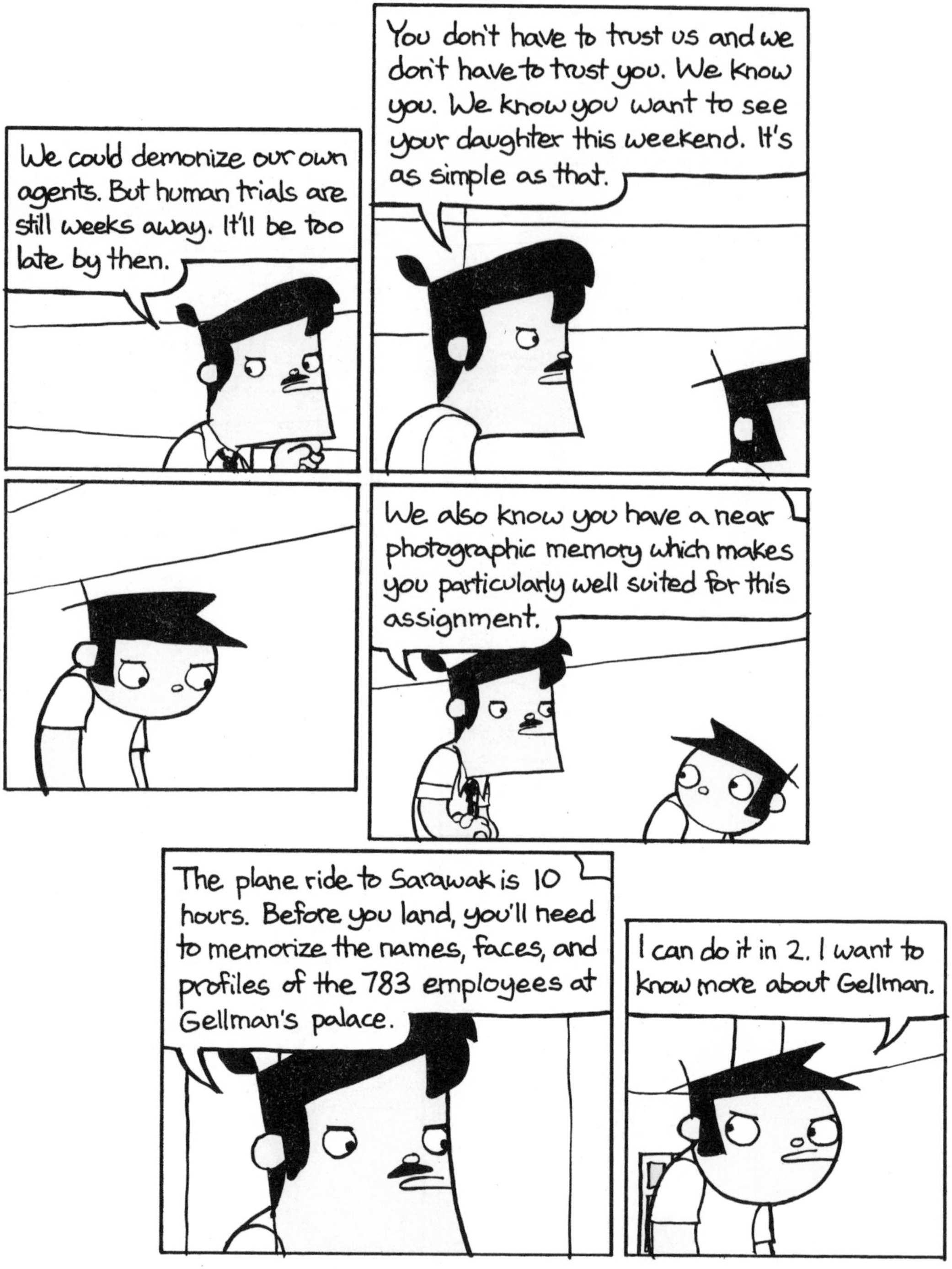

We could demonize our own agents. But human trials are still weeks away. It'll be too late by then.
You don't have to trust us and we don't have to trust you. We know you. We know you want to see your daughter this weekend. It's as simple as that.
We also know you have a near photographic memory which makes you particularly well suited for this assignment.
The plane ride to Sarawak is 10 hours. Before you land, you'll need to memorize the names, faces, and profiles of the 783 employees at Gellman's palace.
I can do it in 2. I want to know more about Gellman.

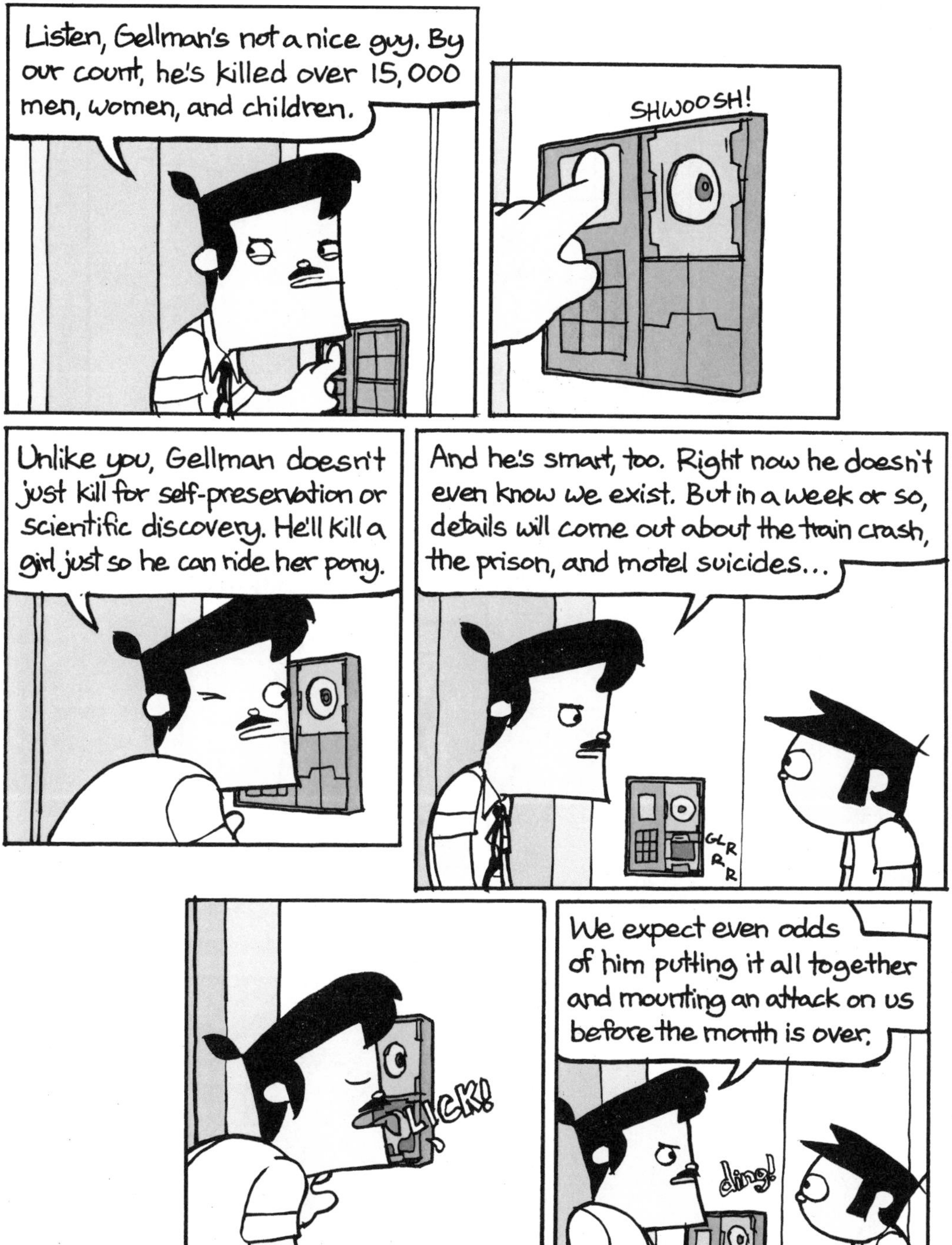

Listen, Gellman's not a nice guy. By our count, he's killed over 15,000 men, women, and children.
SHWOOSH!
Unlike you, Gellman doesn't just kill for self-preservation or scientific discovery. He'll kill a girl just so he can ride her pony.
And he's smart, too. Right now he doesn't even know we exist. But in a week or so, details will come out about the train crash, the prison, and motel suicides...
GLRRR
LICK!
We expect even odds of him putting it all together and mounting an attack on us before the month is over.
ding!

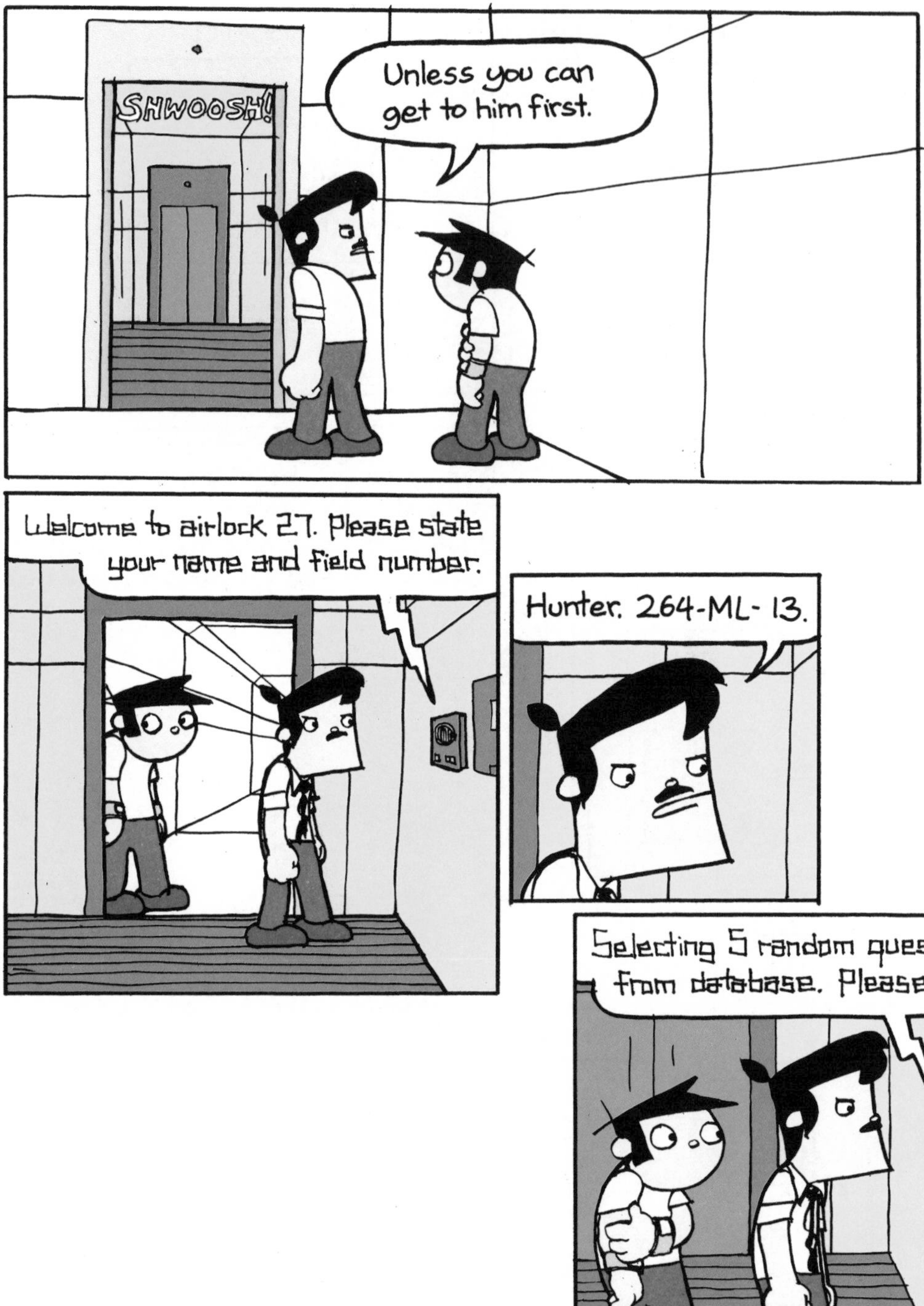
SHWOOSH!
Unless you can get to him first.
Welcome to airlock 27. Please state your name and field number.
Hunter. 264-ML-13.
Selecting 5 random questions from database. Please wait.

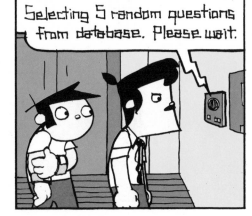

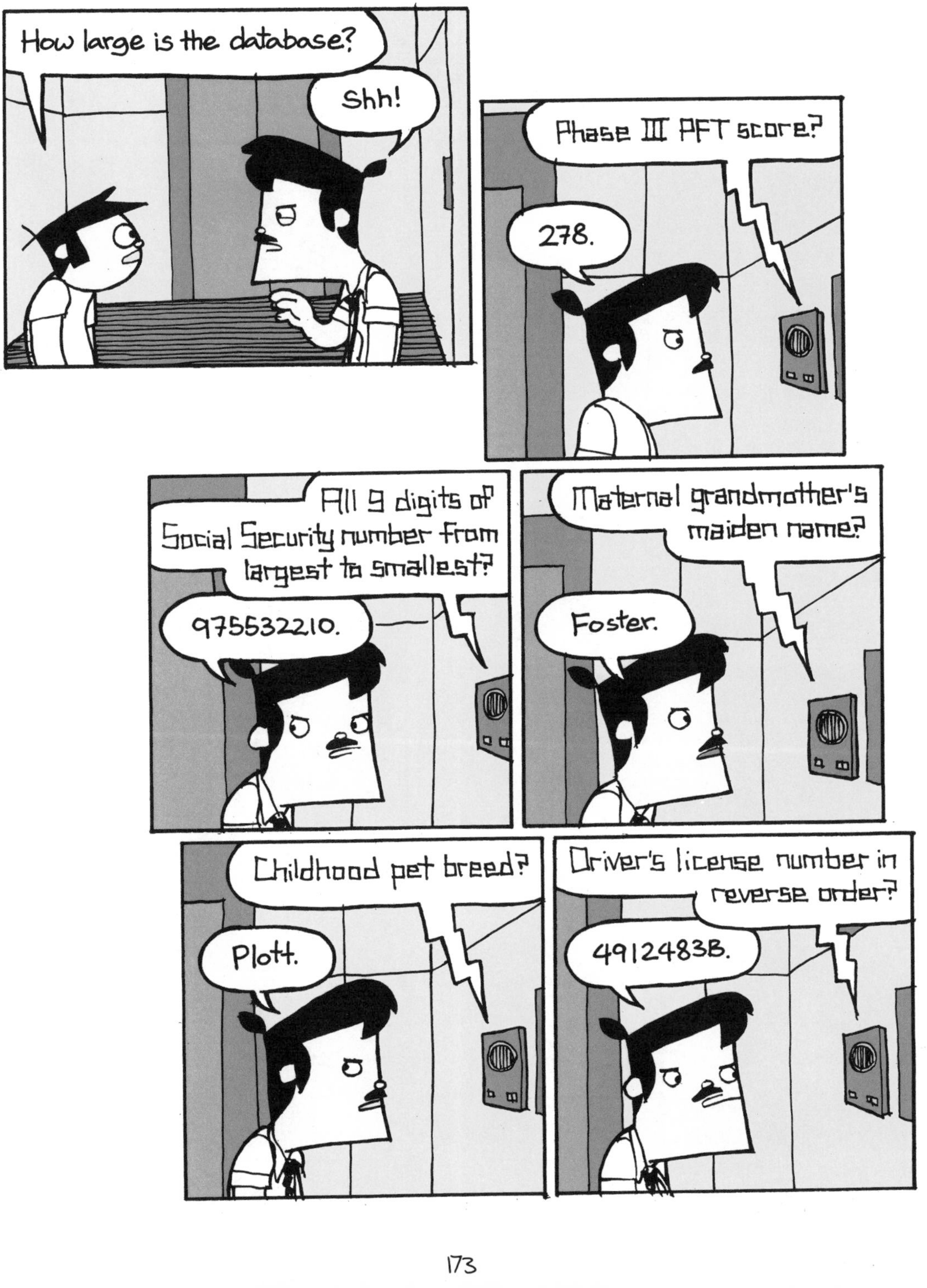
How large is the database?
Shh!
Phase III PFT score?
278.
All 9 digits of Social Security number from largest to smallest?
975532210.
Maternal grandmother's maiden name?
Foster.
Childhood pet breed?
Plott.
Driver's license number in reverse order?
4912483B.

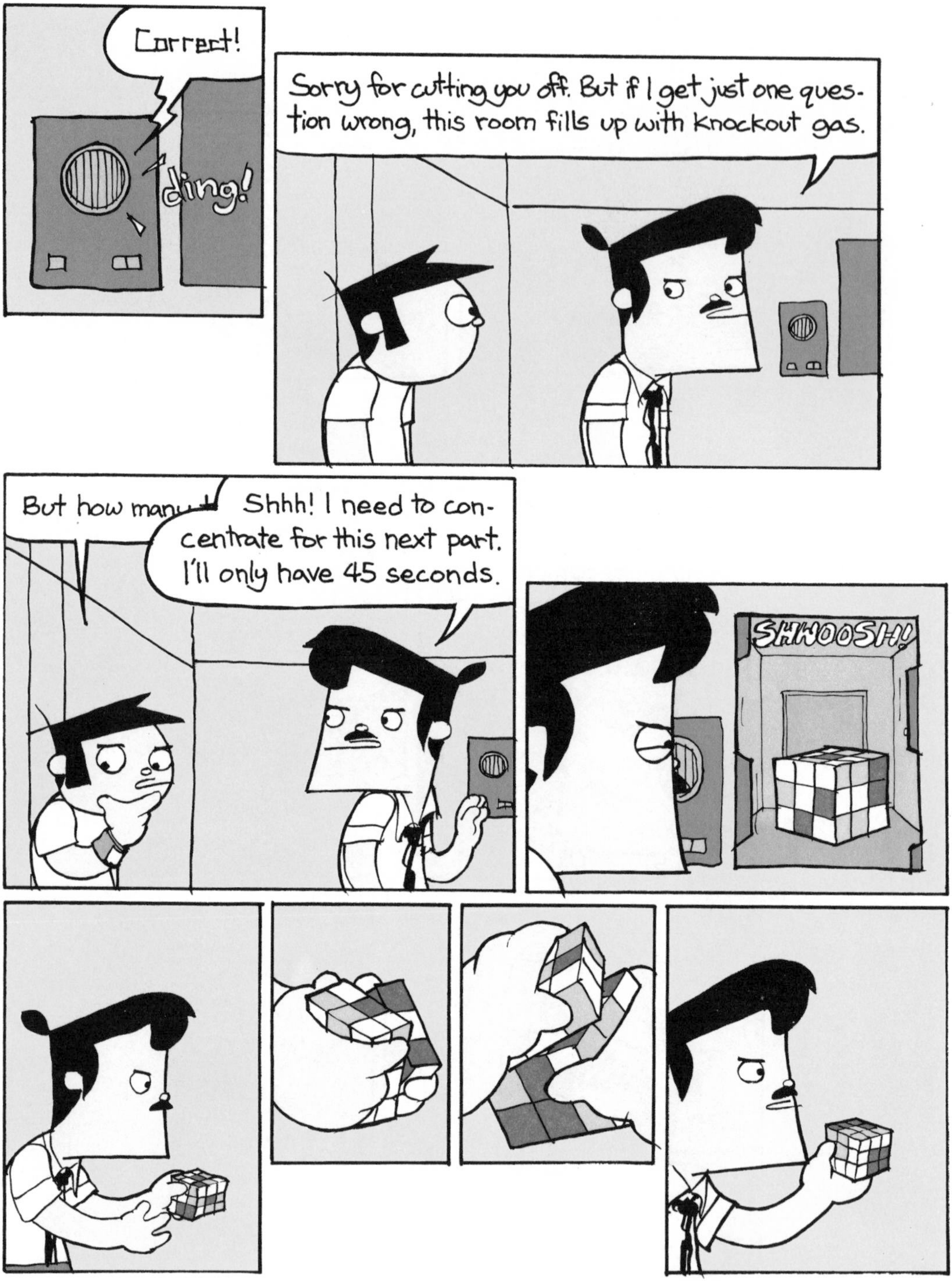
Correct!
ding!
Sorry for cutting you off. But if I get just one question wrong, this room fills up with knockout gas.
But how many t
Shhh! I need to concentrate for this next part. I'll only have 45 seconds.
SHWOOSH!

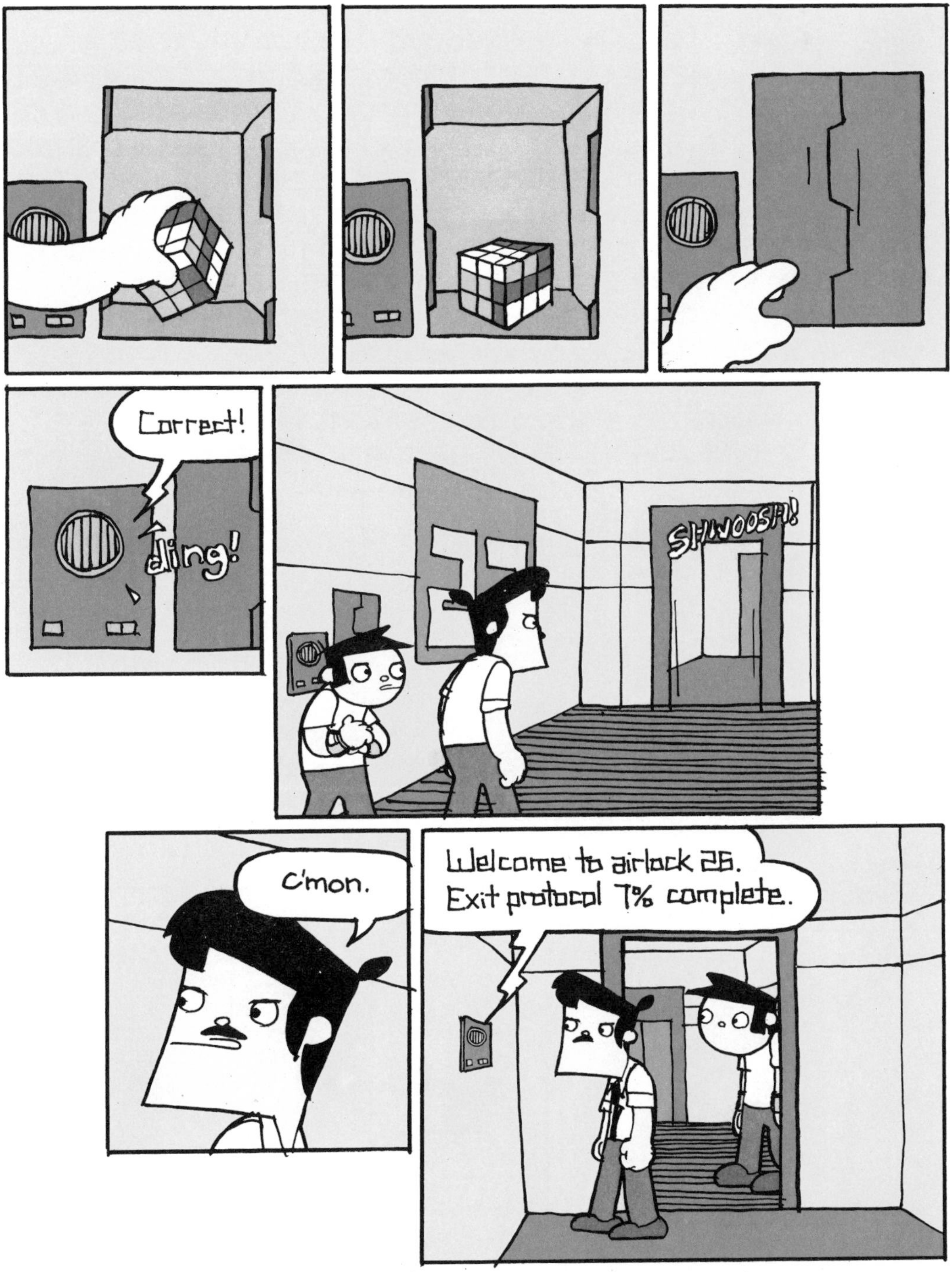

Correct!
ding!
SHWOOSH!
c'mon.
Welcome to airlock 26.
Exit protocol 7% complete.

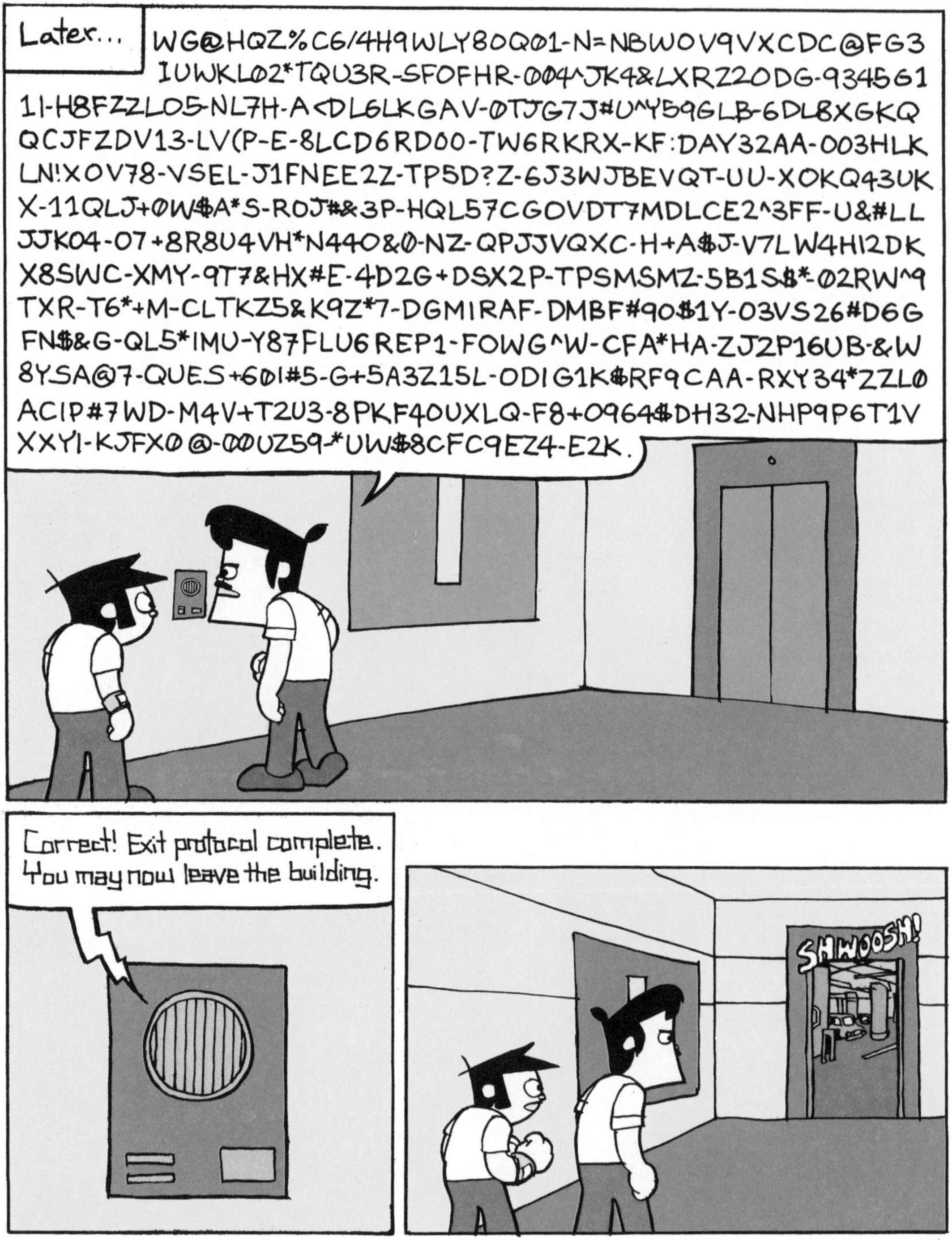
Later...
WG@HQZ%C6/4H9WLY80Q01-N=NBWOV9VXCDC@FG3
IUWKL02*TQU3R-SFOFHR-004^JK4&LXRZ20DG-934561
1I-H8FZZL05-NL7H-A<DL6LKGAV-0TJG7J#U^Y59GLB-6DL8XGKQ
QCJFZDV13-LV(P-E-8LCD6RD00-TW6RKRX-KF:DAY32AA-003HLK
LN!XOV78-VSEL-J1FNEE2Z-TP5D?Z-6J3WJBEVQT-UU-XOKQ43UK
X-11QLJ+0W$A*S-ROJ#&3P-HQL57CGOVDT7MDLCE2^3FF-U&#LL
JJK04-07+8R8U4VH*N440&0-NZ-QPJJVQXC-H+A$J-V7LW4HI2DK
X8SWC-XMY-9T7&HX#E-4D2G+DSX2P-TPSMSMZ-5B1S$*-02RW^9
TXR-T6*+M-CLTKZ5&K9Z*7-DGMIRAF-DMBF#90$1Y-03VS26#D6G
FN$&G-QL5*IMU-Y87FLU6REP1-FOWG^W-CFA*HA-ZJ2P16UB-&W
8YSA@7-QUES+60I#5-G+5A3Z15L-ODIG1K$RF9CAA-RXY34*ZZL0
ACIP#7WD-M4V+T2U3-8PKF40UXLQ-F8+0964$DH32-NHP9P6T1V
XXYI-KJFX0@-00UZ59-*UW$8CFC9EZ4-E2K.
Correct! Exit protocol complete.
You may now leave the building.
SHWOOSH!

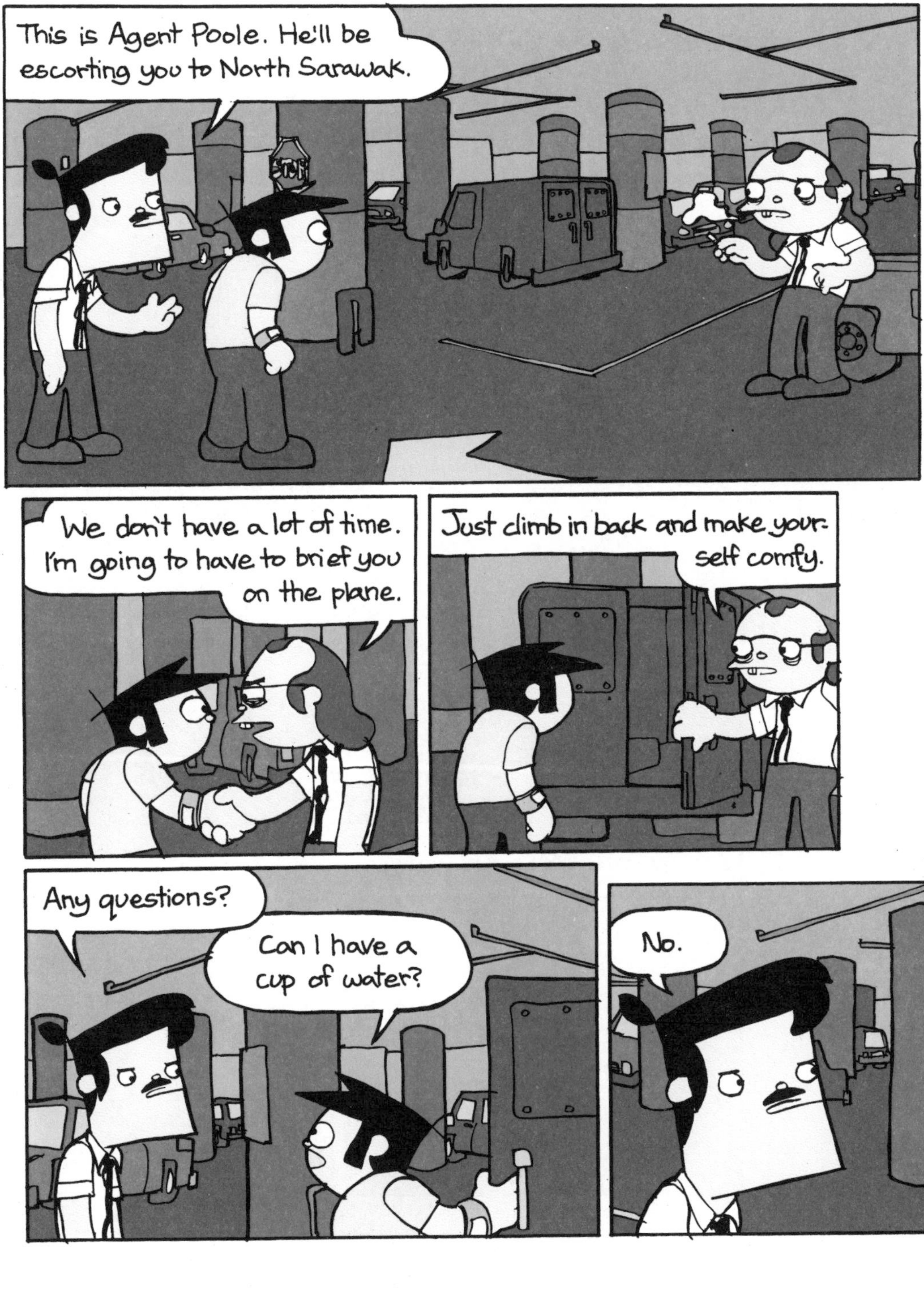
This is Agent Poole. He'll be escorting you to North Sarawak.
We don't have a lot of time. I'm going to have to brief you on the plane.
Just climb in back and make yourself comfy.
Any questions?
Can I have a cup of water?
No.

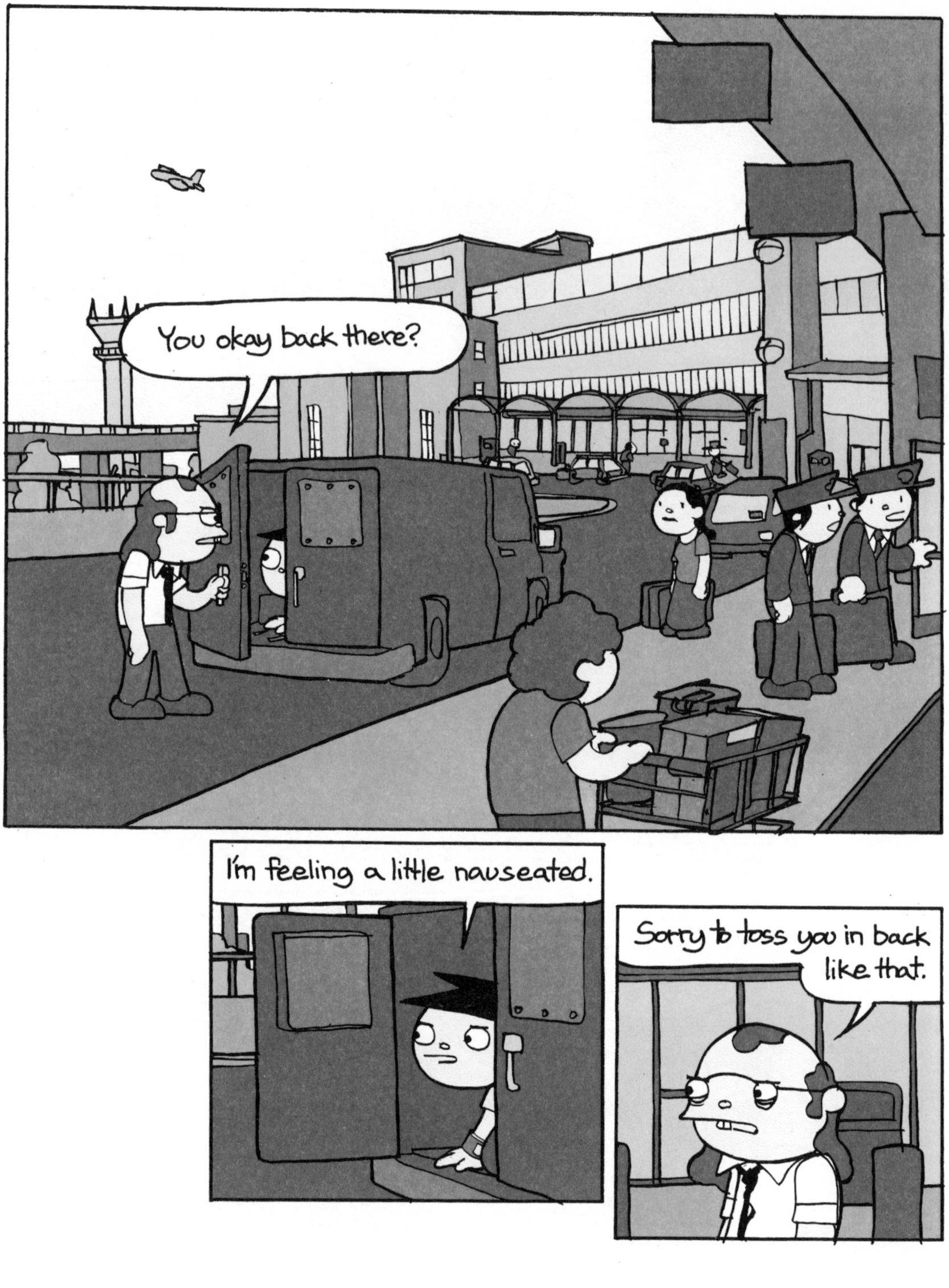
You okay back there?
I'm feeling a little nauseated.
Sorry to toss you in back like that.

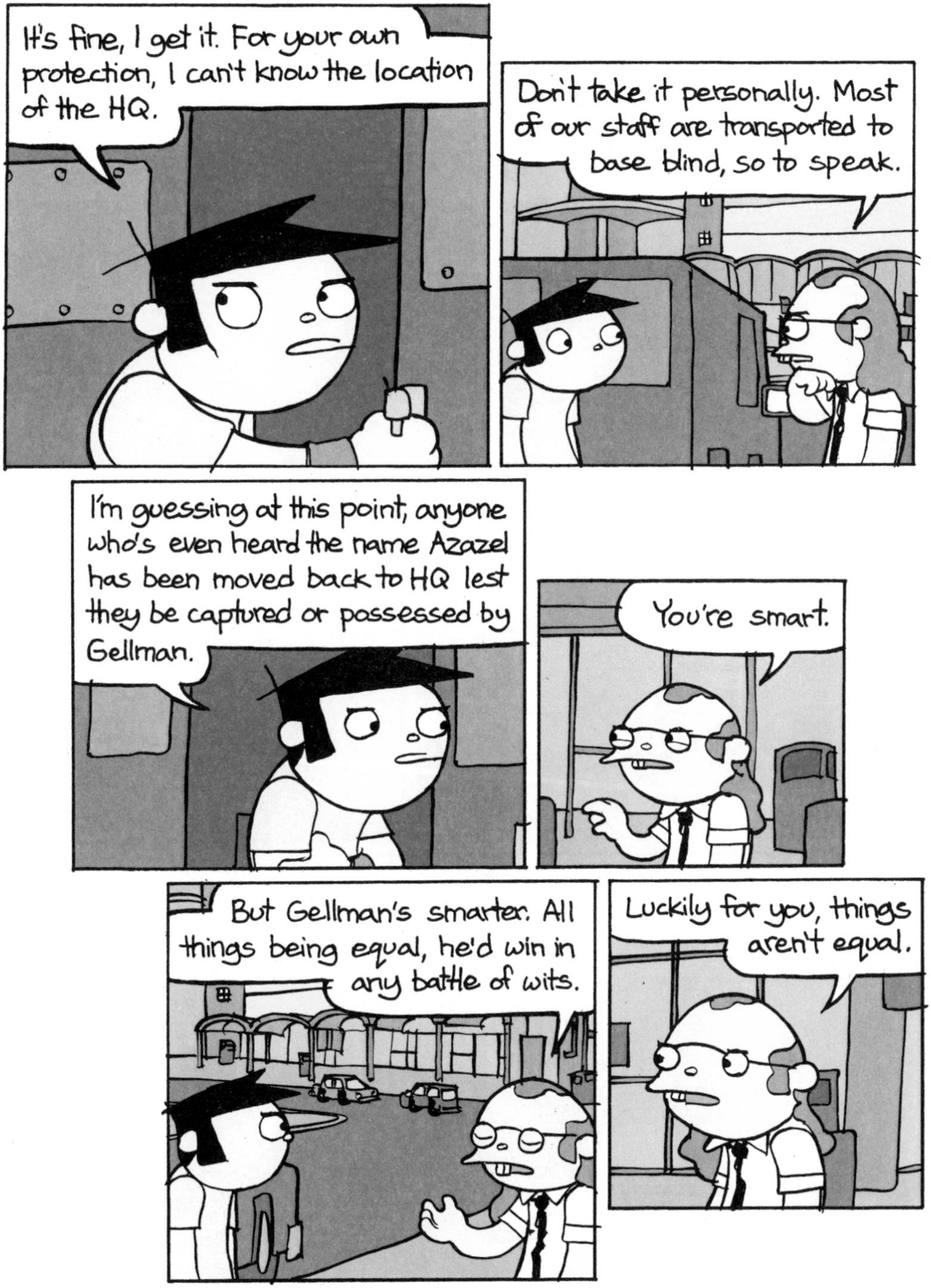
It's fine, I get it. For your own protection, I can't know the location of the HQ.
Don't take it personally. Most of our staff are transported to base blind, so to speak.
I'm guessing at this point, anyone who's even heard the name Azazel has been moved back to HQ lest they be captured or possessed by Gellman.
You're smart.
But Gellman's smarter. All things being equal, he'd win in any battle of wits.
Luckily for you, things aren't equal.

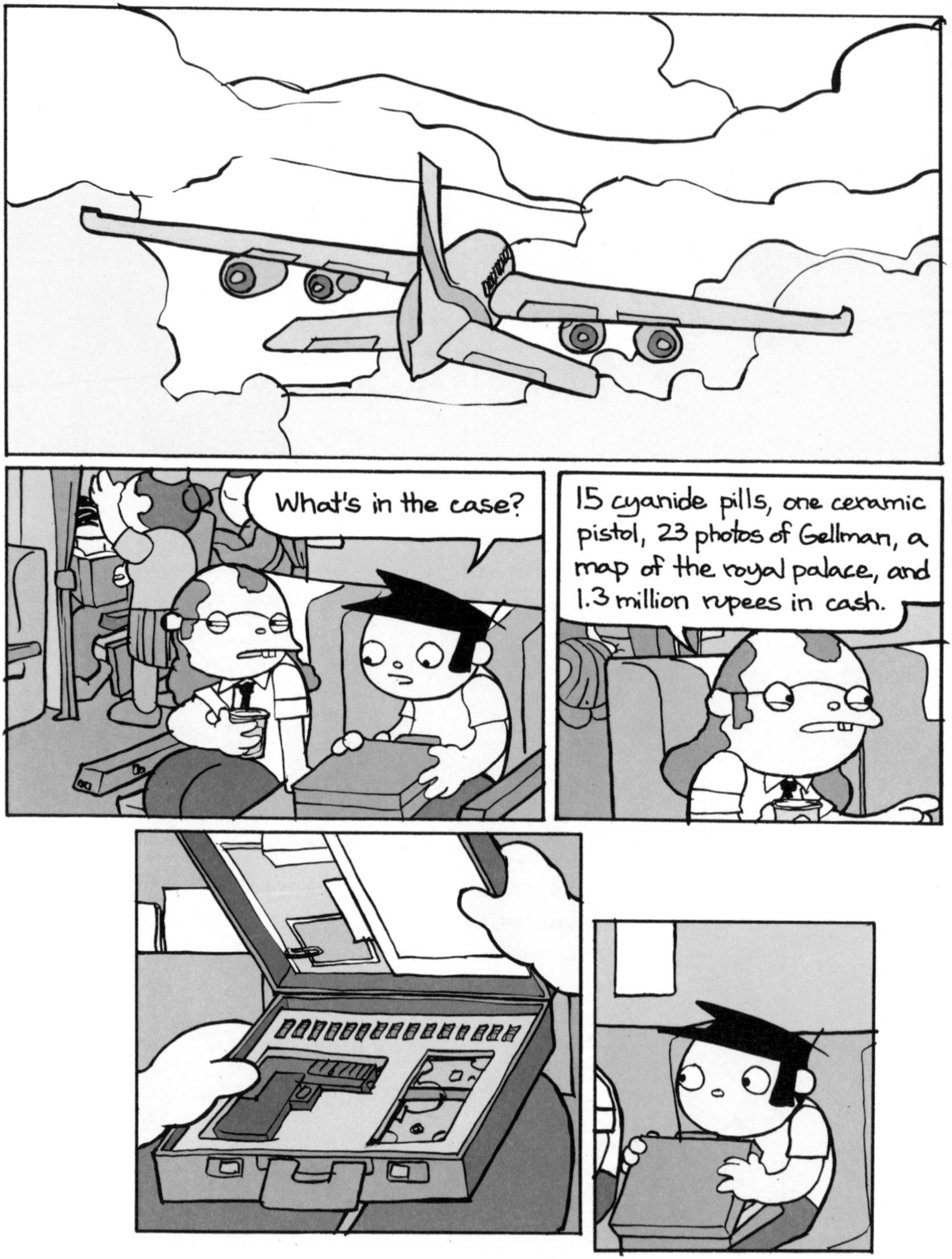
What's in the case?
15 cyanide pills, one ceramic pistol, 23 photos of Gellman, a map of the royal palace, and 1.3 million rupees in cash.

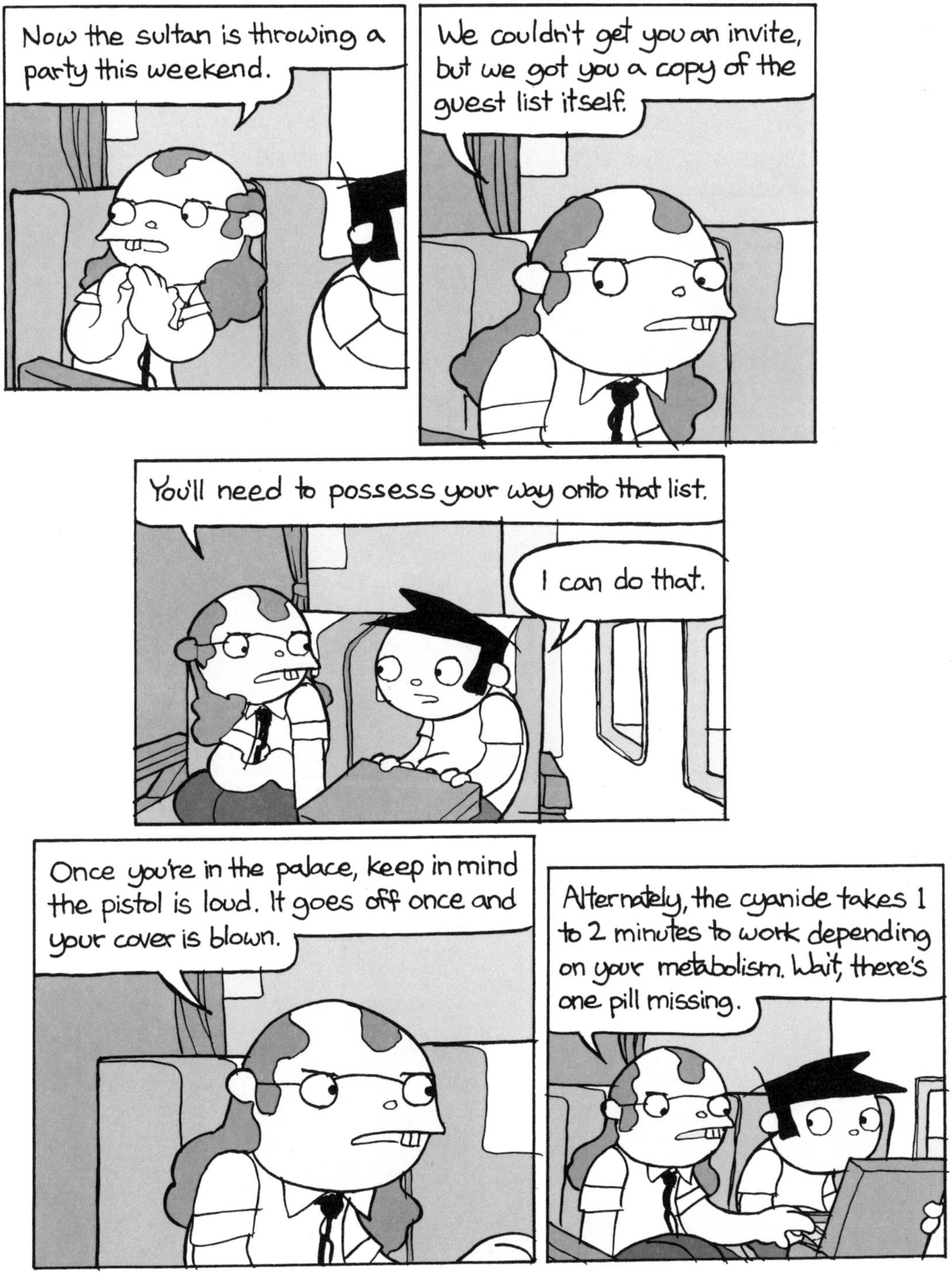
Now the sultan is throwing a party this weekend.
We couldn't get you an invite, but we got you a copy of the guest list itself.
You'll need to possess your way onto that list.
I can do that.
Once you're in the palace, keep in mind the pistol is loud. It goes off once and your cover is blown.
Alternately, the cyanide takes 1 to 2 minutes to work depending on your metabolism. Wait, there's one pill missing.

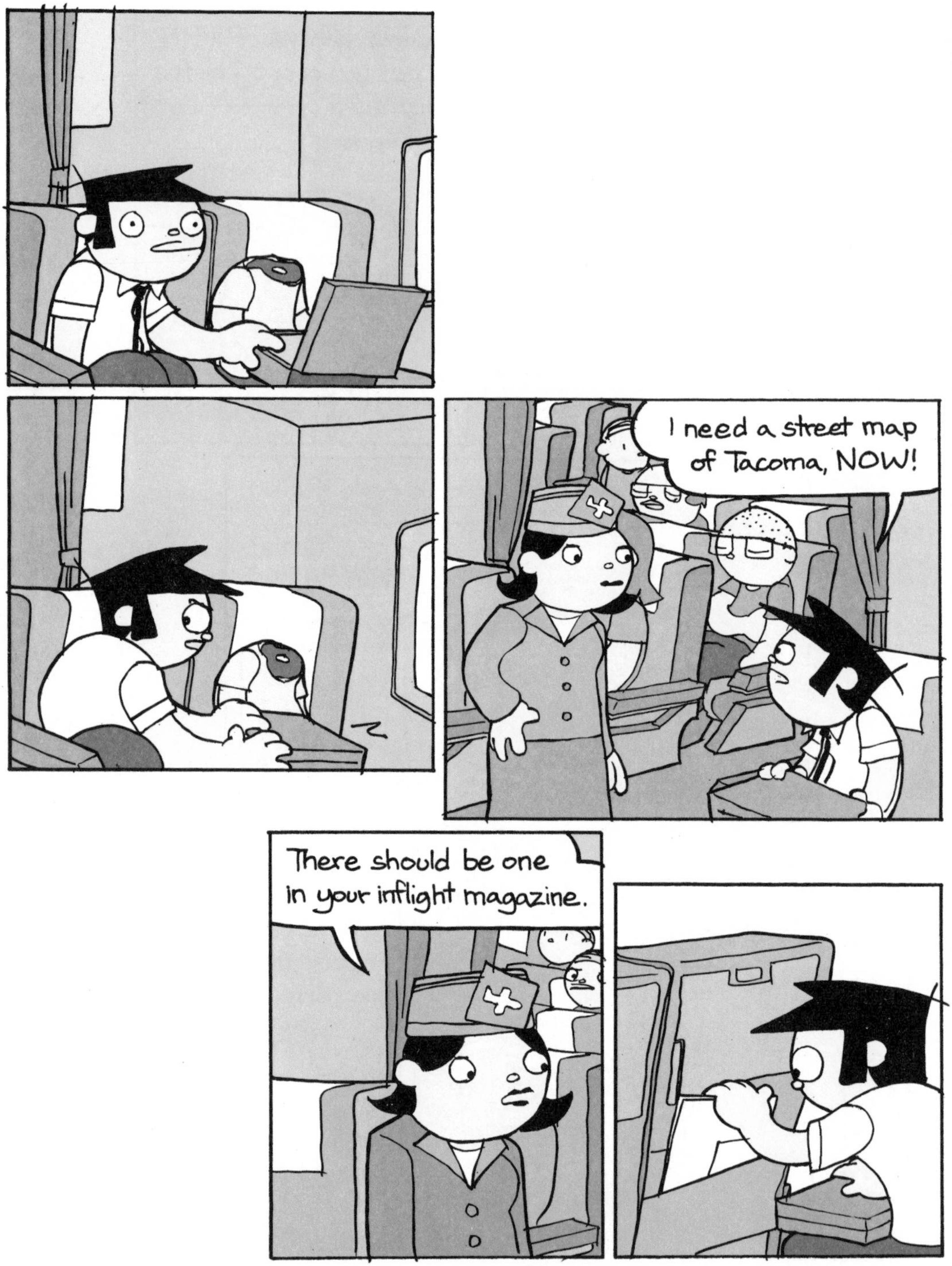
I need a street map of Tacoma, NOW!
There should be one in your inflight magazine.

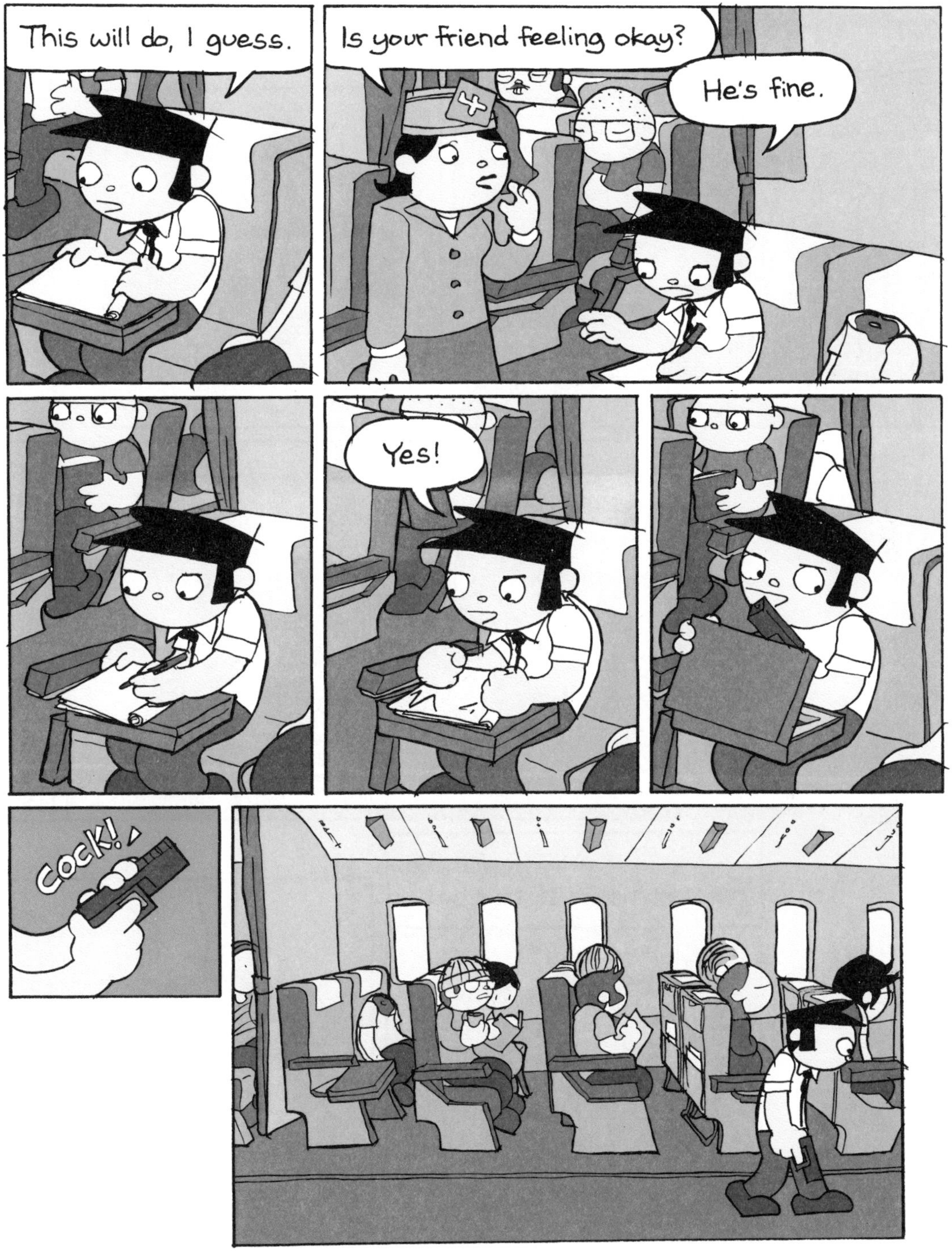
This will do, I guess.
Is your friend feeling okay?
He's fine.
Yes!
COCK!

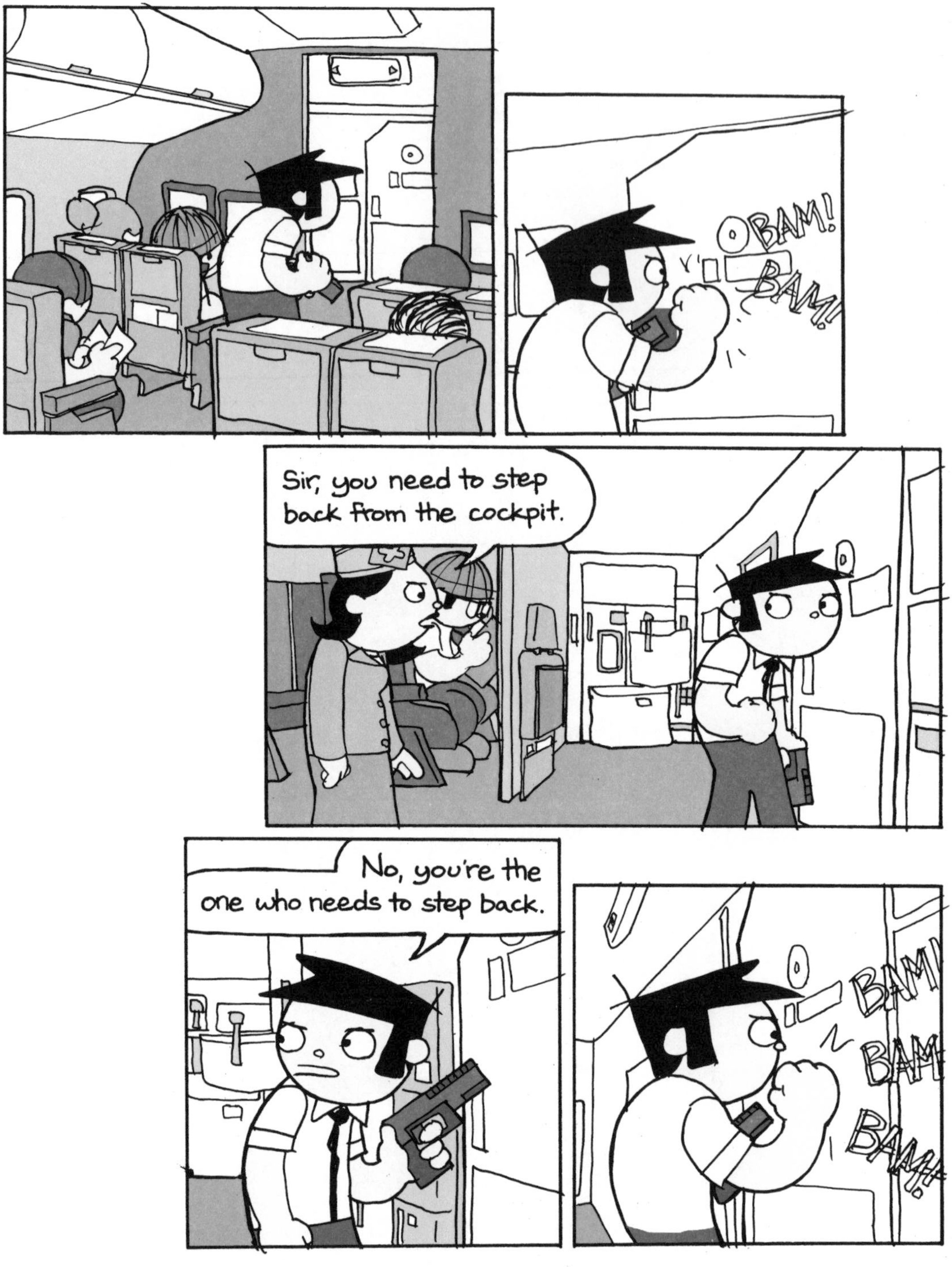
BAM!
BAM!
Sir, you need to step back from the cockpit.
No, you're the one who needs to step back.
BAM
BAM
BAM!

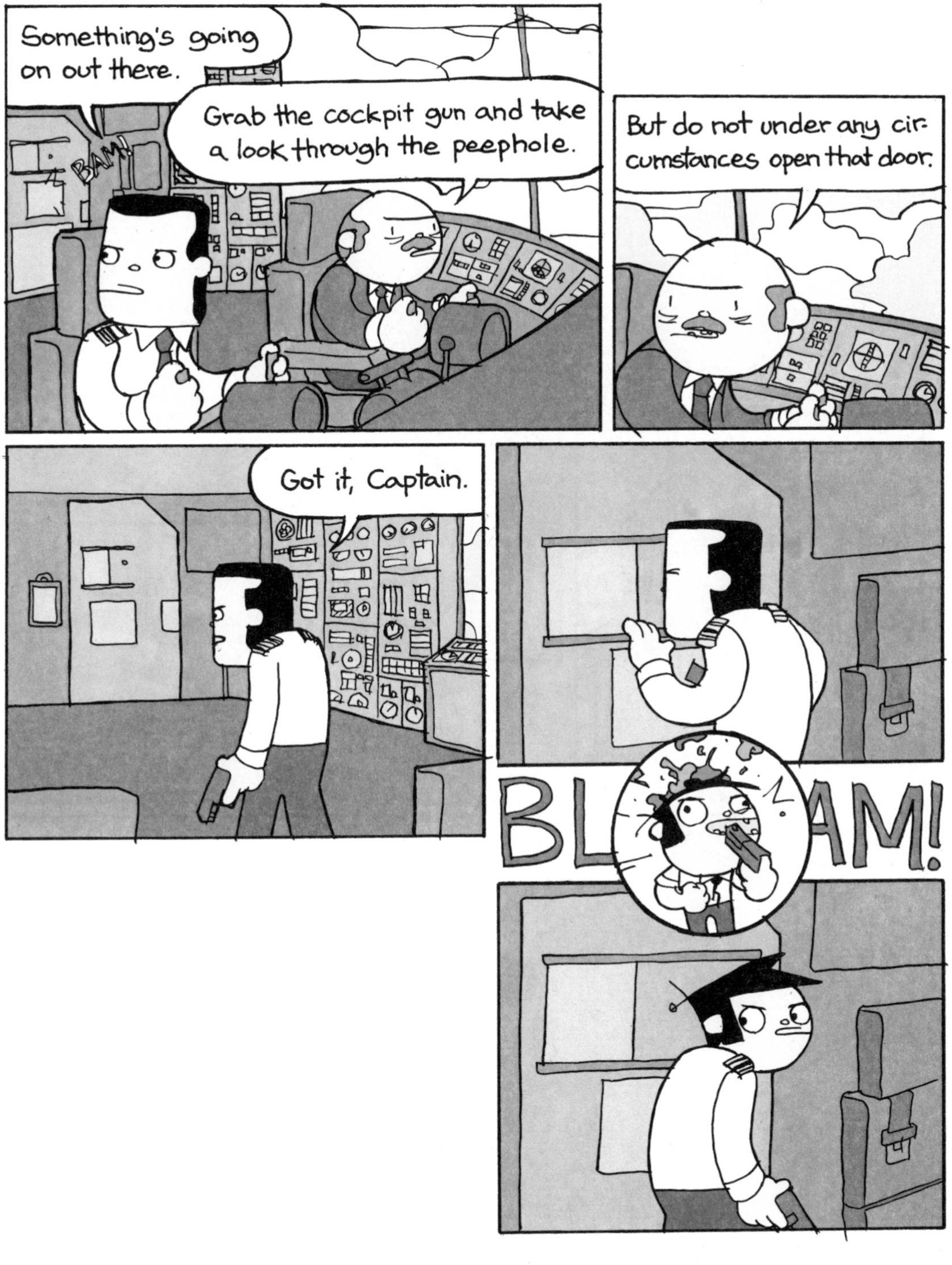
Something's going on out there.
BAM!
Grab the cockpit gun and take a look through the peephole.
But do not under any circumstances open that door.
Got it, Captain.
BLAM!

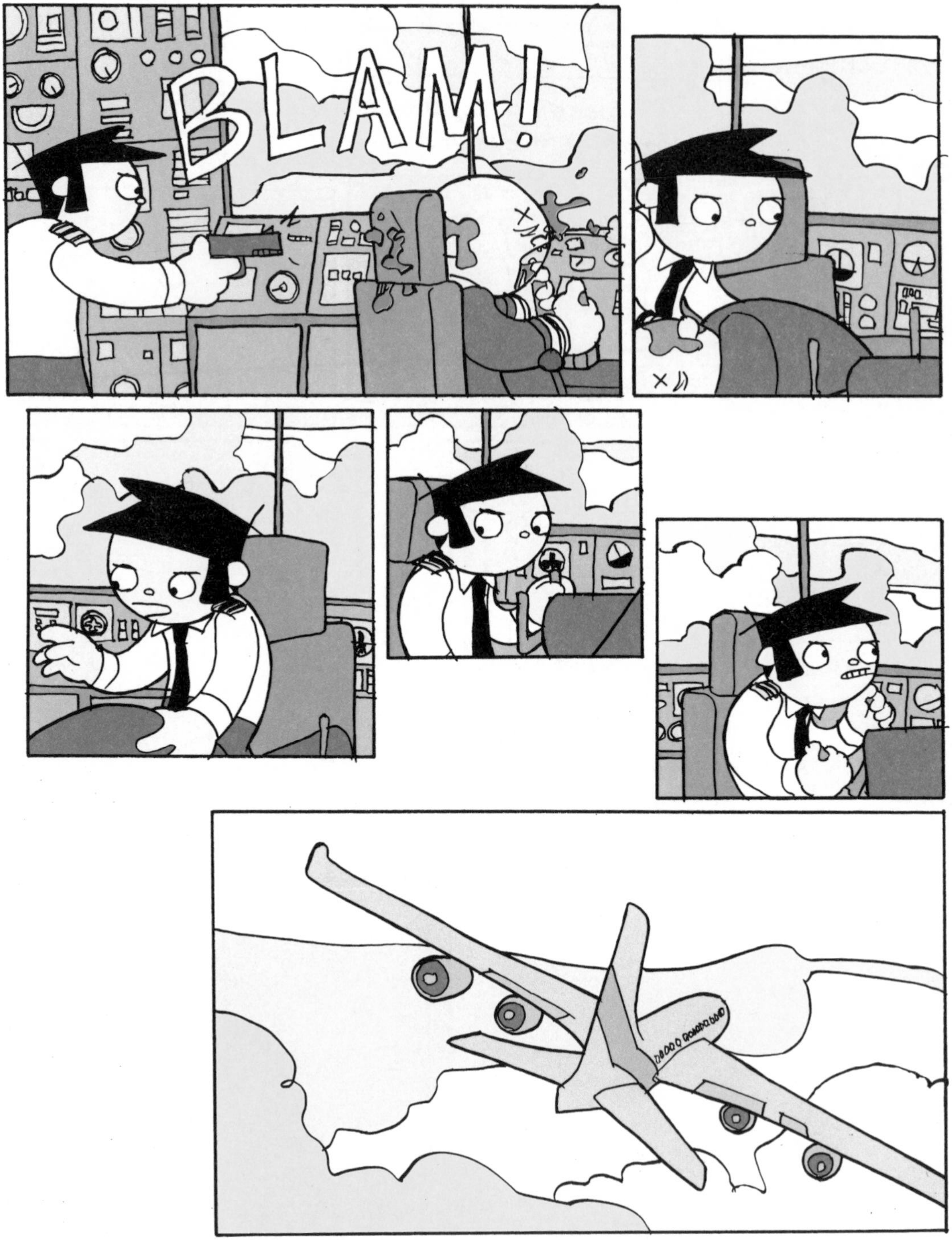
BLAM!

Weeeeeeee!

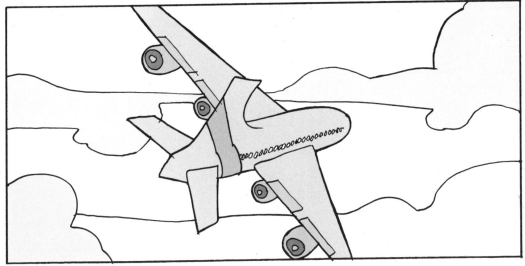

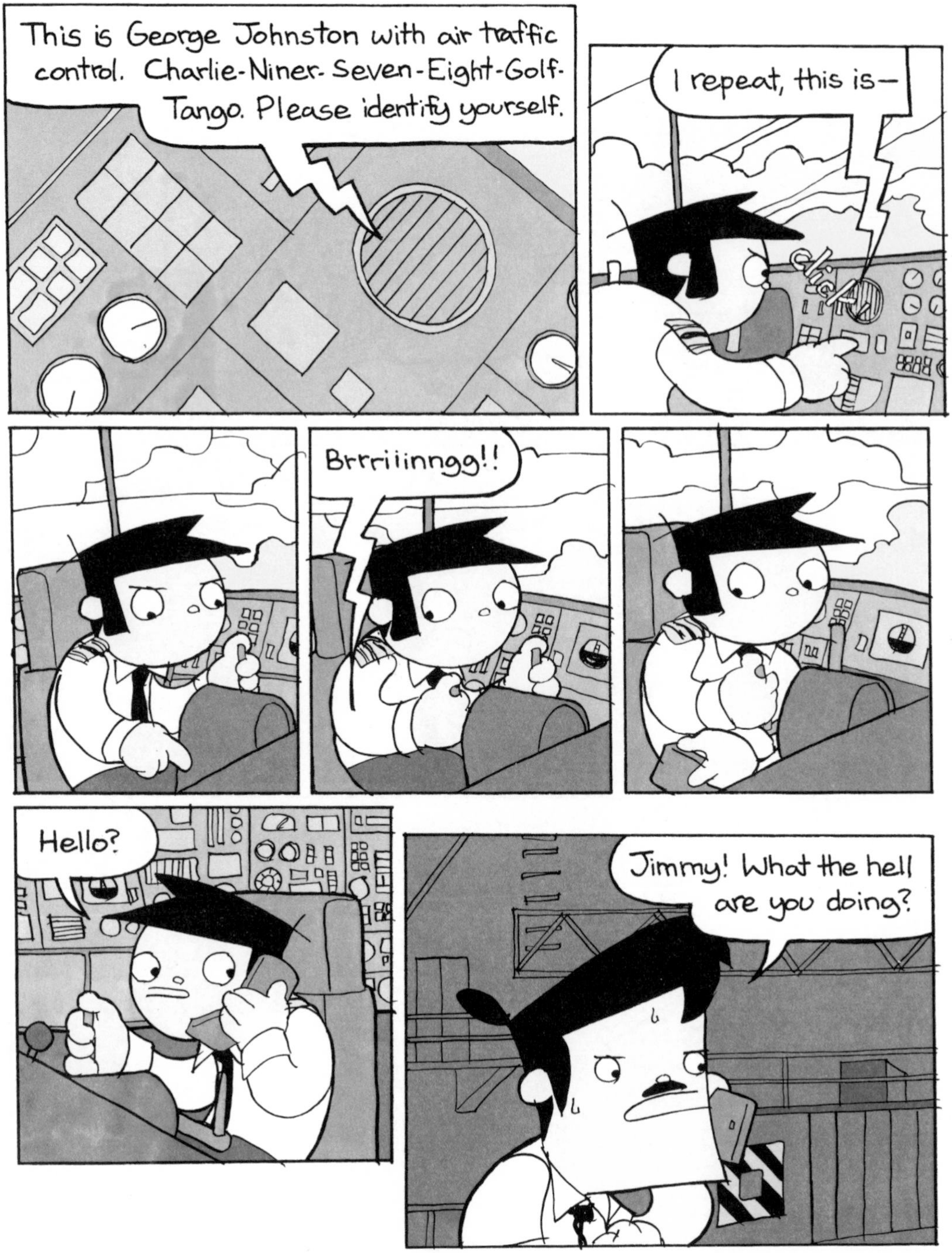
This is George Johnston with air traffic control. Charlie-Niner-Seven-Eight-Golf-Tango. Please identify yourself.
I repeat, this is—
Brrriiinngg!!
Hello?
Jimmy! What the hell are you doing?

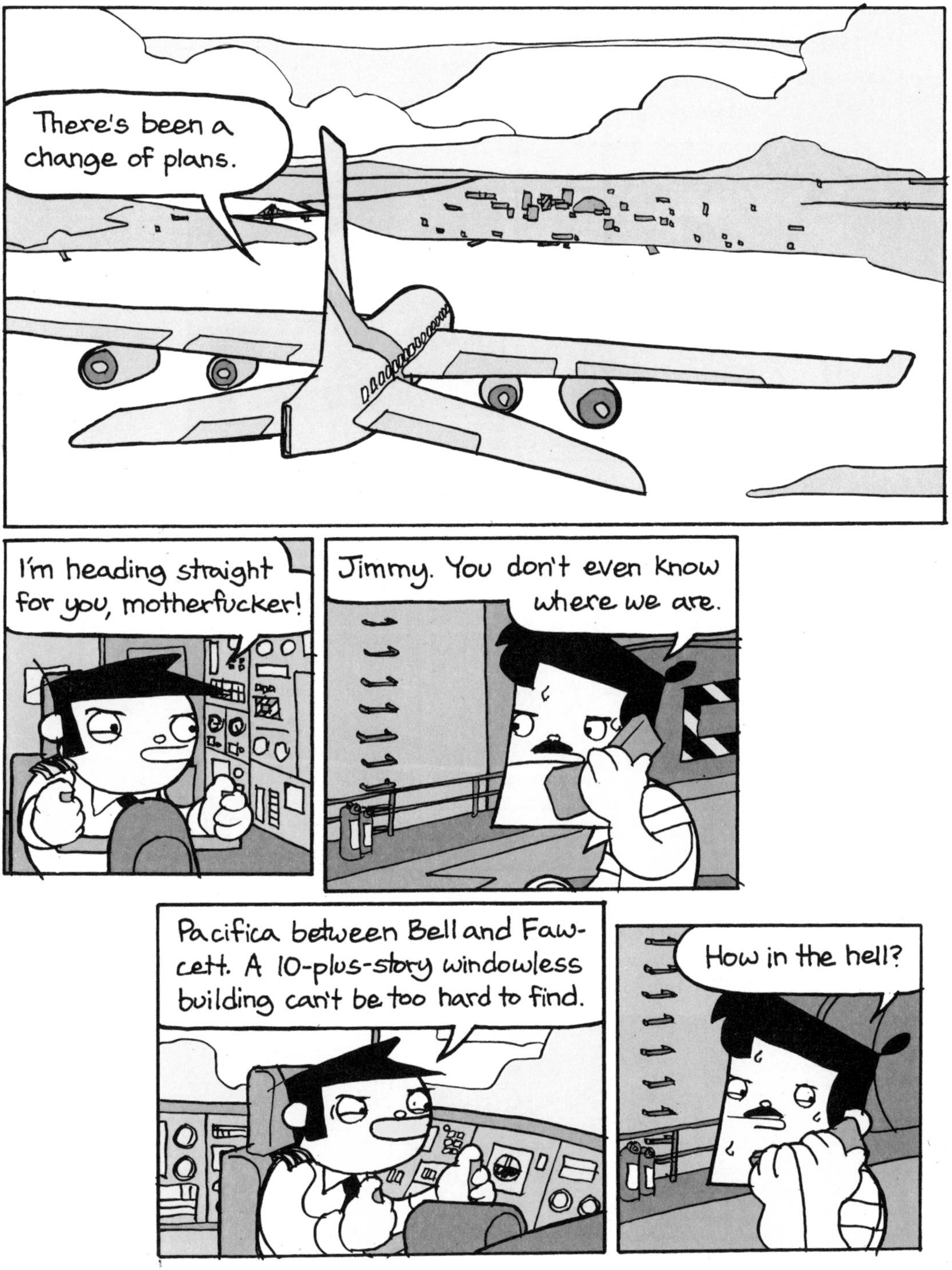
There's been a change of plans.
I'm heading straight for you, motherfucker!
Jimmy. You don't even know where we are.
Pacifica between Bell and Faw-cett. A 10-plus-story windowless building can't be too hard to find.
How in the hell?

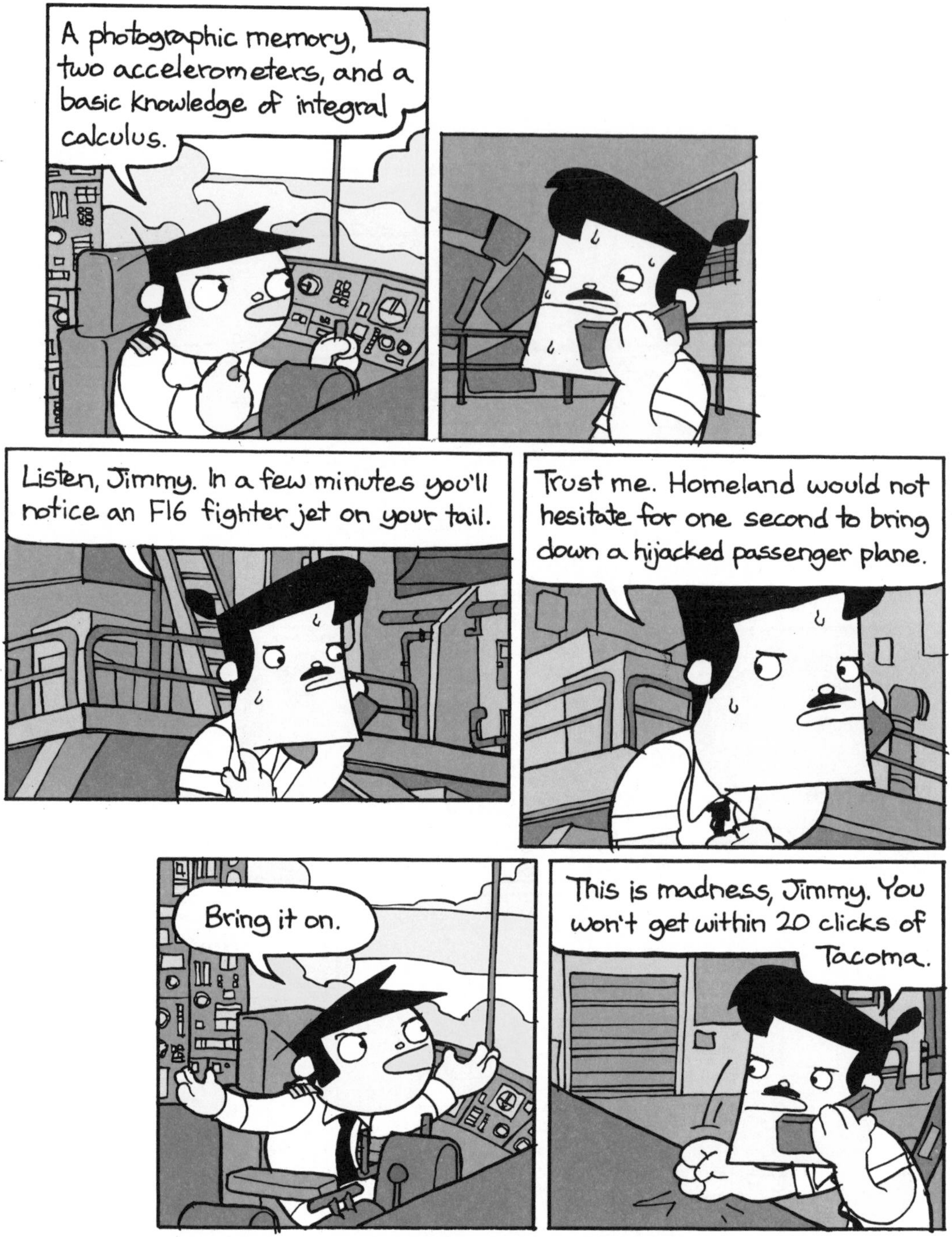
A photographic memory, two accelerometers, and a basic knowledge of integral calculus.
Listen, Jimmy. In a few minutes you'll notice an F16 fighter jet on your tail.
Trust me. Homeland would not hesitate for one second to bring down a hijacked passenger plane.
Bring it on.
This is madness, Jimmy. You won't get within 20 clicks of Tacoma.

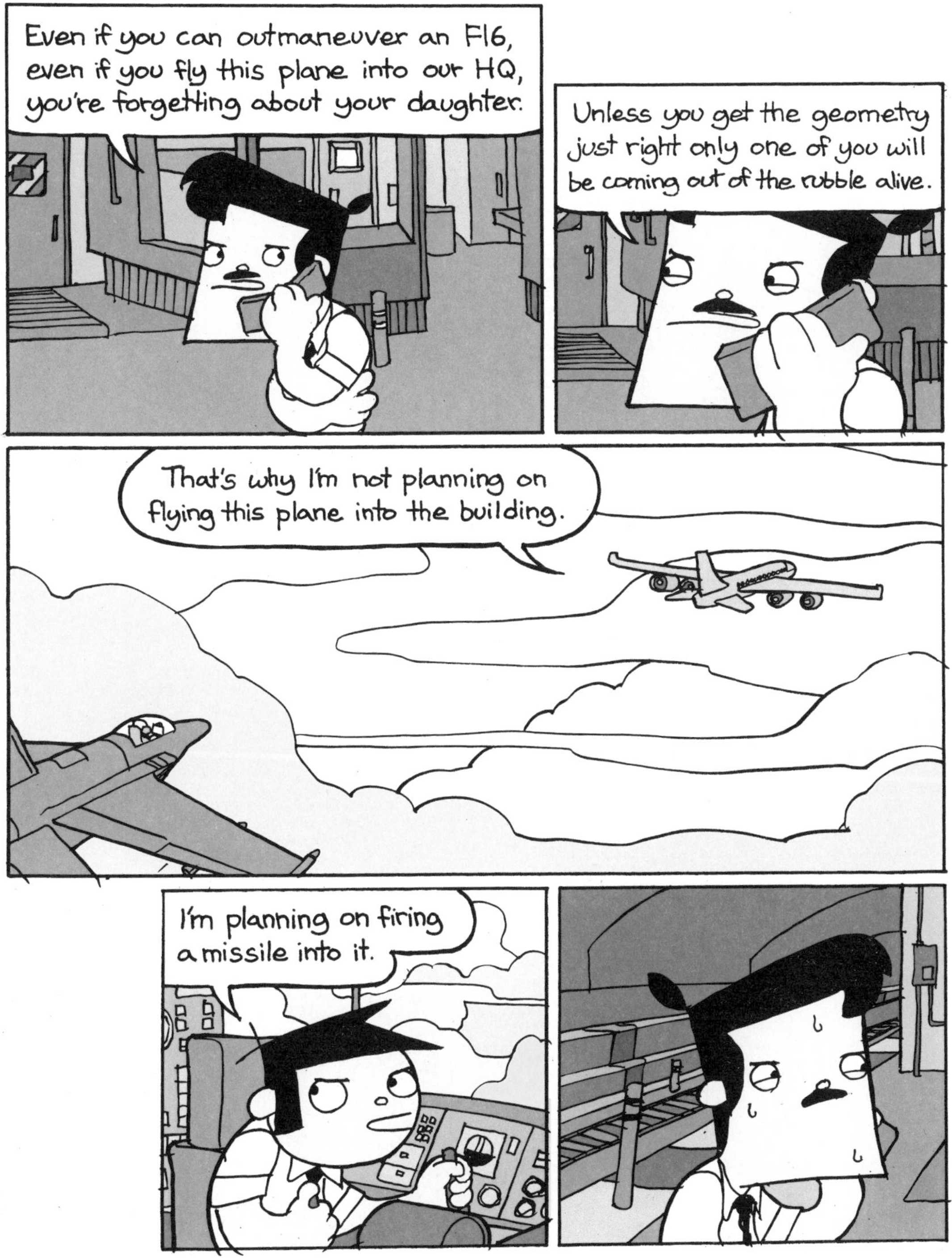
Even if you can outmaneuver an F16, even if you fly this plane into our HQ, you're forgetting about your daughter.
Unless you get the geometry just right only one of you will be coming out of the rubble alive.
That's why I'm not planning on flying this plane into the building.
I'm planning on firing a missile into it.

Jimmy, listen to me. Hello?

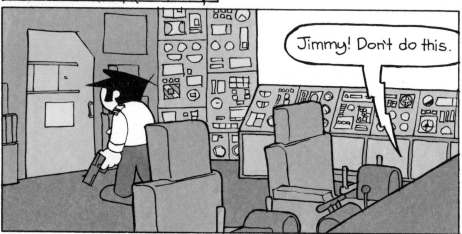

Jimmy! Don't do this.

Captain?

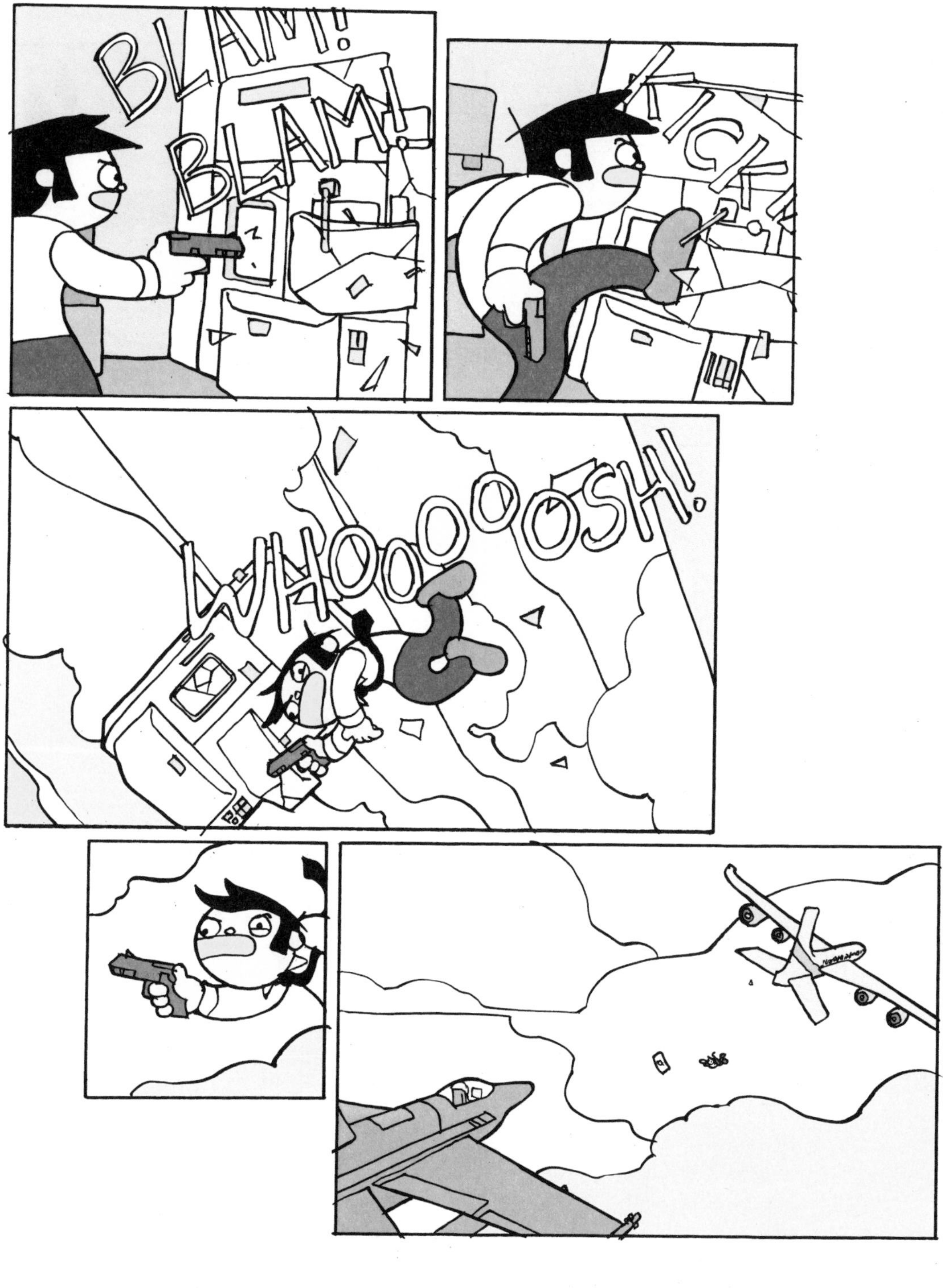
BLAM!
BLAM!
WHOOOOOSH!

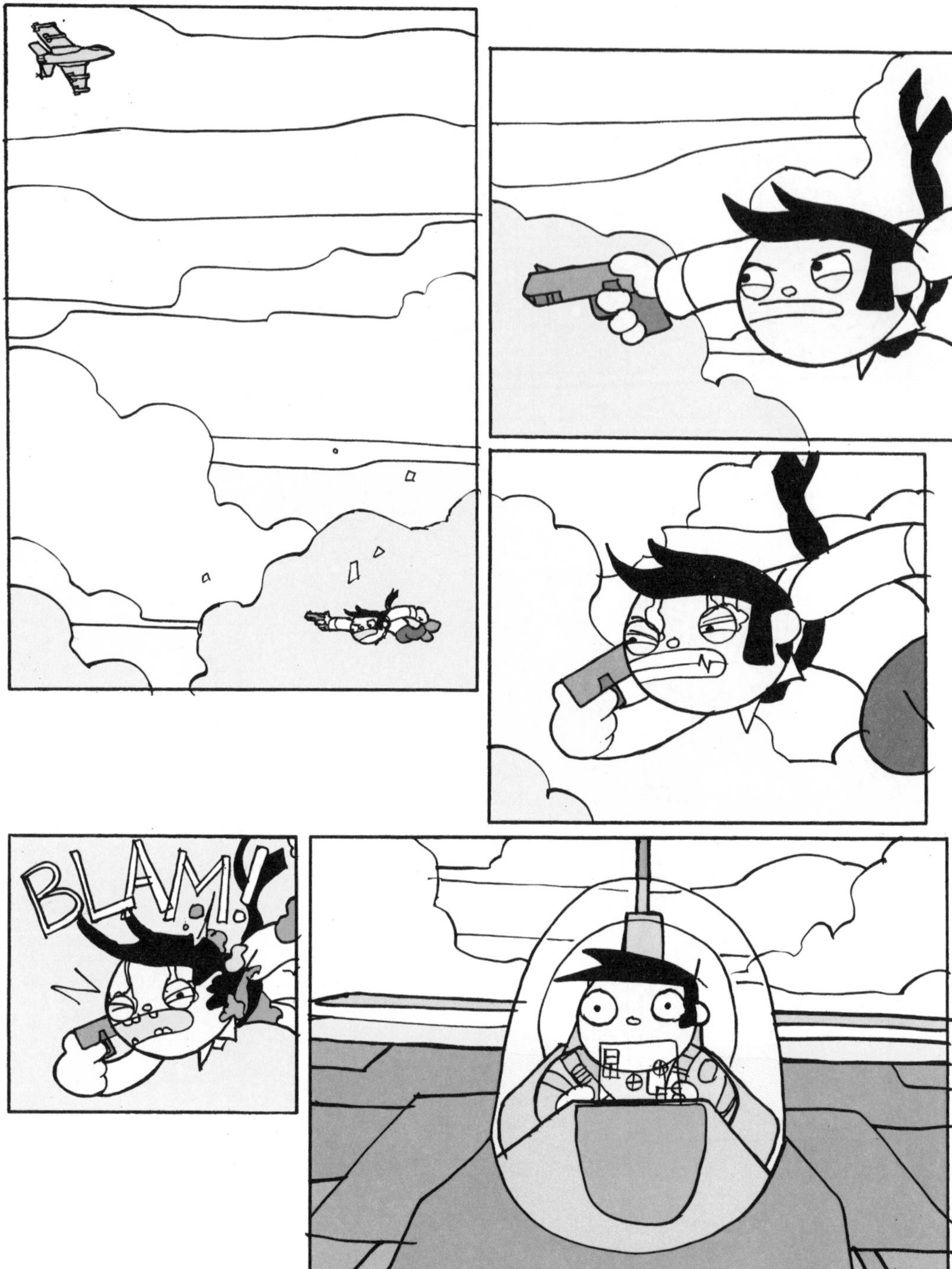
BLAM!

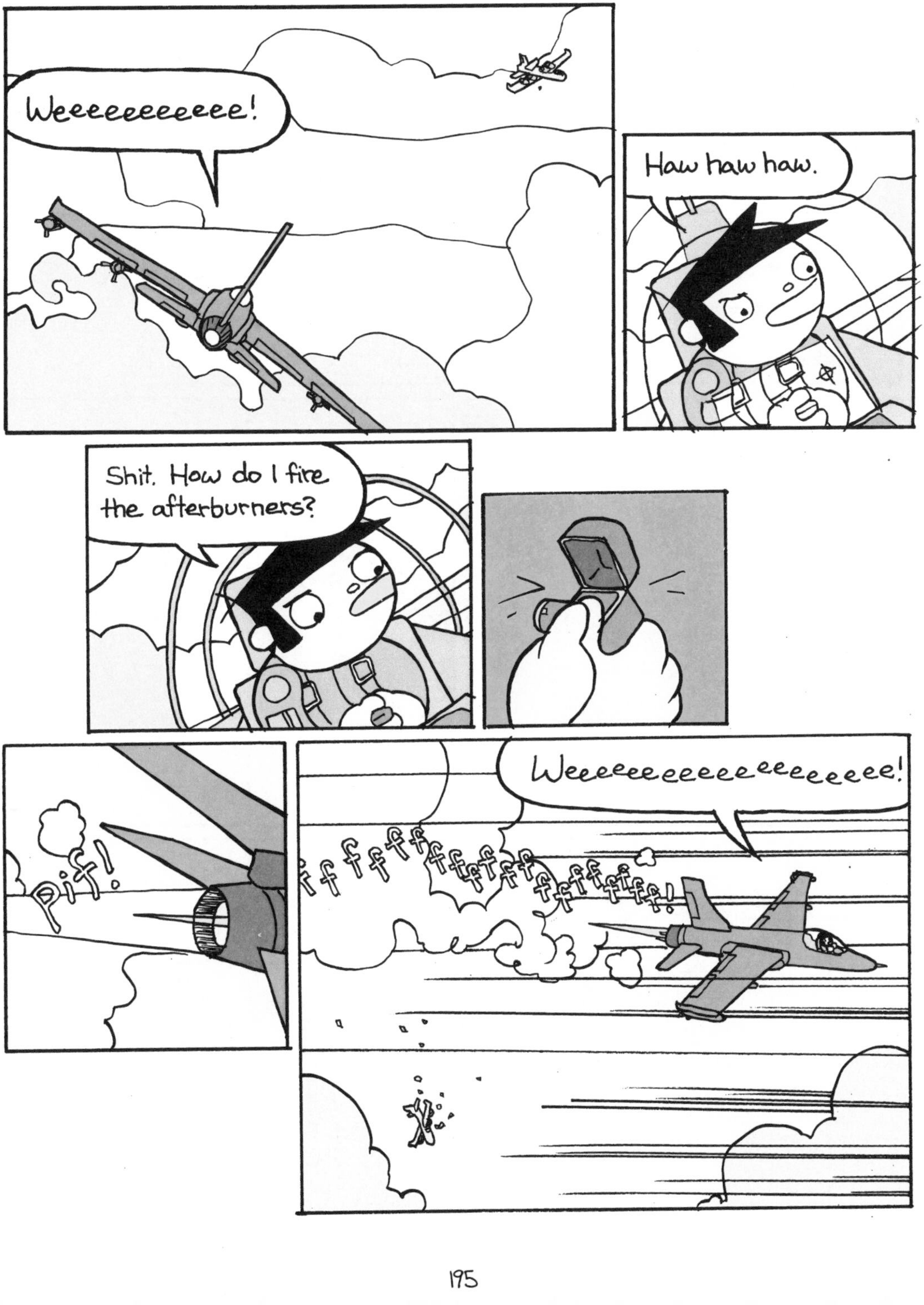
Weeeeeeeeeee!
Haw haw haw.
Shit. How do I fire the afterburners?
pif!
Weeeeeeeeeeeeeeeeee!
ffffffffffffffffffffff!

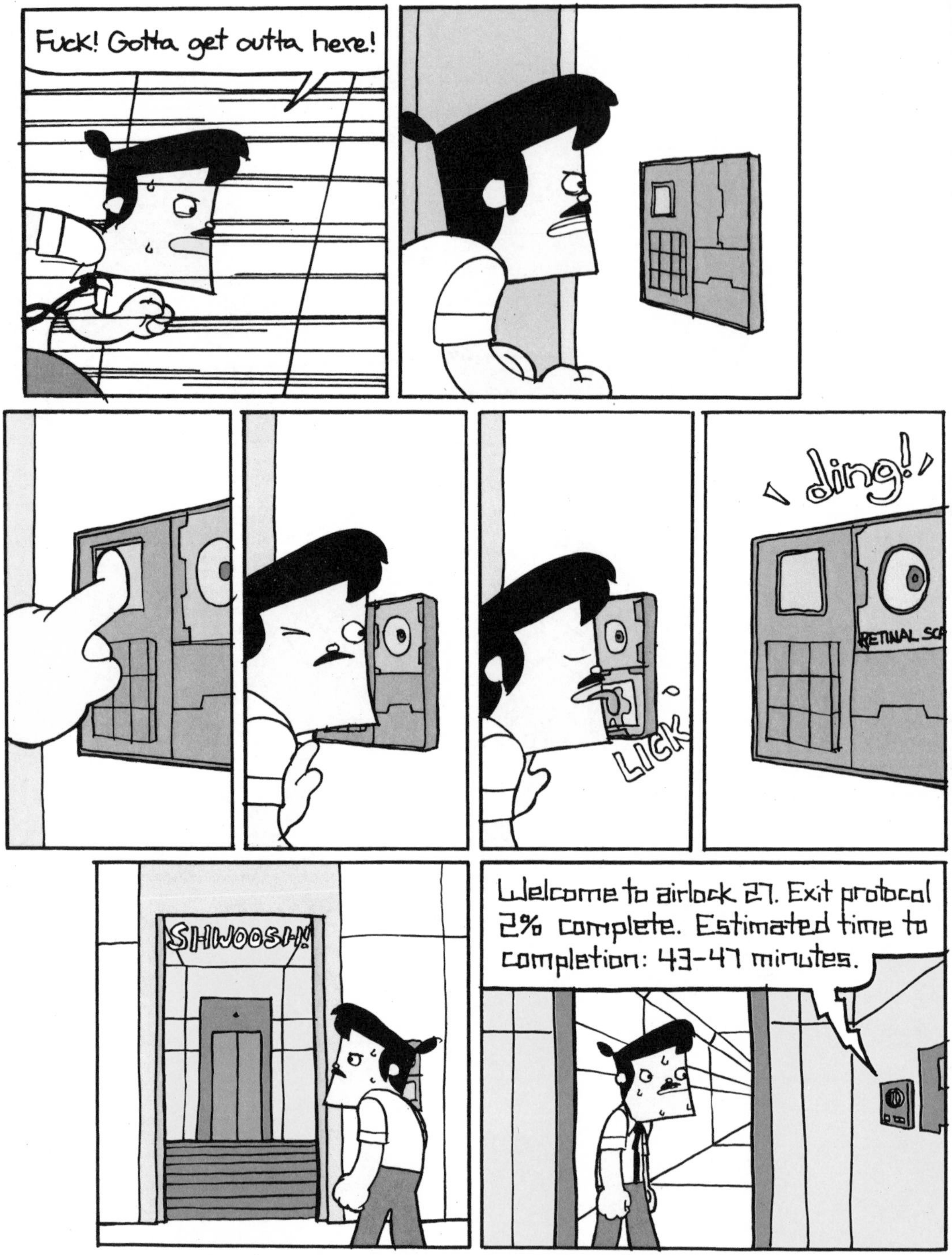
Fuck! Gotta get outta here!
ding!
LICK
SHWOOSH!
Welcome to airlock 27. Exit protocol 2% complete. Estimated time to completion: 43-47 minutes.

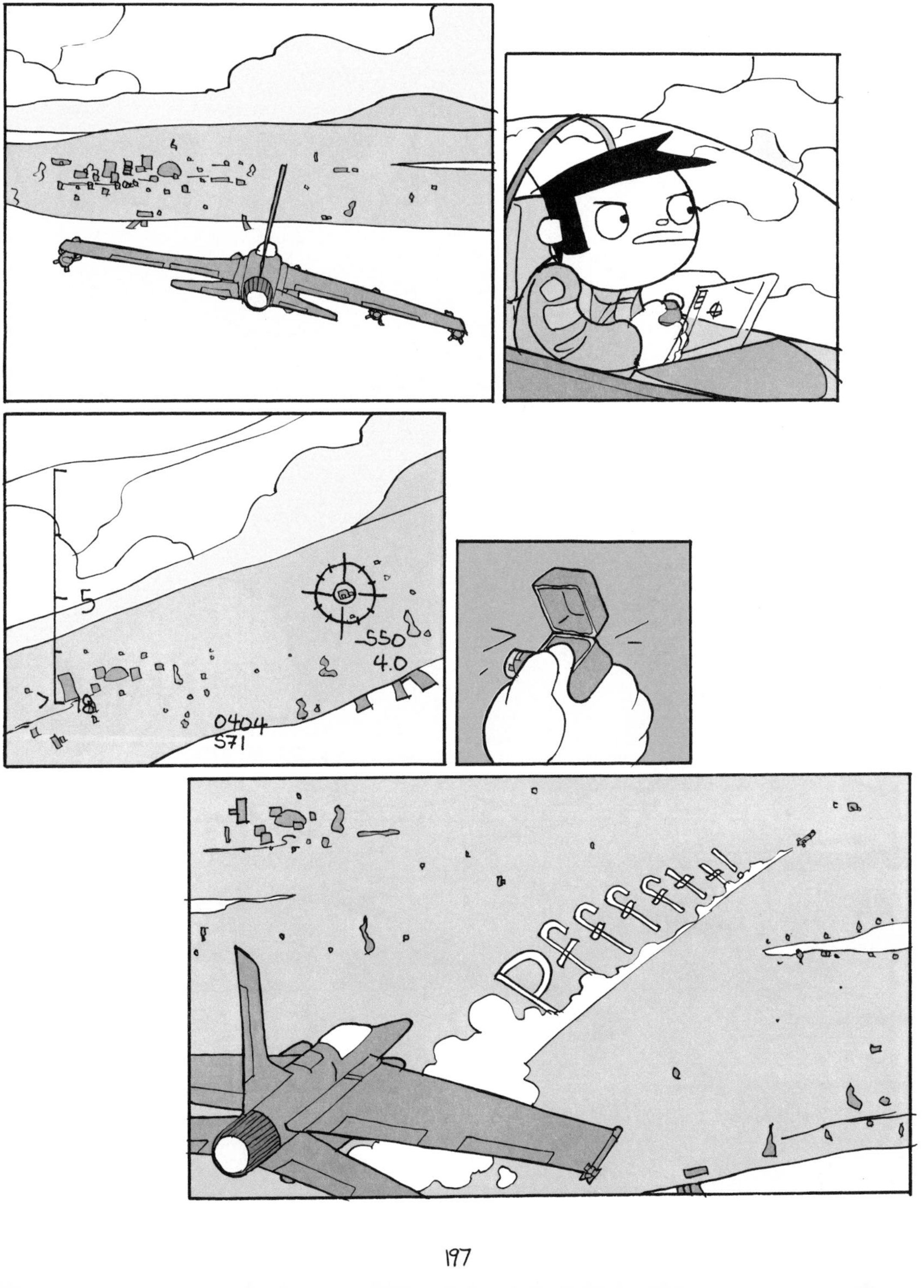

5
550
4.0
0404
571
Pfffftt!

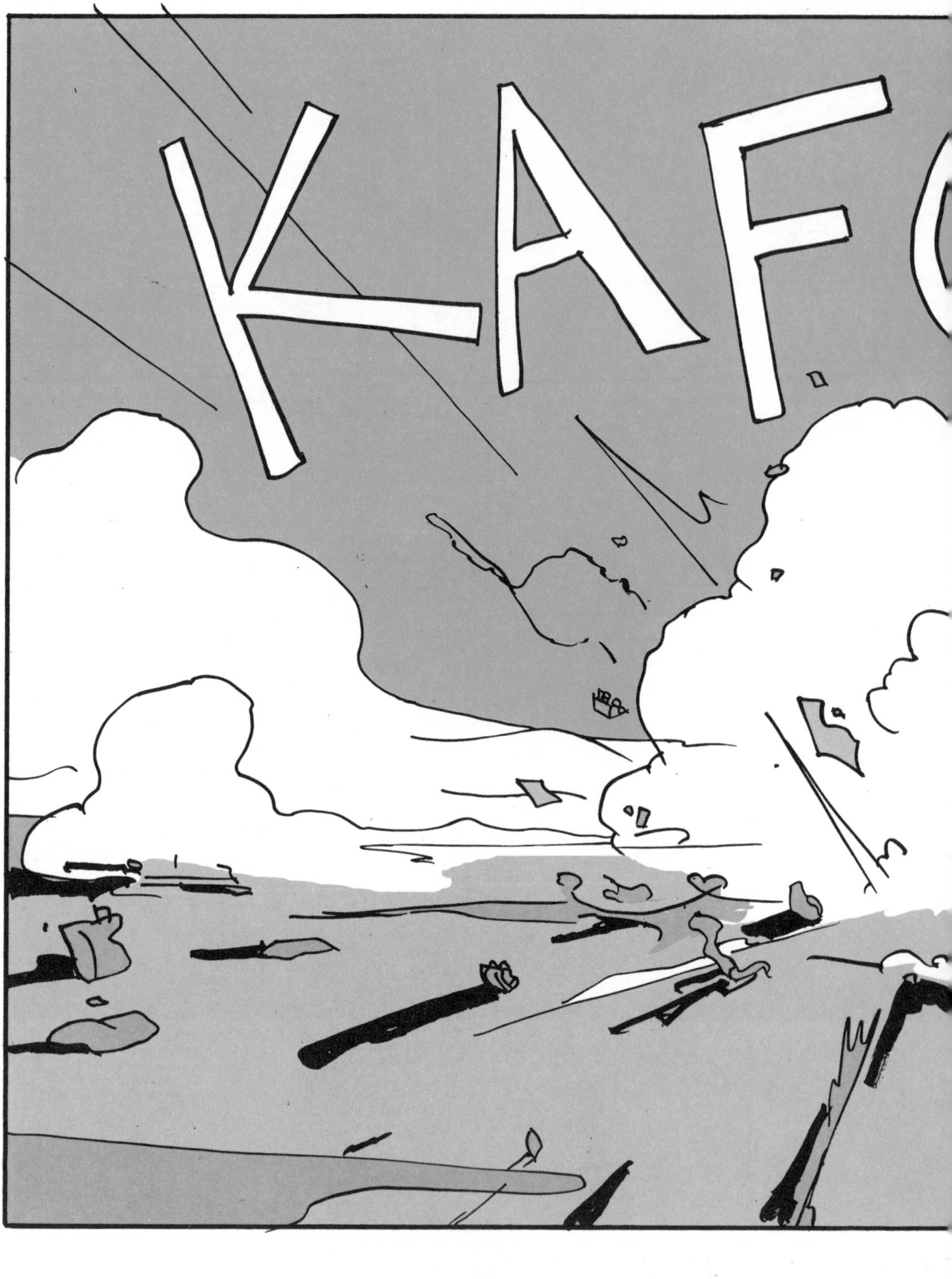
KAF

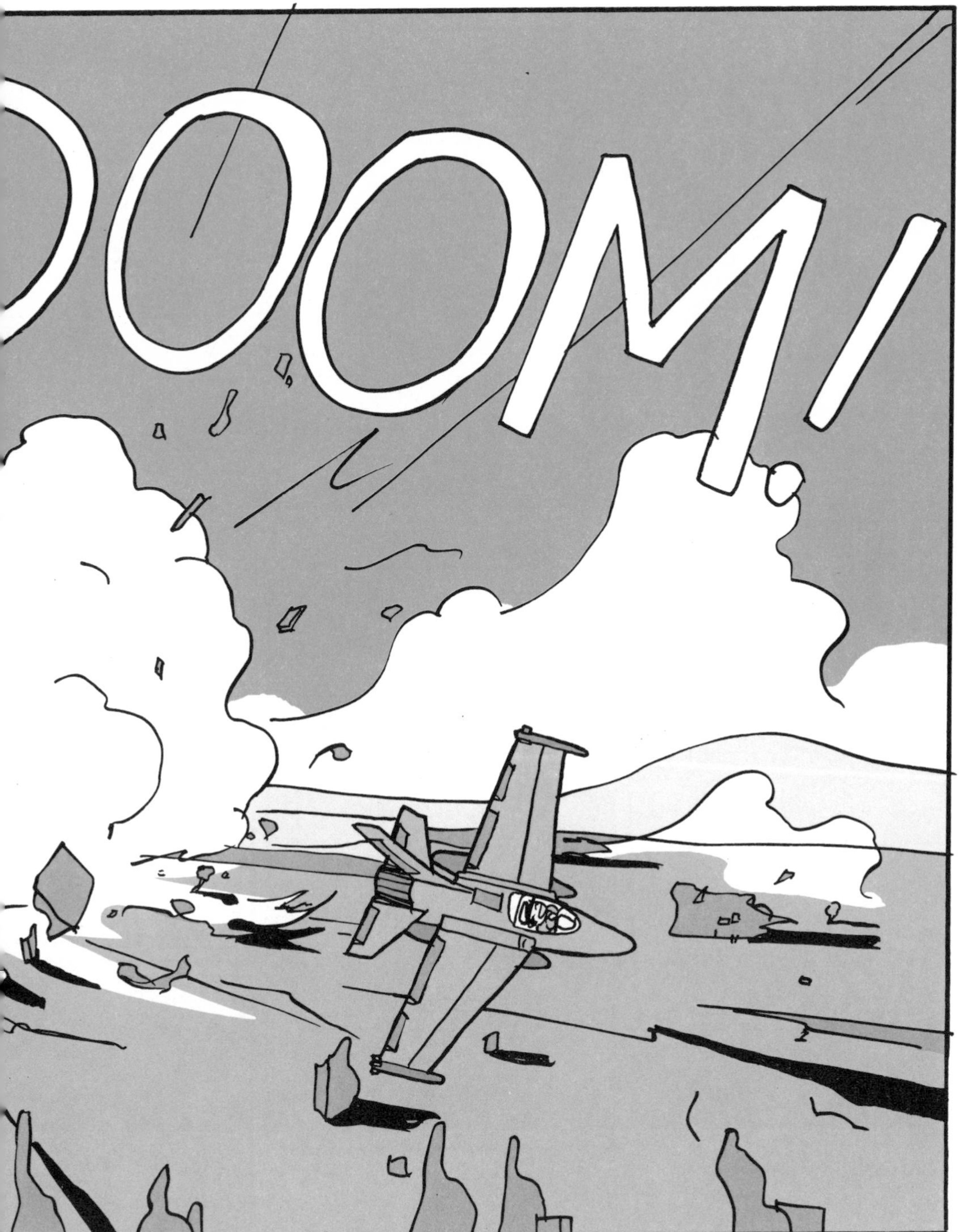
OOOM!

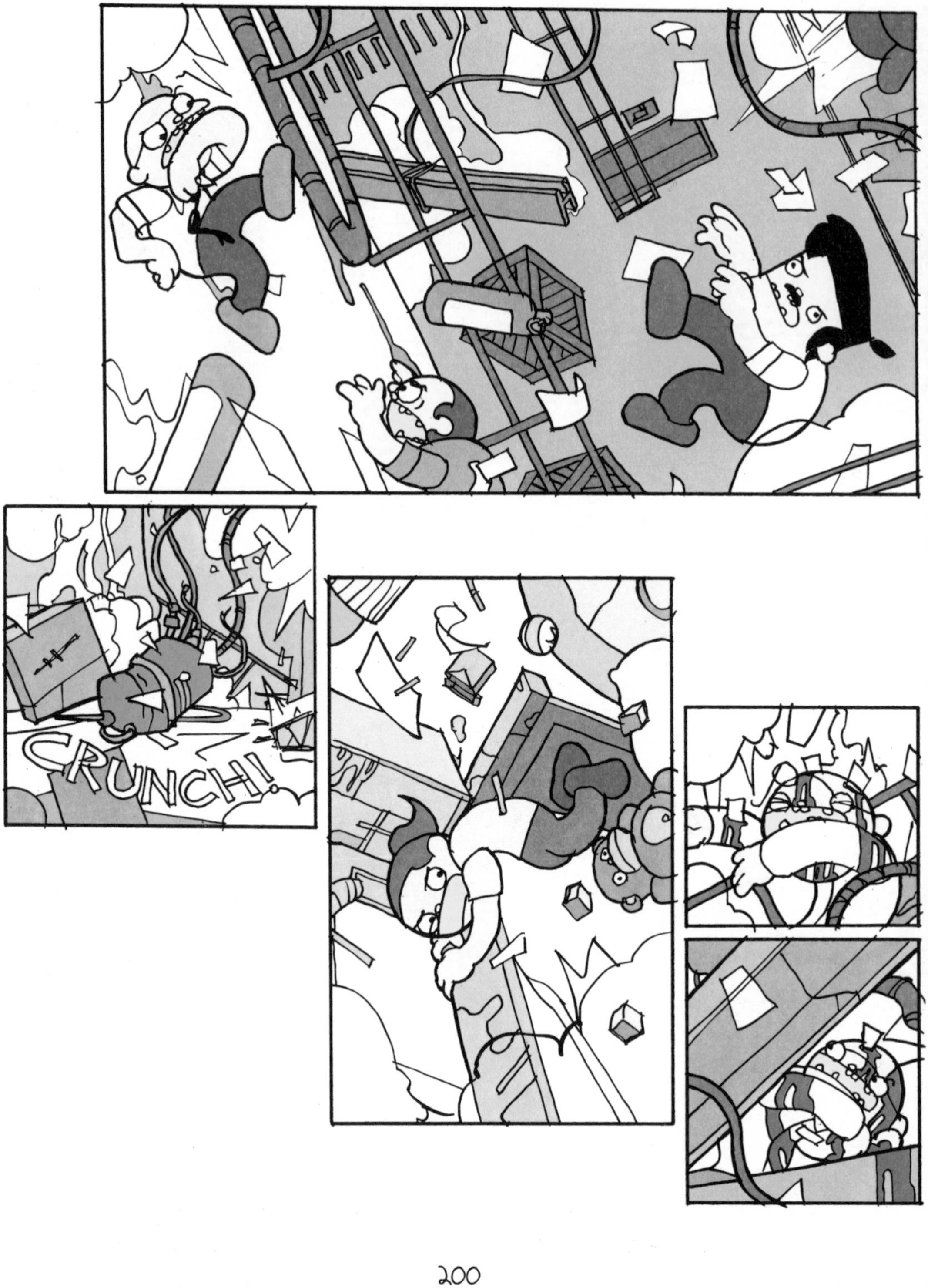
CRUNCH!

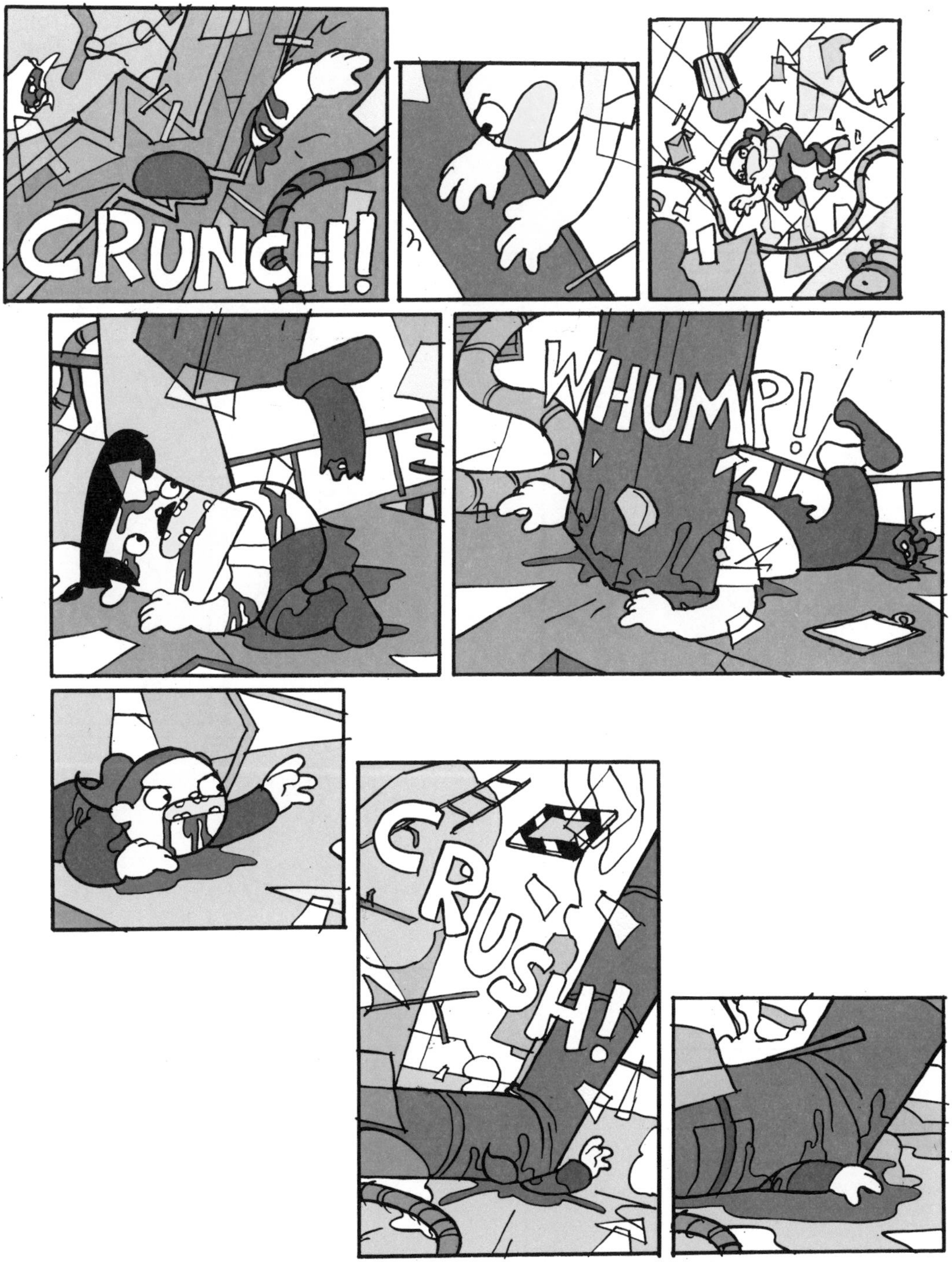
CRUNCH!
WHUMP!
CRUSH!

PEWW!!
POOF!

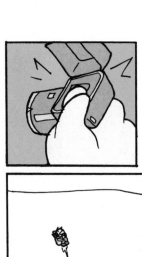

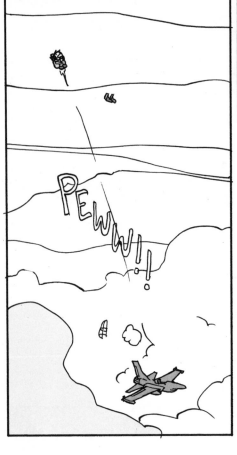

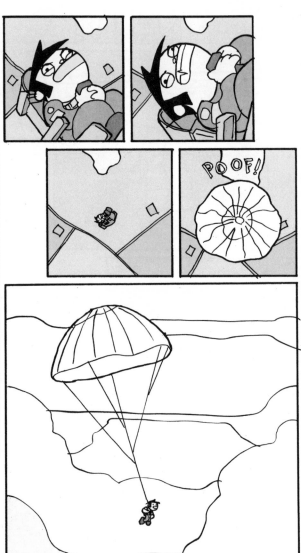

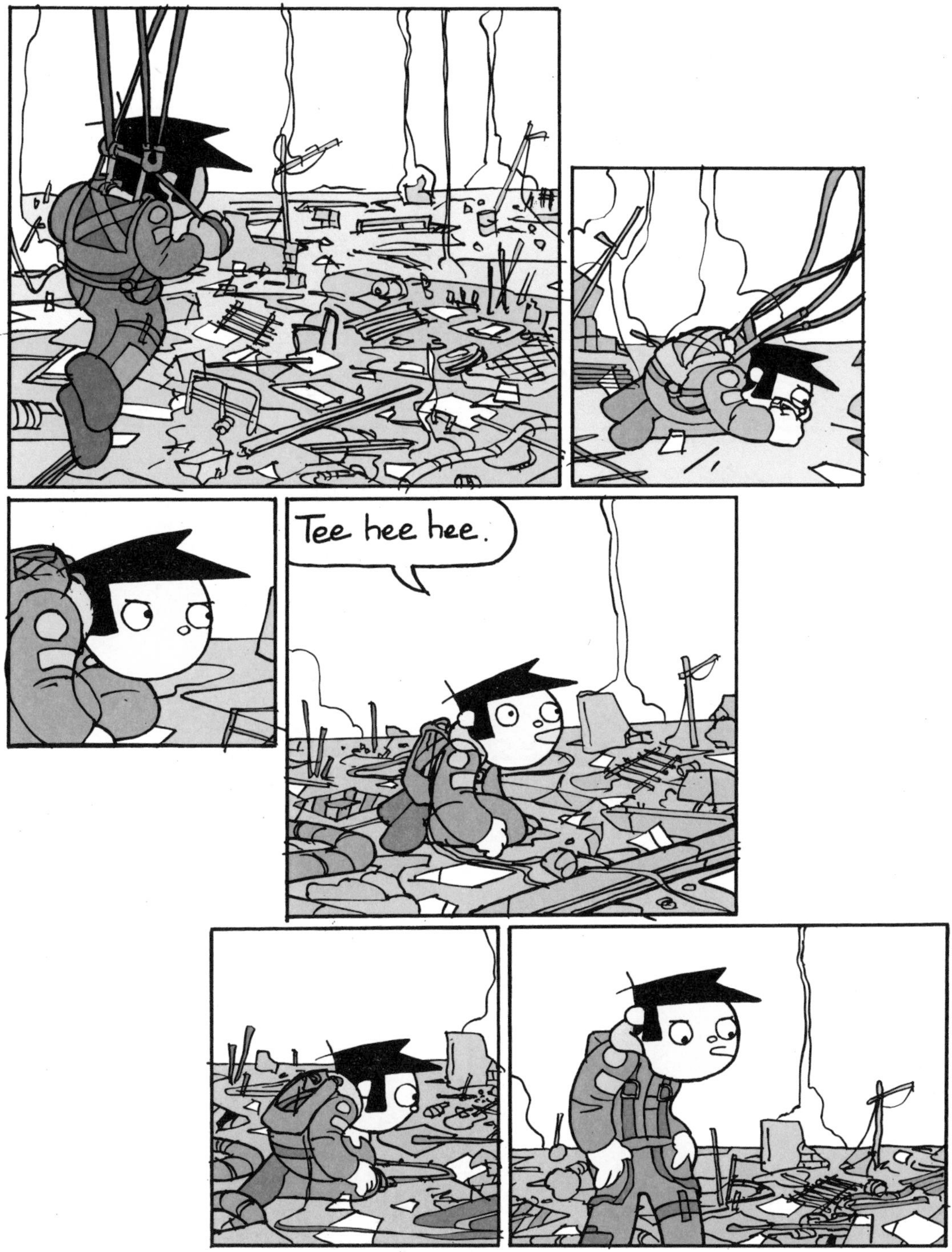
Tee hee hee.

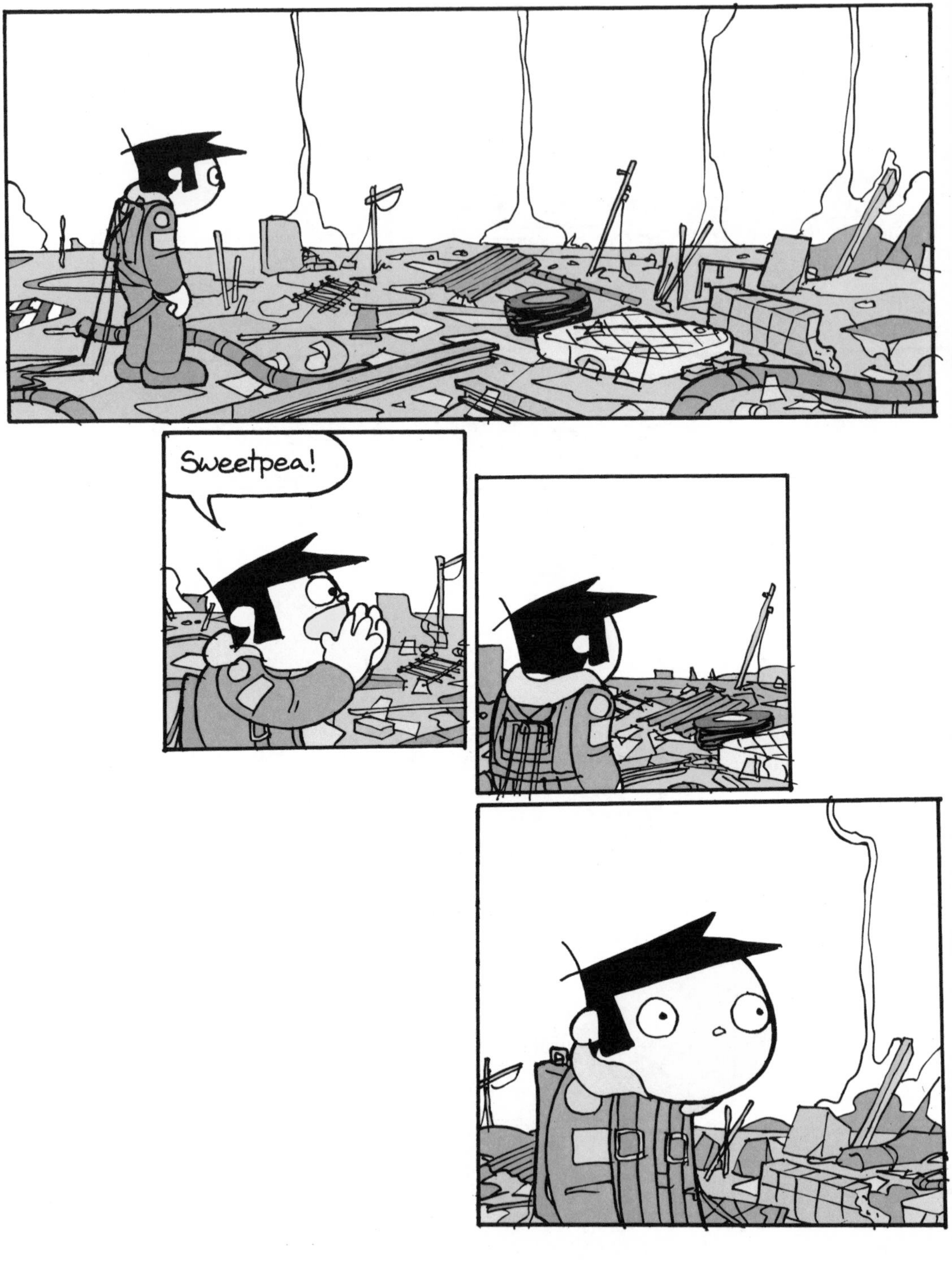
Sweetpea!

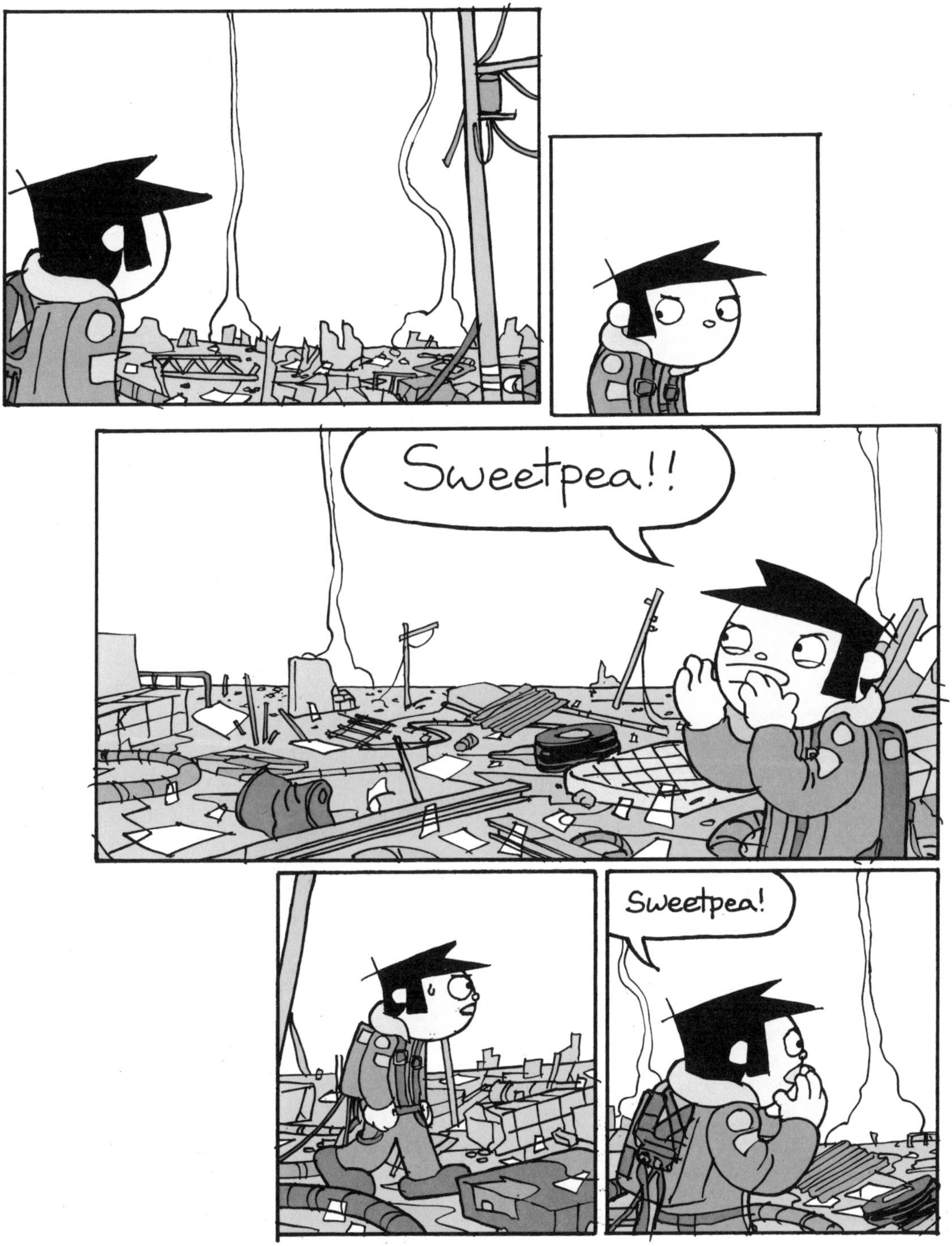
Sweetpea!!
Sweetpea!

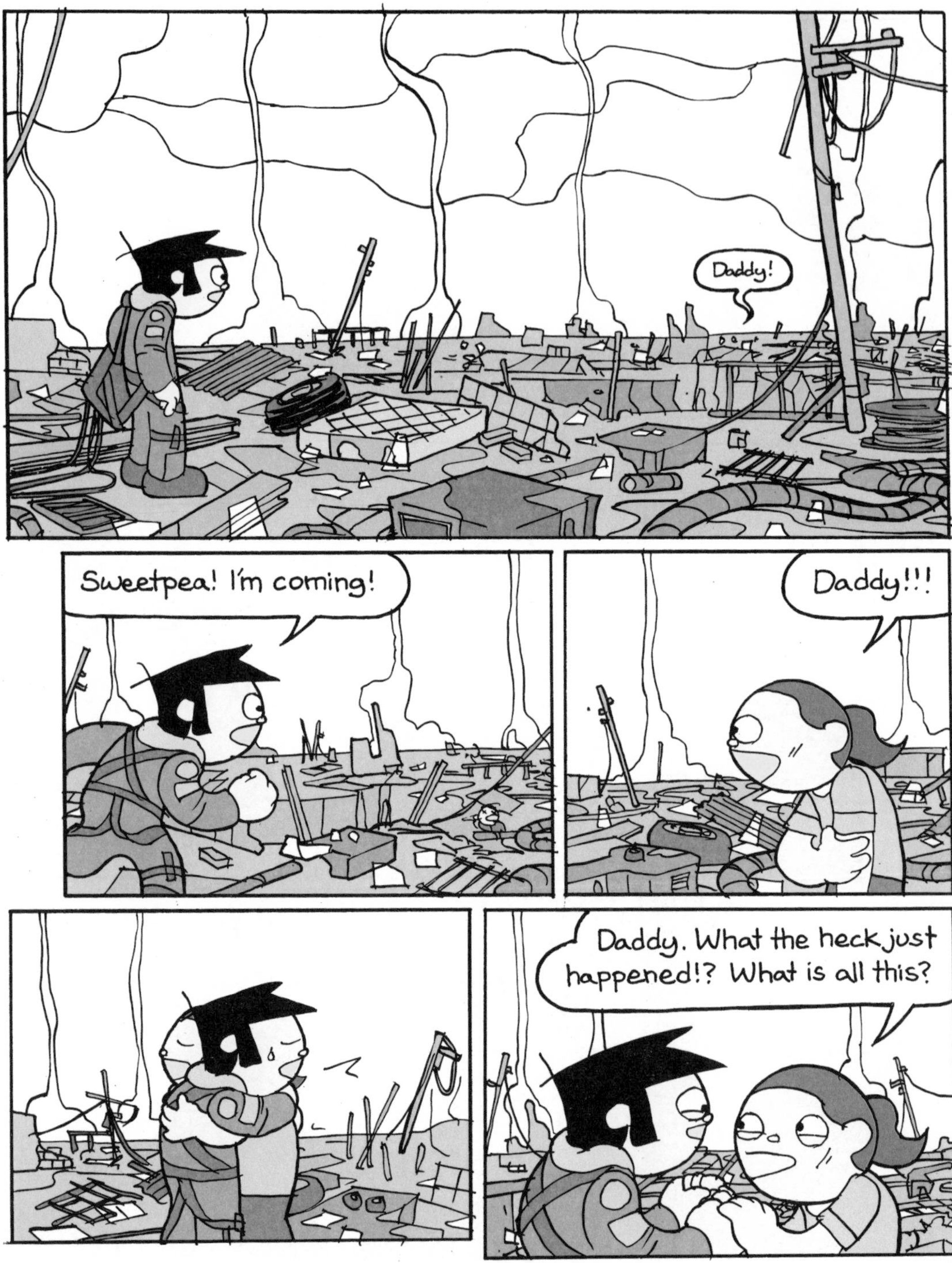
Daddy!
Sweetpea! I'm coming!
Daddy!!!
Daddy. What the heck just happened!? What is all this?

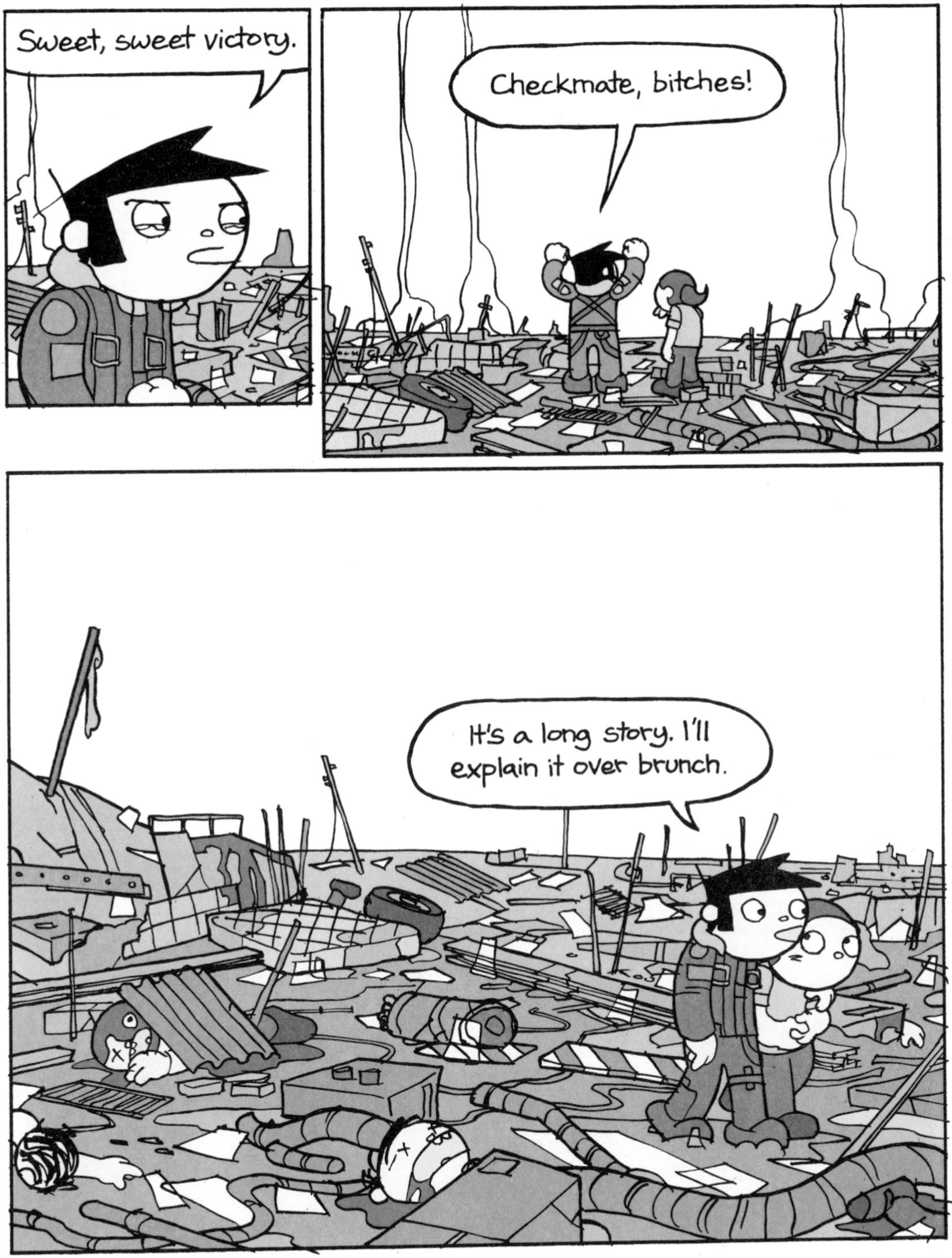
Sweet, sweet victory.
Checkmate, bitches!
It's a long story. I'll explain it over brunch.

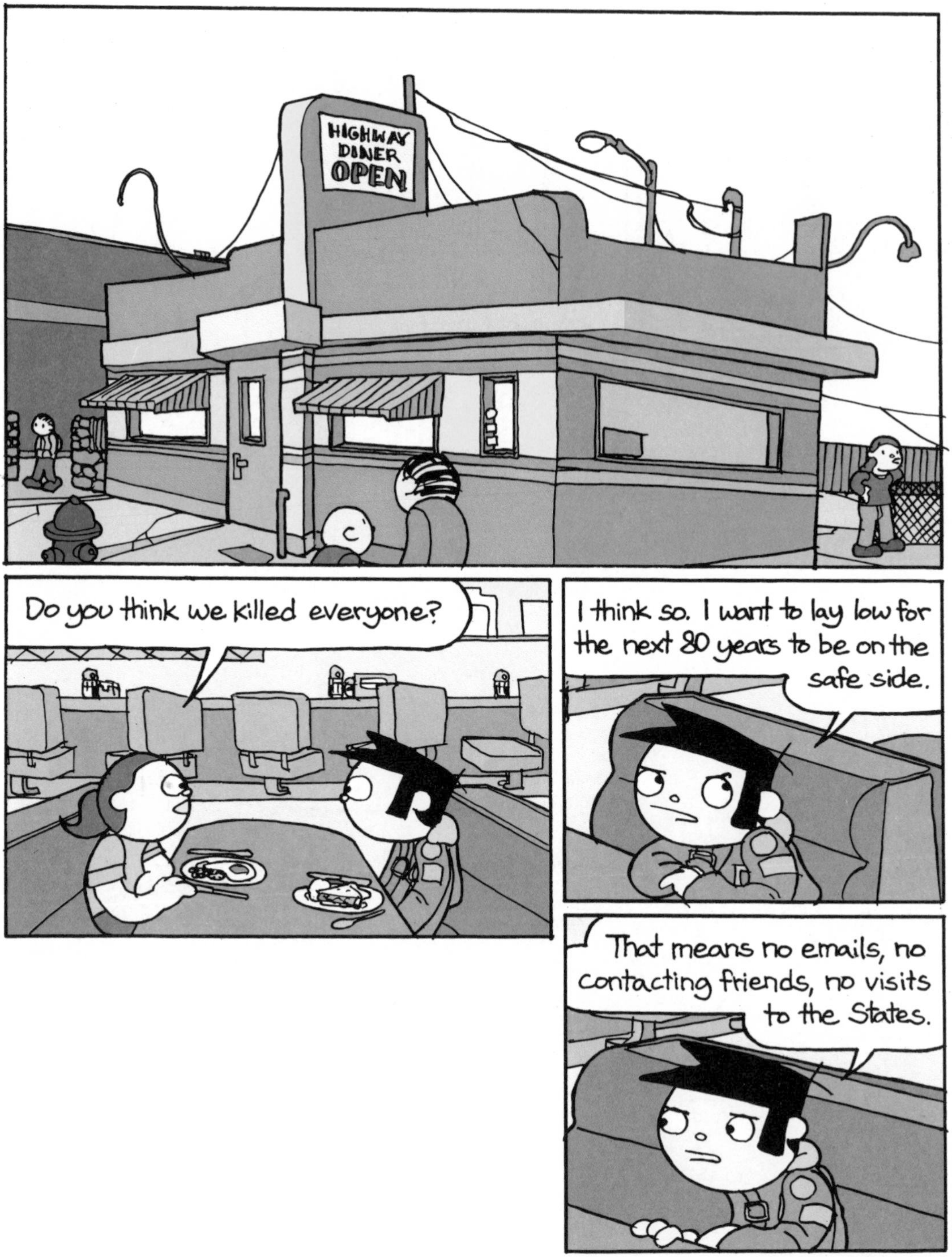
HIGHWAY DINER OPEN
Do you think we killed everyone?
I think so. I want to lay low for the next 80 years to be on the safe side.
That means no emails, no contacting friends, no visits to the States.

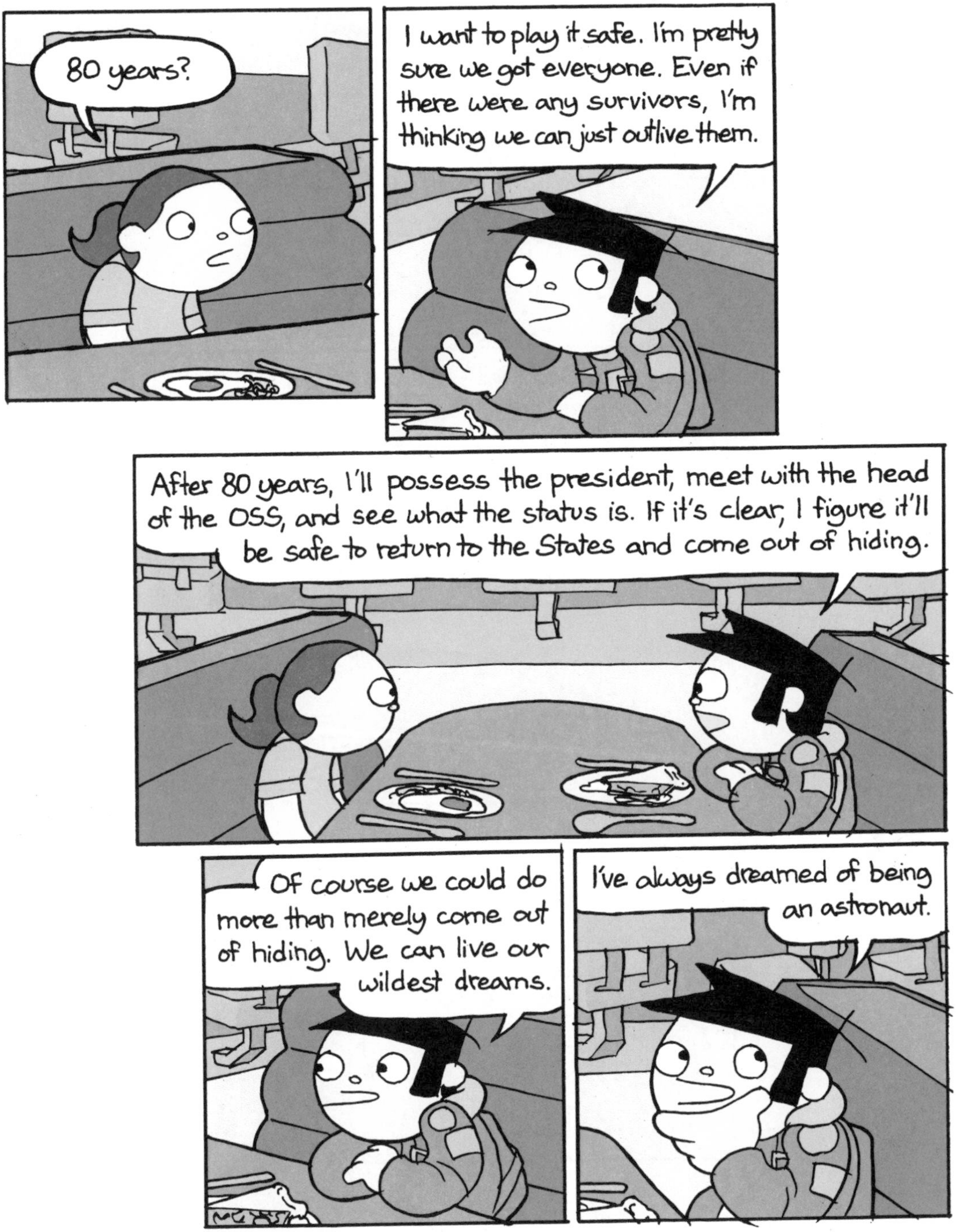
80 years?
I want to play it safe. I'm pretty sure we got everyone. Even if there were any survivors, I'm thinking we can just outlive them.
After 80 years, I'll possess the president, meet with the head of the OSS, and see what the status is. If it's clear, I figure it'll be safe to return to the States and come out of hiding.
Of course we could do more than merely come out of hiding. We can live our wildest dreams.
I've always dreamed of being an astronaut.

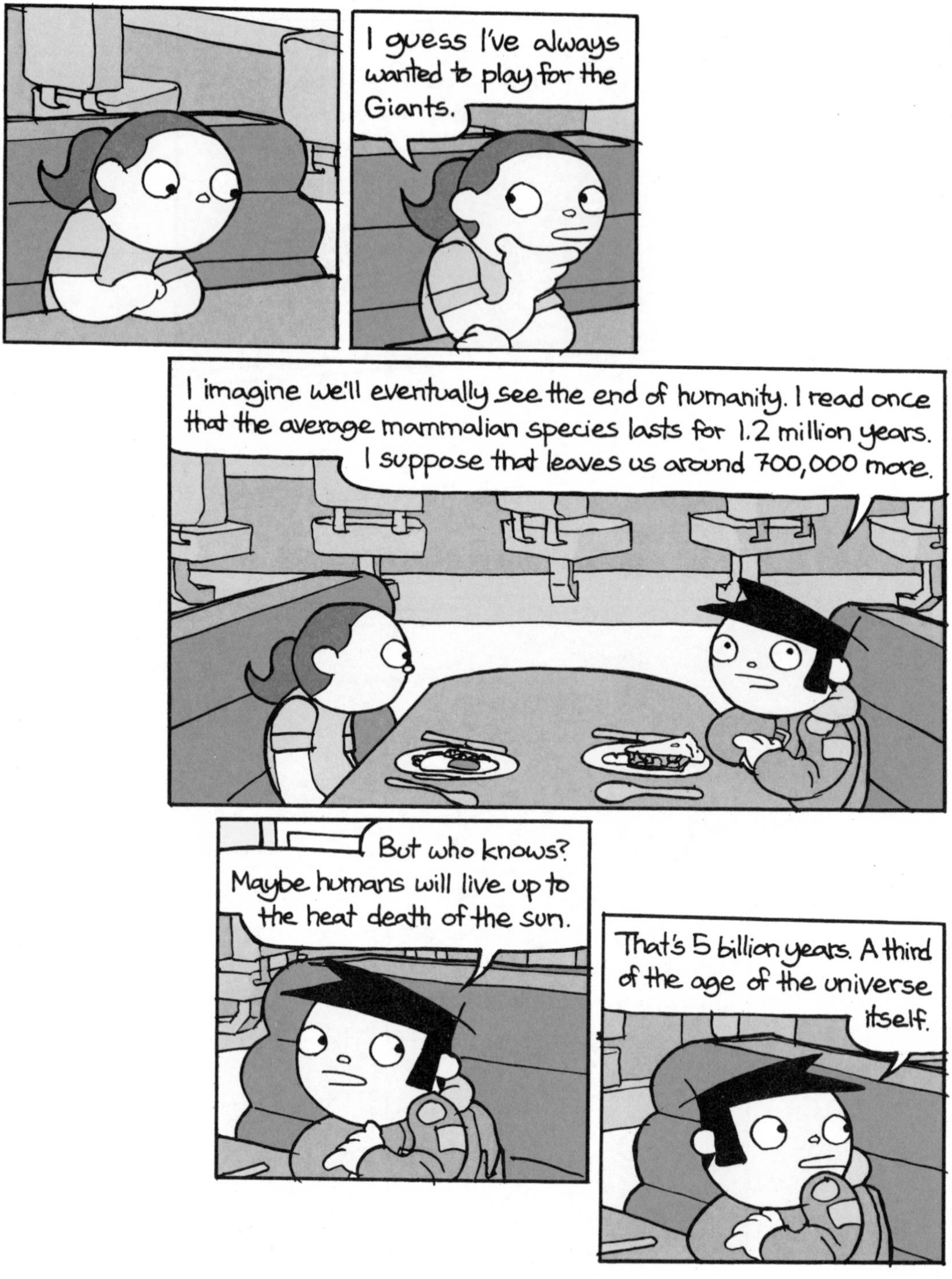
I guess I've always wanted to play for the Giants.
I imagine we'll eventually see the end of humanity. I read once that the average mammalian species lasts for 1.2 million years. I suppose that leaves us around 700,000 more.
But who knows? Maybe humans will live up to the heat death of the sun.
That's 5 billion years. A third of the age of the universe itself.

We don't have to decide right now, but one of us will die and the other will find out if there's humans elsewhere in the universe.

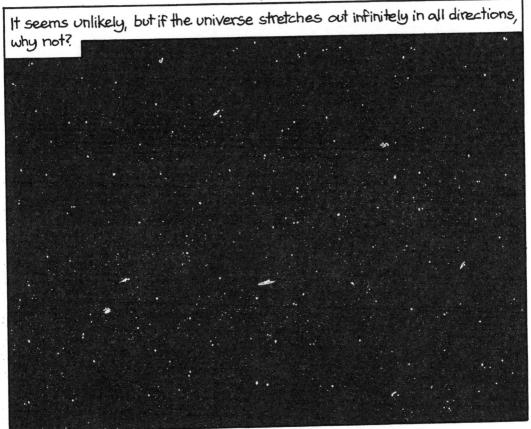

It seems unlikely, but if the universe stretches out infinitely in all directions, why not?

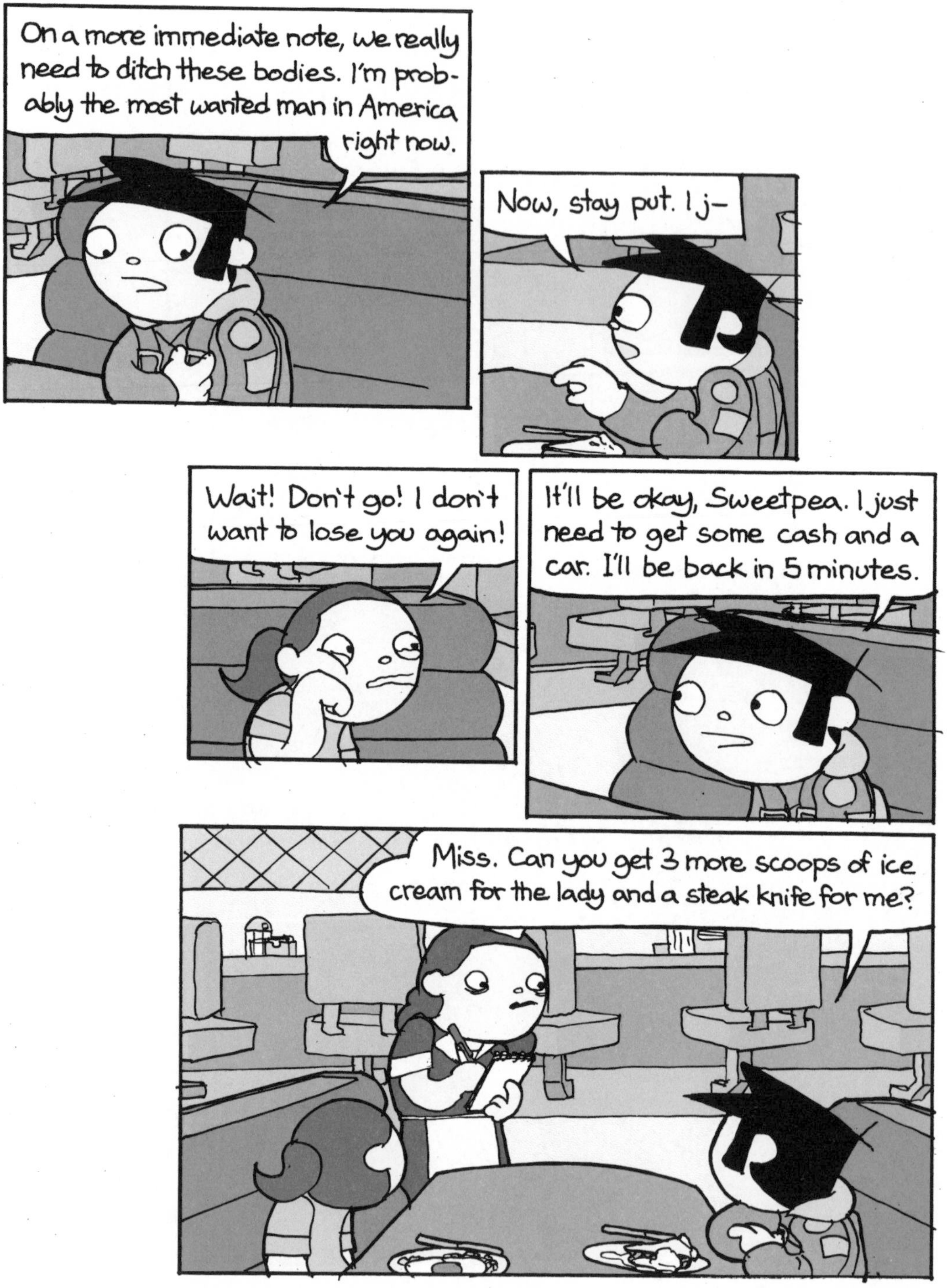
On a more immediate note, we really need to ditch these bodies. I'm probably the most wanted man in America right now.
Now, stay put. I j–
Wait! Don't go! I don't want to lose you again!
It'll be okay, Sweetpea. I just need to get some cash and a car. I'll be back in 5 minutes.
Miss. Can you get 3 more scoops of ice cream for the lady and a steak knife for me?

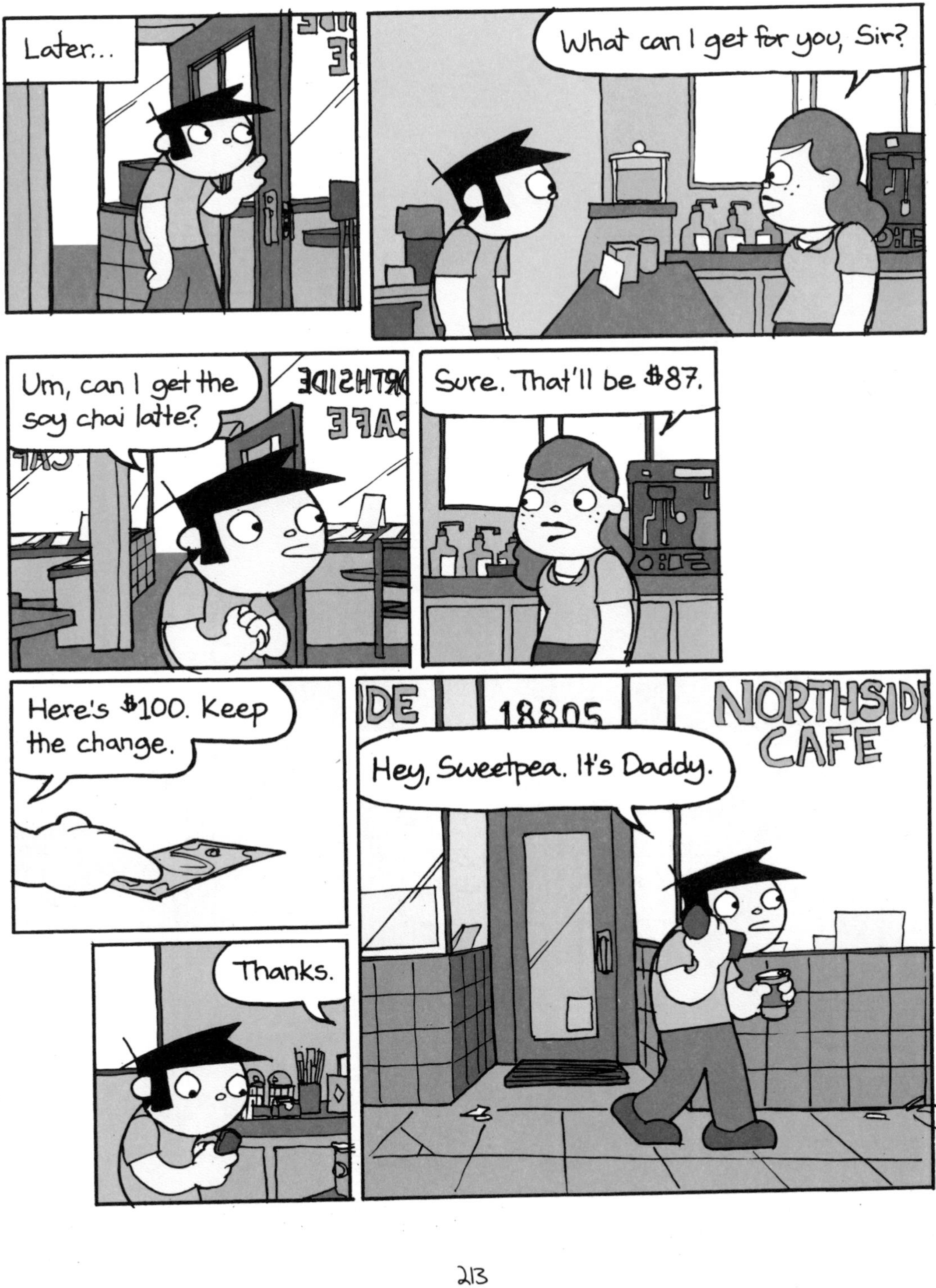
Later...
What can I get for you, Sir?
Um, can I get the soy chai latte?
Sure. That'll be $87.
Here's $100. Keep the change.
Thanks.
NORTHSIDE CAFE
18805
Hey, Sweetpea. It's Daddy.

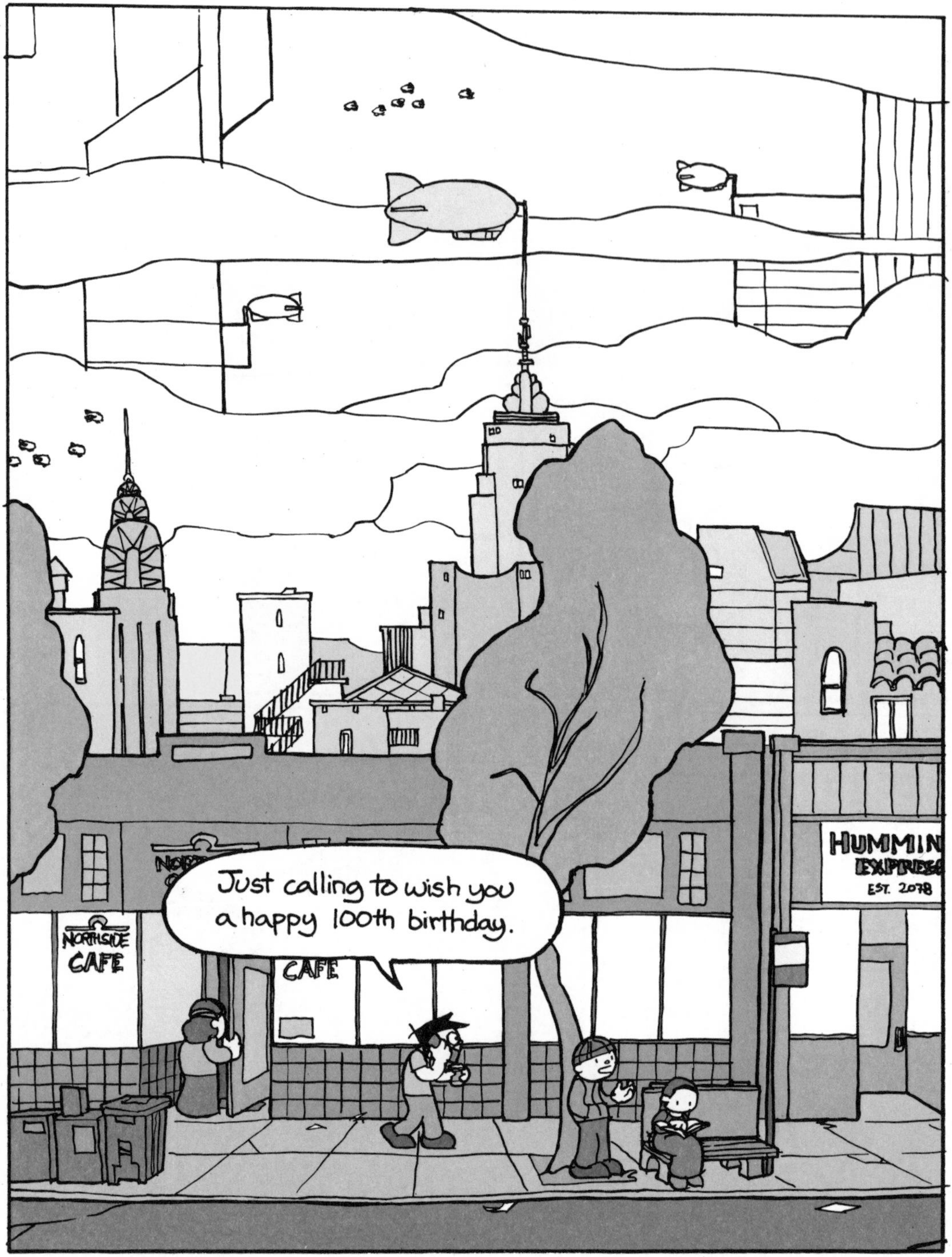
Just calling to wish you a happy 100th birthday.
NORTHSIDE CAFE
CAFE
HUMMIN
EXPRESS
EST. 2078